Management of Health Information: Functions & Applications

SECOND EDITION

Leah A. Grebner, PhD, RHIA, CCS, FAHIMA
Director of Health Information Technology
Midstate College
Peoria, Illinois

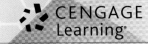

CENGAGE
Learning®

Australia • Brazil • Mexico • Singapore • United Kingdom • United States

Management of Health Information: Functions & Applications, Second Edition
Leah Grebner, Rozella Mattingly

SVP, GM Skills & Global Product Management: Dawn Gerrain

Product Manager: Jadin Babin-Kavanaugh

Senior Director, Development: Marah Bellegarde

Product Development Manager: Juliet Steiner

Senior Content Developer: Elisabeth F. Williams

Product Assistant: Mark Turner

Vice President, Marketing Services: Jennifer Ann Baker

Marketing Manager: Jessica Cipperly

Senior Production Director: Wendy Troeger

Production Director: Andrew Crouth

Content Project Management and Art Direction: Lumina

Cover image(s): INFINITY / Fotolia

For product information and technology assistance, contact us at
Cengage Learning Customer & Sales Support, 1-800-354-9706

For permission to use material from this text or product,
submit all requests online at **www.cengage.com/permissions**.
Further permissions questions can be e-mailed to
permissionrequest@cengage.com

Library of Congress Control Number: 2015953064

ISBN: 978-1-285-17488-4

Cengage Learning
20 Channel Center Street
Boston, MA 02210
USA

Cengage Learning is a leading provider of customized learning solutions with office locations around the globe, including Singapore, the United Kingdom, Australia, Mexico, Brazil, and Japan. Locate your local office at: **www.cengage.com/global**

Cengage Learning products are represented in Canada by Nelson Education, Ltd.

To learn more about Cengage Learning, visit **www.cengage.com**

Purchase any of our products at your local college store or at our preferred online store **www.cengagebrain.com**

Notice to the Reader

Publisher does not warrant or guarantee any of the products described herein or perform any independent analysis in connection with any of the product information contained herein. Publisher does not assume, and expressly disclaims, any obligation to obtain and include information other than that provided to it by the manufacturer. The reader is expressly warned to consider and adopt all safety precautions that might be indicated by the activities described herein and to avoid all potential hazards. By following the instructions contained herein, the reader willingly assumes all risks in connection with such instructions. The publisher makes no representations or warranties of any kind, including but not limited to, the warranties of fitness for particular purpose or merchantability, nor are any such representations implied with respect to the material set forth herein, and the publisher takes no responsibility with respect to such material. The publisher shall not be liable for any special, consequential, or exemplary damages resulting, in whole or in part, from the readers' use of, or reliance upon, this material.

Printed in Canada
Print Number: 01   Print Year: 2015

Rozella Mattingly, retired

To all of my past, present, and future students, who inspire me to continue teaching the next generation of Health Information Management professionals. Each of you has different talents to contribute to this diverse and dynamic career field, some as leaders, and others as followers. May you all find your special niche and thrive as you enter and grow in your careers.

BRIEF CONTENTS

CONTENTS

SECTION II   PLANNING TO MEET INFORMATION NEEDS OF HEALTH CARE FACILITIES   59

4   Planning in the Health Care Setting   61

5   Planning in Health Care: Operational Plans and Tools for Planning   83

6   Management of Financial Resources   97

SECTION III   ORGANIZING TO MEET INFORMATION NEEDS OF HEALTH CARE FACILITIES   157

21 Personal and Professional Career Management   381

Entering health care as a beginning health information manager is exciting. Choosing the workplace environment is no less exciting; the possibilities are so varied. Opportunities for health information managers exist throughout the health care spectrum. *Management of Health Information: Functions & Applications*, second edition, identifies these settings and offers suggestions for rewarding careers. This text is written primarily for students enrolled in health information management courses; it also serves as an important resource for busy managers seeking an update on trends in management. This text will challenge you, the beginning or experienced manager, to look at the management of resources as an art that impacts both your professional and personal life. As you read, think back frequently to past observations of managers and their styles as this text expands your horizons. This will give reality to your learning experiences. Be ready to be intrigued; managing is exciting, stimulating, challenging, and ever-changing.

Management of Health Information, second edition, is structured for use as a primary text in courses where managing health information is taught. Management principles found in introductory management texts are briefly outlined and then an integrated approach to health information management is built from these principles. Readers can maximize their learning experience by concurrently reading a basic management text or taking an introductory management course and by experiencing clinical or practice courses in a health information setting.

The objectives for *preparing Management of Health Information*, second edition, are to:

- Create an understanding of management principles as they apply to various health information management settings.
- Offer students an opportunity to learn through assignments that promote application of knowledge and critical thinking, as well as through Internet exercises that facilitate acquisition of up-to-date information.
- Build managerial skills to complement the technical knowledge from other courses, viewed from a managerial perspective in this text.

The philosophy underlying the fundamental approach of the text can be summarized as follows:

- **Decision Making** is crucial to effective managers. Chapter 3 is devoted entirely to decision making. The steps in making decisions are outlined and then developed further through the use of case studies and review questions. Critical thinking and decision making are embraced throughout the text.

- **Continuous Quality Improvement** is a foundational management concept in health care today. In addition to devoting a chapter to performance improvement in Section V, concepts used in quality or performance improvement are incorporated throughout the text as an integral part of management functions. It is anticipated that continuous quality improvement will become a natural part of management functions, not a concept layered onto present functions.

- **Customer Focus** is integral to all effective managers and organizations. The basic philosophy that health information management departments are part of service organizations evolves throughout this text with the concept that managers serve customers or clients, whatever the setting. Examples used in this text include activities where a department customer may be the physician, an attorney, the patient, a co-worker, an upper-level administrator, or a government regulator.

ABOUT THE SECOND EDITION

Six sections separate the topics in *Management of Health Information*, second edition. **Section I: Introduction to Managing Health Care Information** introduces management functions and theories and includes a chapter on decision making. Sections II through V address the major management functions of planning, organizing, leading, and controlling as they relate to the information needs of health care facilities.

Section II: Planning to Meet Information Needs of Health Care Facilities introduces readers to the concept of planning in the health care setting. Considerations in planning are discussed, such as operational tools, financial resources, policies and procedures, and the physical environment.

Section III: Organizing to Meet Information Needs of Health Care Facilities covers the process of organizing health information services. The organizational model is explained, as is managing employees and technology in the ever-changing health care environment.

Section IV: Leading to Meet Information Needs of Health Care Facilities spans the topics of interpersonal aspects of management, motivating for leadership, and communication.

Section V: Controlling to Meet Information Needs of Health Care Facilities focuses on control and quality and performance improvement in the health care facility.

Special Issues for Health Information Managers are addressed in **Section VI**. These include project management in health care, effective committees, managing change, and personal and professional career management.

FEATURES OF THE TEXT

Each chapter of *Management of Health Information*, second edition, contains the following learning elements:

- **Learning Objectives.** The learning objectives are outcome-based and identify and organize learning expectations for more effective studying.
- **Key Terms.** Chapters open with a listing of terms and phrases that are integral to understanding and mastering the content. They appear in bold type within the chapter, and are included and defined in the **Glossary** at the end of the text.
- **Practice Examples.** Included within select chapters, these features take the learner through the problem-solving process with a real-life scenario.
- **Summary.** Each chapter includes a brief narrative review of the chapter content, with a focus on key points the learner should retain.
- **Critical Thinking Exercises.** These exercises at the end of each chapter reinforce understanding of the key concepts and can be used for self-study or assigned for class discussion. Suggested answers appear in the Instructor's Manual.
- **Application of Theory Exercises**. Designed to promote critical thinking skills, these activities invite readers to put theory into practice and discover if they have truly mastered the content covered in the chapter.
- **Internet Activities.** These internet-based exercises challenge learners to explore information beyond the book, to stay current in the field, and to be aware of changes and updates that affect the profession.
- **Case Study.** Real-world case studies present actual situations a learner might encounter in practice and include a series of questions to guide learners through the problem-solving process. Cases may be used for in-class discussion or assigned for individual practice. Suggested answers to the cases are included in the Instructor's Manual.
- **References and Suggested Readings.** Each chapter includes a list of references or resources for further self-guided exploration and additional information. Students are strongly encouraged to keep up with trends in the career field through reading current journals and web-based research.

LEARNING PACKAGE FOR THE STUDENT

MindTap

MindTap is the first of its kind in an entirely new category: the Personal Learning Experience (PLE). This personalized program of digital products and services uses interactivity and customization to engage students, while offering a range of choice in content, platforms, devices, and learning tools. MindTap is device agnostic, meaning that it will work with any platform or learning management system and will be accessible anytime, anywhere: on desktops, laptops, tablets, mobile phones, and other Internet-enabled devices. MindTap can be accessed at http://www.CengageBrain.com. *Management of Health Information,* second edition, on MindTap includes:

- An interactive e-Book with highlighting, note-taking functions, and more
- Self-quizzes, matching activities, multiple-choice questions, and fill-in-the-blank exercises
- Flashcards for practicing chapter terms
- Computer-graded activities and exercises

TEACHING PACKAGE FOR THE INSTRUCTOR

Instructor Resources

The *Instructor Resources to Accompany Management of Health Information,* second edition, contain a variety of tools to help instructors successfully prepare lectures and teach within this subject area. This comprehensive package provides something for all instructors, from those teaching health information management for the first time to seasoned instructors who want something new. The following components in the website are free to adopters of the text:

- A downloadable, customizable *Instructor's Manual* containing lecture notes, teaching strategies, class activities, answers to Critical Thinking Exercises and Case Studies, and more.
- A *Computerized Test Bank* with several hundred questions and answers, for use in instructor-created quizzes and tests.
- Chapter slides created in PowerPoint® to use for in-class lecture material and as handouts for students

MindTap

In the new *Management of Health Information,* second edition, on MindTap platform, instructors customize the learning path by selecting Cengage Learning resources and adding their own content via apps that integrate into the MindTap framework seamlessly with many learning management systems. The guided learning path demonstrates the relevance of basic principles in health information management through engagement activities, interactive exercises, and real-world scenarios, elevating the study by challenging students to apply concepts to practice. To learn more, visit www.cengage.com/mindtap.

ACKNOWLEDGMENTS

I would like to thank Rozella Mattingly, the author of the first edition, who created a text that was comprehensive and a joy to update. Her hard work and dedication to the first edition was much appreciated.

I would like to acknowledge the continued support of Midstate College for my writing endeavors. I thank my family, especially my husband, Greg, and my children, Matthew and Aaron, for their support and patience as I worked on this project.

I would also like to extend a sincere thanks to Senior Content Developer Beth Williams. She always provided the necessary support, suggestions, encouragement, and assurance. Additionally, I would like to acknowledge the time and efforts of the following reviewers:

Shannon L. Baxa, MS, RHIA, PMP
Associate Professor
Northwestern College
Bridgeview, Illinois

Mona Calhoun, MS, MEd, RHIA FAHIMA
Chairperson
Health Information Management Program
Coppin State University
Baltimore, Maryland

Carline Dalgleish, BS, A, RHIA, AHIMA
Approved ICD-10-CM/PCS Trainer
Educator/Author/Course Development Specialist
Independent Consultant
Arlington, Texas

Kelli Lewis, RHIA
Clinical Education Coordinator
Polk State College
Winter Haven, Florida

Nicole Miller, MS, RHIA
Consultant/Program Director
Trocaire College
Lockport, New York

Martha M. Perryman, PhD, MBA, MT (ASCP)
Professor and Interim Director
Division of Health Care Management
Florida A&M University
Tallahassee, Florida

Kelly Rinker, MA, CPHIMS, RHIA
Faculty
Regis University
Denver, Colorado

Julia Steff, RHIA, CCS, CCS-P
Assistant Professor/Department Chair
Palm Beach State College
Lake Worth, Florida

Karen Norman Williams, MHIM, RHIA, CPHQ, CHTS-TR
Assistant Professor/Program Director
Health Information Technology
Del Mar College
Corpus Christi, Texas

SECTION I

Introduction to Managing Health Care Information

Introduction to the Health Information Management Profession and the Health Care Environment

LEARNING OBJECTIVES

After completing this chapter, the learner should be able to:

1. Identify the major components in a definition of management.
2. Relate management to Health Information Management (HIM).
3. Provide ideas for maintaining knowledge of health care trends.
4. Outline how the HIM career field has evolved over the years.
5. Explain how data and the resulting information are used in health care organizations today.
6. Discuss advocacy and its role in the effective use of health care information.
7. Define a health information consultant's role in alternative delivery settings.
8. List two unique health information needs facing home health care organizations.
9. Give three areas of expertise that HIM professionals offer the home health care setting.
10. Describe several advantages that a computer-based patient record system can offer HIM managers and their customers in the future.
11. Apply the resources that an HIM professional may use for change management.

INTRODUCTION

Management is a concept that goes beyond the traditional understanding of the term. Management includes planning, organizing, and leading organizational activities. When most people think of management, the first thing that comes to mind is somebody in a supervisory or administrative position. It is important for everyone to develop an understanding of management principles for a variety of reasons. Management goes beyond management of people. Management extends into processes of planning, organizing, and leading of organizational activities. As the designated custodian of health records, health information management (HIM) professionals are responsible for planning, organizing, leading, and controlling all aspects of creation, storage, and dissemination of health information. Health informatics and information management (HIIM) refers to the individuals responsible for managing health care data and information in paper or electronic form and controlling its collection, access, use, exchange, and protection through the application of health information technology (IT).

The management skills needed to create an environment that facilitates the timely, accurate, and comprehensive electronic transfer of health care data is a challenge for HIM professionals. In addition, managing the data and subsequent integration of the data into meaningful direct patient care information is only one aspect of the managerial skills needed. Just as crucial to success is the knowledge that entry-level HIM practitioners must have of management theories and practice. HIM professionals make decisions that demand effective planning, organization, motivation, and communication skills. Decisions are enhanced by using controlling tools and time management techniques. Each of these facets of managing requires a degree of human resource interaction. Thus, while automated technologies enhance the careers of health care professionals and offer increased satisfaction, managers continue to need a broad educational core of knowledge. By integrating automated technology skills and management concepts into a framework of professional practice standards, beginning practitioners can fulfill their career goals while meeting customer needs.

Who are the customers to be served by HIM professionals? First they are the patients, their families, and the teams who provide direct patient care within a facility. HIM customers include physicians caring for patients within the facility as inpatients or outpatients. In a broader sense, physicians and their office staff are customers with a variety of information needs that are well served by HIM managers responsible for capture, analysis, integration, and dissemination of health care data.

The teams providing direct patient care include nurses, respiratory therapists, physical therapists, occupational therapists, pharmacists, radiation therapists, and speech therapists. In addition, physician assistants, nurse practitioners, and other specialty nurses work in a variety of settings where timely and accurate health care information is needed.

Customers of health care information also include those professionals performing patient accounting, risk management, utilization review, and performance improvement activities. Integrating the data gathered as patient care is given with the demographic and financial data and making the resulting information available to these professionals are crucial to the long-term health of the facility. Outside of the health care facility, customers may include regulatory bodies and researchers using secondary data.

By integrating a facility's database information and disseminating it, appropriate to each customer's needs, HIM managers serve as **brokers** of health care data. Add to these information needs the demand for research data from many different sources such as physicians, other health care professionals, planning teams, or scientific researchers and then the exciting career possibilities for HIM professionals truly begin to emerge.

> **Broker** A negotiator, an intermediary, or a person entrusted with the transmission of health care data.

Health care decision makers demand timely, accurate information for their professional activities. As bits of data are captured throughout an organization, they may be of little value to decision makers until analyzed and integrated into useful information. Brokers, with HIM knowledge and skill, are the appropriate disseminators of this health care information. The tasks involved in analyzing, integrating, and disseminating information require that HIM brokers manage the resources within their sphere of responsibility to accomplish these objectives efficiently and effectively.

In this chapter, after a detailed definition of management, HIM brokering activities are outlined and discussed. Major health care settings are described in the next section; the unique opportunities HIM professionals have as brokers of information and managers of resources in these settings are outlined.

MANAGEMENT DEFINED

Definitions of management have emphasized the need to manage human beings while accomplishing the objectives of an organization. Because health care settings are increasingly becoming an integral part of today's information/communication society, the definition of management must include all resources, not only people. **Management** is defined as a process of activities for creating objectives and for teaming with people to meet these objectives through efficient and effective use of resources.

As mentioned, this definition uses the term **resources** in its broadest meaning. Health care managers have access to a range of resources, among

> **Management** A process of activities for creating objectives and for teaming with people to meet these objectives through efficient and effective use of resources.

> **Resources** An organization's resources are the skills and abilities of employees, the monies available for producing its products or services, and the physical plant and equipment.

them data and personnel. The terms *efficient* and *effective* are used in this definition because they are crucial ingredients for success in managing with limited resources. These terms complement each other, for one could manage efficiently using the wrong resources for the task and thus not be effective. Or, a manager may be very effective in delivering the services needed but may be organized inefficiently and thus use precious resources wastefully. Whether working in an administrative, managerial, supervisory, or staff-level position, HIM professionals should apply management skills to strive for a balance between effectiveness and efficacy in order to result in efficiency and best use of effort to complete a task. **Effectiveness** is the degree to which stated outcomes are attained, such as coding health records without errors. **Efficacy** is the degree to which a minimum of resources is used to obtain outcomes. An HIM example of efficacy could be that the amount of time (a valuable and limited resource) to complete the task of coding should be limited to a predefined reasonable duration for each account. The HIM perspective with a focus on coding, **efficiency** may be viewed in terms of the number of charts accurately coded within a specified period of time. It is important to effectively complete accurate coding within a predetermined amount of time to meet productivity standards. **Effort** refers to the mental and physical exertion required to perform job-related tasks.

The term *broker* is used in this text to emphasize the roles that data and the resulting information play in managerial activities in health care facilities. A broker acts as an intermediary, managing resources of others. Managing and brokering information in today's health care society brings an exciting opportunity for those who choose a career in HIM. HIM brokers offer managerial expertise in the capture, analysis, integration, and dissemination of data. By learning unique skills for creating timely, valuable information from these data, they broker information to customers. The future holds excitement for the HIM broker who disseminates essential health care information to improve not only the quality of patient care, but also the quality of decisions made throughout the health care organization.

HIM Managing and Brokering Activities

Figure 1-1 details HIM activities and shows the far-reaching consequences as information is disseminated. The flow of information in Figure 1-1 demonstrates how data gathered at each point of patient-caregiver contact in an acute care facility are analyzed, integrated, and then disseminated as valuable information. This portrayal of data through a facility emphasizes HIM managing and brokering activities as captured data are transformed and disseminated to end users. The first column includes professionals or departments where patient care data are generated and initial data capture begins. Here the data become a part of the patient's health record.

Effectiveness
The degree to which stated outcomes are attained.

Efficacy The degree to which a minimum of resources are used to obtain outcomes.

Efficiency The degree to which a desired outcome is achieved within a minimal amount of time.

Effort The mental and physical exertion required to perform job-related tasks.

FIGURE 1-1   Integrated Information Management for Health Information Managers in Acute Care Facilities

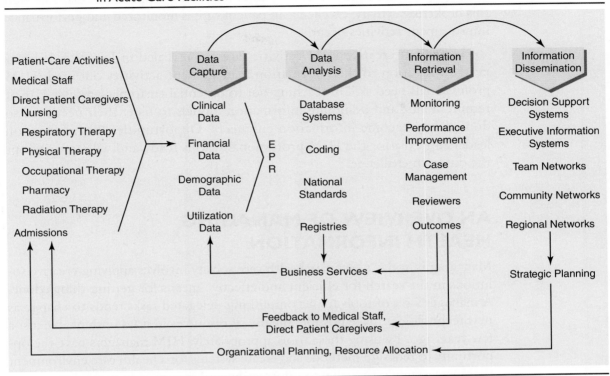

HIM professionals analyze these data, change portions into appropriate format and standards, and then merge the resulting information into database systems and registries. Gleaning information from the electronic patient records for patient-specific coding and abstracting, HIM professionals ensure that business services has the information for timely reimbursement. The coded data are then available in the database systems to integrate for other users.

The fourth column in Figure 1-1 gives examples of the scope of activities taken by HIM managers as the integrated information is shared and utilized for various purposes. Dissemination of information continues and then reaches its major focus in the last column. Patient-care decision support systems are developed or modified as integrated information is shared with patient caregivers. **Strategic planning** decisions are enhanced as information is updated and available in a timely, comprehensive, and meaningful way by upper-level management and members of the board of trustees. Thus, decisions for organizational effectiveness through strategic planning and resource allocation are enhanced.

The flow of information to business services shows the interdependence created by the enterprise network. Not only does business services have timely reimbursement data, but electronic management of receivables can be maintained with the integrated information. Just as important to the health of the

Strategic planning
A planning process that documents long-range objectives, develops activities to achieve the objectives, and allocates resources to those activities.

facility, the flow back to the patient caregivers indicates the continuous pattern of the process and ability to modify clinical decision support systems. Through this brokering activity, excellence in patient care is monitored and performance improvement activities occur.

Important creative HIM activities are not revealed in Figure 1-1, however. In addition to the information management activities outlined, HIM professionals need skill in reaching out to potential customers, assessing their requirements, and designing information models to meet their needs. In so doing, they become information engineers. Opportunities for information leadership exist for the HIM professional who is ready and willing to accept the outreach challenge.

AN OVERVIEW OF MANAGING HEALTH INFORMATION

Managing in today's complex health care society involves applying creative solutions in the search for efficient and effective means for getting things done. A manager's set of tools for accomplishing delegated tasks tends to change as new technologies make possible the use of resources in ways unthinkable just a few years ago. By using these tools appropriately, HIM managers have the opportunity to redesign methods and create systems for a health care environment that increasingly gives value to information and information management.

American Health Information Management Association (AHIMA) The professional organization for health information management professionals.

The HIM industry is the result of evolution from a career field that was more clerical in nature to one that requires professionals to possess higher levels of education and training to broaden the scope from managing records to management of data and information within the records to impact areas beyond the traditional medical records department. In 1991, the American Medical Record Association (AMRA) determined that the changed functions of professionals in the career field warranted a name change to the **American Health Information Management Association (AHIMA)**. The name change reflected the fact that HIM professionals no longer simply manage medical records, but also the information contained in the health records. Management of information extends beyond the health record and the scope of the HIM career field continues to expand outside of the HIM department's traditional function of responsibility for the management and safeguarding of information in paper and electronic form. HIM professionals receive professional training in the management of health data and information flow throughout health care delivery systems. Training is received through a formal degree focus at all levels of postsecondary education. It is also provided through on-the-job training and continuing education seminars. While management of health information starts with information that originates as data elements within the health records, it extends to analysis of data and information in the areas of compliance, technology, and performance improvement. The term *health information* was defined by the **Health Insurance Portability and Accountability Act of 1996 (HIPAA)** Privacy Rule, as any verbal information created or received by a health care provider, health plan, public health authority, employer, life insurer, school or university, or health care clearinghouse that relates to the physical or mental health of an individual, provision of health care to an individual, or payment for provision of health care. HIM professionals are responsible for the care, custody, and control of the health record for such persons or institutions that prepare and maintain records of health care. They are authorized to certify records and supervise all inspections, releases, or duplication of records. This may include being called to testify to the admissibility of the record, verify timeliness, and verify that normal business practices were used to develop and maintain the health record. Continued evolution of the HIM profession has resulted in HIM professionals no longer being limited to managing health information inside of the health care facility, but positions now exist that address public health perspectives through educating health care consumers in the communities to engage in management of their own personal health information.

HIM professionals are no longer limited to simply handling health records, but rather their roles and expertise have grown to include working with all data contained in the records. The combined practices of HIM and IT that affect how data and documentation combine to create a single business record for an organization are known as data management. One product of HIM involvement in data management is the emergence of a new role for HIM professionals. HIM professionals responsible for managing the less technical aspects of data, including data quality and security, are data administrators. Another HIM role, the data navigator, specializes in the development of the graphical user interface used to capture and navigate through the **electronic health record (EHR)** and other systems. The data navigator position has become increasingly critical as new technology has provided the ability for health care consumers to access health information. This development presents not only the challenge of managing the information to be accessed, but also ensuring that the method of accessing is easily understood by laypersons. Another evolving HIM role is the data resource manager, who ensures an organization's information systems meet the needs of people who provide and manage patient services. The HIM professional managing health information in the capacity of a data resource manager must apply management skills and tools that will be addressed in future chapters in order to identify the needs of the people using information so that the necessary health information will be available to those managing patient services. This requires HIM professionals to then collaborate with IT professionals to provide access to the necessary health information. Advances in all aspects of health care present nearly endless opportunities for providers to improve care. IT facilitates this process by ensuring access to globally available data resources.

Health Insurance Portability and Accountability Act of 1996 (HIPAA) The federal law that facilitates maintenance of insurance for health care consumers, protects privacy and security of health information, and controls administrative costs of health care delivery.

Electronic health record (EHR) A digital version of a patient record.

Unique Management Features

Health care organizations have unique features that challenge managers including the complexity of services and the variety of education and experiences of employees. For example, one task in an HIM department may involve manual labor extensively, such as reviewing and processing requests for release of health information. The employee who spends 4 hours a day performing this task may spend another 3 hours at a computer entering data elements abstracted from incomplete records. Teams performing such a diversity of tasks require the HIM professional to use special managerial skills to create an environment of adaptability and flexibility. The demand for accuracy and excellence equally impacts both aspects of the employee activities mentioned above—the manual and the automated. The manager is challenged to create a culture that gives equal value and importance to both highly technical tasks and manual tasks.

Since the mid-1980s, an evolution toward productivity, efficiency, and effectiveness in health care organizations has occurred with accelerating pace. This evolution has led to greater emphasis on cost containment and quality patient care. Increasing productivity, efficiency, and effectiveness in HIM departments is emphasized throughout the text.

INFORMATION MANAGERS IN HEALTH CARE FACILITIES

With the advances in science and technology, greater recognition of the HIM professional as a key component player in the delivery of health care results. Frequently these technological advances allow for preventive care or ambulatory treatment rather than expensive inpatient care. This move will only increase the demand for information flowing to the various health care service organizations such as physician office practice centers, wellness centers, and urgent care centers. As these health care organizations become more complex and more frequently the setting for health care delivery, the need for timely, accurate, and comprehensive information increases.

Definition of Health Care Organizations

Managers of health care information will typically work in health care organizations. However, due to the expanding roles associated with the evolution of the career field, health information managers may work for other types of organizations, too. An organization is defined as a systematic arrangement of people and things to accomplish specific purposes. Health care facilities are seen as organizations where health care professionals come together, with standards and guidelines, to assess, diagnose, plan, and treat patients, and then document these activities. In keeping with these definitions, a major goal for

HIM managers is to provide the resources for managing the information/communication flow within health care organizations such as hospitals.

Delegation of HIM Responsibility

Responsibility for quality health care and optimum performance at all levels of the organization rests with the board of trustees or directors who then delegate responsibility to the president or chief executive officer (CEO). The president or CEO, in turn, delegates responsibility to the managers within the organization. Thus, HIM professionals are delegated their managerial responsibility by the board of trustees or directors of the organization.

Health Care Facilities and Information Needs

With appropriate systems, HIM managers can provide data for clinical decision making at the point of patient care and then make it available as needed through a truly computerized patient record. Direct providers of care perform at optimum when information is at their fingertips and when documentation of their care is entered in the EHR by those same fingertips or by a voice recognition process. As these activities involving patient care are documented and create the information needed by others, the data are analyzed and managed by HIM professionals. In this way, data become information of value and the managers become brokers of accurate, timely, and comprehensive health care information. Obstacles to creating a true EHR are slowly being overcome. HIM brokers, investing in the time to obtain crucial current knowledge, can play a key role in EHR development. As they gain knowledge, they can, for example, educate their teams through in-service training. Giving recognition to employees who expand their knowledge through formal courses is another way to heighten interest in updating technological knowledge.

Health records are made up of many data elements. Data in HIM include items such as dates, narrative items, and images that represent basic facts and observations about people, processes, measurements, and conditions that pertain to management of health care delivery. Table 1-1 lists different types of data that HIM professionals manage. The smallest unique subset of a database is a data element, such as an individual fact or measurement. The level of detail at which the attributes and values of health care data are defined is referred to as data granularity. When considering the term *granularity*, compare how grains of sand make up a beach. Data abstracts are similarly made of many granular data elements. A defined and standardized set of data points or elements common to a patient population that can be regularly identified in the health records of the population and coded for use and analysis in a database management system is called a data abstract. Abstracted data elements facilitate the processes in data analysis for the ability to translate the data into something meaningful. Data elements that have been deliberately selected, processed, and organized to be useful are referred to as information.

TABLE 1-1	Types of Data
Data Type	**Data Description**
Administrative data	Coded information contained in secondary records, such as billing records, describing patient identification, diagnoses, procedures, and insurance.
Aggregate data	Data extracted from individual health records and combined to form deidentified information about groups of patients that can be compared and analyzed.
Demographic data	Information used to identify an individual, such as name, address, gender, age, and other information linked to a specific person.
External data	Data coming from outside the facility that can be used to compare the facility with other similar facilities, such as quality of outcomes for various conditions being treated or surgical procedures.
Health data	Includes both clinical and administrative data (and perhaps other data associated with an individual's health care); also includes aggregate-level health data for secondary uses, such as quality and patient safety monitoring, population health monitoring, research, and reimbursement.
Internal data	Data from within the facility including administrative and clinical data.

HIM professionals strive to ensure data quality and security in all areas of health care delivery. They protect data in both paper and EHRs so that users of data only access on a need-to-know basis and so that the data that are accessed will be used to contribute to a high quality of patient care. Data quality (also known as data integrity) describes the effectiveness and reliability of data as they are used in health care operations, decision support, and planning. Health care data should be complete, accurate, and timely. If health care data are not complete, critical information, such as medication allergies, may be missing and could result in a potentially fatal outcome if a patient is given medication to which he or she is allergic. If health care data are not accurate, this could also result in an unfavorable outcome. Accurate patient matching is critical relative to data quality. Consider the potential result if medication orders for a patient were to end up in the health record of a different patient, whose condition may be worsened by administration of the other patient's medication. Timeliness of health care data could also make a significant difference if a STAT medication order did not make it to the health record right away. Data should also be secure from corruption or modification, either maliciously or accidentally. Data security is the process of keeping data, both in transit and at rest, safe from unauthorized access, alteration, or destruction. Another consideration related to maintaining the integrity of health data that goes beyond protection from alteration or destruction is ensuring access to the data if the primary storage system fails. This includes planning for routine backup of electronic data and contingency planning for unexpected outages or disasters. Improved data accessibility and increased disaster preparedness may be accomplished through a health data repository, which is a database that will provide immediate nationwide access to local data in the event of primary system failure or system unavailability so that providers losing data through a disaster may easily recover it in a timely manner. This concept will be addressed in greater detail in Chapter 15.

Both traditional paper records and EHRs must be protected for the purpose of maintaining privacy and security. The process of controlling access to the information in a database, database management, not only manages the organization and file structure of health information databases but also involves processes to control access to the information through use of passwords. Database management is a critical part of data stewardship. Being a good steward of data is another form of managing the organization's resources. Security also maintains the integrity of EHR data.

Integrity of health record data extends beyond security to also encompass the quality of data. The business processes that protect the integrity of an organization's data during data collection, application (including aggregation), warehousing, and analysis are referred to as data quality management. Poor-quality health care data may contribute to poor-quality patient care, inappropriate reimbursement, and inaccurate data for clinical research. One method of accomplishing this is through a data quality indicator system that records information about the patient and the care provided to the patient, such as vital sign measurements, medication orders and administration records, and diagnoses.

HIM professionals further manage health care data quality through data quality review, including examination of health records to determine the level of coding accuracy and to identify areas of coding problems. The quality reviews may be performed by an HIM professional within the organization or an external auditor may be contracted. If any problems are identified in the review process, corrective action must be taken and coders should be provided with education in order to prevent future similar problems.

Another aspect of managing information performed by HIM professionals in today's health care environment is health data analysis, which is the act of acquiring, collecting, evaluating, and processing health data by utilizing application skills such as database extraction and data analyzing tools to manage information contained in multiple large data sets. As trained experts in health data analysis, HIM professionals are qualified to use application skills to manage, analyze, interpret, and transform health data into accurate, consistent, and timely information. HIM professionals may work as Clinical Data Improvement Specialists, communicating with clinical health care providers concurrent with provision of health care services to ensure quality and specificity of documentation.

Internal data
Data from within the facility including administrative and clinical data.

Another method of managing health care data quality is through health record analysis, that is, concurrent or ongoing reviews of health record content performed by caregivers or HIM professionals while the patient is still receiving inpatient services, to ensure the quality of the services being provided and the completeness of the documentation being maintained. Health records that are found to have deficiencies in the form of missing documents, signatures, or other items are considered to be incomplete. Deficiencies in health record documentation may be so significant that missing data prevent completion of other data and information management processes. Health care providers generally have an incomplete records policy that outlines how physicians are notified of records missing documentation and/or signatures. Incomplete records may be missing important data for other information management processes. This policy generally includes a designation for delinquent health records, which are incomplete records not finished within the time frame determined by the medical staff of the facility. The required time frame for record completion should be documented in the medical staff bylaws, including specification of time frames that designate records to be incomplete versus delinquent. The bylaws should also outline consequences for incomplete and delinquent health records. HIM professionals often develop creative methods to encourage providers to complete records in a timely manner and help the physicians avoid penalties outlined in the bylaws. Failure to measure rates of incomplete and delinquent records, along with addressing data quality compromised by missing information, could result in loss of accreditation, so management of health record data deficiencies is a significant activity for HIM professionals managing data and information. Because of this, it is necessary to include a provision in the incomplete records policy to penalize physicians with delinquent health records. Some examples of physician penalties for delinquent records may include, but are certainly not limited to:

- Suspension of privileges to admit patients to the facility until records are completed
- Inability to schedule new surgical cases at the facility
- Monetary fines
- Revocation of all privileges at the facility and need to reapply after a significant specified time with delinquent records or greater than a specified number of incidences of delinquent records within a designated time frame

HIM professionals need to recognize the impact of managing health care data to facilitate transformation into information and knowledge. This is illustrated in Figure 1-2. Health care data elements must be organized and managed so that they may be put into context for presentation as information. Information is analyzed and understood as knowledge, which combines information and experience in order to give individuals the power to make informed decisions.

FIGURE 1-2   Data-Information-Knowledge Continuum

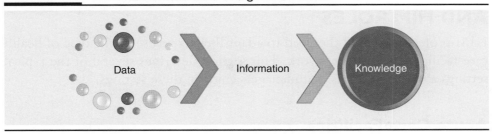

HIM professionals play a key role in the continuum of data to knowledge but are also actively involved in management of knowledge by dissemination to appropriate audiences. Knowledge sources include various types of reference materials and expert information that are compiled in a manner accessible for integration with patient care information to improve the quality and cost-effectiveness of health care provision. Knowledge assets for an organization include printed documents; unwritten rules; workflows; customer knowledge; data in databases and spreadsheets; and the human expertise, know-how, and tacit knowledge within the minds of the organization's workforce. A database that manages raw data and integrates them with information from various reference works is called a knowledge base. A knowledge management system (KMS) provides technology to support the creation, organization, and dissemination of knowledge and expertise to all stakeholders associated with a health care delivery provider. KMS may be incorporated into EHR systems in order to facilitate easy access to knowledge assets by providers in a timely manner. HIM professionals are increasing involvement in applied research activities to develop new methods of knowledge production. In addition, applied research is also being used to address the distribution, sharing, application, integration, evaluation, reflection, adaptation, and sustainability of knowledge.

Advocacy

The role of the HIM professional in health care organizations encompasses several facets of brokering health care information. Advocacy is a major facet of brokering. This includes advocating quality patient care and documentation through the development of a comprehensive, **longitudinal patient record** for every patient.

Longitudinal patient record The creation of a record that encompasses patient health care information from all sources, over time, for use and update by caregivers.

Advocacy includes embracing change and persuading others in the organization to share the enthusiasm. Communication and systems thinking skills will aid the HIM professional in championing change when working collaboratively to identify opportunities for improvement. Developing these advocacy skills will enhance the HIM professional's role in creating cultural change toward the goal of economical quality care and ensuring accurate and useful data as longitudinal EHRs are created.

TYPES OF HEALTH CARE FACILITIES AND HIM ROLES

HIM professionals find the need to adapt their expertise to the type of health care facility in which they work. This section describes several of the typical settings and the positions that managers enjoy in these settings.

Acute Care Facilities

Typically, regional hospitals are structured to meet the health care needs of a regional area, whereas smaller community hospitals meet the basic health care needs of the community. In some instances, community hospitals may specialize in specific therapies or advanced technologies identified as important for the community. Hospitals are considered one of the most complex organizations in modern society (see Figure 1-3). With the governing board holding legal authority and responsibility and with the medical staff making decisions regarding patient care, administration is delegated responsibility for day-to-day operations.

FIGURE 1-3   Organizational Model, Community Hospital

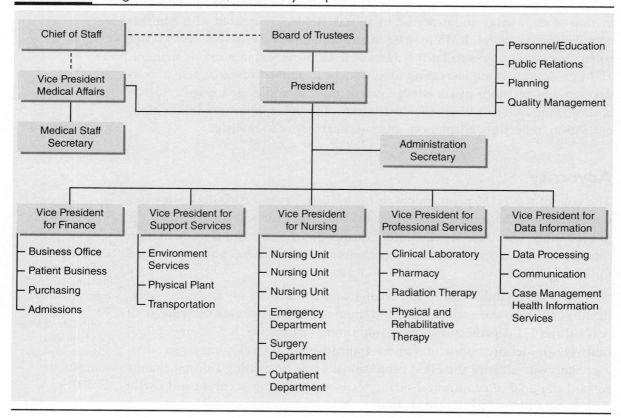

Expanding Roles in Acute Care Facilities

Today HIM professionals are a part of hospital organizations in a variety of positions. Figure 1-4 shows these possibilities.

There are also rewarding careers for HIM professionals as managers of any of the departments listed in Figure 1-4 or as staff professionals within departments. Supervisory or team leader responsibilities within a health information systems department are also fulfilling tasks.

As the health care professional with knowledge of medical science, health data, medicolegal, and information technology, HIMs have an opportunity to expand their roles beyond those listed as the demand for data increases in the health care environment. These expanding horizons offer job enrichment opportunities to HIM professionals while meeting the needs of organizations and communities.

FIGURE 1-4   Possible Positions for HIM Professionals in Acute Care Facilities

1. With advanced degrees:
    Institutional administrators
    Chief information officer (CIO)
    Chief knowledge officer (CKO)
    Chief financial officer (CFO)
    Vice president of operations
    Professor of HIM
    Compliance officer
    Security officer
    Researcher

2. With or without advanced degrees:
    Clinical Documentation Improvement Specialist
    Quality improvement (QI) coordinator
    Diagnosis-related group (DRG) specialist
    Revenue cycle manager
    Coder
    Credentialing specialist
    Manager of an HIM department
    Supervisor of an area within an HIM department
    Electronic health record (EHR) trainer
    Electronic health record coordinator
    Consultant
    Patient advocate
    Patient navigator

Customers of Health Information in Acute Care Facilities

Physician Customers Networking within the organization, especially with the medical staff, brings opportunities for HIM professionals to participate as contributors. Physicians use the services of the HIM department with greater frequency than any other group of customers. By sharing information on new regulations, computer enhancements, work redesign, and other changes, HIM professionals can become valuable resources for physicians.

By listening and encouraging physicians to become involved in change, HIM managers can gather new ideas to improve the information flow to and from physicians. When individuals feel ownership for an idea, they are willing to be advocates for needed changes. The idea can then permeate throughout the facility and a greater understanding of the advantages for change is disseminated. Thus are born the pressures for **paradigm shifts**.

Paradigm shifts
The changes that take place as present models of activity no longer meet the needs, and pressure mounts for a shift to new models.

Upper-Level Administration Customers HIM professionals have information of value to share with upper-level management customers. As opportunities arise for demonstrating the value of specific information for strategic planning, for example, HIM managers can offer to demonstrate the advantages of using these captured data for strategic planning. Then, this first opportunity can be a catalyst for offering additional creative uses of information.

Nursing Customers Another major group of customers is nurses. HIM managers can initiate discussions of information needs and concerns with nursing professionals. Again, listening skills are crucial as nursing professionals verbalize their ideas for the flow of clinical information. Through communication, enhanced clinical information systems that assure a process where data are entered efficiently and accurately can be envisioned. As brokers of information, HIM managers have the expertise to customize reports for meeting specific nursing needs, thus promoting the concept of analyzed data as useful information, not merely data elements.

Patient Finance Accounts Customers Another example of HIM customers is the patient financial accounts staff. By communicating with these people and assisting in their understanding of the body of information available for customized reports to meet their needs, HIM brokers are true advocates. Results of this networking can be improved relationships and improved workflow. By encouraging the patient accounts staff to think of additional information of value to them, HIM brokers have the opportunity to massage the database and customize appropriate reports.

Thus, intrapreneurs who are entrepreneurs within the facility will flourish and create ways of helping others do their tasks through the burgeoning of new methods, technology, and concepts. Managers in other departments have information needs also. By networking, HIM managers can gain knowledge of their activities and then offer appropriate information. The HIM manager's value as a team player will grow as a result of the efficient and effective systems created through the new roles of change agent and broker of health care information.

Customers external to acute care facilities, such as health care planning councils and government agencies, also use data maintained by HIM professionals. As appropriate information is shared with these external customers, the role of HIM managers will be enhanced.

Ambulatory Facilities

An expanding segment of health care organizations involves the diverse group of facilities referred to as ambulatory care settings. These settings include physician office practice centers, urgent care centers, wellness centers, surgicenters, dialysis centers, and other specialty centers. Home health care is discussed in a separate section to emphasize its special features. Employment opportunities for HIM professionals in ambulatory care are increasing. The skills of HIM professionals are needed in ambulatory care organizations to create information systems that will meet a facility's specific needs. As longitudinal electronic patient records develop, health information exchange (HIE) organizations are being created by integrating ambulatory care information into the EHR. HIM professionals have the knowledge to be team players in this development.

HIM professionals may also contract as **consultants** in ambulatory care settings. Consultants can provide expertise in state and federal regulations as they constantly monitor publications for the latest updates. This information is not all that is needed, however. They also monitor trends in health care and accreditation standards and are ready to advise should possibilities for change occur. Strategic planning within ambulatory care organizations is thus enhanced.

Consultant
One who gives professional advice and services in the field of his or her specialty.

Currently, the trend is for physician office practices to merge as specialty or multispecialty organizations or to become part of a larger health care facility such as a hospital. These more complex settings offer employment opportunities for HIM professionals. An alternative to employment, consulting also affords opportunity in physician practice with a shorter-term commitment to planning and implementing office systems that will create efficiency and effectiveness within practice groups. HIM professionals have the knowledge to integrate the resulting information that can lead to enhanced health care delivery and excellence in patient care. As information superhighways become reality, physician office settings will demand the expertise of brokers who can deliver timely, accurate, and comprehensive information through a longitudinal EHR that will extend beyond the HIE into national database systems.

The trends just mentioned emphasize the importance of integrating patient health care information into networks. This health care information from database systems residing in ambulatory care facilities, skilled nursing facilities, and acute care organizations thus becomes available to caregivers. By serving as liaisons among acute care facilities and other health care settings, HIM professionals offer expertise in integrating and disseminating appropriate information.

Skilled Care and Nursing Home Facilities for Long-Term Care

In addition to ambulatory care settings, diverse patterns of organization exist for facilities with inpatient beds for patients not requiring the intensive services of acute care units. The demand for long-term care beds continues to increase throughout the United States. The organizational structure in these settings is less complex than in acute care facilities and predictably there is a narrower range of services.

While the length of stay and level of care in long-term care settings create a somewhat different need for health care information, the patient/resident as a customer continues to be the focus in both long-term care and acute care. To meet customer needs, regardless of the setting, caregivers need timely, accurate, and comprehensive information. Thus, basic HIM standards of practice remain the same and long-term care offers excellent opportunities for HIM professionals. Larger facilities may have the resources to hire full-time HIM professionals to manage their health information systems. Other facilities may utilize the services of HIM consultants.

Home Health Care

Home health care is unique and is a rapidly growing industry. A natural shift from acute care settings to home health care settings has occurred as new technologies make home health treatment increasingly feasible. Cost-containment pressures also demand that care, such as infusion therapy, be given in the least costly health care setting. The expansion of home health care settings is creating opportunities for HIM professionals within these home health businesses. As employees, HIM professionals assist in efficient capture of data from various caregivers and then analyze and integrate these data. This creates the information needed by the caregivers as well as the decision makers within the administrative level of the business. HIM professionals with appropriate backgrounds may find a career in managing home health care businesses very rewarding. Another career possibility in home health care settings is contracting as HIM consultants to assist in creating appropriate health information systems and maintaining them.

Maintaining health information systems and managing the flow of information for health care needs such as advocacy, development, implementation of the EHR, and patient decision support systems will continue to challenge HIM professionals who choose a career involving home health care settings. Unique needs within the home health care settings include remote telecommunication and computer technologies. These can create significant cost savings for home health care businesses as the EHR is developed and integrated into the community network. HIM professionals have the knowledge and skills to plan and implement these systems as management teams struggle to equip their organizations for efficiency and effectiveness in health care. Choosing appropriate hardware and software can be a difficult task; HIM professionals are prepared to assist in these decisions because of their knowledge of information systems and potential vendor applications.

Financial savings can also be realized when automated client care documentation systems are implemented for home health care uses. Well-planned and well-documented policies and procedures are needed as systems are installed. HIM professionals are well positioned to meet their career goals while offering expertise within the home health care setting.

LOCAL, STATE, AND NATIONAL GOVERNMENT AGENCIES

Government agencies can be a part of any of the health care delivery services mentioned in this chapter. Examples are found in the inner cities, Indian Health Service, and prison clinics and hospitals. Some of these have unique needs that merit special mention. Communication skills are especially daily crucial in settings with increased cultural diversity. Also, some facilities give high priority to hiring employees from the local community who may need special training.

These special needs offer HIM professionals an opportunity to be of service in these settings. Training employees in professional standards of practice such as confidentiality of patient information can be very rewarding. When patients are from among an employee's family or acquaintances, adequate training in confidentiality policies and procedures becomes imperative. Also, the wording of policies and procedures should be sensitive to the culture of the community.

As HIEs are developed, data will be captured from all the health care facilities and providers in the network. HIM professionals have an opportunity to advocate the need for standards, security, and decision support systems throughout this network. With the educational curriculum designed specifically to address these issues, the HIM professional is best qualified to perform these tasks and manage this information flow.

EMERGING OPPORTUNITIES FOR HEALTH INFORMATION MANAGERS

Every day all of us are affected in our professional and personal lives by IT. With information and knowledge growing at an ever-increasing rate, HIM professionals face challenges and time constraints just monitoring the latest advances. But this constraint carries with it opportunities to grow, to learn, to innovate, and to excite others as advocates for systems that will improve lives, lengthen lives, and enhance the public health of the nation.

Health care managers can be proactive participants in the effort to review the present structure of patient care, the management of the systems, and the information flow. This effort can lead to paradigm shifts that may create major reorganizational possibilities.

One innovation being tried in a limited number of organizations is a move to **patient-focused centers** where the caregivers in the centers provide all of the care to the patients. The possibilities for assuring quality information as a contributing member of the health care team are exciting. This multidisciplinary team can monitor risk management, utilization management, infection control, and documentation of the diagnosis, procedures, and code assignment. Through a **matrix organizational structure**, the HIM staff can be actively involved in patient-focused centers. The matrix structure is discussed in Chapter 6.

Emerging Opportunities in Reorganization

Rightsizing a health care facility's management structure offers the opportunity to combine departments and create nontraditional alliances. Rightsizing may be synonymous with downsizing; the difference can be that downsizing means deleting services and employees. In contrast, rightsizing means reorganizing for efficiency and effectiveness in meeting customer needs.

In today's information/communication environment the pressure to combine departments and create nontraditional alliances can bring excellence to the workplace and enhance the quality of patient care. HIM managers who are willing to expand their area of control can assume responsibility for such areas as patient registration, business service department, quality management, tumor registry, risk management, medical staff liaison, and utilization management. Such changes will demand HIM professionals with the ability to form teams that can accomplish a combination of these responsibilities and develop a culture where each team member understands the role of the entire team. For teams that avoid turf battles, creativity, innovation, and efficient systems will result. For example, HIM professionals, nurses, and other team members in utilization management can expand their roles by monitoring risk issues, diagnosis issues, and coding details.

An alliance between health information services and business services or patient accounts services can effectively decrease accounts receivable days because of enhanced cooperative efforts. Constraints in such alliances may be

Patient-focused centers
Direct care units where multiskilled health professionals provide all of the patient activities and care, such as admitting the patient, performing diagnostic examinations, caring for the patient, and coding patient diagnoses.

Matrix organizational structure
A design that assigns specialists from departments to work on one or more projects led by a project manager.

due to the lack of knowledge and experience of the managers involved. By taking advantage of formal and informal education opportunities, managers can prepare themselves for expanding roles. Developing the skills necessary to create the cultural changes that alliances offer is crucial to successful alliances.

Innovations in Emergency Departments

Another area where creative managerial ideas can contain costs is data management in emergency departments. Medical care documentation is increasingly important and HIMs who explore enhanced systems for emergency records find that there are systems available that offer legal protocols, financial savings, and administrative efficiency. For example, by using flowcharting and computerized documentation applications in emergency departments, physician time devoted to paperwork can be lessened. These systems can also assist support personnel in their documentation efforts. Using a dictated discharge document for emergency departments can augment flowcharting for the physician and increase the likelihood that complete information on the patient will be included in the record. HIM professionals can network with the caregivers in emergency departments and expose them to opportunities for creating information and documentation systems best suited to their needs.

Emerging Opportunities in Ambulatory Care

A fast-growing ambulatory care center may historically have given low priority to its health care records. Eventually, the inability to have records available for patient care leads to a crisis among the health care providers. Such an organization will find that it needs the expertise of a health information professional.

Planning and implementing appropriate systems for ambulatory care centers can challenge the skills of HIM managers. However, the rewards of seeing effective and efficient systems in place for such diverse health care settings are great.

Concerns continue to be expressed about the quality and effectiveness of information management systems within outpatient facilities. As managed care practices increase and ambulatory health care delivery grows, more emphasis is being placed on effective systems where data integration and networking can take place enterprise-wide and regionally (Gennusa, 1995).

Choosing employment or contracting as consultants with physician practice groups and other ambulatory settings will continue to attract HIM professionals who enjoy the challenges offered. Automated systems created specifically to enhance integrated delivery and continuum of care for ambulatory health care settings will increase and provide opportunities for HIM managers.

Emerging Opportunities in Health-Related Settings

In addition to the opportunities described previously, innovative HIM professionals are enjoying nontraditional roles as emerging needs create new opportunities. These settings include insurance companies, contract research organizations, peer review organizations, recruiting firms, publishing firms focusing on health care, allied health practice firms, state health planning agencies, and pharmaceutical firms. Consulting opportunities are increasing in organizations such as certified public accountant (CPA) firms also. As the need for database management skills increases and regional health data repositories become commonplace, new opportunities for HIM professionals with these skills will emerge.

CHANGE MANAGEMENT

Change management The formal process of introducing change, persuading others to adopt the change, and instill change organization-wide.

As the HIM environment continues to evolve, it is critical that HIM professionals are able to embrace and facilitate change in the workplace. **Change management** is the formal process of introducing change, persuading others to adopt the change, and instill change organization-wide. The health care arena has experienced a sense of constant change over the years. And recently, the dynamic nature of health care has increased. One of the most obvious technological changes in HIM is the introduction of the EHR. Prior to that, HIM professionals had to adjust to computerized record sign-out, deficiency tracking, abstracting, and master patient index (MPI). Coders have benefitted from changes that included encoder software and grouper software that automatically assign groupings and reimbursement information for prospective payment systems based on code assignment. Other changes in health care include new regulations, increased need for higher education, and ease of access to the Internet.

An individual within an organization who believes in an innovation or change and promotes the idea by building financial and political support is referred to as a champion. HIM professionals must manage change in the health care delivery system by acting as champions to promote the skills, education, and knowledge possessed by individuals who have acquired formal education and AHIMA credentials to the medical community in order to further expand roles that HIM professionals may fill in health care organizations. A change agent is an individual within an organization whose primary responsibility is to facilitate change. HIM professionals often act as change agents through volunteer service with AHIMA workgroups that provide members with tools that will allow them to serve as champions for HIM initiatives and other changes occurring in the industry.

Changes in health care originate from a variety of sources. See Table 1-2 for examples of these sources. Change drivers are forces in the external environment of organizations or industries that force organizations or industries to change the way they operate in order to survive. Many are in response to federal and state regulations, such as HIPAA or state-specific Medicaid requirements.

Health care consumers, or people who purchase and/or use goods or services (in health care, a patient, client, resident, or other recipient of health care services is another form of change driver), are more aware of many aspects of health care and have access to a wealth of information through publicly reported

TABLE 1-2	Sources and Examples of Change Drivers in Health Care
Source of Change	**Examples**
Federal Regulations	HIPAA
State Regulations	Medicaid
Community	Opening or closure of large employer
Technology	EHRs
Institutional	New administration Change in organizational structure

outcome data and online resources. Consumer informatics is the field of information science concerned with the management of data and information used to support consumers (the general public) through the use of technology. As health care providers have started to make health information available through patient portals and mobile applications, smartphones are becoming increasingly popular for tracking various aspects of personal health records (PHRs) (e.g., diet, exercise, vaccination dates, and diabetes management). HIM professionals have responded by developing education to help consumers understand both the risks and benefits of electronic management of PHI. The branch of health informatics that addresses the needs of the consumer is known as consumer health informatics. Another area in which health care consumers have become more informed is the need for maintaining a PHR. AHIMA has sponsored a consumer awareness campaign, which educated the consumer about the importance of and need for a PHR. This initiative has been promoted through AHIMA-trained volunteers providing presentations to groups in communities across the nation. In addition, a website, MyPHR.com, has been developed to provide educational information and tools for consumers to create PHRs. This website is constantly maintained and updated by a combination of AHIMA staff members and HIM professionals serving in a volunteer capacity with educational information to help consumers understand the need for a PHR and select the format of PHR that best meets their needs. The AHIMA Consumer Engagement Practice Council has also published consumer guides to provide additional consumer education in lay terms.

Another aspect of health care that has been impacted by consumer awareness is privacy. The Health Privacy Project, a nonprofit organization whose mission is to raise public awareness of the importance of ensuring health privacy in order to improve health care access and quality, created the Consumer Coalition for Health Privacy for the purpose of educating and empowering health care consumers on privacy issues at the various levels of government and consists of patients and consumer advocacy organizations. While health care consumers are generally aware of the Health Insurance Portability and Accountability Act of 1996 (HIPAA), most do not fully understand how it truly impacts them, along with individual state regulations related to privacy. When health care consumers present to providers, they are provided with a copy of the privacy policy and are asked to sign a document that verifies that they received it. However, it is not common practice for the health care provider to explain the policy or even ask if the patient has any questions. Article I of the AHIMA Code of Ethics states that HIM professionals shall "advocate, uphold, and defend the individual's right to privacy and the doctrine of confidentiality in the use and disclosure of information," and Article II states that HIM professionals shall, "represent the profession to the public in a positive manner," which includes serving as an advocate of principles of the profession to the public (http://library.ahima.org/xpedio/groups/public/documents/ahima/bok1_024277.hcsp?dDocName=bok1_024277). Because of this, HIM professionals should play an active role in education of laypersons regarding what they need to know about the HIPAA Privacy Rules and serve as an advocate to help ensure that health care consumers gain a meaningful understanding of privacy policy materials.

Health care consumers are also increasingly aware of quality of care through published information about providers in their communities. One method used by managed care organizations and other health care sectors is the report card, which reports cost and quality of care provided. The consumer-directed (driven) health care plan (CDHP) is a managed care organization characterized by influencing patients and clients to select cost-efficient health care through the provision of information about health benefit packages and through financial incentives. In addition, the Joint Commission Agenda for Change is an initiative focused on changing the emphasis of the accreditation process from structure to outcomes. The term *center of excellence* is used to identify a health care facility selected to provide specific services based on criteria such as experience, outcomes, efficiency, and effectiveness. Tertiary and academic medical centers are often designated as centers of excellence for one or more services such as organ transplantation.

Medicare has developed a method to address not only quality of care but also cost for treatment of Medicare beneficiaries. This has been accomplished through Accountable Care Organizations (ACO), which are organizations of health care providers accountable for the quality, cost, and overall care of Medicare beneficiaries who are assigned and enrolled in the traditional fee-for-service program. ACOs include physicians, hospitals, and other providers of health care services. Participation is voluntary for providers through several types of ACO models.

As health care in the United States continues to evolve, roles of HIM professionals are also further diversified. Medical treatment methods are developed through clinical research. In a similar manner in the nonclinical side of health care, HIM professionals are also involved in applied research. This is a type of research that focuses on the use of scientific theories to improve actual practice, as in medical research applied to the treatment of patients. The increasingly dynamic nature of health care delivery in the United States has increased the need for HIM professionals to engage in applied research to develop improved processes and identify best practices in managing all aspects of health records.

SUMMARY

Management is defined as a process of activities for creating objectives and for teaming with people to meet these objectives through efficient and effective use of resources. For the HIM professional, data and their management are the focus of the management process. In the HIM profession, the term *management* extends beyond the general assumption of simply managing human and material resources, but rather it also goes as far as managing information. This function is the result of evolution of the HIM profession from managing records to managing the information contained in the records and other broader aspects of health care. This evolution has been accompanied by new opportunities and challenges in management of health data. The term *broker* is one way to describe the role HIM professionals play as disseminators of health care information. Current knowledge is crucial for managing data and disseminating information. Reading, networking with other HIM professionals and other members of the health care delivery teams, and attending professional meetings are excellent methods for enhancing this needed professional growth.

The priority given to health care information in quality patient care throughout diverse settings is expected to increase as timely, accurate information is demanded. The federal government is expected to continue in its role as catalyst toward a true EHR. HIM professionals are well qualified to participate in developing and implementing this transition. Advocating quality patient care, confidentiality, security, effectiveness, and efficiency are also important roles for the future HIM professional. Being prepared for and accepting additional responsibilities within health care organizations during the transition will ensure HIM managers a role in the Workplace of the Future.

The flow of information/communication networks will continue to be crucial to success within organizations, within HIEs, within regional health care systems, and eventually within international health care markets. As the health care environment continues to experience introduction of new technology and new regulations, HIM professionals must embrace change management and act in the capacity of change agents to promote career field changes to convince others to also embrace the change.

CRITICAL THINKING EXERCISES

1. Explain why HIM managers of the future can increasingly describe themselves as health information brokers.
2. List three methods HIM professionals can use to keep their knowledge current, and discuss the benefits of each.
3. Contrast the terms *efficiency* and *effectiveness* in the framework of health information management.
4. Describe several major management skills that will be needed by HIM brokers of the future.
5. Offer three ways an affiliated acute care organization differs from a freestanding ambulatory care organization and three ways in which they are similar.

APPLICATION OF THEORY EXERCISES

1. Reflect on the evolution of the HIM career field into the current industry practices and outline your predictions of what further evolution of the career field may involve over the next 10–20 years.

2. Choose one of the ambulatory care settings and discuss present and future opportunities for HIM professionals in this setting.

INTERNET ACTIVITY

Search for journal articles or other published information about recent and upcoming changes in the HIM career field. Summarize your findings and discuss how you might act as a change agent to champion these changes immediately after graduation as you enter a new position in a department with seasoned HIM professionals who have not embraced the concept of change.

CASE STUDY

You are the Director of HIM at a 400-bed acute care hospital. One of the responsibilities of your position is to oversee the management of health record completion. As you review monthly reports, you notice that the incomplete and delinquent rates have been steadily increasing and are reaching the maximum limit designated in the institution bylaws. You realize that you must do something to impact change in this trend. Develop three creative methods of addressing the problem that you may present at the next Health Record Management Committee meeting for approval as a new process.

REFERENCES

AHIMA Code of Ethics. (2011). http://library.ahima.org/xpedio/groups/public/documents/ahima/bok1_024277.hcsp?dDocName=bok1_024277

Gennusa, C. (1995). Outpatient HIM practices improve as managed care increases. *Advance for Health Information Professionals,* 5(10), 23.

SUGGESTED READINGS

AHIMA (2014). Strategic Plan 2014-2017: Driving the Power of Knowledge. http://library.ahima.org/xpedio/groups/public/documents/ahima/bok1_050165.pdf

AHIMA (April 2011). The medical record, 1941: Times change, but Huffman is still right. *Journal of AHIMA,* 82 (4), 88.

Butler, M. (May 2014). Adapt or disappear: AHIMA's reality 2016 has a new mission to transform the HIM workforce through education—or else. *Journal of AHIMA,* 85 (5), 24–29.

Dimick, C. (August 2012). Health information management 2025: Current "health IT revolution" drastically changes HIM in the near future. *Journal of AHIMA,* 83 (8), 24–31.

Johns, M. L. (September 2006). In the winds of change, principles provide a steady course. *Journal of AHIMA,* 77 (8), 36–38.

CHAPTER 2

Management Theories for an Integrated Management Model

LEARNING OBJECTIVES

After completing this chapter, the learner should be able to:

1. Define and describe the universal process approach to management.
2. Define and describe the five traditional management functions.
3. Explain how the operational approach to management applies to HIM professionals.
4. Explain how the behavioral approach to management applies to HIM professionals.
5. Explain how the systems approach to management applies to HIM professionals.
6. Describe how other approaches to management apply to HIM professionals.

INTRODUCTION

A strong foundation upon which to build an integrated model of management is developed in this chapter. This foundation begins with the scientific management approach developed in the early 1900s and builds on theories proven valuable throughout the twentieth century. Blending the best of these past and present theories into an **integrated model of management** creates the principles for HIM managerial success in today's information/communication society. To build the integrated model of management for HIM managerial success, the best of these past and present approaches are synthesized into a useful framework.

Integrated model of management
A model that uses the best features of information theories to develop a healthcare management model that integrates new technologies into the management model of the future.

First, the chapter prepares a foundation for integrated management concepts by briefly describing the major management approaches, and, second, it develops further selected past and present theories that contribute to an integrated management model.

GENERAL MANAGEMENT THEORIES

Figure 2-1 outlines selected management approaches and theories developed during the twentieth century. From these approaches, useful theories are incorporated into an integrated model of management that is of value in managing HIM activities today.

As the body of management knowledge and practice outlined in Figure 2-1 continues to evolve, management theories will continue to build on the comprehensive knowledge already tested and in practice. At the same time, new theories are being developed as research continues and paradigm shifts occur. For example, HIM managers are facing a paradigm shift as traditional roles for HIM departments change to information/communication roles. In the past, the departmental roles were largely involved in filing and retrieving medical records, coding, transcription, and release of information. These structured activities were best accomplished utilizing process and systems approaches to management. Technology, cost containment, and evolving expectations of upper-level management that HIM professionals have a broad range of valuable information create pressures for a paradigm shift in today's society. The challenge for HIM managers is to embrace those aspects of the new ideas that will continue the development of a professional management style, while retaining an open mind that invites future creative growth. An integrated model of management offers the opportunity for meeting these challenges successfully.

FIGURE 2-1   Selected Management Approaches

Scientific Management Approach

- Relationships between people and their work:
  - Eliminate wasted motions or activities to increase productivity.
  - Use incentive pay for reaching standards.
  - Choose the employee best suited to a task to perform that task.
  - Use the correct tools or techniques for a task.
  - Schedule complex tasks through use of devices such as the Gantt chart.

Human Resources/Human Relations Approach

- Relationships between people and among groups of people:
  - Adopt acceptance view of authority—the willingness of subordinates to accept authority.
  - Focus on social behavior and satisfaction among employees.
  - Satisfy human needs in the workplace with development of an employee's full potential.
  - Motivate employees and thus increase productivity.
  - Use communication tools effectively.
  - Develop work groups for specific tasks.

Quantitative Approach Theories

- Apply statistical models to solve complex problems.
- Use computer simulation for decision making.

Process Management Approach

- Use functions of planning, organizing, leading, and controlling to describe management activities that integrate several previous theories.

Systems Approach Theories

- Recognize internal and external environments as important to decision making.
- Manage the input of labor, capital, and materials into the organization as they are transformed into finished products or services.
- Integrate various theories of management.

Contingency Approach Theories

- Use appropriate managerial approaches for different situations and conditions.
- Use participative management appropriately.
- Accept new ideas that fit the situation such as continuous quality improvement techniques.

Universal process approach to management A management approach based on the assumption that all organizations, regardless of size or type of ownership, are guided by the same general rational management processes.

The **universal process approach to management** is based on the assumption that all organizations, regardless of size or type of ownership, are guided by the same general rational management processes. This approach may be applied to general situations, as most organizations have some sort of division of labor, chain of command, and designated authority. However, caution must be exercised to recognize that all organizations are far from equal, even within the same industry or specialization in the career field. Basic HIM functions, such as coding or release of information, may be approached similarly to an extent.

Henri Fayol's Five Traditional Management Functions

Henri Fayol, a French engineer at the turn of the twentieth century, identified five traditional management functions—planning, organizing, directing, coordinating, and controlling—to accomplish the major processes of management, which includes planning, organizing, and leading organizational activities. Fayol was not only an engineer but also a successful administrator who was able to apply classical managerial functions to activities at many levels in most industries.

Planning The management function concerned with defining goals, establishing strategy, and creating plans to guide the coordinated effort of employees to meet the goals.

Planning is an examination of the future and preparation of action plans to attain goals. HIM professionals plan for workplace changes to be consistent with the dynamic nature of the career field. Recent changes in HIM that have required a significant amount of planning in nearly all healthcare settings and in various levels of healthcare organizations include transitioning to the EHR and moving from ICD-9-CM coding system to ICD-10-CM and ICD-10-PCSc coding systems.

Organizing The management function that determines what tasks are to be done, who shall do them, the reporting structure, and at what level decisions will be made.

HIM professionals perform the process of **organizing** through coordinating activities. For example, HIM professionals coordinate workflow processes, continuing education meetings, and staff schedules. Workflow processes are addressed through careful scheduling to ensure staff coverage is able to perform tasks that are necessary to complete tasks necessary for each step in the processes. HIM professionals serving as regional, state, or national educational meeting coordinators must organize speakers according to tracks that present content for specific categories.

Controlling The management function that ensures activities are being accomplished as planned and corrects any significant deviations.

Monitoring and maintenance of a project's structure comprise the management function of **controlling**. An EHR implementation project requires a significant amount of controlling throughout the processes involved. While planning and organizing provide the initial groundwork for EHR implementation, controlling carries on the process to make sure the plans are carried out accordingly. An HIM professional performing the function of controlling monitors the progress of the project and maintains organization of the project.

Leading The management function involved in motivating employees, directing others, resolving conflicts, and selecting effective communication channels.

Leading is the management function in which people are directed and motivated to achieve goals. Leading is not reserved for those in management positions, but may be accomplished by any HIM professional in the workplace or other leadership position. An important example of leadership roles for HIM professionals is volunteer service for AHIMA, a component state association (CSA), or an associated regional HIM organization. Henri Fayol also established 14 principles of management as key points in the formulation of administrative approach to management. These are outlined in Table 2-1 as they relate to HIM professionals. These functions have evolved over time and other theorists may describe them slightly differently, such as some may refer to leading as "directing," and others may include the task of staffing as a function of management.

TABLE 2-1 HIM Examples for Fayol's Principles of Management

Management Principle	Example
Division of work	HIM professionals generally work in specialized areas, such as coding and release of information.
Authority	The HIM department has a director who gives orders for work to be completed by employees in the department in a responsible manner.
Discipline	HIM professionals may be penalized for breach of confidentiality.
Unity of command	HIM employees report only to one supervisor.
Unity of direction	HIM employees work in accordance with the mission statement and vision of the organization or department.
Subordinator of individual interests to the general interest	Employees are treated equally and fairly, avoiding favoritism or preferential treatment.
Remuneration	HIM employees are paid a salary that is comparable and competitive to similar positions in other facilities in the region.
Centralization	HIM employees play a role in decision making with the manager.
Scalar chain	Chain of command is outlined in an organizational chart, which clearly designates reporting relationships.
Order	All resources necessary for all processes in the HIM department are well-organized and distributed equally to ensure all employees have the ability to complete work.
Equity	All employees are treated equally, regardless of position.
Stability and tenure of personnel	Hiring and retention efforts ensure that qualified employees have appropriate training for the positions.
Initiative	Employees are encouraged to seek opportunities to learn new skills.
Esprit de corps	Employees work together, supporting an environment of teamwork.

Each of the management approaches outlined in Figure 2-1 has points of validity that meld into the unifying view of management that creates a foundation for HIM professionals. The diversity of ideas so evident in current management texts is the result of past and current research and the testing of management concepts over time. Synthesizing this diversity into an integrated view of management for HIM managerial success in healthcare organizations is not only exciting but also rewarding. Each of the management approaches is now briefly discussed.

A Scientific Approach

Scientific approach Scientific procedures for finding the best way to accomplish a task, introduced by Frederick W. Taylor.

Early in the twentieth century, modern management theory was born with the publication of books describing scientific management research theories. These **scientific approach** theories became widely accepted by managers. The emphasis of these researchers was on eliminating waste and inefficiency in manufacturing and other labor-intensive industries. As the relationship between people and their work became the guiding philosophy, standards were set for repetitive tasks. In each instance, these standards were developed by management and researchers as the one best way of performing a task. Performance was then compared to these standards. Experiments in hand-and-body motions in laying bricks, for example, helped eliminate wasted motions and thus increase productivity (Robbins, 1994). Choosing the best tools and the right employee for a task resulted in significant increases in productivity.

During the early 1900s, Frederick Taylor, Frank and Lillian Gilbreth, and Henry Gantt became well-known for their scientific management research. Frederick Taylor believed there was one best way to do a task and his research focused on giving workers the right tools for the task, training them in the one best way for doing the task, and motivating them through wage incentives.

Operational approach A management approach that concentrates on improving efficiency of processes and elimination of waste

Scientific management is a principle that states that the best management is a science based on laws and rules and secures maximum prosperity for both employer and employee. Scientific management theory is an operational approach to management that was initially developed by an industrial engineer, Frederick Taylor, in the late 1800s in an effort to increase efficiency in the workplace through development of standardized processes. An **operational approach** to management concentrates on improving efficiency of processes and elimination of waste. The focus of management theories following the operational approach discussed in this section are scientific in nature, based on measurable standards and time management. This is important in today's healthcare environment with a focus on utilization review and managed care.

Taylor's work was inspired by his observations of work being done without any defined system when he worked in a machine shop. He noted that lack of defined processes did not facilitate coordination of seemingly random processes that were performed through the plant. Similar issues exist in other professions, including health care, without standardized processes. The four main foci of Taylor's work addressed standardization of processes, time studies of tasks, systematic selection and training, and incentive pay. The scientific approach to management involves evaluation of processes to identify and eliminate waste of labor, time, and other resources in order to improve efficiency (Kreitner & Cassidy, 2013). This approach is applied in many aspects of performance improvement in HIM, not only to improve efficiency but also to promote higher quality outcomes.

Over the years, HIM professionals have used applied research to identify standardized processes that work best for various areas of practice. Accreditation organizations, such as the Joint Commission, have also developed standards that must be followed in health care. These standards are based on scientific-based research as well. Taylor also introduced the management theory of "initiative and incentive," demonstrating that offering an incentive provided workers with increased initiative to meet the assigned goals. While financial incentives seem obvious, Taylor also explored the impact of other incentives. The topic of incentives used in the HIM profession will be addressed in detail in Chapter 7. One of these incentives focused on managerial involvement. If management realizes factors impacting processes and associated managerial tasks, it will facilitate completion of tasks by subordinates. Taylor's four foci of management are outlined in Table 2-2 as they relate to HIM professionals.

Frank Gilbreth, assisted by his wife, Lillian, continued Taylor's work with focused studies on tasks within processes to identify potential steps that could be streamlined or eliminated (Kreitner & Cassidy, 2013). An HIM application of this would be a detailed examination of processes in the department to

TABLE 2-2   Taylor's Four Foci of Management

Taylor's Four Foci of Management	HIM Applications
Develop standardized work processes based on scientific study of each process involved.	"Best practices" are published and provide guidelines for various HIM tasks.
Systematically select, train, and develop each employee rather than making them learn processes and tasks on their own.	New employees go through a training schedule that involves shadowing in each area of the department, followed by mentoring in the area in which they are hired for a designated period of time.
Provide supervision and guidance for each worker in order to ensure that the processes are completed appropriately.	Team leaders in specialized areas in the HIM department
Divide work equally with managers applying scientific management principles to assist in planning work, while workers perform assigned tasks and are appropriately rewarded.	Coders in an HIM department are designated as inpatient or outpatient. All of the coders with the same designation are evaluated according to the same productivity standards.

determine areas of significant delays or duplication of efforts. For example, an HIM department that had been outsourcing cancer registry tasks changing processes in the workflow to eliminate the need to outsource the task and have the coders perform cancer registry abstracting since they are already reviewing the records for coding. Another contributor to scientific management was Henry Gantt. Gantt was the creator of the **Gantt chart**, which is a graphic tool used to plot tasks in project management that shows the duration of project tasks and overlapping tasks. The Gantt chart is a valuable tool used to identify timelines for tasks to be completed in projects as a means of time management (Kreitner & Cassidy, 2013). Figure 2-2 provides an illustration of a Gantt chart for a simple software purchase and implementation project. The Gantt chart will be discussed in greater detail in Chapter 16. Gantt was also responsible for the introduction of the concept of providing a minimum wage in order to recognize that human resources are valuable assets to completing tasks and provision of services (Kreitner & Cassidy, 2013). This was based on the premise that workers are more receptive to being rewarded by a fair wage for their work, as opposed to using punishment for not achieving goals as a

Gantt chart A bar chart that graphically shows the work planned and completed on one axis and the time span on the other

FIGURE 2-2 Gantt Chart

	Jan	Feb	Mar	Apr	May	Jun	Jul	Aug	Sept	Oct	Nov	Dec	Jan
Assessment	■	■											
Assess staff readiness	■												
Assess financial resources		■											
Survey Clinical Staff			■	■									
Research Vendors		■	■	■	■								
Order Software						■							
Software Installation							■	■					
Forms redesign				■	■	■	■						
Train pilot team								■					
Implement pilot team								■	■	■			
Gather feedback							■	■	■	■	■	■	■
Make adjustments/ changes									■	■			
Implement complete organization												■	■

means to motivate. The concept of minimum wage continues to be pertinent across all industries. As the HIM industry continues to expand into additional specializations and professionals are earning higher degrees, the issue of fair pay is a concern from several perspectives. As minimum wage increases, higher level trained professionals do not always get pay increases. HIM professionals are broadening their scope of practice through education and training, but sometimes encounter situations where others in the same roles with different training background may be paid differently, either higher or lower. Equal pay between genders also continues to be a concern, even in the female-dominated HIM profession.

Henry Gantt suggested offering a bonus to the manufacturing foreman, as well as the workers, when the standard was met or exceeded. He also introduced management to a graphic bar chart for use as a scheduling device. The Gantt chart continues in use today for planning and controlling projects. Details on using Gantt charts are outlined in Chapter 5.

Modified management concepts based on scientific approach concepts continue in use today and have increased importance as efficiency and effectiveness are given priority in healthcare organizations. The concepts from the scientific approach that are incorporated into the integrated management model are outlined in Figure 2-1.

Human Resources and Human Relations Approaches

The concepts that focused on human behavior and managing were partially developed and publicized during the same period as the scientific researchers were sharing their ideas. However, **human relations approach** enthusiasts focused on the social relationships in the workplace. They challenged the traditional view of authority—the view that authority comes from above. In its place, these researchers presented an acceptance view of authority—the view that authority comes from the willingness of subordinates to accept it (Robbins, 1994). The human relations approach is a management philosophy emphasizing the shift from the previously discussed less personal-focused view of workers to concern for their satisfaction at work. This approach examines human systems as systems that are organized relationships among people. The behavioral management theories focus on the employee, rather than the process.

Human relations approach An approach that emphasizes the important role humans play in the success of an organization, and states a satisfied employee will be a productive one.

These theories were further developed as group norms and behaviors were studied during the 1920s to 1950s and results were published by different groups within the broad **human resources approach**. The growing human relations movement focused on behavior and employee satisfaction. Research showed that employees were positively influenced by group standards and security. The human relations movement emphasized a belief that a satisfied employee will be productive. Motivational behavior and productivity became the focus of many research studies. One example from the 1930s became

Human resources approach A managerial approach that focuses on human behavior.

famous as the Hawthorne studies. Although the initial focus of the studies involved productivity and change in the physical environment, the results showed that productivity increase occurred when supervisors developed effective human relations skills that included cooperative effort with employees (Robbins, 1994).

Edward Deming was an engineer who maintained balance in his life by also being a musician, for which some of his works have been recognized. One of the most recognized managerial accomplishments of Deming was his role in the Ford Motor Company's shift to focusing on quality in the 1980s. His approach emphasized the importance of management being involved in the processes of quality improvement. Deming further developed organizational management theory with inclusion of human component by promoting teamwork and employee involvement in continuous improvement processes. Deming promoted participative management in quality improvement activities (TQM/ quality circles) and popularized the plan-do-check-act (PDCA) cycle, which is a performance improvement model originally developed by Walter Shewhart, a physicist often referred to as the "father of quality control statistics." See Figure 2-3 for a diagram of the PDCA cycle. Shewhart used scientific management approaches to develop processes on which many of the current day quality control practices are based. Shewhart cited the importance of checking quality of products following normal completion of processes. This practice is very similar to the healthcare focus on quality of patient care outcomes. If an unfavorable outcome occurs in a healthcare organization, the key processes involved in the outcome are examined for the purpose of correcting issues that led to the unfavorable outcome. This will be addressed in greater detail in Chapter 13.

FIGURE 2-3   Plan-Do-Check-Act (PDCA)

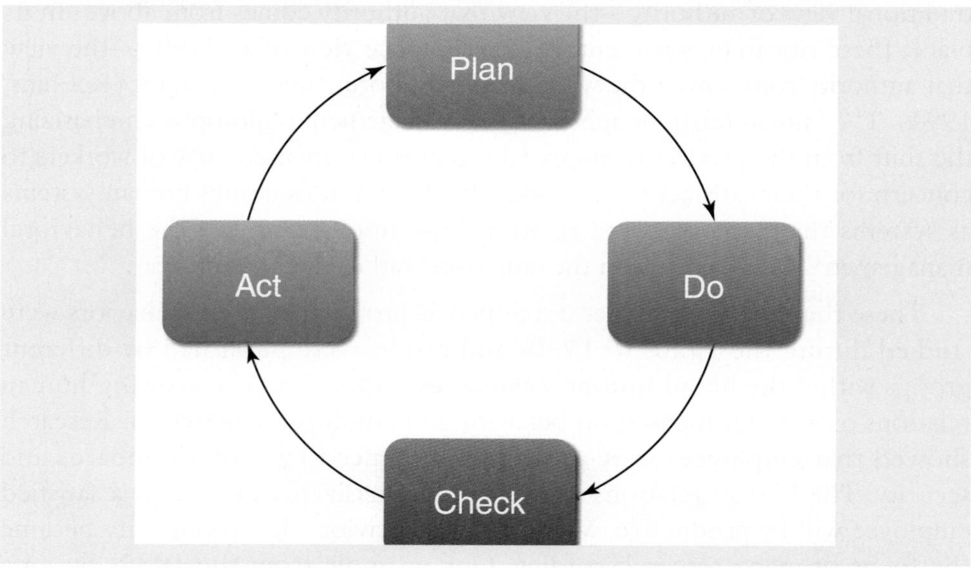

The PDCA cycle indicates that activities should be planned prior to doing them. After doing an activity or completing a task, it is necessary to check and ensure that the activity or task was completed according to the plan and the intended objectives are met. Any areas identified that may provide a higher quality outcome or more efficient process should be incorporated in the planning step the next time the activity or task is completed. The PDCA cycle is continuous.

An HIM example of the PDCA cycle may be applied to the release of information (ROI) process. The planning step involves planning the process and design of associated forms. Doing includes completing the steps and forms of the ROI process. After completion of the ROI process, the HIM professional might identify something that may need to be improved in the process.

Peter Drucker is known as the father of modern management. His management theory focuses on motivation of employees. Drucker's perspective is that motivation comes from the individual and that the manager can merely hinder the individual's motivation or assist by removing potential obstacles (Dunn, 2010). For example, if an employee is frustrated about a situation, the manager may offer to listen to the employee's concerns and respond by taking appropriate actions to alleviate the problem, if it is within the manager's scope.

Abraham Maslow proposed a hierarchy of five human needs with the highest being self-actualization (Robbins, 1994). Managers who accepted the human relations approach attempted to develop organizations where employees could meet their needs and develop their full potential. Maslow's hierarchy of needs is discussed in greater detail in Chapter 13.

Modified human resource management concepts have a firm base of support in today's healthcare organizations. Motivation, human relations, group behavior, and communication within organizations continue to gain managerial importance and are a part of the integrated model of management.

A Quantitative Approach

Quantitative approach solutions to management problems began during World War II and continue to be useful in decision making. Applications of statistical models, information models, and computer simulations make this approach valuable for complex problems that are measurable and welldefined. In Chapter 5, specific quantitative management models are discussed as part of the integrated model of management.

A Process Approach

In the 1960s, Harold Koontz detailed a **process approach** that synthesized major theories into an integrated whole. Koontz defined the process approach as management performing the functions of planning, organizing, leading,

Quantitative approach The use of quantitative techniques, usually computerized, to improve the decision-making process.

Process approach A process where management performs the functions of planning, organizing, leading, and controlling in a circular and continuous manner.

and controlling. He interpreted these four functions as being circular and continuous (Robbins, 1994).

Several researchers took this process approach a step further into a modified process approach to management. They used the same four functions, although they gave them different names or divided them for greater detail. Thus began the integrated view of management theories that continues to be modified through research and new technology (Robbins, 1994).

The Systems Approach

Systems approach A theory that views an organization as a set of interrelated and interdependent entities.

The **systems approach** theory views an organization as a set of interrelated and interdependent parts. This management theory, developed in the mid-1960s, is a way of approaching the job of managing holistically. This approach views inputs and outputs for organizational activity in much the same manner as physiologists view the body in a state of equilibrium. The inputs would be material, labor, and capital. These are transformed in the process and become outputs or finished products and services. As in physiology, forces in the environment can place restraints on the organization (Drucker, 1990).

Ludwig von Bertalanffy explored theories related to different types of systems in the areas of art, biology, medicine, culture, physics, and general systems. He combined the overlapping similarities in these systems in his general systems theory, indicating that the purpose of his theory was to provide an explanation of nature of systems, whether they are physiological, biological, or sociological. Bertalanffy's general systems theory stated that systems of any kind consist of many components that must work in a cooperative manner to accomplish the purpose of the system as a whole. Any deviation within a normally functioning system results in feedback, which impacts other related systems (Bertalanffy, 1975).

An HIM department is a system that contributes to the larger system of the healthcare organization as a whole. However, the HIM department is also made up of several smaller systems, such as coding, release of information, and transcription. Each of these smaller systems generally has several employees completing specific functions. If the normal functioning within one of these areas occurs, such as an employee in the coding area having unexpected time off for bed rest during pregnancy, not only are the rest of the employees in that area impacted but the situation may also impact staff in the rest of the HIM department and will likely have an impact on the unbilled accounts of the organization, which will impact the finance department and overall financial situation of the organization as a whole.

Closed system Systems that are not influenced by their environment and do not interact with their environment.

Open and closed systems are contrasted in this approach. The **closed system** is neither influenced by nor interacts with its environment. Since healthcare organizations are dynamic systems that interact with and are influenced by their environment, they are referred to as open systems.

Stakeholder is a name given to any entity with a stake in the future of an organization. For healthcare organizations, as **open systems**, input comes from several stakeholders—the community, employees, physicians, and researchers. Healthcare organizations are significantly influenced by their environment. Much of this influence is in the form of constraints, such as mandates from government agencies. When the organization successfully ensures coordination of all its parts and meets the needs of stakeholders and the constraints of the environment, the output or service should meet customer expectations (Robbins, 1994).

The perspective of an open system is that variables exist outside of the organization of planned processes (Kreitner & Cassidy, 2013). In the HIM field, these variables may include government regulations, economic changes in the community, or natural disasters. For example, a large employer in a community may change insurance plans, which could translate to most of the employees being forced to seek services from a different provider in the community.

However, due to the dynamic nature of the healthcare environment and rapid expansion of the scope of HIM practice, it is necessary to consider approaches beyond previously assumed limits. Creative and innovative approaches are being developed in the career field. HIM professionals must possess strong troubleshooting and problem-solving skills to tackle new issues that arise in the workplace, many of which they were not trained for during their formal education. They may be technology-related or may simply be the result of introducing new processes or organizational cultural changes.

The **Peter Principle**, named after the 1993 book by Laurence J. Peter, is a cynical belief that employees will advance to their highest level of competence, and then be promoted to their level of incompetence, where they will remain. AHIMA has published their Vision 2016 initiative, which has a strong focus on the importance of developing the HIM career field beyond previously accepted terminal degrees and areas of competence. HIM professionals are being encouraged to pursue higher degrees and obtain training in areas that have previously been limited to other healthcare specializations. The Peter Principle can easily be overcome if HIM professionals continue to encourage their peers to accept the belief that they are capable of achieving competence in higher level positions and areas previously somewhat foreign to the career field.

The Contingency Management Approach

The **contingency approach** steps beyond the systems theories and recognizes that situational variables will arise that require managers to use different approaches to solving problems. The contingency approach to management recognizes the fact that alternate approaches to situations may be necessary. The management theories presented in the previous sections of this chapter

Stakeholder Any constituency in the environment that is affected by an organization's decisions and policies.

Open systems Dynamic systems that interact with and respond to forces in the environment.

Peter Principle Cynical belief that employees will advance to their highest level of competence, and then be promoted to their level of incompetence, where they will remain.

Contingency approach An approach that recognizes and responds to situational variables as they arise.

participative management
A management style where managers consult with employees and use their suggestions in making decisions.

Internal environment
Forces within the organization but outside the department that potentially affect the department's performance; factors within the department that affect its ability to perform effectively and efficiently.

External environment
Outside forces that potentially affect a department or total organization's performance.

Empowerment
The process of increasing the decision-making discretion of employees.

are approached in a "one size fits all" manner. This approach is not based on specific theory, but rather that management activities should be determined on the basis of each unique situation. While a manager may prefer to follow one of the more defined management approaches, the contingency approach identifies the need for an alternative method of addressing situations (Kreitner & Cassidy, 2013). For example, circumstances occur that demand immediate answers and leave no time to ask for employee participation in the decision-making process to solve a problem. The contingency approach encourages managers to meet such a demand appropriately, and honestly share the background circumstances and the decision with employees. Managers will then be committed to a **participative management** style but accept that it is not appropriate or possible in every situation (Robbins, 1994).

Because the contingency approach represents the value of using the best management theory to meet the circumstance a manager is facing, it encourages the paradigm shift faced by the HIM managers. As information/communication technology and cost containment become the focus of upper-level management, HIM departments need to be redesigned or perhaps even reengineered to meet the new demands. Thus, the emphasis becomes focused on the situation, on the **internal** and **external environments**, and ultimately on a creative solution that breaks with traditional roles.

The contingency approach to management predominates as theories are integrated into the management model. Interwoven into the fabric of this approach are quality improvement theories, innovation and change theories, participation and **empowerment** theories, and ethical standard theories. This integrated approach creates a unifying framework that allows managers to meet today's challenges and explore tomorrow's opportunities.

SUMMARY

HIM professionals experience a wide variety of situations in the workplace. The management theories presented in this chapter—behavioral, contingency, operational, scientific, systems, and universal process, should provide guidance on how different situations may be approached. Selection of one approach over another will depend upon both individual preference and organizational culture, along with the circumstances of each situation. Productivity was a major thrust for many of the early management researchers. Productivity certainly remains important today as managers

plan objectives that must be accomplished with limited resources.

The scientific management approach was developed early in the 1900s by researchers who focused on eliminating wasted activities, using incentive pay, and choosing the best employees and tools for a task. Human relationships in the workplace became important to researchers of the human resources approach, which developed an acceptance view of authority, focused on satisfying the needs of employees, motivating employees to improve productivity, and using communication tools and work groups effectively.

Quantitative approach theories focus on statistical models for solving complex problems and the use of computer simulations to enhance decision making. The four management functions of planning, organizing, leading, and controlling were developed by process management theorists for describing management activities that integrate selected theories to create a balanced view. Theorists of the systems approach to management emphasized the internal and external environments of organizations for inputs and outputs that resulted in finished products or services.

Advocates of the contingency approach to management use selected theories from previous approaches to appropriately meet managerial situations or conditions. Participative management grew in importance with work teams and quality improvement techniques.

An integrated approach to management for HIM professionals combines these major features from past and present approaches and includes quality improvement ideas, transition ideas, empowerment ideas, and ethical standard ideas. This framework offers HIM managers and brokers the tools for meeting the challenges of paradigm shifts as healthcare organizations face the pressures of change.

CRITICAL THINKING EXERCISES

1. Choose one major management theory and explain its value by building an integrated model of management.
2. Give four typical stakeholders who offer input to managing a healthcare organization.
3. Explain why healthcare organizations are considered open systems under the systems approach to management.
4. How does a participative management style fit into the contingency approach to management?
5. Discuss the role mentors can play in teaching both management theory and practice.

APPLICATION OF THEORY EXERCISES

1. Compare and contrast the management theories presented in this chapter.
2. Interview an HIM professional to find out examples of situations encountered in the workplace, along with a management style most effective for each.
3. Develop a Gantt chart for planning steps involved in writing a research paper.

INTERNET ACTIVITY

Search online to find at least two articles that present situations in which HIM professionals have had to apply to the contingency approach. Provide a brief summary of the situations and how the contingency approach was used.

CASE STUDY

You are new to the position of Vice President of HIM for a large chain of healthcare facilities. As you have assessed the current situations in the HIM departments at each facility, you have met with the HIM Directors, all of whom do not believe that AHIMA Vision 2016 presents realistic goals for any of their employees because they feel their employees have reached their greatest potential and believe that they will not be successful if they try to pursue any kind of additional training or promotion. Describe how you would address this situation.

REFERENCES

Bertalanffy, L. v. (1975). *Perspectives on general system theory: scientific-philosophical studies.* The International Library of Systems Theory and Philosophy. New York: G. Braziller.

Drucker, P. (1990). *Managing for the future.* New York: Truman Talley Books.

Dunn, Rose T. (2010). *Dunn & Haimann's healthcare management* (9th ed.). Chicago, IL: Health Administration Press.

Kreitner, R, & Cassidy, C. (2013). *Management* (12th ed.). Chapter 2 The Evolution of Management Thought. Boston: Cengage Learning.

Robbins, S. (1994). *Management* (4th ed.). Englewood Cliffs, NJ: Prentice Hall.

SUGGESTED READINGS

Burns, L. R., E. H. Bradley, & B. J. Weiner, (2012). *Shortell & Kaluzny's health care management organization design & behavior* (6th ed.). Clifton Park, NY: Cengage Learning.

Liebler, J. G. & C. R. McConnell. (2012). *Management principles for health professionals* (6th ed.). Sudbury, MA: Jones & Bartlett Learning.

CHAPTER 3

The Art of Decision Making and Problem Solving

LEARNING OBJECTIVES

After completing this chapter, the learner should be able to:

1. Explain differences between strategic planning decisions and day-to-day problem-solving decisions.
2. Describe problem seekers and ways they manage differently than problem avoiders.
3. Outline the steps in the decision-making process.
4. Differentiate conditions for certainty, risk, and uncertainty.
5. Describe the pressures facing decision makers in satisficing rather than using total rationality.
6. Illustrate well-structured problems and contrast these with ill-structured problems.
7. Explain how to create programmed decision-making tools for teams and contrast these with nonprogrammed decision-making methods.
8. Identify advantages and disadvantages of team decision making.

INTRODUCTION

Developing decision-making skills for meeting organizational needs now and for the future is a crucial component to managerial success. The art and science of decision making is a central element in the planning function of the integrated model of management, and these skills permeate the other managerial functions as well. Were HIM managers to record every decision made during just 1 week, they would discover a lengthy list. Encompassing much of the daily activities of managers is this pervading relationship of decision making and successful management.

This chapter emphasizes both of these phases in making decisions—daily activities decisions and strategic planning decisions. Appropriate decisions made during the strategic planning phase can lessen the stress during the daily activities decision phase. Also, daily decisions made in anticipation of problems will lessen the need for crisis decision making and related stress. In reality, problems will arise regardless of the skill used during planning, so problem-solving expertise for these daily activities decisions is very much needed. Increasingly, the highest level of decision-making skills is needed for planning the future direction of the department and/or the organization.

Problem-solving steps that assist managers in making the best possible decisions are outlined in this chapter. Also, the types of problems faced by managers are contrasted. Suggestions for different approaches to decision making for each type of problem give insight into ideas managers can use. To summarize, the chapter discusses how using a participative management style for solving problems can have lasting advantages.

DECISION MAKING IN PLANNING AND DAILY PROBLEMS

Problem-solving process See decision-making process.

Problem seekers Managers who actively look for opportunities to alleviate potential problems before they occur.

The paradigm shifts occurring in today's health care environment make the **problem-solving process** during the strategic planning phase particularly important. As managers face growing unsolved problems in the health information management workplace, the dichotomy between actual and desirable situations creates pressure for changing a present paradigm. The manager who can forecast and generate ideas for shifting to a new paradigm is helping to create the exciting health care environment of the future. This task is hard work.

Strategic planning in itself is also hard work, with commitment needed to take the plan through to a satisfactory decision. **Problem seekers** are found to have a higher level of commitment to strategic planning. Problem seekers who actively look for opportunities to plan, anticipate, and solve possible problems before they occur have the potential for becoming exceptional managers.

At the other extreme are **problem avoiders**, who may ignore signals of possible problem eruption. Several causes for this avoidance may be valid. They may include (1) time constraints, (2) delegation of responsibility to others who are also too busy, or (3) a perception that upper-level management will avoid the problem also. Once problem avoiders recognize the value of a team approach to finding solutions, they can share the responsibility.

Problem avoiders Managers who tend to ignore signs of problem eruption.

In the daily work environment, crises occur and problems erupt when reality fails to equal the desired situations. In other words, there is a difference between what is and what should be. An example in a health information department is when the manager finds the work flow suddenly faltering in one section due to excess absenteeism. Action to bring the actual and desired situation back in balance can be taken by the manager and, ideally, with the participation of the team within that section. The solution may include asking that budget funds be allocated for hiring a temporary employee through the human resource department. This example shows that few problem-solving decisions are truly made in isolation. Here the manager, the team, the human resource department, and the person to whom the department reports may all be involved in solving this problem.

The absenteeism problem may have been entirely unanticipated. However, a crisis need not occur if the manager plans ahead with the human resource department for budget allocation to use an on-call resource person in such situations. Some managers use on-call professionally trained resource persons to meet such emergencies. When professionals prefer only part-time employment, this can be a viable short-term solution to obtaining well-trained employees to solve an absenteeism problem.

THE PROCESS OF DECISION MAKING

Several steps are included in the **decision-making process**. While decision making is defined as making a choice between two or more alternatives, a more complete description includes the whole process as shown in Figure 3-1. The process is shown in seven steps. In actuality, the decision process encompasses the first five steps; the last two steps can be considered actions taken as the result of the decision. They are included because action following the intellectual work is crucial to the success of the decision.

Decision-making process A series of steps that include identifying a problem, developing and analyzing possible alternatives, selecting the best alternative, and monitoring its effectiveness.

Abbreviated versions of the process may be adequate for a personal decision, such as when plans begin for enjoying a 2-week vacation. Looking at alternative vacation spots may be the major decision-making step taken. In contrast, managers need to immerse themselves in all seven steps outlined when choosing among alternatives for all but the simple problems. As these

FIGURE 3-1   The Decision-Making Process (Based on Robbins & Coulter, 2012)

1. Define the real problem after awareness of the symptoms.
2. Set criteria for making the decision while analyzing available information.
3. Generate relevant alternative solutions to the problem.
4. Analyze and evaluate these alternatives.
5. Select the best alternative for a solution.
6. Implement the chosen alternative.
7. Monitor and evaluate the decision's effectiveness.

steps are discussed in detail, decisions appear to be made in isolation. This, of course, is not true. Managers deal with an interrelated network of problems and solving one problem may have implications that impact others. The busy professional must keep a broad and integrative perspective as decisions are made.

PRACTICE EXAMPLE

As each of the steps is explored in detail, a practice example problem is used to create a climate for discussing decision-making skills. This example problem discusses the response to a budgetary committee mandate that the HIM department plan a budget with three fewer full-time equivalent (FTE) employees than the present year. The management team begins strategic planning to rightsize the HIM department for the coming year. The focus will be on increased efficient and effective workflow systems throughout the department. The team, at its first meeting, plans the strategy for beginning the seven-step decision-making process.

1. *Define the real problem following awareness of the symptoms.* The organization's problem in the example is a facility-wide budget constraint while the focused problem for the HIM management team is preparing a plan with a budget showing three fewer FTE employees. The actual problem to be faced, however, is inefficient or ineffective work methods where redesign for cost containment is possible. In this example, problem awareness of the symptoms came with a falling patient census and then crystallized with the budget committee action to rightsize the facility. At this awareness phase, the HIM management team develops sensitivity to facility and departmental events that show discrepancies between actual and desired situations. Perceptual skills enable the manager to collect and interpret cues from these events for beginning identification of the problem. At this step, a decision may be made that no further action is needed. In the example, of course, this is not a viable alternative.

As details of the problem are defined, these are documented by the team. It is also helpful at this point to begin listing objectives for returning to the desired situation, which may actually be a revised desired situation, as mandated in the problem.

A management team approach is being used in the example as one way to solve problems. Certainly managers make decisions by themselves in many instances. However, using a team approach, when applicable, has several advantages that are discussed later in the chapter. The use of a team keeps the decision making at the lowest level in the organization possible—where the activity takes place.

2. *Set criteria for making the decision while analyzing available information.* Using a team approach to solve the problem, the managers next empower employees in each section to review the department's philosophy and objectives and then set priorities for action. For example, having staff available from 7 A.M. to 11 A.M. to assist physicians in record completion activities may be a priority activity that is not negotiable.

3. *Generate relevant alternative solutions to the problem.* At the next management team meeting, there is a consensus that section meetings should be encouraged and the team managers of each section plan should meet and generate ideas. Reviewing present systems critically can open windows of opportunity. Listening to the experiences of others, reading journals for ideas, and talking to vendors—these activities will assist the team in generating alternatives. **Creativity** is crucial in this step as the final solution can only be as good as the quality of the alternatives chosen for review. Looking at creative alternatives opens doors and expands the possibilities for a workable solution.

Every employee has creative abilities when empowered to work in an atmosphere of trust, freedom, and security. Certainly for some people creative ideas appear to come as a "bolt from the blue," but creativity mostly incubates as a person becomes saturated with information. By choosing to organize the concepts into new and meaningful relationships, creative ideas surface.

Since every system in the HIM department is involved in this example, step 3 is a time-consuming activity. The section teams generate ideas for more efficient and effective systems. These ideas are analyzed by the management team.

4. *Analyze and evaluate these alternatives.* Some alternatives may require capital funds, some may involve other departments, and some may suggest reengineering the workflow completely. This step is also time-consuming as the managers network and further develop ideas for possible solutions. Alternatives to consider further are those that have the greatest number of desired results possible and the fewest undesirable consequences.

Three conditions are present as this analysis is undertaken: **certainty**, **risk**, and **uncertainty**. Ideally, all decisions would be made with certainty; unfortunately, that is not the norm. Estimations of how likely it is that certain events will occur and then acting on those estimates in a risk environment is much more likely. At the far extreme is uncertainty, where the decision maker has

Creativity A thinking process that combines ideas in a unique way to produce new and original concepts.

Certainty A decision situation in which the manager can make a correct decision because the outcome of each alternative is known.

Risk The decision maker has some information but must calculate the likelihood of specific outcomes.

Uncertainty A situation where the decision maker has no certainty about the probabilities associated with the situation.

(Continues)

PRACTICE
EXAMPLE

(Continued)

several variables lacking certainty. It is then very difficult to estimate the positive or negative impact of alternatives. Decisions on the alternatives may be influenced more by the personality of the manager. An optimist is more likely to choose an alternative that will maximize the benefits, with the uncertainty factors of less weight. Risk factors associated with alternatives can have probabilities assigned to them, which allow managers to use computer software to assist in the decision-making process. Further discussion of computer-assisted decisions is found in Chapter 5. In the example, the management team analyzes the alternative brought forward by the sections.

5. *Select the best alternative for a solution.* In this step of the process, the decision maker should ask four questions as outlined in Figure 3-2. The first question regards no choice, which is always a possibility: Is the best choice one of doing nothing? This choice may be taken if it is perceived that no action will provide the most desirable result. Should this alternative be rejected, then the remaining three questions are relevant. Doing nothing is not a viable solution in the example since the budget committee has mandated change.

The second question asked is whether and to what extent each alternative will contribute to achieving the objectives that were documented in step 1. Again the responses to this question should be expressed in terms of possible results. In the example, the management team continues to encourage section teams to participate during this analysis phase.

Economic effectiveness is considered in the third question. Not all decisions relate to maximizing the use of available resources, so this may not be a criterion for every decision. Since some team efforts are interdepartmental, it is important to ask the fourth question as team members may be unaware of the resources available in another department.

The last question seeks in very practical terms the feasibility of implementing an alternative that appears to have the highest positive factors. Should an alternative pass the test posed in question 3 regarding economic resources, this fourth question can focus on available expertise. A decision to automate aspects of the HIM department workflow systems to reduce labor may be one alternative considered by the teams in the example but could fail if the expertise for implementing such a program is unavailable.

FIGURE 3-2   Questions to Ask in Selecting the Best Alternative

1. Is the best choice one of doing nothing?
2. To what extent will each alternative contribute to achieving the objectives documented in step 1?
3. To what extent will each alternative contribute to economic effectiveness by maximizing use of available resources?
4. To what extent is expertise available to implement the alternative with the highest positive factors?

Asking and seeking answers for these four questions increases the chances that a good decision among the appropriate alternatives will be made. Involving all those affected by the forthcoming changes as decisions are made at this step will ease the transition into step 6.

6. *Implement the chosen alternative.* In our example, employees were actually lost through attrition rather than by outright layoffs. And, the alternative chosen was to reorganize the record analysis section. First, the teams worked with the medical staff to decrease the number of elements looked for in a discharged record. Guidelines developed by the American Health Information Management Association (AHIMA) were used to acquaint the medical staff and the department staff with acceptable practice. By networking and through journal review, the team generated ideas for streamlining discharged record procedures. By implementing these ideas, cost savings were achieved.

Nursing representatives were invited to share their expertise on the team and joined in the cost-saving effort by accepting specific record completion tasks at the point of patient care. The coding section staff also suggested ideas for shared responsibility during concurrent coding and accepted these completion tasks. Using these combined efforts, the rightsizing task was accomplished and the team eliminated the three FTE positions within the time frame requested by the budget committee.

The change was implemented when one record analysis team member moved away and two others were retrained for other positions in the department as employees left. The team planned biweekly meetings for 2 months to discuss any implementation difficulties that might arise.

Frequent team meetings during this transition period kept the managers aware of potential problems that could retard successful implementation.

7. *Monitor and evaluate the decision's effectiveness.* Through a **continuous quality improvement** program, this step can be incorporated into each section's regular monitoring activities. The loop becomes complete as any problems that develop are taken back to step 1 for solution.

> **Continuous quality improvement** A health care term that is patient or employee focused, used to describe a constant cycle of improvement.

RATIONALITY IN DECISION MAKING

The busy manager is expected to behave rationally, objectively, and logically when following the seven steps in decision making. But, is it realistic to assume that managers know all the alternatives available and all the consequences each alternative might bring to the situation? The **rational model in decision making** expects managers to maximize every choice in decision making. This model fails the test of reality since, in a manager's real world, time constraints may not allow for full development of all possible alternatives with analysis of the consequences of each alternative, if implemented. Other factors may also create blocks to total rationality and are discussed below (Robbins & Coulter, 2012).

> **Rational model in decision making** A model where the manager behaves rationally in making decisions by following the steps and maximizing every alternative before the final decision is made.

Managers may have a combination of reasons for deviating from the path of total rationality. For instance, their values, backgrounds, past experiences, and interests all work to influence perceptions as alternatives are explored. Expectations of others and the organizational culture can create distortions and encourage maintaining the status quo. Another possibility is that a past decision and its results may be a component of the current problem. This situation may escalate a manager's commitment toward one of the alternatives in an effort to demonstrate that an earlier decision was correct. Using a team approach to solving problems can minimize these constraints to some extent. When a manager or team uses the seven-step model in theory, but takes shortcuts because of limitations outlined above, the result is more likely to be a satisficing decision rather than one that maximizes all available information.

CONTINGENCY APPROACH TO DECISION MAKING

The contingency approach to management is outlined in Figure 2-1. Additional aspects of the contingency approach to planning are discussed in Chapter 4. For this discussion, a description of some of the unique features of contingency management that relate to making decisions is helpful. First, the type of problem and decision a manager faces can determine the reaction to it. Some decisions can be made that efficiently solve well-structured problems with a minimum of effort. However, there are ill-structured problems that demand time-consuming additional knowledge. These factors show the value of contingency theory, where the approach to a problem is contingent on the type of problem.

For example, when managers perceive there are new opportunities for growth in computer technology that would enhance managerial decisions, they get excited. But, then they find new computer purchases are contingent on other decisions to be made by upper-level management. Extra time and effort may be required to develop viable alternatives when so many other factors are involved. This is especially true when managers are involved in exploring a new technology such as an electronic patient record (EPR).

Two types of problems arise in this situation. The decisions for problem solutions can be separated into two categories. First are routine or **programmed decisions** for handling well-structured problems. The second category of decisions can be described as **nonprogrammed decisions**, where contingency management approaches are especially useful. Here the problems tend to be unique and nonrecurring.

Programmed Decisions

An example will give focus to this type of decision. An annoyed attorney telephones a release-of-information team member to complain that a record he needs for court the next morning has not yet been delivered. Because this

Programmed decisions A repetitive decision that is documented to handle routine problems.

Nonprogrammed decisions Decisions that are unique and thus require custom-made solutions.

situation has occurred in the past, the section team has created a procedure for solving this problem. There is no need to review the seven-step process with the developing of alternatives. Team members need only follow the step-by-step procedure, first by accessing the database to find when the request was received. Then they can check whether the release of confidential information was included with the request, and when the information was sent. Armed with this information, the team member can respond to the attorney and then meet the attorney's needs—following the procedure. The decision for this team member is a routine programmed one.

As procedures are documented for programmed decisions, they include **rules**. The procedure mentioned in the situation above would include a rule that sets parameters on what is a valid release form. Rules explicitly state what can and cannot be done. Programmed decisions can be made with efficiency and effectiveness when procedures are in place to guide in the resolution with explicit rules.

Rule An explicit statement that requires definite action be taken or not taken in a given situation.

Policy statements are also used in developing procedures. A policy sets parameters for making a decision, thus allowing the technician to use judgment. In contrast, a rule allows for very little interpretation. For example, a rule regarding the patient's signature on a release form before sharing health record information leaves little room for judgment. However, a policy stating that "Every attorney is treated courteously and promptly" gives the technician direction and guidelines while allowing opportunity for discretion in that treatment.

Nonprogrammed Decisions

Managers need skill in handling unique and nonrecurring problems that require a custom-made solution, contingent on the situation. HIM managers find opportunities to develop these skills as new technologies create system capabilities unheard of before the 1990s. When unsolved problems are occurring with the present dictation system, for example, an opportunity for a nonprogrammed decision is created. Certainly all seven steps in the decision-making process are utilized as the managers empower the transcription team to join in developing a strategy for purchasing the latest in dictation technology for the best price and service available in the area.

In reality, most problems faced by managers fall between fully programmed and nonprogrammed decisions. A measure of individual judgment is needed, even in programmed decisions, while components of nonprogrammed decisions make use of structured procedures that could be considered a programmed approach. Upper-level management bears responsibility for the majority of decisions involving unique and nonrecurring problems. At the lower level in the organization are the teams responsible for sections where the more routine decisions are made. Only the difficult decisions are passed up to the managers.

As the examples show, standardized procedures facilitate organizational efficiency; managers and the section teams appreciate them for this reason. They allow decisions to be made at the lowest level possible within an organization. This process is cost-effective and creates an environment where employees feel empowered and in control of their activities.

A TEAM APPROACH IN DECISION MAKING

Teams have been mentioned frequently in this chapter as participating in making decisions. These teams or groups may be called task forces, section teams, multidisciplinary teams, study groups, work groups, or committees. This team approach brings advantages into the decision-making process. The axiom that two heads are better than one holds true here. A first step is reaching out to the team performing the activity in question. This puts the manager in touch with the best perspective as the discussion begins. Increasing the possibilities for diversity of opinion in this way strengthens the process and also brings the true problem into focus. Typically, a wider range of alternatives results from this diversity of ideas, with increased opportunity for creatively solving the problem.

In addition to the section team, other teams can be formally assigned specific tasks. To include professionals from other specialties on these teams may be crucial to the success of the project. This multidisciplinary group can bring valuable insights from different perspectives into the problem-solving process. Shared understanding of the problem leads to creative solutions. Another benefit of the multidisciplinary team approach is the mutual understanding of the challenges and opportunities facing the various specialty groups as they work together. Also, this democratic model can be perceived by the employees as more legitimate, thus increasing acceptance of the eventual solution and facilitating a smooth implementation phase.

Used appropriately, teams can successfully tackle many problems. But, there are some drawbacks to group decision making that must be considered. First is the increased time factor and the cost of each employee's time to attend meetings. Also, busy professionals may feel there is no time for another committee. Managers must plan these team meetings carefully and ensure that they move at a brisk pace. An experienced **moderator** can decrease negatives by seeing that vocal individuals do not dominate the meetings and that social pressures to conform are minimized.

Moderator A person skilled in group techniques who leads a committee or group through a decision-making process.

Electronic meeting A committee or group meeting where decisions are made with linked computer technology.

One last drawback is that group responsibility for the final decision releases any single individual from that burden. Again, the moderator can reinforce team/individual responsibility for the decision.

Electronic meetings provide methods that can give anonymity, honesty, and speed to the decision-making process through electronic voting. This technique and others for group meetings are discussed in detail in Chapter 18.

SUMMARY

Decision making is described as choosing between two or more alternatives. Decisions are needed when an actual situation fails to match the desired situation. Managers make critical choices when planning effectively, but decision making also permeates all the other functions of management. Committees or teams meet for strategic planning sessions where the future direction of the department or organization is decided. Philosophies and objectives result and future decisions are made based on these strategic plans.

In contrast, day-to-day decisions are made in shorter time frames. These decisions complement those made during the planning function. As unsolved problems surface during day-to-day activities, pressure mounts to make a paradigm shift that creates the need for further strategic planning decisions.

Problem seekers generate opportunities for solving problems before crises arise, whereas problem avoiders tend to ignore signals that problems are surfacing. Problem avoiders may be overworked and under pressure. By using a team approach, problems can be solved at the lowest level of the organization possible, thus freeing the management team for other pressing tasks. Seven steps that assist managers in making decisions are outlined and discussed. This process then becomes a loop that can lead to awareness of problems before they become crises.

As alternatives are analyzed and evaluated, those favored have the greatest number of desired results and the fewest undesirable consequences. Managers weigh the alternatives in an environment of risk, since few decisions are made with the certainty that the desired results will follow. Uncertainty is the third condition to consider. Mathematical computer models can be used by assigning weights to these conditions. Use of these models when making quantitative decisions gives assurance that all factors are considered in the final decision.

In totally rational situations, managers make decisions that maximize the economic payoff, because all information in each alternative is available. In reality, the pressures faced by managers cause them to make decisions without full information; thus, they choose the alternative that is considered good enough at the time. This is called a satisficing solution.

Employees facing well-structured problems have procedures for solving them. These procedures include consideration of rules and policies and allow day-to-day problem solving at the lowest level possible. Problems that are ill structured require unique solutions and therefore demand the attention of managers. Decisions are made contingent on the variables surrounding the problem.

The day-to-day problems offer opportunity for managers to use a team approach in creating tools, such as procedures and manuals that will allow for programmed decisions when these problems are well structured. With ill-structured problems, use of nonprogrammed methods is more likely. Managers must monitor current and future technologies constantly for optimum use of appropriate new tools.

Empowering section teams with a voice in the decisions that affect their daily activities offers many advantages. Managers create an environment of openness and trust by respecting the ideas and concerns voiced by teams.

CRITICAL THINKING EXERCISES

1. Why can the group decision-making process be both efficient and effective?
2. Give three reasons why top management in a health care organization would encourage department managers to document a wide range of programmed decisions for their staff.
3. Interpret the meaning of the phrase *satisficing decision* and then describe a decision you have made recently that aligns with its assumptions.
4. Consider the steps of the decision-making process; identify one step, if any, that is more important than the others. Defend your answer.
5. Discuss the value of encouraging group members to share differing ideas as they explore alternative solutions to a problem.
6. State reasons why managers may not routinely anticipate difficulties before they become problems.
7. Compare the use of rules and policies in managerial action; explain the difference between these tools.

APPLICATION OF THEORY EXERCISES

1. You are the director of an HIM department. Having recently moved to the EHR, plus eliminated the old paper records through a combination of scanning and microfilm, your department has newly available space from the room previously used for paper record filing. You are considering a remodel of your department. Apply the seven steps outlined in Figure 3-1, to decisions involved.
2. Explain the rationale for avoiding a difficult decision, hoping the problem will go away. Discuss advantages or disadvantages for tackling the problem immediately.
3. Think of several decisions you have made in the past week. Describe the conscious steps you took in the process of reaching the final decision for each.

INTERNET ACTIVITY

Do an Internet search to find electronic tools or software that can be used for both individual and group decision making. Describe at least two of the options that you find.

CASE STUDY

Complaints have come to the department manager regarding timeliness of requests for patient information and a decision must be made.

Three months ago, Community Hospital opened a 24-hour urgent care center 10 miles away in a rapidly growing community.

Kent Jones, the health information services manager, took part in the planning that included the use of a combined record and one patient identification number. The decision was made to use electronic sharing of patient records between the facilities; however, at present it is necessary to fax some portions of the record upon request. In the past month, Kent has received four complaints from the urgent care center that records were not faxed in a timely manner.

There are 26 employees in health information services. Three full-time employees care for record activity during the day, with one employee devoted to record activity during the evening shift, when a team leader and four other employees are usually in the department. During the 11 P.M. to 7 A.M. shift, one employee cares for the department and picks up the discharged records from the patient care units. This time away from the department averages 1 hour. Adding additional employees is not an option, since there is a hiring freeze in place.

Kent envisions an increase in the requests for record information as the patient load at the urgent care center increases and realizes the assumption of his management team that this activity could be absorbed without adjusting work schedules was in error.

Prepare to assist Kent in solving this problem using the steps outlined in this chapter.

REFERENCES

Robbins, S., & Coulter, M. (2012). *Management* (11th ed.). Upper Saddle River, NJ: Pearson.

SECTION II

Planning to Meet Information Needs of Health Care Facilities

CHAPTER 4

Planning in the Health Care Setting

LEARNING OBJECTIVES

After completing this chapter, the learner should be able to:

1. Define the management function of planning.
2. Apply time management techniques in situations encountered by HIM professionals.
3. Explain differences between formal and informal planning.
4. Distinguish between strategic and operational planning.
5. Describe contingency planning and its advantages in health care management.
6. Define organizational vision and its role in the mission statement.
7. Explain how departmental objectives flow from organizational mission statement, goals, and objectives.
8. Identify the four components of SWOT analysis and describe the steps in analyzing the environment.
9. Outline major steps in the planning process.
10. Define transitional planning.
11. Describe use of a business plan.

INTRODUCTION

Planning is a crucial element to success in professional career choices and in personal growth. Planning is just naturally a part of daily activities. Think back to the decision-making process in making your career selection. You chose a college to meet that career goal and then planned details for reaching personal objectives. This planning may have involved formal planning concepts as long-range goals were documented on the road toward a chosen career path. This section on planning includes tools for increasing the certainty of success in meeting professional goals in the workplace and personally.

This chapter starts by discussing time management. Then, the discussion moves to the broad foundations of planning that give this management function the importance it deserves. The discussion outlines the different types of plans that managers use and various methods for using these planning tools appropriately. Next, strategic planning is described in detail as a part of the planning process. The transitional planning section focuses on the opportunity to redesign systems for a smooth transition through a paradigm shift. Lastly, developing a **business plan** as discussed in this section will be especially helpful to entrepreneurs and intrapreneurs.

TIME MANAGEMENT

Time is a resource each of us has in equal allotments; how the precious minutes are used is up to us. Although the phrase *saving time* is frequently heard, managers can only spend time—saving it is not an option. When engaged in each of the four management functions—planning, organizing, leading, and controlling—HIM professionals utilize time as a resource. Time is a resource that must be carefully managed due to the limited nature. HIM professionals, especially those in management position, are often assigned to numerous committees in health care organizations. Increasing responsibilities in the workplace, as well as maintenance of an effective balance between work and personal schedules, requires development of effective **time management** skills of planning sufficient amounts of time for tasks according to appropriate priorities.

The HIM profession is comprised of a wide range of functions, each demanding attention and activity from busy managers. This heightens the awareness that time is a valuable resource. When a variety of activities simultaneously confront busy managers, they tend to focus on the most urgent ones—not necessarily the most important. This can create tension for managers. By taking a few moments to focus on end results and then setting priorities and delegating appropriately, managers can schedule their time and their staff's time most effectively.

Because time expended in an HIM department is so closely tied to the budget, managers can experience stress when budget allocations and time used to accomplish objectives are not in alignment. For example, HIM managers and employees can be pressured to meet deadlines—such as 3-day billing information submission without adequate coding and reimbursement staff—but they lack the staff resources for success in this instance. Stress related to time management can also be caused by other factors, and suggestions for reducing such stress are outlined in this chapter.

Implementing the tools and techniques for time management gradually leads to confidence. HIM professionals soon find that setting priorities and delegating tasks to empowered employees are integral to the functions of planning, organizing, leading, and controlling.

Planning personal activities for the day, for the week, or for the year mandates that managers choose how time will be expended. When the return on invested time is considered just as important as the return on invested money, managers begin to give increased value to this scarce resource. Unfortunately, while employees experience automation and other job enhancements with resulting higher productivity, managers are frequently asked to increase their responsibilities and effort without comparable job enhancements that would increase managerial productivity. Thus, the managerial tasks are increased, creating a demand for efficient use of time. This situation is especially true in health care, where the trend is to reengineer with flattened organizational structures, adding to the responsibilities of middle management. This increased responsibility offers an additional reason for health information professionals to utilize time management principles wisely.

A look at possible time wasters in the typical HIM department gives focus to the principles for effective time management. Figure 4-1 provides a list of common time wasters that can keep HIM professionals from prioritized activities already planned for the week. These time wasters are, in part, uncontrollable since they are responses to legitimate requests, problems, or demands

FIGURE 4-1   Potential Time Wasters for HIM Professionals

1. Technology issues
2. Unplanned interruptions
3. Personal interruptions
4. Poorly communicated directions
5. Need to seek missing information
6. Meetings
7. Lack of motivation
8. Lack of organization
9. Poor time management skills

Response time
Uncontrollable time spent responding to requests, demands, and problems initiated by others.

initiated by someone else. The time needed to complete these uncontrolled requests is called **response time**. When response time can be shortened, discretionary or controllable time is increased.

Increasing discretionary time is the goal as the time wasters outlined in Figure 4-1 are scrutinized for action. A closer look at the challenges outlined in Figure 4-1 offers insights that can be helpful in reducing these time wasters.

Technology Issues

There are a variety of issues that HIM professionals may encounter with technology, which may be potential time wasters. Computers may need to be rebooted. The printer or copy machine may develop a jam or need toner. If the Internet is needed for a task, the connection may be slow. All of these things take away time, during which an employee may have been otherwise productive.

Unplanned Interruptions

Certainly not every crisis situation can be avoided. The goal is to decrease their frequency and disruption. During the planning functions, programmed decisions can be documented for the teams. Recurring problems can then be handled by the teams in line with the policies. Managerial planning reduces the frequency of crisis situations and increases discretionary time for both managers and employees.

Personality differences offer a plethora of ways managers choose to handle interruptions. Some managers gradually make everyone aware that they have an open-door policy except for time periods needed for concentrated work. Choosing a special time of day when the door is closed for an hour or two is then accepted well. Managers who choose to close their doors for longer periods can be accepted well also when they increase their visibility by employing management by walking around (MBWA) techniques. Appropriate assertive comments to upper-level management can also lessen interruptions. Comments such as, "Thank you for deferring our conversation this morning while I was busy completing the medical staff report" lets upper-level management know that you will inform them when important items take precedence over interruptions.

Personal Interruptions

Most workplaces have policies regarding personal phone calls, visitors, and other forms of personal interruptions during the workday. Many prohibit employees from using cell phones and even require that cell phones be turned off in the workplace. Emergency situations do happen occasionally, which may require the employee to be contacted at work. However, it is important that employees not only have plans in place for childcare or elder care, but they should also have a backup plan in case something happens with the routine practice.

Poorly Communicated Directions

When providing instructions to employees regarding tasks that need to be completed, it is necessary to use terminology that clearly defines every step in the process and all materials needed. The manager should also verify that the employee understands what is intended by the instructions.

Need to Seek Missing Information

Many reports and projects are monthly or yearly requests and it is possible to plan and organize for them. The amount of time between running these reports and completing these projects may allow for forgetting necessary details involved in producing the desired results. Documenting what is needed and having this information routinely gathered will reduce the time wasted in preparing for the next report. Taking a critical look at each project when it first arrives can provide impetus for asking questions and setting in motion the gathering of material and information. Then, when there is time to work on the project, the information and material will be ready.

Meetings

Chapter 18 offers suggestions for effective meetings. Poorly run meetings that are chaired by someone else challenge the members to create a climate that encourages change toward effectiveness. Additionally, not all meetings are necessary, or too many members may be added to committees. Meetings take employees away from otherwise productive time. When forming committees or determining invitees to meetings.

Lack of Motivation

Employees lacking motivation may find other distractions that take away from productive time. Lack of motivation may be intrinsic or extrinsic. Intrinsic motivational issues may be due to personal problems, illness, or even a lack of interest in the type of work. Extrinsic factors may include interpersonal conflict in the office, poor management, or a wide variety of other factors. Chapter 14 addresses methods of providing motivation for employees.

Lack of Organization

The tools and techniques described in the next section offer ideas for putting disorganization and procrastination on notice that they will not be tolerated. Personality types tending toward disorganization can take small steps toward using these tools and techniques; time management enhancement makes the effort worthwhile.

Poor Time Management Skills

Time is a valuable and limited resource, which is easily wasted if an employee has poorly developed time management skills. As a manager, it may be necessary to mentor employees to prevent wasted time. Employees may feel overwhelmed if given several tasks to complete without the ability to assign priorities to each. This may result in an employee spending a little bit of time on one activity, then jumping to the next, and then the next, without spending enough time on any of the tasks to make sufficient progress.

By utilizing effective time management techniques themselves, HIM managers are role models for the team members. When emphasis is given to reducing time-wasting habits through in-services, bulletin boards, newsletter spots, and e-mails, additional impetus can quicken the pace of change. The raised awareness level regarding time management encourages employees to look for time wasters and eliminate them.

One way to raise awareness is by creating incentives for teams who ferret out time wasters; this creates enthusiasm. Allowing the members to initiate action when specific team members have time-wasting habits offers advantages. For example, when one employee is habitually taking longer to perform a task, such as opening correspondence and keying in information, the members may request a time and motion study for opening and sorting the correspondence.

Team leaders can reduce time wasters by ensuring:

1. Orientation and training are thorough.
2. Instructions are clear and documented so team members do right things right the first time.
3. Policies and procedures are current and understood by team members.
4. Duplication of activities is minimized.
5. Socializing and personal activities are reserved for break and lunchtime.

TOOLS AND TECHNIQUES FOR TIME MANAGEMENT

To some extent, time management remains an individualized process. Just as each of the time wasters in Figure 4-1 can create greater difficulty for some HIM professionals than others, so the tools and techniques outlined in this section have greater usefulness for some managers than they will have for others. This situation relates to personality types, for HIM professionals carry their personality types into the workplace and their methods for handling time management are as varied as their personality types. By utilizing the tools and techniques outlined in Figure 4-2 that best match their personality organizational types, busy managers can develop time management plans that will increase discretionary time.

FIGURE 4-2   Tools and Techniques for Time Management

1. *Activity log:* Keep an activity log in 15-minute intervals for at least 2 weeks to determine how time is spent. It can be on an appointment calendar or automated log. Record as activities are done, not at the end of the day. At the end of each week, categorize the activities and total the minutes. Analyze how time is spent and look for time wasters. This log analysis brings into focus how time is actually spent and offers opportunity for change.

2. *Objectives:* Plan or update personal and departmental objectives. List activities that need to be initiated to accomplish objectives needing action; include deadlines when appropriate.

3. *Desk file/computer file:* Use the file drawer in your desk as a working file, not just for storage. Prepare file folders for items that are frequently used for quick reference—a file for each employee or team—to drop in an informal note of commendation, concern, or family item, for example. Prepare a file folder for each unfinished project or request that now resides on top of the desk and place it in the drawer. Keep the top of your desk work space clear except for the item being done at the moment.

    Complement use of the desk file with a computer file. Since requests come in hard copy in many situations, a desk file cannot be totally replaced in most facilities.

4. *Master list:* Create a master list or "to do" list either on computer or in an $8\frac{1}{2} \times 11$ inch ruled binder. Attack clutter and stacks on the desk first, then activities from the list of objectives, and subsequently periodic reports. Indicate the date that each item made the master list and a deadline for completion.

    a. Go directly to the master list when accepting a request and write it down; do not record on small pieces of paper.

    b. Cross through items as they are completed; tear out the page when the majority of items on it have been completed; rewrite unfinished items and dates, when using a binder; on a computer, move completed items to an inactive list or delete completely.

    c. Keep the master list available at all times as a working document; review it before leaving for the day to set priority projects for the next morning.

    d. Prepare a file for daily mail items that cannot be cared for at once. Place items on the master list with the date and completion date, when necessary.

5. *Daily organizing techniques:* By taking the actions outlined above, the desk is now uncluttered, the working files are out of sight in the drawer or on the computer, and the master list is less than two pages. Discretionary time is increasing, and some daily organizing techniques can increase that time even further.

    a. *Beginning-of-day planning:* The real slaves of time are those who dash in at the last minute every morning, stressed and out of breath. What a difference arriving at least 10 minutes early—at least most mornings—can make. Those 10 minutes offer the opportunity to look at the appointment log (computer or desk calendar) for the day. Make sure items needed for appointments are ready, and note on the master list any items that still need completion. Review the master list for priority items for the day. Circle or star those that

(Continues)

(Continued)

have the highest priority. Check any messages that may have come in; record or discard appropriately. Now, meet the challenges of the new day.

b. *Mail techniques:* It may be helpful to delay checking e-mail until high priority items have been completed. Paper mail for the department can be sorted by a receptionist, secretary, or team manager. Choose the best time of day for the mail and concentrate on it then. Label and place in the "out" basket any items that need rerouting. Place items in working file folders as needed; have folders for committee meetings or team meetings and place items in these folders for future announcements or discussions. Choose to delegate requests when possible. Scan magazines, journals, or reports for key information; clip articles for later reading and place in the "to read" basket. Find time to read and share them.

There are a variety of methods that may be used for time management purposes. Individuals commonly use planners to keep track of meetings, deadlines, and other important items on schedules. Planners are available in a variety of forms from a small pocket or purse size to a large wall size. Technology has enhanced and facilitated this type of time management in many ways. Calendars are now frequently maintained in electronic format and are easily synchronized among computers, smart phones, and tablet devices. In addition, others may be granted access to an electronic calendar and may also send invitations to meetings or other events. Electronic calendars may be configured to display alarms for reminders of meetings, along with sending e-mail alerts to others included in the meetings or events.

In today's hectic workplace environment, it is not unusual for individuals to encounter multiple events that are scheduled at the same time or tasks with similar deadlines. Because of this, it is important to be able to identify priority rankings for tasks and events. Table 4-1 outlines a method of classifying activities according to priority.

TABLE 4-1   Priority Ranking Matrix

	Not Urgent	**Urgent**
Important	Priority 2 Important but not urgent These items must be addressed or completed in order to accomplish goals, but lack the urgency of priority 1 tasks.	Priority 1 Important and urgent Do these tasks immediately Emergencies High-priority meetings
Not important	Priority 4 Not important, not urgent These items are time wasters and should be avoided.	Priority 3 Not important but urgent These are items that are either not scheduled, such as interruptions, or are tasks that are busy work that are not critical.

Reducing stress related to time pressures can increase productivity for HIM professionals and increase their feelings of well-being at the same time. A couple of stress-reduction techniques include two techniques that relate to time management: (1) slow down and (2) tackle problems one by one, not all at once. To slow down need not mean to get less done. Slowing down better relates to increased efficiency through the tools and techniques outlined in Figure 4-2. There will be increased discretionary time to slow down and enjoy other aspects of the health information profession and career goals.

Tackling problems one by one is valued advice for beginning the morning thinking time, when the challenges for the day can seem overwhelming. By creating a mindset that prioritizes the tasks and then concentrates on one task at a time, busy managers reduce stress for themselves and set the tone for the staff as well. Each manager must choose the most effective work schedule for himself by understanding his productivity cycle. Doing the most difficult priority item at the time of day when energy levels are highest is important. Also, big projects like the budget have many individual items that can be tackled one by one, delegated, or divided into tasks that better fit the schedule. By always thinking of big projects in terms of divided units, HIM managers can reduce stress and not waste time slots that may be just long enough for one divided unit, but not for a whole project.

PLANNING DEFINED

One reason for planning is to get from where we are to where we want to go. Knowing the goal, setting the objectives, developing the strategy, choosing methods for achievement—these are components of planning. Or, it could be said that planning is choosing the ends or what is to be done, as well as the means or how it is to be done. Thus, planning lays the foundation for organizational activity. The health care organization may be a consulting firm; it may be a new home health care facility; or it may be a large inpatient facility. HIM professionals can choose involvement in the planning associated with each of these three examples of health care organizations.

Planning involves the six universal questions: Who? What? Where? When? Why? How? Planning does not stay behind closed doors; it is a communicated, coordinated effort. When every person concerned knows where the organization is going and what they must contribute to reach the objective, they will become a part of the team effort.

Formal and Informal Planning

A manager carries around in her head some plans for the day's activities. Several are probably not written down anywhere and have no objectives formally tied to them. They are examples of **informal planning** that occur in every

Informal planning The planning done by managers that is not formally documented for present or future use.

FIGURE 4-3 The Planning Process

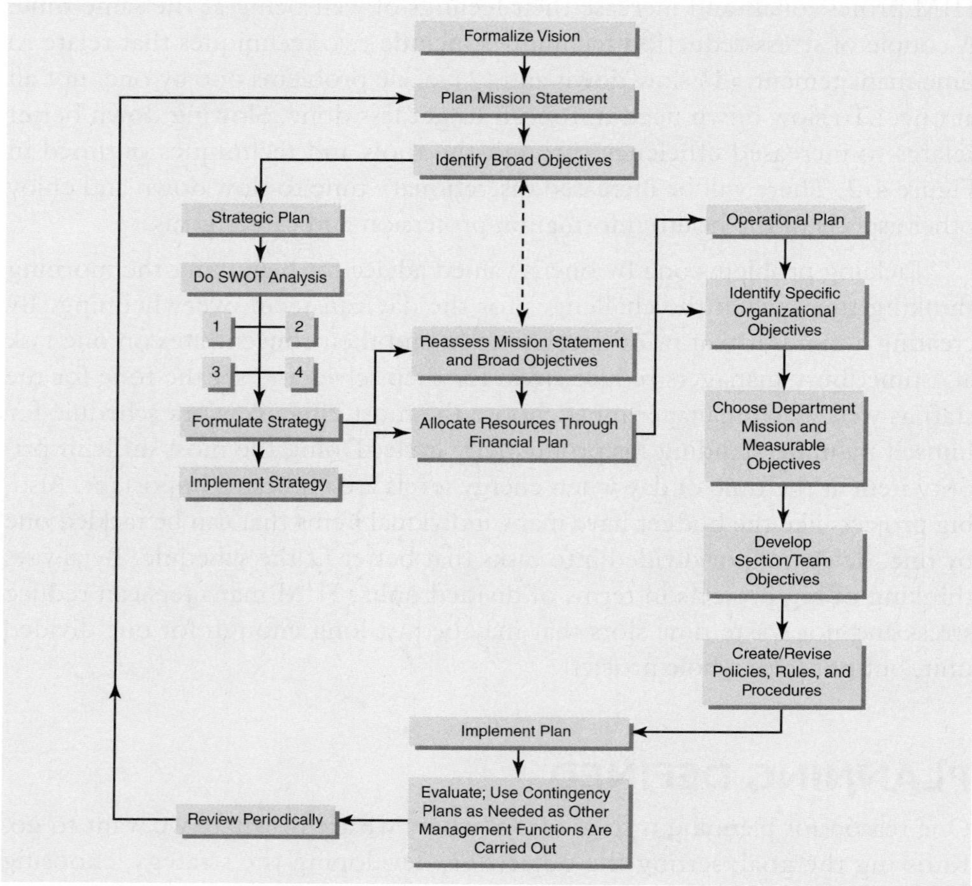

Entrepreneur A
person who con-
ceives a product or
service idea, pursues
opportunities for in-
novation, and starts
an organization.

Intrapreneur A
person who creates
an entrepreneurial
spirit within an
organization.

organization. Even an **entrepreneur** catching a vision of the future may not formally document that vision and the plan for getting there until after the company is established. This circumstance can also occur with **intrapreneurs** in HIM departments. They may not document ideas for creating a profit center within an HIM department until formal requests for space or capital equipment demand formal planning. Planning, as discussed here, refers to the formal type of planning with goals and specific objectives documented and shared.

Figure 4-3 shows how transforming the vision into the mission statement is the first step in the planning process. During the strategic planning phase, the mission statement is subject to revision.

Strategic and Operational Plans

Another type of management related to planning is strategic management, which is planning and decision making based on long-term organizational objectives and the organizational mission. Strategic decision making is generally performed by those in higher administrative levels in the organization, such as the boards of directors, chief executive officers, and top-level executives. These decisions are directly related to the organization's strategic plan. A strategic plan is a formal documentation by the organization's leadership that states objectives based on the organizational mission, vision, and goals in order to set the strategic direction of the organization. The approach to strategic planning is generally dependent upon the size, structure, and culture of the organization. While the strategic plan is finalized and documented by top executives in an organization, many organizations involve input from lower levels of management, or even all employees.

Strategic planning sessions generally start with a reflection on the mission, vision, and values for the purpose of determining a strategy, or course of action designed to produce a desired business outcome. Mission statements are often accompanied by statements of the organization's values and a vision statement. This organizational **vision** presents a picture of the desired future that sets a direction and rationale for change. Long-term objectives, referred to as strategic goals, are set by an organization to improve its operations. These are able to be linked directly to the mission statement of the organization. Some strategic goals may build on planning from previous years and some may be new. Occasionally, strategic planning may involve radical changes that involve changing the mission statement.

Vision An idealized goal that proposes a new future for an organization.

Strategic planning brings focus to the organization's vision and provides direction toward the goal. As long-range plans are developed, it is the strategy that will create this plan into action and eventual results. We can consider strategic planning as a bulldozer at a construction site, making the moves, converting the goals into accomplishments. In the health care setting, where the product includes a variety of services, strategic planning will determine which services or products to offer. As these plans are shared, members of the organization are directed toward these goals.

Strategic plan documentation may also include a strategy map, which documents relationships between the specific areas of the organization and strategic goals. The strategy map is not only a useful planning tool, but it also may contribute to quality improvement activities by outlining documentation of the strategic goals for further analysis. The organization's strategic plan documentation should include a strategy map of the cause-and-effect relationships related to the organizational strategic plan. This includes action steps that must be taken in order to achieve the strategic plan. All activities related to strategic initiatives of the organization or department should be shared through strategic communications. Some examples may include promotion of a new service being provided by the facility, implementation of electronic health record (EHR) systems, or change in the mission statement.

In contrast, operational planning tends to be short term. This type of planning identifies specific details for achieving the objectives outlined during the strategy or long-term planning phase. For example, an HIM department's operational plans for the month may include specific objectives for maintaining the 3-day submission of patient information for billing despite the vacation plans of a coding technician.

Strategic planning is emphasized in this chapter and operational plans are covered in detail in Chapter 5.

Short-Term Versus Long-Term Planning

As the examples in the section above show, long-term plans are typically strategic and are usually documented for 5 years or more. In contrast, the time frame for short-term planning is 1 year or less. Plans that cover 1–5 years may be called intermediate plans. Despite these traditional time frames, managers should realize the value of flexibility. Should any internal or external environmental changes occur, appropriate adjustments may be needed in the plans. This is particularly true in the volatile health care environment.

Contingency Approach to Planning

From the previous discussion, the value of a contingency approach that gives flexibility to formal planning can be observed. Just as Chapter 3 showed the value of developing contingencies in the decision-making process, so these examples show the advantages of adjusting to forces within and without the organization when planning for the future.

STRATEGIC PLANNING

Mission statement The documentation of the purpose of an organization.

Developing a strategic plan for the organization begins with the **mission statement**. It is the strategy that transforms long-range objectives into action and reality. The mission statement and objectives are the good intentions, but these can lie dormant. The strategic plan is the bulldozer that turns the mission statement and objectives into accomplishments. One key to the bulldozer action is the leader who skillfully translates the mission and long-range objectives to the team. The team then joins the leader in converting these objectives into strategies and then into action at the department level. Each team member needs to feel a commitment for that goal in order to say, "I contributed to the goals of our department, our organization."

Strategic planning for the health information manager is exciting but demanding. A vision for the future may be glimpsed only by a manager. It may at first be an unclear vision to have innovative technology in the department for maximum productivity and effectiveness. As the vision becomes focused, the management and team will formalize the strategic plan by documenting the goals for enhancing productivity and effectiveness. Another goal may be to maintain the long-term prosperity of the department.

The organization and the department managers will plan the goals for flexibility because of possible health care system changes in the external environment. The manager understands this dynamic environment and thus builds into the plan the flexibility to anticipate and act quickly. Networking, reading, listening, and empowering teams for knowledgeable input—these activities will allow the manager to reflect on complex issues. Skillful, quick, appropriate, and intuitive responses will be forthcoming as strategic plans are developed. Thus, for effective planning, goals must be clearly defined. The strategic plan will then blend with environmental pressures to create long-term effective results.

Developing Strategy from the Organization Mission Statement

A vision of the future has been mentioned several times as the starting point for a strategic plan. This vision, when documented in the formal planning process, is identified as a mission statement. From the mission statement, the objectives are developed. While the mission statement encompasses the broad vision at the organization level, the objectives flowing from it tend to become more specific. As can be seen in Figure 4-3, strategic planning flows from the mission statement, and when complete, requires reassessment of the mission statement.

In a health care facility, planning strategically may begin with upper-level management setting the tone for the process by asking department managers to assist in communicating the vision and developing the organization's mission statement. Department managers may then be asked to develop strategies that would be unique for their departments. The resulting mission statement lays the foundation not only for the facility but also for the objectives of the department. In other facilities, upper-level management may first develop the mission statement and then ask managers to plan specific departmental goals using this statement with their teams.

For the entrepreneur just starting a business, strategic planning may occur as the vision is formalized into a mission statement before the major objectives are developed for the new firm. From these beginnings, the entrepreneur formulates the choices for future direction, setting the stage for action, forecasting the future. Through strategic planning, the risks can be minimized and the resources allocated for accomplishing these broad goals. It is most important that the strategic plan include the resources necessary for implementation.

Developing the Goals or Objectives from the Mission Statement

The next step in strategic planning is to assess the broad goals or objectives that managers will use to create operational plans. These terms—*goals* and *objectives*—can be used interchangeably. They refer to the outcomes expected and desired from the activities of the organization, from a specific area within the organization, or even from an individual. The proposed objectives will be reassessed and revised during analysis and development of the strategic plan.

As service organizations, health care facilities have products that are intangible. Their mission statements frequently express a desire to heal the sick in a global setting. The domain of the organization is thus defined in very broad terms. This gives managers an opportunity to prepare goals or objectives that describe how areas of responsibility are a part of the mission of the facility. They should be designed by focusing on what the organization does best—that is, the areas of competence.

For example, Peter Drucker describes an emergency department struggling to create an overall goal that became, simply, "to give assurance to the afflicted" (Drucker, 1990). This is operational; it is a goal around which a culture can be created. Translating that goal into policies and procedures for team implementation changed the focus of every employee in the department. With the major focus on giving assurance, the team changed the flow of patient care, and when Drucker wrote his book, *Managing Non-Profit Organizations*, this emergency department had a qualified person seeing anyone who came through the door within 1 minute—that is the only way to give initial assurance in an emergency situation (Drucker, 1990).

This change to a customer-driven goal became a reality because upper-level management revised the mission of the hospital and then actively demonstrated their willingness to encourage departments to make cultural changes. They also empowered middle managers to set the pace for change within their **span of control**.

Span of control
The number of employees a manager can direct with efficiency and effectiveness.

Because the mission statement tends to be a long-range vision, the more specific objectives can be long-, middle-, and short-range goals that have a tendency toward contingencies. Thus, they can be adapted as the environment changes. Certainly regulatory changes can create a need for revisions in an objective. By periodically reviewing the forces in the external environment, managers can anticipate regulatory or other changes and have contingency plans ready for intervention.

Leaders in health care today can expect to revise or completely change strategic plans as the environment in which they operate changes.

Analyzing the Environment

In order to answer the universal questions of who, what, why, when, where, and how, it is now necessary for managers to further develop a strategic framework by analyzing the environment. Knowing the opportunities and threats in the environment allows managers to align the organizational activities with that environment to enhance success. The framework includes an analysis of the strengths and weaknesses of the organization or department. This thinking process model is frequently called **SWOT analysis** because it puts together the strengths, weaknesses, opportunities, and threats to show how to best serve customer needs. These four components are used to analyze the environment with the following two-step SWOT process:

Step 1. Strengths and weaknesses: By looking inside the organization, managers can answer the questions: Where are we now? What unique skills and tools do we have that will give us advantages in meeting our customers' needs? Where are the weak areas in our organization? Answering these questions, in concert with step 2—the opportunities and threats in the environment—gives insights into whether the organization's strengths can indeed meet the needs of the customers.

A strong organization culture can be a strength if its emphasis aligns with an environmental opportunity. For example, during expansion, a record-copying service may have a culture that embraces hospital department employee satisfaction. Thus, it would commit to equipment that would enhance relationships with these employees, possibly including having each copying service representative use computer software for tracking copies made for specific requestors and for making this information available to the department in a timely manner. This procedure could be a distinct advantage if analysis of the environment showed an opportunity in the expansion area because of past poor relationships with other copy services.

Included in exploration of strengths should be documentation of the core competencies. The objectives for the organization or department must be linked to the core activities that will accomplish the stated objectives. An organization or department is only as strong as its weakest core competency. A core competency can change suddenly, such as the changes in federal regulations in the 1980s, which suddenly changed coding expectations. Many HIM departments found they lacked competence in the coding accuracy demanded when the prospective payment system became a reality with billing linked to diagnosis codes.

Step 2. Identifying opportunities and threats: Identifying opportunities and threats in the environment is the second step for health care planners. However, this step is most effective when done in concert with step 1. It allows planners to focus on those strengths and weaknesses that will have the greatest impact on opportunities or threats in the environment. For example, the HIM department managers in a hospital where there is a large ambulatory care department would want to define environmental opportunities and threats relative to the caregivers and patients in ambulatory care as a high priority.

Health care managers will also identify opportunity and threat possibilities relative to legislative and regulation changes. Monitoring legislative activity and factoring in flexibility that can respond to sudden changes in the environment gives planners a strategic advantage.

SWOT analysis
An analysis involving an organization's strengths and weaknesses and the opportunities and threats in its environment.

Through professional organizations, HIM managers are offered the opportunity to monitor proposed legislation and to influence regulations through the activities of legislative affairs offices. Journals and newsletters from other health care organizations also give the current status of such activities. These informational tools are very helpful to health care planners performing SWOT analysis.

Formulating and Implementing Strategy

Once the SWOT analysis is documented and communicated, the management team can begin to plan the strategy that will allocate resources to accomplish the objectives that have been reassessed and revised in response to the analysis. The strategy is then transformed into operational plans where the action takes place.

STEPS IN THE PLANNING PROCESS

A review of Figure 4-3 shows the major steps in the planning process, from formalizing the vision of the organization down to the contingency planning involved during evaluation of the plan. As specific organization or department objectives are created, it is crucial that they be in measurable terms. The language should be clear and specific. It is helpful to compare each objective with one that is well stated, such as the choice of words used by President Kennedy in the 1960s: "man on the moon by the end of a decade." Or compare it to the mandate for nationwide automated records.

After the objectives are planned by each section/team, policies and rules will need review and revision. Again, professional organizations and other health care organizations have information on changes in the environment that may need incorporating into these policies and rules. The procedures for the team members are revised to reflect an emphasis on the objectives that give direction for the future. Chapter 6 covers these aspects of planning.

As stated in Chapter 2, planning is a function managers do in their daily activities. In reality, planning covers all functions of management. As the strategic plan is implemented, the procedures that flow from the objectives become a part of the organizing, leading, and controlling functions.

As the plan is evaluated during the controlling function, contingency planning may be required as environmental forces change. Anticipating change and preparing contingency plans will assist busy managers in this step. As the planning process cycle is repeated, adjustments are made at each step to reflect the strengths, weaknesses, opportunities, and threats of the future. This cycle appropriately covers all the management functions during the process.

TRANSITIONAL PLANNING

Transitional planning is a process that offers a new paradigm for planning that will begin by designing a bridge to the future and to a new system for health care. This process stretches beyond strategic planning to meet the demands for changes in incentives and focus. HIM professionals have an exciting opportunity to participate in this transition to a health care system that will emphasize full-continuum health care with priority given to preventive and health-oriented services. As this transition from inpatient, disease-oriented services to the new paradigm occurs, incentives will change. Information systems (ISs) of the past that created data to assist strategic planners in assessing the environment for competitive advantage and marketing designs will need changing. Transitional planning will focus instead on information necessary for building cooperative regional health care delivery systems.

Involved in the planning for these new systems will be a broad base of stakeholders: health care organizations, physicians, other health care providers, payers, regional businesses, and the public. Sophisticated software systems will be needed to create the information base demanded by these regional planners.

Transitional planning A process that offers a new paradigm for planning that begins by designing a bridge to the future.

Developing the Vision for a Transitional Planning Model

Transitional planning refocuses on a vision that asks health care organization planners to place ethical issues on the discussion table as incentives change. A healthy population, well educated in preventive care, will have value over sophisticated advertising planned for repairing a disease-specific group. These ethical issues will be reflected in the mission statement. Visionaries will create regional networks with a focus on avoiding duplication of services. These networks can involve all the responsible parties in a commitment to an efficient and effective health care delivery system. This participative process will create a framework that includes a redesigned health care system, not just a piecemeal adaptation of an old system.

Assessing the Environment

During the transition phase the assessment of present delivery models, attitudes of responsible parties, internal operations, and external change will be ongoing and must be integrated into the plan for bridging to the new paradigm. As integrated regional networks are built, this assessment will reveal where the planners must focus energies to effect success.

Opportunities for HIM professionals will grow as network ISs become an increasingly crucial component of the new paradigm.

Transition Plan Creation

Priorities will be set, strategies planned, and objectives created toward the final phases of the assessment component. Commitment to new incentives, changed risks, and the new paradigm will require outstanding communication skills. Managers with organizational development skills and team-building skills will be highly valued during this period.

Implementation Plan Creation

Building the infrastructure completely will depend on where the external environment has led. At this phase of the plan, the forces creating the change toward full-continuum health care should have most of the incentives in place. Implementation will inevitably lead to repeating the cycle of transitional planning toward the next paradigm shift.

Rural areas of the United States are leading in creating regional collaborative centers for expensive diagnostic and therapeutic equipment. This type of collaboration will increase the transitional demand for the EHR and timely regional record transfer to a total EHR. As the regional information/communication structures become operational, new ventures toward the national network will be created. This new paradigm will include participative planning groups with a broad community-based commitment to quality, timeliness, efficiency, and effectiveness.

DEVELOPING THE BUSINESS PLAN

Intrapreneurs and entrepreneurs alike need to develop business plans for their ventures. Business publications tell of the high failure rate among small business in the first 5 years of operation. Frequently, the documented reason for failure is inability to implement good management processes. Taking time to write out a detailed business plan assists the entrepreneur in thinking through all of the details that lead to success.

Developing a Business Plan Within the Organization

While the enthusiasm for an innovative idea is still bubbling, the first question intrapreneurs should ask is, "Is there a demonstrated need that will be met by developing this idea into a project?" Financial constraints in today's health care environment demand that there be a substantial need. The plan must show that this substantial need can be met in a cost-effective manner. So, the next question is, "Will the project be cost-effective?" Should the intrapreneur have uncertainty as to how these two questions might be answered by upper-level management, now is the time to put out some feelers, ask questions, sow

FIGURE 4-4 The Business Plan

1. Executive Summary (Manager's or Team's Summary):

   Exact name of business or project, specific nature of the business.

2. Mission Statement: Planned accomplishments and goals.

3. Description of the Business or Project: Who will manage the business?

   What is the product or service offered, the risks involved? Where will the business be located? Why is the business unique, why can it succeed? When is startup? (business timetable of key events) How will funding occur, how will risks be addressed? How will legal or conflict-of-interest threats be met?

4. Target Market, Sales, or Service Market Penetration:

   Market survey to assess need, competition, changing needs, and/or constraints.

5. Financial Plan and Projected Budget:

   Operating budget for first year; projections for 5 years.

   Projection of savings, a break-even chart.

   Projected balance sheet; profit and loss statement.

6. Evaluation Plan:

   Tools for monitoring effectiveness and efficiency.

---

seeds, and emphasize the perceived problem. Empowering a team to brainstorm ideas will enrich the problem-solving aspects of the project and thus enhance the documentation.

A resounding "yes" to the two questions above is a green light for the project at this point. Figure 4-4 outlines basic steps in a business plan; these can be adapted for a project. The executive summary can be identified as the manager's summary or the team summary. This introduction or summary should identify the exact nature of the project. An innovative name for the plan could be chosen that will give team members a sense of identity and ownership.

Next the HIM professional leads in planning the mission statement for the project—the goals in broad perspective. Blending the ideal with the practical aspects of the project can inspire creation of a mission statement for employees, medical staff, and upper-level administration. Selling the project to the major stakeholders is one burden of the mission statement; it needs careful thought. From it comes the operational plan.

The project is described in step 3. Some aspects of the universal questions will need more or less detail, depending on the project. For example, a project involving ISs will emphasize the capture of data and brokering data dissemination to the stakeholders as information of value to them. In today's competitive health care environment, step 4 is crucial. For instance, should the project involve offering transcription service to local medical office practices, a survey to determine present transcription activity, future needs, problems with present services, and legal constraints will be needed. Also, IS capabilities will need to be addressed.

The intrapreneur may wish to involve the chief financial officer (CFO) in developing strategy for step 5. The break-even chart will be closely scrutinized by the stakeholders. The real challenge may be to explore and document savings that may not be evident at first glance. For example, a department developing an automated chart-tracking system needs input from all the sections in the department for complete documentation of time and cost savings.

Employees want to know their extra effort is noticed: What better way than to set target dates for evaluation of the project? Let them choose rewards at these interim steps. Involve all the stakeholders with feedback and ideas for adjustments. Of course, the budget process is also an evaluative tool as projection figures are reviewed.

Developing Entrepreneurial Business Plans

Increasingly, HIM professionals are becoming entrepreneurs. For example, small consulting firms are being developed and are offering a variety of services through publicizing in the major HIM magazines and state newsletters. These entrepreneurs need professional expertise, in-service teaching ability, and business acumen to interest clients, employees, and investors. The business plan outlined in Figure 4-4 will enhance the probability of success in all three of these areas.

SUMMARY

Planning, in some form, is used by managers every day, starting with effective time management. The importance of the long-range planning function is evident in organizations of any complexity. In the dynamic health care environment of today, the advantages of contingency plans are stressed. Maintaining flexibility as changes occur and paradigms shift will be increasingly necessary.

Strategic planning flows from the vision and mission statement of the organization to set the tone for the future. The objectives written in response to the strategy become increasingly specific down through the organization. When individual employees plan objectives and goals for the time period with the manager, these will be aligned with the broad objectives of the organization. Just as important, when the process is participative, employees will understand how individual objectives help accomplish those broad objectives. Strategic planning is cyclical; before the next budget period, the process is repeated.

Part of the planning process is an analysis of the strengths, weaknesses, opportunities, and threats facing the organization, referred to as a SWOT analysis. When the internal and external environments are analyzed frequently, planning is enhanced.

Transitional planning goes beyond traditional strategic planning to assist managers in paradigm shifting. In today's changing health care scene, HIM professionals have the opportunity to participate in the transition by advocating ISs to meet new demands and by preparing to work with new tools and knowledge. Networking among all health care givers should ensure a longitudinal patient record as the EHR is developed.

Business plans are structured documents to give focus to planners. Intrapreneurs anxious to bring about change by adopting a new system use business plans to formalize their requests. Entrepreneurs need detailed business plans for providing a directional map to future success.

CRITICAL THINKING EXERCISES

1. Explain how an organization's mission statement, strategic plan, and overall objectives relate to one another.
2. Give examples for using informal planning in a manager's daily activities, then explain when formal planning would be more appropriate.
3. Describe the major steps in strategic planning and document reasons why each step is important.
4. Define the terms *objectives* and *goals*, then discuss their importance in strategic planning.
5. Describe the steps in a SWOT analysis. Give examples that show the value of SWOT analysis in strategic planning.
6. Describe your nonverbal and verbal responses to the HIM manager who says, "Plan? I seldom have time to plan. I live from day to day just attempting survival."
7. What are the components of a detailed business plan?

APPLICATION OF THEORY EXERCISES

1. Make a list of activities that you did yesterday. Identify items in the list according to the priority that they were when you completed them. Should any of the activities been ranked as a higher or lower priority than as they actually were completed? Create a list of activities that you need to do tomorrow and assign priority ranking to each. At the end of the day, review the list to evaluate how well you adhered to your plan. Analyze your findings to determine what you could have done differently or how you plan to do things differently when planning in the future.
2. Your management team is giving priority to automating chart tracking during strategic planning meetings. Write out possible major objectives the team members should consider as they prepare for a presentation to top management.

INTERNET ACTIVITY

Search online for time management tools. Describe any that you find that best fit your personal situation.

CASE STUDY

Jackie and Sandra began a long-term-care consulting firm 5 years ago in a retirement region. They now have six employees: two RHIAs and four RHITs. They now have consulting contracts with 35 long-term-care facilities and have developed a reputation for excellence.

During a meeting with the employees, Jackie and Sandra commended them for the effort each had contributed to the success of the firm. In planning for the future, Jackie and Sandra then asked the employees to share with them ideas on expanding the business by revising the vision. One option they had discussed and now shared was that of expanding their geographic region into another state. This would mean actively marketing to long-term-care facilities beyond their present region and hiring additional staff.

Bryan said he had been listening to employee conversations at a nearby hospital and learned that there was a need for additional home health care personnel and resources in the region. Hospital utilization management staff expressed concern with the difficulty of referring patients promptly to home health care firms. Bryan thought developing and managing home health care as a separate cost center would fill this market niche and offer challenges to each of them.

Ann shared an experience she had at one of the nursing homes. Two physicians were telling her how difficult it was to hire knowledgeable office staff and retain them. Ann suggested expanding their business into physician offices. She felt they had the expertise to manage practice offices and train competent staff. Ann further stated that when she mentioned this need to a physical therapist who recently joined a group of fellow therapists in opening an office, her friend responded that such a service would be welcomed by them also. Then he related the difficulty they were having finding competent office managers.

Jackie, Sandra, and their staff have three options to consider as they undertake strategic planning:

1. Develop a SWOT analysis for this consulting firm.
2. Make assumptions regarding the region and factors that relate to each of the three options.
3. Choose one of the options and prepare a business plan for the firm.

REFERENCE

Drucker, P. (1990). *Managing non-profit organizations.* New York: Truman Talley Books.

SUGGESTED READING

http://library.ahima.org/xpedio/groups/public/documents/ahima/bok1_050165.pdf

CHAPTER 5

Planning in Health Care: Operational Plans and Tools for Planning

After completing this chapter, the learner should be able to:

1. Describe the scope of operational planning.
2. State the advantages of including team members in planning.
3. Identify major factors in planning operational objectives.
4. Outline major ingredients of the MBO system.
5. Give several advantages for using Gantt charts and PERT networks.

INTRODUCTION

This chapter begins the next phase of the planning function, which is operational planning. Operational planning is concerned with short-term plans that specify details on how the strategic or transition plans, described in Chapter 4, will be implemented. During the strategic planning function, resources were allocated to meet the broad objectives chosen for the organization. Now the scope is narrowing and the management team develops specific plans for a department or cost center. These operational plans will focus on departmental objectives and then on resource allocation to meet the chosen objectives. Finances, personnel, and other resources are considered as these detailed plans materialize.

PREPARING OPERATIONAL OBJECTIVES

section and team managers Managers whose span of control covers one section of a department or one team within a section or a department; also called team leader, team coordinator, section leader, or section coordinator.

Creating specific and measurable departmental objectives in harmony with the organization's strategic goals and objectives may seem daunting to managers initially. But the HIM manager, who begins by learning all the steps in the process and then exerts mental effort toward visionary leadership, will be ready for the challenge. Including **section and team managers** in the process makes it a participative effort. Reinforcing the vision and goals of the organization and communicating priorities for the coming year are the manager's activities that build consensus and a sense of ownership by the management team. Since the operational objectives are subject to final approval by the budget committee, the HIM manager ensures that the team understands this limitation.

After the managers are familiar with the steps in the operational planning process and in setting organizational objectives, team members become involved in the planning. This is where the brainstorming ideas for the operational objectives begin. The sections within the department can meet as independent groups first and then bring their ideas to a larger group meeting. Here priorities are set and objectives are chosen for the budget committee.

Strategies for holding successful meetings are outlined in Chapter 19. By following these strategies, managers can defuse tensions that may begin to develop when one section or team appears to lose importance. As priorities change and rightsizing occurs, one section may necessarily be downsized and another given added responsibilities and financial gain. Figure 5-1 emphasizes

FIGURE 5-1   Levels of Planning Objectives

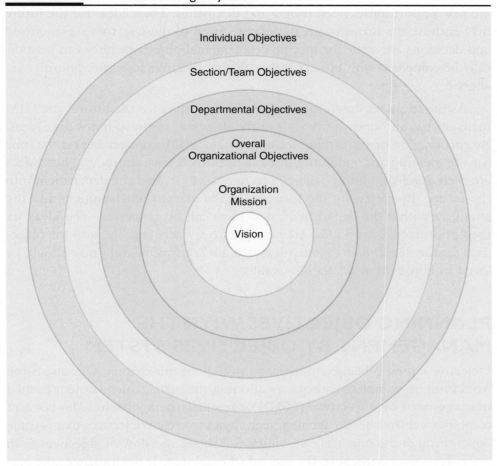

the integrated process as the vision and mission of the organization are communicated to each level.

For example, coding/reimbursement sections grew in importance and staffing in most hospitals during the 1980s under the prospective payment system. In the 1990s, it became necessary to cut staffing because of increased automation and streamlining of the functions performed. At the same time, additional staffing was needed for concurrent record completion activities. When the department objectives show, in clear measurable terms, the rationale for such decisions, tensions can be defused. Managers can demonstrate a balanced perspective by verbally reinforcing the value of each section/team and of each individual employee to the total organization.

As this process occurs, documents created during the SWOT analysis described in Chapter 4 will assist in developing operational plans. First, the objectives or goals regarding the future are broken down into operational terms. Next, the list of factors or threats that could hinder implementation of the objectives is identified to keep the plans realistic. Contingencies that could create new opportunities need review and discussion. These ideas for the future may enthuse the teams to greater effort. As all of these factors are discussed and decisions are made for specific departmental objectives, they can periodically be compared with broad organizational objectives to ensure priorities are aligned.

As the teams sit down to plan specific objectives for the future, the HIM manager has an opportunity to lead the discussion toward innovative ideas. By encouraging brainstorming techniques, the HIM manager can set the tone for the meeting and guide the discussion into creative thought. These ideas are then developed into possible objectives that can lead the department into the future. By reviewing the forecasts in the external environment and the strengths within the department, new ideas can be generated. The ideas are then prioritized. Lastly, ideas are incorporated, where feasible, into the objectives for the department. Those ideas that are not feasible right now should be saved and brought into later discussions.

PLANNING OBJECTIVES WITH THE MANAGEMENT BY OBJECTIVES SYSTEM

Management by objectives (MBO)
A system where performance objectives are jointly planned by manager and employee with periodic review of progress and rewards based on this progress.

Results management See management by objectives (MBO).

Objective setting is being emphasized throughout this chapter. Our discussion would not be complete without mentioning the management system termed **management by objectives (MBO)** or **results management**. This concept combines a cluster of management techniques to create objectives that cascade down through the organization. Figure 5-2 shows this flow of objectives from upper-level management to the individual employee. It demonstrates the participative activity throughout with overlapping circles at each level. The communication and feedback network shows the bottom-up aspect as well as the top-down aspect as objectives are planned. Originally named by Peter Drucker, MBO emphasized his belief that every individual should participate in planning the goals for the workplace (Longest, 1990).

As shown in Figure 5-2, the levels of the organization are meshed together as the setting of objectives flows downward through the communication network. The beginning of the cycle lies with the mission statement. The flow of upward feedback brings ideas from the individual employees clear up to the top of the organization for input as objectives are developed.

Research indicates that a commitment from all levels of management to the participative process enhances personal motivation for achieving results. Because of upper-level management communication, the mission of the organization flows downward as objectives become a link to the more specific departmental objectives at the next level. Figure 5-2 emphasizes the participative culture by overlapping the circles. In this way, each employee can share an

FIGURE 5-2   Flowchart of Management by Objectives (Results Management)

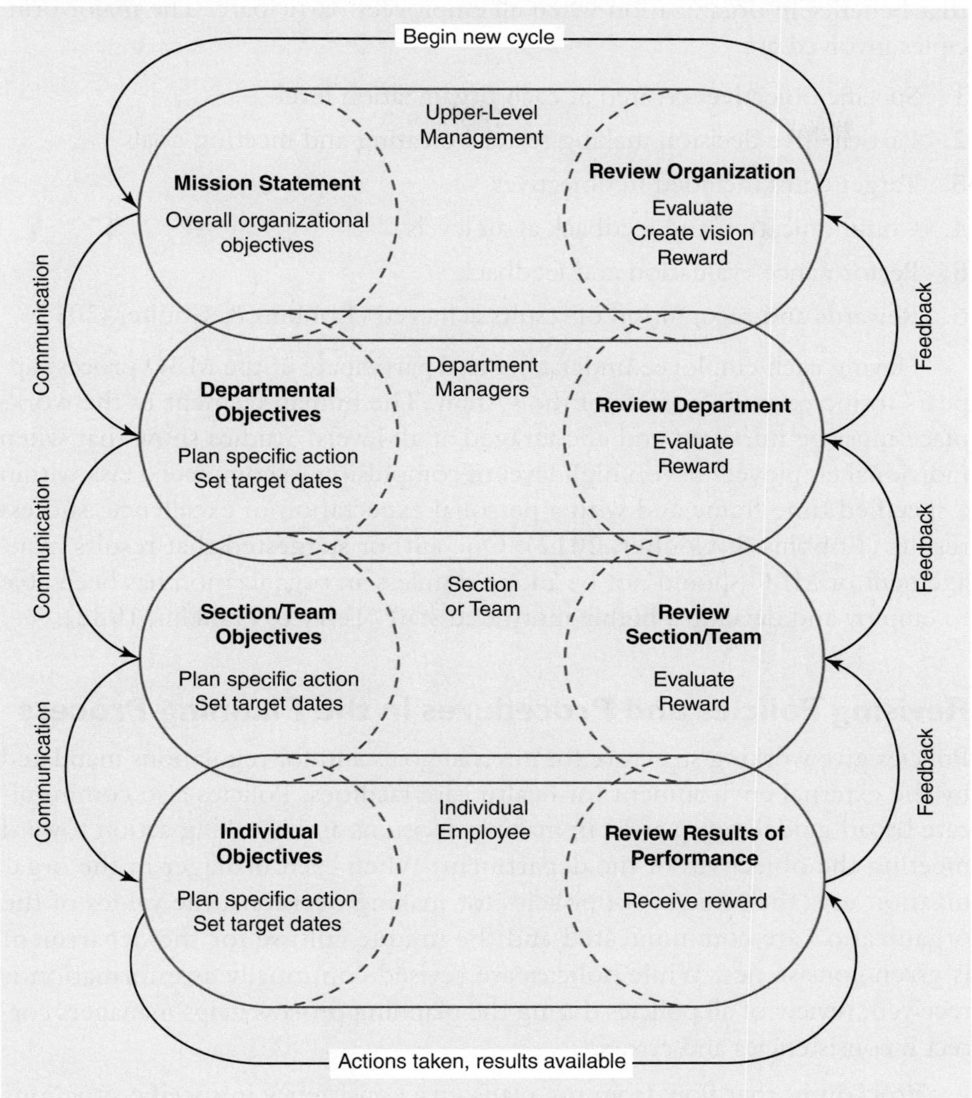

understanding of the organizational mission. Thus, individual objectives are part of the big picture and become the focus of activity.

The plan of action calls for periodic review of the results, with performance evaluation at each level as feedback flows upward. Because employees know what to expect and have helped develop the plan for action and target dates, they are committed to striving for quality results. Their rewards can then be seen as fair and equitable.

A new cycle begins as results are fed upward and upper-level management reviews them and begins the next strategic planning process.

In summary, MBO takes selected management principles into a process that benefits an organization when all employees participate. The major principles involved are:

1. Specific objectives created at each organization level
2. Participative decision making toward creating and meeting goals
3. Target dates included in objectives
4. Communication and feedback at all levels
5. Performance evaluation and feedback
6. Rewards and recognition of results achieved (Robbins & Coulter, 2012)

Having each employee understand and participate in the MBO process appears to increase the success of the system. The human element in the workplace must be nurtured and encouraged at all levels. Studies show that when individual employees have a high level of compulsion to complete a task within a specified time frame and with a personal expectation of excellence, success results (Robbins & Coulter, 2012). One author suggested that results management or MBO should not be adopted unless an organization has been able to employ and develop a highly motivated staff (Terry & Franklin, 1982).

Revising Policies and Procedures in the Planning Process

Policies give working structure for internal goals and for regulations mandated by the external environment for health care facilities. Policies also communicate broad guidelines to assist in making decisions and in taking action toward meeting the objectives of the department. When each manager in the organization uses the same set of policies for making decisions, the values of the organization are communicated and the unique culture for the department is given consistency. While policies are revised continually as information is received, review of all policies during the planning process helps managers correct inconsistencies and errors.

Procedures that flow from the plans give consistency in specific situations and they also need review. Since they give precise guidelines for daily employee activity, frequent revisions and accuracy are mandatory. Each employee should have a handbook with the latest revisions. Revisions are especially important in the coding/reimbursement section where guidelines are mandated by new technology or federal and state regulations. The mechanics for planning and documenting policies and procedures are covered in Chapter 7.

Implementing and Monitoring the Plan

As discussed earlier, the last step in the process is evaluating the results as changes occur. Figure 4-1 emphasized the value of correlating the budget to desired performance results. A review of the evaluation tools for monitoring may show the need for revision also. The team members can assist in reviewing the present tools and suggesting new ones. Planning data capture at the time the task is done allows for efficiency in analyzing and integrating subsequent results. When automation is available for this step, timeliness can be a realistic goal and adjustments can be made promptly.

TOOLS AND TECHNIQUES TO ASSIST IN MANAGERIAL PLANNING

Operational planning tools help managers to be more effective. Some of these tools and techniques may be used in strategic planning also. Two techniques to assist managers in scheduling are the Gantt chart and the **performance evaluation and review technique (PERT) network**. Scheduling includes preparing a list of planned activities, the order of completion, who is to do each activity, and the time needed to complete each.

Other tools involve mathematical models that are often computerized. They assist managers in making complex decisions. These managerial tools are part of the quantitative approach to management mentioned in Chapter 2. Through sophisticated software, these models offer alternative solutions and then the computer program chooses the best alternative according to the information given.

Performance evaluation and review technique (PERT network) A diagram that graphically shows the relationships among the various activities of a project and estimates the time needed for each activity.

Gantt Chart

Henry Gantt was an engineer at Bethlehem Steel during the early 1900s and worked with Frank and Lillian Gilbreth to increase worker efficiency. One of the tools Gantt developed during this scientific management era continues in use today, in modified form, for scheduling. Called the Gantt chart, it compares progress of a project at different points in time. Targeting these decision points in a project is most useful (Robbins & Coulter, 2012). The Gantt chart can be reviewed at any point in the continuum as shown in Figure 5-3. This figure illustrates a simple example of how this scheduling tool assists a team in monitoring progress. It outlines the tasks for a team involved in a 3-month project to plan a reception for area physicians to publicize a home health care unit opening.

The Gantt chart forces the team to address all facets of the project and to assess whether the timing of each task is on schedule. As the figure shows, at the 2-month team meeting, activities 1 and 2 have been completed on time. However, one speaker had not yet been confirmed for activity 3. Activities 4 and 5 have been started and the team discussed a problem with the order for printed napkins. The coordinator was asked to monitor this order in 1 week. As planned, activity 6 will be completed during the third month. The chart shows that activity 7 was initiated by the host and hostess and confirmations were received.

FIGURE 5-3   Gantt Chart for Home Health Care Reception. Reviewed at the End of 2 Months

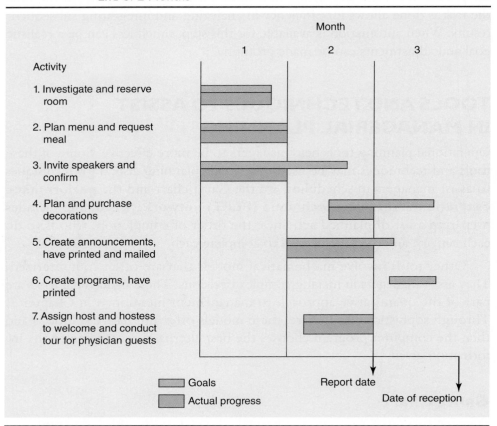

PERT Network Analysis

When activities are relatively independent of one another and are few in number, the Gantt chart is helpful as a scheduling tool. When a project has many activities and they are interdependent, program evaluation and review technique (PERT) is preferable (Longest, 1990). Although a software program can

PRACTICE EXAMPLE	Installing a computerized incomplete record system is used in this example. While there are many details to manage in such an installation, the PERT chart will be used to diagram major events and activities involved. In this way, the manager and his staff can estimate when the new system can be operational and where major monitoring should occur.
	In this example, simultaneous exploration of an automated system occurs involving the medical staff and the HIM department. At a medical staff meeting, several physicians suggested that the facility automate the incomplete record completion system. They described the experience of another facility, Children's Hospital, that has recently installed an automated system. About 40 percent of the medical staff is also on the staff at Children's Hospital and staff

members are enthusiastic about the new system. Administrators stated they will meet with the HIM manager and discuss the possibility.

At the same time, the HIM manager has been networking with the manager at Children's Hospital and has visited the hospital to look at the system. The manager had prepared a proposal for inclusion of a computerized incomplete record system in the next capital expenditures budget.

This proposal would replace the current system in which incomplete records are filed by physician name on shelves in the work room. Four employees are on the physician record activity team, which is responsible for incomplete records. The team would need training in any new system and procedure changes involved. Technicians who are cross-trained to work in any area of the HIM department would also need training if the new system were approved.

The initial meeting with administration produced a consensus to proceed with the proposal. Next, the HIM manager met with the physician record activity team and empowered them to assist in the planning. One request from this meeting was that temporary employees be hired to assist in the routine work flow while the team members were trained.

The team also emphasized the need for additional workstations in the work room since the incomplete records in the new system would all be in electronic format. The decision was made to remodel the work room, take out the shelving, and add three additional workstations. The plant manager and physician record activity team were involved in the planning and implementation of the project. At this point, the HIM manager prepared the PERT network shown in Figure 5-4 for tracking activities.

As can be seen in Figure 5-4, events are outlined in the rectangles and the activity for reaching each event is identified with an arrow. Above each arrow is an estimated time, in weeks, for completion of the activity. For example, it is estimated that event E, to hire temporary employees, is needed 2 weeks before the employees will complete training. Should event F, installation of the training computers, be delayed, then event E should also be delayed to allow efficient use of the temporary staff.

Looking for the critical path on the PERT network is the next step. The critical path is the longest path in weeks to accomplish the activities. In this simple chart there are only three pathways, so each needs to be calculated as follows:

1. A-B-C-E-H-J-K equals 10 weeks.
2. A-B-C-F-H-J-K equals 13 weeks.
3. A-B-D-G-I-J-K equals 15 weeks.

The calculations show pathway 3, at 15 weeks, is the critical path, indicated in Figure 5-4 by heavy lines. Should any of the activities on this pathway be delayed, the project completion date will be delayed. However, should an activity in pathways 1 or 2 be delayed, the HIM manager can review the PERT network and determine whether there will be a delay. The slack time for pathway 1 is 5 weeks and for pathway 2 it is 2 weeks. Because of the interdependence of pathways 1 and 2, should the delay be between events B and C, both pathways are affected and would need review.

FIGURE 5-4   PERT Chart for Incomplete Record System Installation

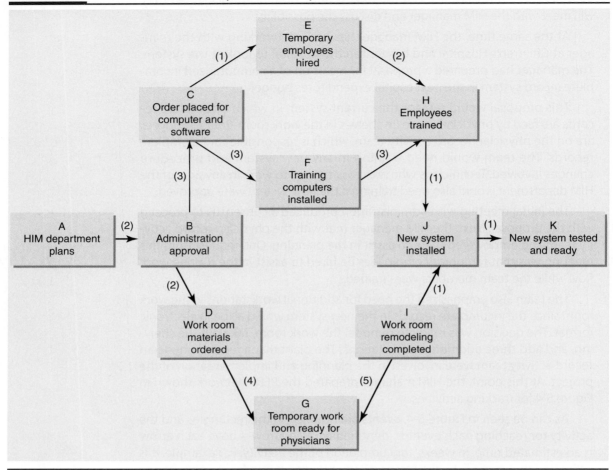

be used to create a complex PERT model, the example in Figure 5-4 reviews the manual steps of creating a simple PERT model for understanding the process. The practice example gives details of PERT activities.

In this simple example, the HIM manager can make adjustments manually. Software programs for PERT networks can handle hundreds, even thousands, of events and activities and then adjustments are made by computer.

When estimations of the time for completion of activities are uncertain, a further enhancement can be used. By creating three different time estimates, managers can improve their planning skills. This is accomplished by having an optimistic, a most likely, and a pessimistic time for each activity. The shortest time length is called optimistic, the middle time length is called most likely, and the longest time length is called pessimistic. In Figure 5-4 the times given are considered most likely.

Delays in activity completion have been discussed; the opposite is also a possibility. Should it take less time to complete an activity along the critical path, then the HIM manager can review the PERT network and make adjustments that could mean completion of the project ahead of schedule.

Mathematical Models as Planning Tools

Other tools involve mathematical models that are often computerized. They assist managers in making complex decisions. These managerial tools are part of the quantitative approach to management mentioned in Chapter 2. Through sophisticated software, these models offer alternative solutions and then the computer program chooses the best alternative according to the information given.

As a part of the team involved in planning a project, one of these tools may be useful in arriving at the best decision. These tools include break-even analysis, queueing theory, probability theory, linear programming, and simulation. Complex planning tasks involving many variables can be completed efficiently using these quantitative tools. There are several books available that cover these topics in detail.

A break-even analysis evaluates the costs of a project or activity for comparison with the projected outcome or benefits to determine if the outcome will be greater than or equal to the costs. If the costs are determined to be greater than the projected outcome or benefits, the project or activity may not be carried out. Queueing theory uses mathematic algorithms to predict anticipated waiting times for various resources necessary for operations. Probability theory is used to generate mathematical probability of possible outcomes. Linear programming is a mathematical model that uses linear relationships to determine the optimal outcomes based on geometric calculations. Simulation involves performing activities in a test or other non-real-time environment to determine an estimate of time to complete the activities.

SUMMARY

This chapter begins with a focus on operational planning at the department level. The concepts include short-term plans and the resources needed to fulfill the planned objectives. This implies that the budgeting process is intimately tied to planning.

Emphasis is given to participative management by involving the sections and teams in planning objectives that affect their work. At this level, objectives are specific and measurable. Use of SWOT analysis keeps the teams' focus on priorities. Encouraging employees at all levels to share creative ideas and demonstrating the value of their ideas are important managerial concepts in this integrated planning model. Setting objectives at each level within the MBO system outlines a thrust of participative management that can lead to productive results.

Two quantitative planning tools, Gantt charts and PERT networks, examples of which were provided, are valuable tools for successfully planning and completing projects. Using software programs that assist in decision making when there are many variables involved in planning gives added value to these models.

CRITICAL THINKING EXERCISES

1. Describe differences between a top-down approach to creating objectives versus a bottom-up approach.
2. Discuss potential conflicts between objectives being planned by financial services and those planned by HIM department managers in a large hospital.
3. Develop a Gantt chart for one of your class projects.
4. Explain why the critical path in a PERT network is so important.
5. Give two examples where automation would lend valuable assistance in solving managerial problems.

6. How would you respond to the statement, "It is impossible to plan when we do not know what we are going to be doing next month."
7. Explain the value of participative managerial concepts when coordinating a group effort.
8. Think of the person to whom you were responsible in your last position. Give some operational planning activities you observed that manager doing.

APPLICATION OF THEORY EXERCISES

1. Compile a list of individual objectives that are operational in nature related to completing your education.
2. Interview an HIM professional involved in planning a project. Document the tools being used in planning this project and in carrying it into implementation.
3. Outline an operational plan for the transcription section of an HIM department.

INTERNET ACTIVITY

Research the mathematical models that were discussed at the end of this chapter and provide an example of a situation in which each may be used.

CASE STUDY

The last Joint Commission report for Community Hospital was unfavorable with regard to employee ongoing education. Top executives admitted that they set other priorities and the managers concurred. Overall the report was very good and the managers were pleased but determined to focus on education during the coming year.

With this mandate, upper-level management developed one corporate objective relating to education as the budget process for the coming year began. This corporate objective read:

> *Corporate objective III*: To educate health care professionals within the enterprise to meet the health care needs of society and to define 5-year plans to meet educational needs for the several professional groups.

The corporate objectives were distributed and discussed at a meeting with middle managers. The responsibility for developing departmental objectives for the coming year was delegated to the managers. Community Hospital culture was participative in nature, and the flowchart in Figure 5-1 describes the communication process as the managers shared the vision with the teams and the team leaders empowered individual employees to offer suggestions.

1. Develop ongoing educational objectives for health information services to meet corporate objective III for the coming year.
2. Develop ongoing educational objectives for the major teams in the department for the coming year.
3. Choose two professional employees that you know and develop educational objectives for each of them for the coming year.

REFERENCES

AHIMA e-HIM Workgroup on the Transition to ICD-10-CM/PCS. "Planning Organizational Transition to ICD-10-CM/PCS." *Journal of AHIMA* 80, no.10 (October 2009): 72–77.

Longest, B. (1990). *Management practices for the health professional* (4th ed.). Norwalk, CT: Appleton & Lange.

Robbins, S., & Coulter, M. (2012). *Management* (11th ed.). Upper Saddle River, NJ: Pearson.

Terry, G., & Franklin, S. (1982). *Principles of management* (8th ed.). Homewood, IL: Richard D. Irwin.

CHAPTER 6

Management of Financial Resources

LEARNING OBJECTIVES

After completing this chapter, the learner should be able to:

1. Outline HIM activities related to revenue cycle management.
2. Interpret coverage guidelines for insurance and government-funded payment systems.
3. Discuss the impact of HIM functions related to finance and accounting.
4. Explain the value of a budgeting process.
5. Contrast fixed budgeting versus variable budgeting.
6. Contrast incremental budgeting versus zero-based budgeting.
7. List the major factors for success in budgeting development.

HIM professionals play a variety of roles in managing the financial aspects of health care. Financial management in health care extends beyond basic management principles as it is important to fully comprehend various payment systems and the ability to manage the revenue cycle. This chapter will discuss revenue cycle management, government-funded payment systems, finance and accounting principles, and the budgeting process.

REVENUE CYCLE MANAGEMENT

The **revenue cycle** is a set of events that occur and repeat routinely as information and data about patient health and financial information moves through, into, and out of a health care provider for the purpose of determining compensation, or reimbursement, for services. The charges generated from providing health care services, which generate earned and measurable income are referred to as revenue. HIM professionals play an active role in **revenue cycle management**, which is the management of all contributing functions, both administrative and clinical in order to capture, manage, and collect revenue or payment from provision of services to patients. The goals of revenue cycle management include increasing cash flow and decreasing accounts receivable.

Unbilled Accounts

Reports that list patient encounters that have ended but for which a final bill has not been prepared are reviewed by HIM professionals on a regular basis. Unbilled accounts, which have not been billed and are not included in accounts receivable, may be identified on the accounts not selected for billing report, a financial report that is generated on a daily basis for the purpose of identifying and tracking accounts to find out whether they may not be billed or be ready to be billed yet. This report is generated from a combination of discharge data and patient accounting data. Accounts appearing on the report are analyzed by HIM professionals to determine if the accounts have not been billed because of coding backlog, or if the delay is the result of a provider documentation deficiency. Another report reviewed by HIM professionals in the revenue cycle management process is the discharged, no final bill (DNFB) report, which includes all patients who have been discharged from the facility but for whom, for one reason or another, the billing process is not complete. Aging of accounts, which involves a determination of the period of time that

Revenue cycle
A set of events that occur and repeat routinely as information and data about patient health and financial information moves through, into and out of a health care provider for the purpose of determining compensation, or reimbursement, for services.

Revenue cycle management
Management of all contributing functions, both administrative and clinical, in order to capture, manage, and collect revenue or payment from provision of services to patients.

has lapsed since the bill was sent to each payer, is also common practice in revenue cycle management. The final accounts receivable balance divided by an average daily revenue is referred to as days in accounts receivable.

Charge Reconciliation

Charge reconciliation, which is the act of reviewing all of the charges that have been entered for claims submission through charge entry, is a process that HIM professionals perform in order to ensure that all procedures, supplies, and services are available and transfer to the claim form. Part of this process involves **charge capture**, which is a process of collecting all procedures, supplies, and services provided during delivery of patient care. Charges are the dollar amounts actually billed by health care facilities for specific services or supplies and owed by patients. A charge code is the numerical identification of a service or supply that links the item to a particular department within the **charge description master (CDM)**. The CDM, which is also called a **chargemaster**, is a comprehensive computerized list that contains information about several aspects of all items that the organization may charge for the health care services and procedures provided to patients. Figure 6-1 provides a sample of a small portion of a CDM. The CDM includes a charge code, which is a number unique to each facility for the purpose of identifying each charge. The logic of the charge code assignment is defined by the facility and is often

Charge reconciliation The act of reviewing all of the charges that have been entered for claims submission through charge entry.

Charge capture A process of collecting all procedures, supplies, and services provided during delivery of patient care.

Charge description master (CDM) A comprehensive computerized list that contains information about several aspects of all items that the organization may charge for the health care services and procedures provided to patients.

Chargemaster Charge description master.

FIGURE 6-1   Chargemaster

Number	Description	Department	Rev Code	CPT Code	Unit Price
111111234	PELVIS 1 VIEW	20	320	72170	770.00
111111235	PELVIS 3 VIEWS	20	320	72190	900.00
111111245	SACROILIAC JOINTS	20	320	72202	1,050.00
111111246	SACRUM	20	320	72220	1,150.00
111111247	COCCYX	20	320	72220	1,150.00
111111248	SACRUM & COCCYX	20	320	72220	1,150.00
111111275	STERNUM	20	320	71120	7,450.00
111111276	STERNO/CLAVICULAR JOINTS	20	320	71130	725.00
111111290	RIBS BILATERAL	20	320	71110	1,210.00
111111305	ACROMIOCLAVICULAR JOINTS	20	320	73050	700.00
111111450	HIP BILATERAL COMPLETE	20	320	73520	1,500.00
111111451	HIPS & PELVIS INFANT	20	320	73540	600.00
111111502	CHEST PORT 1 VIEW	20	324	71010	850.00
111111503	CHEST PORT 2 VIEW	20	324	71020	970.00
111111550	ABD PORT 1 VIEW	20	320	74000	740.00
111111551	ABD PORT 2 VIEW	20	320	74010	950.00

arranged according to department. The item description is identical to or as similar as possible to the code description for the item in the CPT or HCPCS coding systems. The CPT or HCPCS code is hard-coded into the chargemaster for many items, which means that the codes are automatically assigned through the chargemaster, as opposed to soft-coding, in which a coder looks up the code to assign manually. Revenue codes, which are three-digit reference codes for Medicare billing, are included to appear in the billing information to reflect the type of services and area in which services were provided.

INSURANCE AND GOVERNMENT-FUNDED PAYMENT SYSTEMS

Medicaid Assistance with medical coverage for low-income families and individuals, established by Title XIX of the Social Security Act.

Medicare Federally funded program established to assist with health care costs for Americans 65 years of age and older and those with disabilities or end-stage renal disease, established by Title XVIII of the Social Security Act.

Medicare administrative contractor (MAC) Contracting entity that administers the Medicare program for designated regions.

Medical necessity Documentation to justify that a medical procedure or service will benefit the patient's medical well-being or have a positive impact on the ability to diagnose and treat a medical condition and that the procedure or service is consistent with the medical community's accepted standard of care.

Another important part of revenue cycle management is having a strong working knowledge of insurance programs and government-funded payment systems. **Medicaid** provides assistance with medical coverage for low-income families and individuals. The Medicaid program was established by the addition of Title XIX of the Social Security Act and is jointly funded by both state and federal governments. **Medicare** was established through Title XVIII of the Social Security act in 1965 as a federally funded program established to assist with the health care costs for Americans 65 years of age and older and those with disabilities or end-stage renal disease. **Medicare administrative contractors (MACs)** were established in 2011 Medicare Part A and Part B as contracting entities to administer the Medicare program, replacing previous carriers and fiscal intermediaries.

Prospective Payment Systems

HIM professionals are educated and trained to apply their skills in any type of health care setting. Similar general principles apply in most settings, but one area that is important to recognize that is unique to each setting is the prospective payment systems (PPSs) on which reimbursement is based. Payment systems for different health care settings are outlined in Figure 6-2 along with the basis of reimbursement for each payment system and data set that identifies documentation elements that are required for reimbursement purposes. Details of each payment system are provided on the Center for Medicare and Medicaid Services (CMS) website.

Medical Necessity

Medicare and others providing reimbursement for health care services require to document **medical necessity** of services being billed. Documentation of medical necessity provides justification that the procedure or service will benefit the patient's medical well-being or have a positive impact on the ability to diagnose and treat a medical condition, and that the procedure or service

FIGURE 6-2 Prospective Payment Systems

Setting	Payment System	Data Set and Documentation Instrument/Reporting System	Basis of Reimbursement
Physician Office	Resource-Based Relative Value Scale (RBRVS)	None	Medicare Fee Schedule
Outpatient	Outpatient Prospective Payment System (OPPS)	None	Ambulatory Payment Classification (APC)
Inpatient Acute Care Hospital	Inpatient Prospective Payment System (IPPS)	Uniform Hospital Discharge Data Set (UHDDS)	Medicare severity-diagnosis-related groups (MS-DRGs)
Skilled Nursing Facility	Skilled Nursing Facility Prospective Payment System (SNF PPS)	Minimum Data Set 2.0 (MDS 2.0) Data collection in Resident Assessment Instrument (RAI), reported through Resident Assessment Validation and Entry (RAVEN)	Resource Utilization Groups, Version III (RUG-III)
Inpatient Rehabilitation Facility	Inpatient Rehabilitation Facility Prospective Payment System (IRF PPS)	Data collection in Inpatient rehabilitation Facility Patient Assessment Instrument (IRF-PAI) reported through Inpatient Rehabilitation Validation and Entry System (IRVEN)	Case-mix groups (CMGs)
Long-term care hospital	Long-term care hospital prospective payment system (LTCH PPS)	None	Medicare severity-long-term care diagnosis-related groups (MS-LTH-DRGs)
Home Health	Home Health Prospective Payment System (HH PPS)	Data collection in Outcome and Assessment Information System (OASIS) reported through Home Assessment Validation and Entry (HAVEN)	

is consistent with the medical community's accepted standard of care. Hospitals have traditionally employed entry-level staff members, often with no formal education or training, to work in patient registration. However, the need for medical necessity documentation requires knowledge of coding and billing regulations, along with a thorough understanding of medical terminology, pathophysiology, and other concepts related to coding.

Payment Rejection

Just because a health record has quality documentation, coding is accurate, and medical necessity is reflected on the bill, it is not a guarantee that reimbursement will occur. Rejection may result if the submitted bill is not accepted by the payer, although corrections can be made and the claim resubmitted. When a bill has been returned unpaid for any of several reasons, such as lack of coverage or inaccurate coding, it is referred to as denial. Some reasons for denial include inaccurate coding, lack of insurance coverage, no documentation of medical necessity, or sending the bill to the wrong insurance company.

Case-Mix Index

HIM professionals are also concerned with the quality of clinical documentation because of the impact on case-mix index (CMI). CMI is the average relative weight of all cases for a provider for a specified period of time. It provides a reflection of the acuity level of the patients treated by the provider and the intensity of services delivered. CMI allows for the patient population for a provider to be compared with other groups. CMI is calculated by dividing the sum of the weights of diagnosis-related groups for patients discharged during a given period by the total number of patients discharged.

Managing Health Care Documentation

Recovery audit contractor (RAC) A governmental program whose goal is to identify inappropriate payments to providers for services delivered to Medicare beneficiaries.

Another concern of HIM professionals, related to documentation and reimbursement is the **Recovery Audit Contractor (RAC)** program. This is a governmental program whose goal is to identify inappropriate payments to providers for services delivered to Medicare beneficiaries. Improper payments may be overpayments or underpayments. Health care documentation integrity is the characteristic or extent to which health care documentation adequately and accurately reflects the condition of the patient, decision-making processes of the clinician, and health care services that were rendered. Health care providers should have a general health record documentation policy that outlines documentation practices within the facility. Clinical documentation is any manual or electronic notation (or recording) made by a physician or other health care clinician related to a patient's medical condition or treatment. Clinical Documentation Improvement (CDI) is a set of processes developed for the purpose of improving the specificity and accuracy of clinical documentation. One of the goals of CDI that impacts HIM professionals is to allow greater specificity and accuracy of coding for diseases and procedures performed on patients. This is generally accompanied by a Clinical Documentation Improvement Plan (CDIP), which is a program in which specialists concurrently review health records for incomplete documentation, prompting clinical staff to clarify ambiguity that allows coders to assign more concise disease classification codes.

FINANCE AND ACCOUNTING PRINCIPLES

The healthcare industry is highly dependent upon management of financial resources. HIM professionals serve a variety of roles to support financial management in health care organizations. In order to understand the full picture of health care finance, it is best to break it down to explore each area separately first.

Managing Financial Data and Information

Each department within an organization collects data to be used for both departmental and organizational purposes. Beyond that, the state and federal government collects and analyzes data submitted by health care organizations and related entities. Financial data in health care may include, but is not limited to that related to charges for patient care delivery, actual cost of care, reimbursement for care, salaries, operating expenses, and assets. As the scope of HIM career opportunities expands, there is a growing need for HIM professionals to develop an understanding of how financial data are generated, maintained, and used. Most health care organizations have a financial information system that is used to collect, store, and process financial data. Financial data stored in the financial information system can be used for generation of reports to be used for analysis of financial data or communication regarding the status of specific financial aspects of the organization. Users may compare report information to financial indicators that are used for comparison purposes to determine how a department, service line, or organization measures against defined target levels.

Basic Accounting Functions Addressed by HIM Professionals

Collection, recording, and reporting of financial data are known as **accounting**. The financial professionals in organizations work with financial data by following generally accepted accounting principles (GAAP), which are principles or standards that are recognized in the accounting industry to define procedures for processing financial data and creation of financial reports. While HIM professionals do not need to completely understand all details of GAAP, it is necessary to know some of the basics as they may relate to financial aspects impacting or being impacted by HIM activities.

Accounting
Collection, recording, and reporting of financial data.

    Basic principles of accounting that HIM professionals may encounter include a general knowledge of accounts payable and accounts receivable and budgeting processes. Accounts payable (A/P) are the accounts for which the organization owes to another entity. These are often represented in financial statements as liabilities or expenses. Accounts receivable (A/R) are accounts created for entities owing payment to the organization. HIM has the ability to impact this aspect of the organization's financial management through activities related to unbilled account management. A balance sheet is used to reflect assets and liabilities for the entity. It reflects the current state of balance between the assets and liabilities. A sample balance sheet is illustrated in Figure 6-3.

FIGURE 6.3 Balance Sheet

Memorial Hospital

Balance Sheet

Assets

Cash	100,000
Accounts receivable	400,000
Buildings	5,000,000
Equipment	3,000,000
Inventory	500,000
Total Assets	9,000,000

Liabilities

Accounts payable	750,000
Building mortgage	8,250,000
Total Liabilities	9,000,000

THE BUDGETING PROCESS

Operating budget A budget developed for the purpose of planning routine, and some nonroutine, expenses and revenue for the upcoming fiscal year.

Capital budget A budget developed for larger assets that are part of the strategic planning process.

Cash budget The combined operating and capital budgets.

An **operating budget** is developed for the purpose of planning routine, and some nonroutine, expenses and revenue for the upcoming fiscal year. Items included in an operating budget may include, but are not limited to, salaries, supplies, utilities, and noncapital purchases. A **capital budget** includes larger assets that are part of the strategic planning process. Items that may be included in a capital budget may include real estate, buildings, and equipment. The operating and capital budgets are combined into a **cash budget**. This provides a comprehensive picture of all projected cash flow for the organization in the upcoming fiscal year.

Financial reports are generated to communicate the financial status for specific areas of the organization. These may be automatically generated on demand or for defined budget periods, such as monthly, quarterly, or annually. Annual reporting should be identified as following either a calendar year or a fiscal year. A calendar year is the period that starts January 1 and runs through December 31, while a fiscal year may be defined by an organization as its official accounting period. A fiscal year may be an actual calendar year, or it may be defined differently, for example, October 1 of the current year through September 30 of the following year. The fiscal year is normally defined according to factors impacting various financial and operational factors. The fiscal year is normally divided into quarters for reporting purposes.

Bottom-Up Budgeting Process

Given the complexity of hospitals, the time span for completing the hospital budget process is typically several months and begins with a review of the mission statement, goals, and major objectives. In other health care organizations, a shorter time frame may occur. Depending on the management style of upper-level management, this may be a **bottom-up budgeting process** where first-level and middle-level managers have the opportunity to share in setting priorities during the initial phase of planning and priority information gathering. With the opportunity to share their concerns and ideas in the early stages of the process, these managers embrace an ownership in the process. To avoid disappointment later, however, decision makers should use terms such as *concerns, ideas, suggestions,* and *input.* Negative feelings will follow if first-level managers and their teams perceive their specific goals and objectives are rejected outright. The first planning principle in Figure 6-4 emphasizes the need for this participative effort (Longest, 1990).

Bottom-up budgeting process A philosophy that encourages participation of all employees in planning priorities and objectives for the budget year.

Top-Down Budgeting Process

A **top-down budgeting process** can also be effective when effort is taken to communicate the objectives and priorities of the organization for the budget year. Middle-level managers then have a greater responsibility for giving their teams a sense of ownership as the components of the departmental budget are planned. Many health care organizations use a combination of these top-down and bottom-up budgeting processes. After the initial idea generating phase, the broad priorities are set by upper-level planners. Each department can then negotiate for its share of the budget.

Top-down budgeting process A philosophy where upper-level management plans the priorities and objectives for the budget year and disseminates these to others in the organization.

Future Budgets for Information/Communication Systems

HIM professionals have a special role in monitoring organizational objectives for any mention of information systems. Because of the importance of planning for newly integrated systems, HIM managers must be ready and participate in planning these capital expenditures. Correct decisions made during this process can mean success later. Capital expenditures refer to

FIGURE 6.4   Planning Principles for the Budgeting Process

1. Make the budgeting process participative.
2. Use strategic plans in developing operational budgetary needs.
3. Keep budgets as flexible as possible.
4. Base budget figures on factual information.
5. Keep budgets easy to understand.
6. Tie budgets to desired performance results.

major purchases of buildings or equipment. The cost of an item determines whether it falls into this category. For example, items over $5,000 may need to go through the capital equipment budget process. As facilities transition toward information/communication commitments, budgets will reflect this commitment.

Once the focus for the budget period has been outlined, preparation for the numerical details begins. Traditionally, HIM departments were labeled nonrevenue-producing departments. This is no longer true under the prospective payment system. HIM departments are now revenue departments. Managers can effectively show the impact their departments have on reimbursement and on cash flow. Also, departments with specific expertise, such as in transcription or record storage, may become revenue producing in another way—such as by offering a service to the medical office practice community.

Fixed Versus Variable Budgeting

Fixed budget
A budget that assumes a fixed level of services, sales, or productivity.

Variable budget
A budget that recognizes and gives consideration to adjusting costs as volume fluctuates.

The concept of a **fixed budget** assumes a fixed level of activity or volume over the period of the budget. Planners predict this fixed level as the budget is prepared. In contrast, the **variable budget** recognizes that a number of costs vary with the volume of activity, and flexibility is built into the budget. Thus, variable budgets represent flexible standards that can be realistic goals for managers as costs and activity are monitored periodically (Robbins & Coulter, 2012).

Either of these types of budgets can be powerful management tools; during the planning function, they keep the team focused on strategic goals, objectives, and priorities. During the controlling function, budgets facilitate performance evaluations and results-oriented control. In a stable environment, the fixed budget clearly outlines the resources that are allocated to a specific purpose, and the controlling function can be very straightforward.

Fixed Budget Approach

Fixed budgets can be effectively applied in facilities such as a health maintenance organization (HMO) setting. Once the rates have been set and clients have been estimated for the budget period, the allocation of those resources must be carefully planned and controlled. Department managers need fairly accurate forecasts as they take careful short- and long-range views of departmental needs for the future. A balanced perspective of needs and alternatives for meeting these needs is best created with input from the team members. In this way, visionary changes or anticipated regulatory requirements can be discussed and incorporated into the budgeting process. Having to go back and ask for additional funds when federal regulations require an additional piece of datum is a stressful experience. This is especially true when the proposed requirement was published in the *Federal Register* 6 months earlier, leading to an unwanted label—that of crisis manager.

Variable Budgeting Approach

When patient activity is unstable, a flexible or variable budget can lead to prompt action in keeping costs down when patient activity is decreased. Using a reliable temporary agency for the peak periods can keep the backlog to a minimum when patient activity peaks. Another alternative is to build **flex time** into the budget for special projects that must be accomplished. For example, a manager planning conversion to automated information systems technology can use the extra employee hours effectively if the slow time corresponds with the conversion time. A flexible budget is not an invitation to spend, however. The variables in the cost schedules are tied to the patient census or other revenue streams.

Chief financial officers usually have preferences for the type of budget the facility will complete. Organizational tradition is frequently another factor in the type of budgeting process used. Keeping detailed appropriate information from one budget period to the next assists the HIM manager in setting the stage for negotiating in the new budget period regardless of the type of budget used. Computer applications can make this task efficient. Team manager procedures should include tracking activities to capture data for information that is needed periodically for a variety of needs such as the budget. Monitoring and evaluation are the last components of the budget process.

Incremental Budgeting Versus Zero-Based Budgeting

Incremental Budget Approach

As the budget for a facility is developed, year after year, the majority of allocations become standardized. For instance, the new patient folders that will need to be ordered for the budget period are estimated and the manager does not question the need to include folder costs in the budget. The budget allocated for folders will not vary greatly from year to year and an inflation factor is just added each year. This is an example of an **incremental budget** where funds are allocated to departments based on the amount in the budget for the present period.

Thus, with the incremental or traditional budget, funds are allocated to the HIM department on the basis of what was budgeted the previous period and only incremental changes beyond an inflation factor are reviewed. Should the manager be seeking to identify inefficiency and waste in the department, budget data are not particularly helpful under this approach (Robbins & Coulter, 2012).

Flex time Flexible work hours where employees work a specified number of hours per week, but are free, within limits, to schedule their own hours.

Incremental budget A budget that allocates funds to departments for the new budget period based on allocations of the previous budget period.

Zero-Based Budget Approach

Zero-based budgeting (ZBB) A budgeting system where each budget request requires justification in detail regardless of past allocation.

One company, in an effort to become more efficient, developed **zero-based budgeting (ZBB)**, which required managers to justify budget requests each budget period. This company, Texas Instruments, was successful in becoming efficient; however, a modification of ZBB became less costly for the company (Robbins & Coulter, 2012). In its pure form, ZBB requires managers to justify all budget requests in detail each budget period. Allocations from the previous year are not considered. The burden is shifted to managers to justify all requests as the budget is developed. Requests are grouped into decision packages by the department managers and then planners rank them according to their value in meeting the goals of the organization.

A decision package may be quite detailed and include a breakdown showing effort levels and alternatives for reaching each level. For example, the team responsible for coding and reimbursement considers spending $30,000 during the current year in efforts to obtain physician final diagnoses promptly. The team's decision package for the new budget year might propose a second alternative—spending only $20,000. This reduction could be achieved by taking only three trips per week to physician offices. In contrast, the team might propose spending $40,000 by dedicating an additional technician for 2 hours every morning to ensure records are available for physicians to complete. The package would then estimate the average turnaround time for completion under each of these three alternatives.

At the first effort level, the cost would remain at the present level, $30,000; the turnaround time at present averages 36 hours. The second effort level, or alternative, has a cost of $20,000; the estimate for turnaround time might be 48 hours. The third effort level would cost $40,000 with a projected turnaround time of 24 hours. With this information, the budget committee can make a decision based on the priority given to prompt completion of final diagnoses.

An adaptation of zero-based budgeting is most likely the budget process facing health care managers. Here the budget committee plans the budget process and develops the adaptation chosen for use in the organization as budget planning time approaches. Rarely is the pure-form ZBB process seen in health care organizations. Since the pure form of ZBB requires managers to justify each line item in their request, it is quite expensive in terms of time and detail. Certainly, it imposes a rigorous approach as managers evaluate budget needs and prepare decision packages for upper-level management.

For these reasons, an adapted version of zero-based budgeting is frequently used. This approach asks managers to justify specific line items where variables exist. The goal of management, especially in an era of rightsizing and financial restraint, is to use the budgeting process for allocating limited resources effectively and fairly.

While a modified ZBB has advantages over the traditional budget, there are drawbacks—it increases paperwork and preparation time. And, political concerns are not totally eradicated; managers can still inflate the benefits of their pet alternatives. However, its value in managing declining resources makes it especially popular with health care managers today (Robbins & Coulter, 2012).

A review of the principles outlined in Figure 6-1 reinforces the importance the budgeting process plays in the planning function. These principles are applicable for HIM managers in health care facilities and for small business owners alike. Effective budgets are not viewed as just time-consuming paperwork but as tools that turn strategic planning into action at every level of the organization.

MAKING THE PLANS OPERATIONAL

Typically, there is a time lag between submission of the budget proposal and final approval during which additional information may be requested quickly. Budget committees have hundreds of details to synthesize into one package and need all the facts at hand as decisions are made. Thus, managers should expect last-minute requests and allow time to give priority to them.

Once final approval has been received, the management team sets the tone for implementing any additional changes for the revised objectives and new budget. Every person involved in the changes must understand the plan and have the opportunity to become excited about it. When opportunity for change comes, resistance comes trailing along. As employees are involved in the planning, organizing, and implementing of the change at their level, they have the opportunity to commit to change, which can lower resistance. Of course, revising policies and procedures is a crucial component for success of the plan and the changes involved.

SUMMARY

Revenue cycle management is a critical set of functions performed by HIM professionals, as it has a direct impact on the financial well-being of the health care facility. Government and private payer systems require HIM professionals to maintain a working knowledge of guidelines on which reimbursement is based.

Management of documentation is a significant contributor to accurate reimbursement. HIM professionals must be aware of the impact of functions, such as coding, have on the overall financial picture of the organization, as HIM professionals may work closely with the finance department to address issues in these areas.

CRITICAL THINKING EXERCISES

1. Give several differences in the budget you would prepare for a consulting business plan and the budget an HIM department director would be creating in a hospital with 50 employees.

2. List some items in a departmental budget that have flexibility, depending on patient activity.

3. Compare incremental and zero-based budgets.

4. Identify items that should be considered for inclusion in an HIM department budget.

APPLICATION OF THEORY EXERCISES

1. Your department is behind in completing the coding and billing for your hospital, how would you prioritize the work of your coders to maximize their efficiency?

2. As the manager of the Health Information Management department you receive a copy of a letter of denial from ABC Insurance Company for patient Joseph Barker, date of birth October 10, 1938. On January 4 of this year, Mr. Barker was seen in the hospital emergency department for chest pain. In a review of the medical information, you discover that the information sent to the insurance company on the claim form is not correct and many departments that treated the patient did not send their information to the billing system.

Write a letter of appeal to an insurance company for the denial of a claim for services.

INTERNET ACTIVITY

Medicare is a federally funded health program established in 1965 to assist with the medical care costs of Americans 65 years of age and older as well as other individuals entitled to Social Security benefits owing to their disabilities. Medicare is administered by the federal government by the Centers for Medicaid and Medicare Services (CMS). CMS maintains two websites for information on Medicare services, payment and reimbursement; one is designed for Medicare beneficiaries and the other is designed for providers and organizations. Visit both websites and identify what services are covered by each. Compare and contrast the ease of use and information on both sites.

www.medicare.gov

www.cms.gov

CASE STUDY

Based on the following information, create a proposed budget for year 2:

- Recent merit pay increases (usually 0–5% provided annually) have resulted in the following salaries:
  - 2 coders each at $15/hour
  - 1 coder at $14.50/hour
  - Lead coder salary, $50,000/year
  - 2 release-of-information specialists each at $13/hour
  - Director salary, $75,000/year
  - Physician record assistant at $14/hour

- Credentialing specialist salary, $37,000/year
- 2 data quality analyst salaries, at $15/hour
- Scanning clerk at $12/hour

- Additional equipment was obtained in month 6 at a rental rate of $200/month.
- The ability to fax records electronically will be available at the start of budget year 2.

	Budget Year 1 ($)	Actual Year 1 YTD 3rd Quarter ($)	Budget Year 2
Revenue			
Record release fee income	150,00	125,000	
Expenses			
Salaries (including overtime)	375,000	300,000	
Benefits	550,000	425,000	
Contracted audits	100,000	50,000	
Equipment rental	4,000	3,200	
Supplies	5,000	4,500	
Education	6,000	3,000	
Postage	2,000	1,250	

REFERENCES

Robbins, S., & Coulter, M. (2012). *Management* (11th ed.). Upper Saddle River, NJ: Pearson.

Longest, B. (1990). *Management Practices for the Health Professional* (4th ed.). Norwalk, CT: Appleton & Lange.

SUGGESTED READINGS

Casto, A. B., & Forrestal, E. (2013). *Principles of Healthcare Reimbursement* (4th ed.). Chicago: AHIMA.

Davis, N. (2011). *Revenue Cycle Management Best Practices*. Chicago: AHIMA.

CHAPTER 7

Planning Policies and Procedures

After completing this chapter, the learner should be able to:

1. Explain the differences between rules and policies and how each relates to objectives.
2. Discuss the value of documenting procedures into manuals in the work environment.
3. Give several reasons for creating an open-mode environment for employees.
4. Outline guidelines for developing departmental rules and policies that will conform to organization-wide rules and policies.
5. Describe the steps for creating rules and policies to cover unique problems.
6. Identify the steps for successfully revising department procedures.
7. Defend managerial decisions that empower teams to revise their own procedures.
8. Give examples of alternative health care settings where HIM consultants need skills in writing policies and procedures.
9. Describe the main features of the narrative format for writing procedures.

INTRODUCTION

Some managers find creative enjoyment in outlining a plan of how a task is efficiently undertaken and then documenting each step. There are also those who are energized to creative effort while thinking through how a task is to be done, but lose the energy quickly when it comes to documenting the steps and putting policies and procedures into actual sentences. One management style is not necessarily preferable to the other, just as no one person can possess every managerial quality.

However, effective managers can honestly explore and accept their own strengths and weaknesses. They understand the need to complement their weak areas by hiring employees with strengths in those needed skills. This can be especially crucial when a manager has weak writing skills. By actively choosing assistants, supervisors, and/or team leaders who have strong skills in writing and documenting, strong management teams may be built.

Walk in any department and ask to review the procedures for a specific task in the departmental **manual**. You will quickly discover the importance given to this aspect of managing. Compare the procedure with related policies in the manual and then with actual tasks being performed by the team. When high priority is given to planning policies and procedures and keeping user-friendly manuals readily available to employees, this will be evident through observations. Manuals may be either hard copy or electronic in format.

Manual A book containing policies, rules, and procedures for a department, a section, a team, or an employee. Also called a handbook, guidebook, or data quality manual.

There are a variety of different types of manuals that may be found in an HIM department. A general department manual provides an overview of each of the different specialty areas within the department, while additional manuals may be developed for each of these areas, such as a coding manual or a release of information manual. Insurance companies provide carrier manuals to share information about policies and procedures for submission and processing of claims. A compliance manual includes information about HIPAA Privacy, HIPAA Security, and other pertinent federal, state, and local regulations.

Or, explore the documentation qualities of a consulting firm; ask to review the sample policies and procedures for a specific HIM task and the priority given to documentation will soon become evident. The writing expertise of consultants is frequently in demand because long-term care and ambulatory care facilities also need well-documented rules, policies, and procedures for accrediting and licensing purposes. An effective consultant also emphasizes the value of updated manuals for the day-to-day activities of the facility.

DEVELOPING RULES, POLICIES, AND PROCEDURES

The examples detailed in the Introduction show the value of documenting policies and procedures in various health care settings. Developing concise steps for HIM departmental activities can increase productivity, efficiency, and effectiveness. Policy and procedure manuals will increase in value as automated systems replace manual activities, which is another excellent reason to devote time and effort to preparing them.

Managers have found several advantages for documenting rules, policies, and procedures and making them serve as useful tools in the workplace. These advantages are identified in Figure 7-1 and are referred to throughout the remainder of the chapter.

In Chapters 4 and 5, policies, rules, and procedures were mentioned as flowing from the objectives developed during strategic planning activities. Policies and rules thus allow for a consistent pattern of behavior within organizations as objectives are embraced. These strategic planning goals and objectives give direction to the operational goals and objectives within the department and subsequently to the procedures.

Policies Defined

Policies are guides that establish parameters for making decisions. They allow for judgment and interpretation on the part of managers. For example, a human resource department policy stating that, "The HIM department wage scale shall be competitive with that in the community" leaves room for interpretation. Staying competitive with several other organizations in the beginning wage for medical record technicians, for example, does not require

FIGURE 7-1   Reasons for Documenting Rules, Policies, and Procedures

1. Encourage teamwork.
2. Promote clarity, consistency, and continuity of performance.
3. Provide excellent information for training programs.
4. Establish standards and expectations against which actual performance can be monitored.
5. Serve as a central database for adding, revising, or deleting rules, policies, or procedures.
6. Release managers, supervisors, and team leaders for departmental planning or other activities by saving time spent answering repetitive questions.
7. Serve as source documents for inspection by accrediting and licensing agencies.
8. Become working benchmark documents and thus serve as a warning signal for potential problems and quality improvement actions.

a manager to begin a new employee at a specific wage. It does insist that the manager review community wages and choose a beginning wage within the range discovered in this review. Parameters are thus set for managerial action.

Rules Defined

A rule differs from a policy in that it is written as an explicit statement that tells managers what they ought to do officially or outlines what they should not do. Rules limit specific actions. HIM managers find rules give direction to many facets of their work. For instance, the federal rules regarding medical codes that are to be used for specific surgeries or diagnoses leave no room for a coding technician to use personal judgment in assigning such codes. In addition, these specific rules allow vendors to develop coding software with precision. Such federal standards give consistency across the country in the development and use of coding rules and policies.

Procedures Defined

Once the rules and policies are developed to give substance to the objectives, then procedures are needed. Putting action into the plan, a procedure is a series of interrelated sequential steps that give the necessary details for meeting one aspect of an objective.

Empowering the teams assigned to perform specific tasks by encouraging them to document their role in meeting an objective increases the opportunity for complementing strength and weakness traits across the group. The team can assign a member with special writing skills the task of updating the policies and procedures for the manual. Using the strengths of this team member increases the effectiveness of the total team effort. At the same time, the team needs the organization's protocol for writing procedures and for making changes in policies and rules for incorporation into the manual.

Assuring that the team has the tools for performing tasks empowered to them is a responsibility of the manager. This includes having computers available for maintaining the procedure manual with timely updates. As rules and policies are disseminated or created by the team, procedures are developed or revised to give them action. Steps for data gathering to monitor effectiveness of the rule or policy should become a part of the procedures. Including this evaluation tool as rules, policies, and procedures are developed emphasizes the expectation that quality improvement techniques will increase the team's effectiveness.

In an HIM department, there are activities that frequently overlap among teams. Communication is crucial as employees on different teams need access to updated procedures that affect their work. As coordination across the teams occurs, an added bonus is the interaction that encourages understanding of another team's tasks and pressures. This also promotes cohesiveness among the employees and enhances the team spirit as well as the total departmental spirit.

Manuals as Tools

Within a department or a firm, policies, rules, and procedures that affect all employees are gathered into a departmental or organizational manual. A copy of this manual is then made available to each employee. It may be called a handbook, a guidebook, or a manual. HIM managers grow accustomed to the term *manual* as regulatory agencies use manuals for disseminating information and accrediting agencies refer to manuals in their requests for information. One of the more technical teams in a department may prefer *data quality manual*. Having the team feel ownership of this instrument by naming it and updating it is more important than the name itself.

Creative Manual Writing

How do managers invite creativity into the work setting? Creative writing author, John Cleese, suggests managers create an **open-mode environment** for employees that encourages creativity and original thinking (Cleese, 1991). By contrast, well-defined tasks are typically performed in a closed mode of thought as little creativity is involved.

Open-mode environment A specific work space that encourages creativity and original thinking.

To create an atmosphere where an employee can move to an open mode of thought, Cleese suggests that managers:

1. Provide a specific work space away from the demands of the daily routine.
2. Set specific time periods for using this space.
3. Eliminate the fear of making a mistake.
4. Allow the employee freedom to express humor.

Cleese emphasizes that once the task has been completed and documentation submitted, the employee must return to a closed mode of thought to effectively carry out the new or revised procedure.

WRITING POLICIES AND RULES

As already noted, policies and rules are developed from the operational goals and objectives in the department. These were created or updated from the strategic plan of the organization. For example, the procedures for hiring new employees are developed from the objectives of the department. These objectives were developed from the organization's overall goals and objectives. Hiring high school graduates who have completed at least one applied computer course may be a goal of the organization. The department would, consequently, include this rule in the manual and in the position descriptions.

The example mentioned above shows how specific and explicit a rule can be. There is no leeway for the manager. Rules apply to specific situations. On the other hand, a policy is a guide that gives parameters for the decision-making process. The policy has a broader scope. Either policies or rules may derive from organizational culture, social, or ethical considerations. These facts are reinforced here to set the stage for getting them down in written form.

Sources of Information

HIM managers monitor a variety of sources for information that will assist in updating rules and policies within their area of responsibility. The human resources department publications are one important source. Some rules and policies can be considered programmed decisions or **standing-use plans**. They assist managers in repetitive and routine decisions where a problem is well structured and relatively simple. When a manager takes action in line with such a standing-use plan, she can be confident the decision treats employees equally. The format for writing these standing-use policies may come from the human resources department as well as from the revised policies.

Standing-use plan
A plan that is created when repetitive or routine decisions are made; also called programmed plan or decision.

Other sources for standing-use policies are those mandated by regulators or by standard professional practice. These policies must be updated when regulations or standard professional practice guidelines change. They are reviewed with employees periodically. In this way, they assist in creating the culture of the department. When new or revised rules and policies are presented, time should be allowed for discussion about their unchanging nature. Empowering the teams to participate in formulating policies and rules when appropriate gives a sense of ownership to employees.

The new rule outlined above for hiring a high school graduate with an applied computer course is in response to an internal environmental change. An example of a revised rule necessitated by the internal environment would be when changes are made in data system configurations and rules or policies need revision as a result.

External environmental changes impact the workplace when federal regulators or professional organizations enact or publish changes that affect the role of HIM professionals. For example, in response to the Patient Self-Determination Act (passed in the early 1990s), a rule for giving patients information about advance directives might be stated, "A copy of the information sheet, *Right of Patient to Make Decisions Regarding Medical Care*, will be given by admitting officer to each patient admitted for treatment in this facility as mandated by the Patient Self-Determination Act." This rule gives an explicit statement that specifies:

What:	*Right of Patient to Make Decisions Regarding Medical Care*
When:	On admission
Where:	Admitting office

Why: Mandated
Who: Patient
How: Information sheet

Similarly, a policy for in-service education on advance directives could be part of the HIM department's manual and could be stated, "Employees of the HIM department will receive in-service education regarding advance directives and the Patient Self-Determination Act." This policy allows the manager to choose the type of in-service best suited to the needs of the department. Judgment is also allowed in how and when to present advance directives information to new employees. No specific time frame is given in this policy.

In another example, setting policies for scheduling vacation times throughout the year can be facilitated through team effort. The total department policy can be broad, with a statement such as, "Coverage of priority tasks during an employee's absence will be planned before final vacation approval is given." Within a specific team, such as record retrieval, a more specific rule can refer to having someone available to retrieve records during certain time periods.

Considerations for Writing Rules and Policies

Organizational rules and policies will become a major part of a department's manual. The guidelines in Figure 7-2 can assist in writing departmental policies and rules that will be in conformity with those of the organization.

One challenge for writing rules and policies lies with those infrequent problems that arise. Problems that require unique solutions, those with little structure, or those where specifics change, frequently need decisions that are nonprogrammed. The decision-making process outlined in Chapter 3 is needed for developing rules and policies to handle these problems. As mentioned

FIGURE 7-2   Guidelines for Developing Rules and Policies

1. Review any regulations that mandate specific wording of a rule or a policy as the result of required or prohibited courses of action.
2. Set boundaries for action that are as broad in scope as possible.
3. Construct rules and policies to reinforce goals and objectives, yet be flexible enough to accommodate a changing climate.
4. Include any applicable legal constraints that apply and document source of information.
5. Develop a strategy for handling conflicting accrediting and regulatory policies.
6. Show consistency throughout the manual in tone and format.
7. Review the manual periodically, especially for needed revisions because of accrediting body updates or other reasons.
8. Date the replacement pages for new or revised policies and rules. Include the signature of the person approving the change.

earlier, a nonprogrammed decision is a synonym for a single-use plan. When possible, decisions made for unique problems should be documented. The documentation for these single-use rules and policies may be kept in the manager's manual only. For subsequent unique problems, the manager may refer to these policies to gain insights into making a specific decision.

WRITING PROCEDURES

Specific, chronologic procedures flow from the policies and rules. Procedures outline how tasks will be accomplished by listing a series of related steps or tasks to achieve a specific purpose. First, the action must be described. Second, what must be done and under what circumstances should be explained. Not only is the person doing the procedure identified, but other team members who contribute in some way are also included. As mentioned earlier, for some procedures, interdepartmental personnel who contribute to the task are also included.

Procedures are valuable tools for managers as they standardize tasks that are repetitive. They give uniformity to tasks regardless of who performs them. Also, they are of value for giving confidence that personnel training is complete. Lastly, they facilitate performance appraisal and quality improvement efforts.

Revising Procedures

The need to revise procedures occurs with greater frequency than writing a totally new procedure. As tasks are performed and data are gathered that relate to their accomplishment for the performance of employees, problems inevitably surface. Through quality improvement techniques, managers and teams can focus on solving problems. When steps in a procedure are involved in the problem, updating the procedure once the decision is made assures that employees will have the best tools available for creating uniformity and excellence. And, of course, the updated procedures give documentation for later monitoring during the fourth management function—controlling. Concepts of quality improvement techniques are covered in Section V, where the controlling function of management is discussed.

Gathering information from every person involved in the procedure is the first step in revision. The data already available have typically shown the problem. Now the team can assist in solving the problem by focusing on the customer, the service, and the desire for excellence. Managers can listen to those ideas and assist in incorporating the chosen solutions into the revision. Lastly, the manager can give recognition to the team for creating excellence that results in better procedures and happier customers.

After the difficult task is completed, the manager can enjoy the satisfaction of accomplishment with the team. Rewards may be appropriate. For example, when physicians are the customers, visibility is important. This could be achieved by allowing the team to disseminate creative notices of any changes that impact physician patterns of practice. This action would enhance physicians' perception that the team truly desires to serve their needs. The manager can then encourage the physicians to verbalize their appreciation directly to the team members.

Writing New Procedures

Concurrent with any reengineering of department systems or installation of new systems is the demand for documenting the necessary steps to make the change useful. After the policies are developed or revised, the managers would use the decision-making steps outlined in Chapter 3 to incorporate the new tasks into the work setting. Alternatives are explored, always focusing on the customers who will use the information, the records, or whatever the new system produces.

Again the teams involved should make all the decisions appropriate for their level. An implementation team with members from several sections of the department may be used to assist in creating the process. As mentioned earlier in this chapter, by choosing the person with the best skills for documenting these procedures, successful implementation is enhanced.

It should be emphasized that when responsibility is given to a team member for this writing, recognition of the extra effort needed must be given. A team member can become discouraged very quickly if no release time is given from routine tasks. The value of the manual to the team and the department is such that the budget should reflect time allotted for preparing the new procedures and revising the manuals. When creative thought is needed, the employee should be given both time and space for an open-mode environment.

An alternative to the use of a team member is to assign the revision of manuals to a resource person. This person may be a professional who performs a broad range of activities when employees are ill or on vacation. Should such a resource person be chosen to perform procedure writing, the manager would include technical writing expertise in the skills section of the job description for that position. Job descriptions are discussed in Chapter 10.

It is possible the new system being implemented will alter the department functions so dramatically that even the mission of the department will need changing before the policies and procedures are developed. Enthusing employees to make such a major change is a challenge facing many department managers today as regulations mandate the use of computerized systems. By emphasizing that these changes can be opportunities for greater service to the department's customers, managers can gain the support of the team. HIM professionals can share their enthusiasm for the opportunities being created by changing health care patterns.

HIM professionals who choose a career in consulting for long-term care facilities, physician office practice, urgent centers, or surgery centers will find writing skills very important. Consultants meeting with the administrators of such facilities will likely be asked questions relating to procedure writing. In fact, administrators may ask to see samples of procedures prepared by the consultant. Not only are consultants involved in the training of health record employees for these settings and need procedures for this training, but they typically provide the manuals to assist these employees when the consultant is absent.

Format for the Procedures

In some organizations, standardized formats are already in place for writing procedures. If not, managers can explore different formats with the management team and then assist in choosing the most useful model for departmental procedures. Introducing the team to sample procedures with different formats can be helpful. A narrative sample format is shown in Figure 7-3. It shows selected portions of the procedure for a department receptionist.

As shown in Figure 7-3, the narrative style used is an outline form with action verbs beginning each statement and explanations or notes written in paragraphs. A narrative style is used most frequently for HIM department procedures.

Outline Format Using All Numeric Style

The outline format used in Figure7-3 is an alphanumeric format. Some writers prefer to use an all-numeric format as shown below, in brief:

1.   Request ...
1.1.   Show ...
1.1.1.   Pull ...

Abbreviated Narrative Format

An abbreviated narrative form uses *key steps* and *key points* to emphasize the content of a procedure. This style is useful when detailed explanations are needed and the steps in the action are easily described in a few words.

It is especially valuable for training manuals. The rationale behind a step can be detailed under key points. The example below is just one step in a release-of-information procedure:

Key Step	Key Points
Open correspondence and sort.	Different types of requests for information are separated for efficient input into the computer—attorneys, insurance companies, other health care givers.

FIGURE 7-3   Procedure for Department Receptionist

Objective: The Health Information Management Department responds to customer requests courteously, professionally, and promptly while following rules and policies for confidentiality.

Date of Preparation: _____

Revision Date: _____

Person Responsible: _____

Signature: _____

I.   Voice Mail

   a.   Listen to voice mail messages before 8:15 a.m. each workday.

      i.   Document messages as needed for follow-up.

      ii.   Respond to messages appropriately and promptly.

         1.   Refer to appropriate team for answers as needed.

         2.   Retrieve information and return calls.

         3.   Inform the supervisor or team leader of any messages containing potential problems.

   b.   Check voice mail periodically throughout the day and follow steps in a above as needed.

      Note: The dial tone on the telephone has a beep in it when there is a message waiting in voice mail. By checking for this beep at the end of the workday, all messages can be cleared before the counter is closed.

II.   Telephone Calls

   a.   Answer the telephone by the third ring.

      i.   Identify yourself after stating, as appropriate, "Good morning or good afternoon, Health Information Management Department."

      ii.   Offer courteous assistance to the customer. If unsure of the answer, refer to supervisor/team leader. Never say, "I don't know." Always offer to find an answer.

      iii.   Ask if there is anything else you can do for the customer before hanging up.

   b.   Talk with any customer on hold at least once every 30 seconds.

III.   Walk-in Customers

   a.   Smile and offer help to the customer.

      i.   Telephone the employee to come to the counter and meet the customer when the workstation is out of sight.

      Note: Customers are thus escorted while in the department, so they are not wandering about.

      ii.   Offer a chair to the customer if there is a wait.

      iii.   Ask if you can do anything further for customers before they leave.

   b.   Use a professional attitude at the reception counter at all times.

      i.   Avoid gossip.

      ii.   Refer to employees respectfully.

      iii.   Maintain confidentiality policies.

Action Verbs

Action words give procedures vitality and meaning. Using the best action verb can challenge the writer. Below are some verbs that are frequently used for departmental procedures:

Check	mail	destroy
Verify	send	show
Distribute	compute	gather
Issue	obtain	use
Place	read	pull
Write	input	forward
Provide	prepare	telephone
Fax	request	record
Decide	print	receive
Open	stamp	flag
Respond	refer	offer

Page Numbering

For ease in revising the manual, page numbering is best done by section, with each section identified by letter. Thus, the page numbers for Section A would begin with A-1, A-2, and so on. An index is also helpful. Dividers can be used to separate the sections.

Advantages of using computer software and laser printers are evident in the finished product. Proofreading can be done using the computer and then special graphics can give a professional look to the manual. Loose-leaf binders that will survive constant use can be purchased. These allow for update insertions with minimal waste. Manuals should be user-friendly and readily available to everyone.

When these steps are followed, employees can feel ownership of their manuals. Managers and team leaders who keep a high awareness level of the need for procedure revisions can succeed in keeping manuals user-friendly and current. When employees see the manual as a baseline tool for quality improvement, they will want to incorporate the revisions into their day-to-day activities. Through these efforts, managers are focusing on outcomes-based management.

SUMMARY

Documentation through the use of rules, policies, and procedures serves several needs for the HIM professional. These tools promote teamwork and consistency. They provide a base for training programs and serve as a standard for practice. They offer effective and efficient use of a manager's time and play a role in quality improvement.

Whereas policies are guides that set parameters for making decisions, rules are explicit statements that set the direction for action. Writing or revising rules, policies, and procedures can be a participative task where the manager or team member with technical writing skills is selected. Appropriate tools and an open-mode environment enhance the activity.

Policies and rules should be consistent with the goals and objectives of the organization as well as the more specific objectives of a department. And, in fact, the entire manual is best developed and written consistent with the culture of the organization.

Standing-use rules and policies assist in meeting well-structured problems with speed and efficiency. But they must be updated when changes occur in regulations or standard professional practice.

Nonprogrammed decisions have unique problems and require the decision maker to use the decision-making process. These single-use rules and policies should be documented in the manager's manual for reference.

Procedures flow from the rules and policies and give direction to daily activities. They need frequent updating as change occurs. Each team member performing the activities should be involved in the planned changes. By recognizing a team's efforts to maintain a user-friendly current manual, the manager enhances team spirit.

Writing skills are a strength for consultants, since ambulatory care settings and long-term-care facilities need this expertise. The documentation also gives direction to employees in these settings when the consultant is absent.

A narrative format is useful for writing procedures. While procedures may necessarily follow organizational guidelines in their preparation, they should be user-friendly and effective. Action words, abbreviated sentences, and frequent updates give them value.

Computer software, printers, and loose-leaf binders give a professional look to documents. If computer capabilities are used appropriately, making revisions and subsequent dissemination of revised or additional pages will be efficient and effective.

CRITICAL THINKING EXERCISES

1. List several of your attributes that you feel have contributed to creative ideas in your past experiences. Compare these with attributes you feel contribute to your skills in explaining activities in written form.
2. List eight advantages managers have when they choose to document rules, policies, and procedures.
3. Give several examples where standing-use plans would be valuable for a consulting firm that contracts with long-term care facilities.
4. Define policies and explain how policies differ from rules.
5. Outline four steps managers can take to enhance an open-mode environment for creative writing.
6. Describe the narrative style of procedure writing and give an actual example of statements showing the flow of activity.

APPLICATION OF THEORY EXERCISES

1. Prepare a policy for releasing health information for patient requests.
2. Ask to review a manual in an HIM department and then document strengths and weaknesses of this manual using Figure 7-1 as a guide and standard.

CASE STUDY

You just started working in a position as director of HIM for an acute care facility and you discover there are no documented procedures. Explain the steps you would take before writing the procedures. Write a basic procedure for releasing health information to patients.

INTERNET ACTIVITY

Search online for benchmark data for medical coding and outline your findings.

REFERENCES

Cleese, J. (1991). And now for something completely different. *Personnel*, April, p. 13.

CHAPTER 8

Planning the Physical Environment

LEARNING OBJECTIVES

After completing this chapter, the learner should be able to:

1. Define the term *ergonomics* and give several reasons for applying ergonomic principles when designing or remodeling the HIM work environment.

2. State the reasons for implementing an ongoing inventory of equipment and furnishings in an HIM department.

3. List the specialists best prepared to participate in the design of a new department or a remodeling project; give ways the expertise of these specialists can be useful.

4. Outline the principles used to create a space model that can lead to success in planning the new environment.

5. Give examples of the tools used in planning a remodeling project or new construction and explain ways HIM managers would use these tools.

6. Present a space model for an HIM department, defend the placement of each section within the department, and describe how automated technology placement is considered.

7. Discuss the value aesthetics play in the work environment and how the efforts of interior designers can impact the comfort and satisfaction of employees.

INTRODUCTION

When customers enter a health care facility's HIM department for the first time, what initially catches their attention? Is it the interior design? Is it the lighting? Is it the friendliness? Would a first-time customer immediately feel he would enjoy interacting with the staff again? Should not customers leave the department with a desire to return again and again for service? What steps can managers take to create an attractive positive atmosphere?

The term *physical environment* refers to the components of the workplace that include office furniture, cubicles, lighting, temperature, appearance, and noise control. All of these aspects of the workplace must be carefully planned to facilitate development of a workplace that allows for workers to complete required tasks in a workspace that allows proximity to individuals completing the previous and following tasks in a process, provide a safe environment, and have a workplace that is comfortable and pleasing for staff working in the area. The physical layout of the HIM department has evolved with the career field. Previously, the HIM department was generally limited to a centrally located HIM department. Now, the centrally located HIM department still exists in most places, but HIM professionals also work in other areas of the facility and even have home offices.

Department managers can set the tone of friendliness and helpfulness by their own attitudes, thus permeating the culture of the whole department. This positive tone should then become evident to all who enter. But the tone of friendliness and helpfulness can be jeopardized by the physical appearance of the department, and customers may leave with mixed feelings about the service. The physical appearance of the work environment is discussed in this chapter as ideas for creating a pleasant work environment are suggested. With appropriate planning, managers can design workplace settings that will enthuse employees and create goodwill in customers.

First, the current trends in the work environment and the factors to consider when change becomes a possibility are discussed. Considerations include an assessment of the present department design and an inventory of furniture and equipment. Concerns employees may feel about the anticipated change and how their work environment may be affected are discussed.

In the next section, ergonomics, an applied discipline, is offered as an important component in planning for either remodeling or new construction. Assessing the present department design is the next phase of the redesign project and the major assessment features are outlined. The formal planning begins with a discussion of the appropriate participants and the setting of priorities.

The next section includes a plan of action for undertaking the project and **space modeling** for the new department design is roughed out for discussion. Fourteen principles for planning the layout are detailed. Next the tools needed for creating and sharing the documentation are discussed. These include graph paper, templates, computer software programs, and architectural symbols.

As the space model or layout is shared with the planning committee, possible constraints to the project are likely to become an issue, so this probability is documented. Creating the space model itself, using the tools and ergonomic principles, is then detailed. Working and reworking the layout as ideas are introduced makes this part of the project a challenging one. The concepts discussed here for creating a floor plan in an acute care HIM department can transfer to designing a new one in any alternative setting.

Space modeling
The layout model created to depict the plans and decisions made for a physical environment that includes ergonomic principles.

CURRENT TRENDS IN PHYSICAL ENVIRONMENT DESIGN

There are a variety of factors to be considered when planning the physical layout of an HIM department. There are also differences in the consideration of the layout if it is a new department space that is being planned for the first time versus remodeling an existing department. Planning the physical layout may be accomplished through the use of computer software that provides the ability to enter measurements of rooms, locations of doors, windows, electrical outlets, and permanent equipment. Once the available space has been established, office furniture and movable equipment may be added to scale and easily rearranged in the program to determine the most appropriate layout to meet workflow needs within any space restrictions. When planning the physical layout of the department, other variables must also be considered, such as fire code and Americans with Disabilities Act (ADA) requirements for the amount of space between desks.

Two major legal aspects impacting the design of work environments for HIM professionals are the ADA and the Occupational Safety and Health Administration (OSHA). Creating a safe workplace for each employee must be a major consideration when remodeling or new construction is contemplated. The concern is also that customers entering the department have a safe environment with accessibility, when caring for their health information needs. As priorities are developed, HIM managers will want to work closely with the human resources department as plans take shape—reviewing and revising details for compliance with current regulations. The facilities management department, which is responsible for the physical components of the facility, should also be involved. This department is also sometimes referred to as plant operations or even health care facility engineering. The reason for this part of the organization to be involved is the need to coordinate all activities involved in any changes or new construction in the facility. There are various aspects that need to be considered, including electrical; heating, ventilation, and air conditioning (HVAC); maintaining compliance with any building codes or fire codes; and ensuring that all areas are accessible to be compliant with the ADA. The facilities management department not only provides input related to the functional oversight of the HIM department as a stand-alone department, but also ensures that the department is developed in a manner that contributes to the overall operational efficiency for the institution in an environment that is safe for patients, staff, and visitors.

The OSHA has regulations that must be followed carefully in all workplaces. OSHA formed as a result of the Occupational Safety and Health Act of 1970 (OSH Act), which addresses a wide variety of circumstances that may be encountered in any type of work environment. For example, employees should not only be provided with ergonomically correct furniture and supplies at the workstation, but training for proper use of these items should also be included. Some organizations provide routine mandatory training related to ergonomics in order to help prevent injuries. This training may include information about proper positioning, exercises, and general safety.

Another OSHA requirement is the Hazard Communication Standard (HCS), which requires employers to provide detailed information related to potentially hazardous substances that may be encountered in the working environment. This information must be addressed in a document commonly referred to as the Material Safety Data Sheet (MSDS), which should be provided on OSHA Form 174. Some examples of substances requiring MSDS encountered by HIM professionals include, but are not limited to, toner for printers and copy machines, correction fluid, and cleaning fluids. While these items may not seem to be obviously harmful, it is important to have MSDS information in case of a reaction that occurs through skin contact or accidental ingestion, contact with eyes or other mucous membranes, or inhalation. The MSDS must address information in 16 sections, which are as follows (see Figure 8-1 for an illustration of a sample MSDS template that incorporates the required sections):

- Identification
- Hazard(s) identification
- Composition or information on ingredients
- First aid measures
- Firefighting measures
- Accidental release measures
- Handling and storage
- Exposure controls/personal protection
- Physical and chemical properties
- Stability and reactivity
- Toxicological information
- Ecological information
- Disposal considerations

FIGURE 8-1   Sample MSDS Template

IDENTITY *(As Used on Label and List)*	Note: Blank spaces are not permitted. If any item is not applicable, or no information is available, the space must be marked to indicate that.			
Section I				
Manufacturer's Name	Emergency Telephone Number			
Address *(Number, Street, City, State, and ZIP Code)*	Telephone Number for Information			
Date Prepared				
Signature of Preparer *(optional)*				
Section II—Hazardous Ingredients/Identity Information				
Hazardous Components (Specific Chemical Identity; Common Name(s))	OSHA PEL	ACGIH TLV	Other Limits Recommended	%*(optional)*
Section III—Physical/Chemical Characteristics				
Boiling Point		Specific Gravity ($H_2O = 1$)		
Vapor Pressure (mm Hg)		Melting Point		
Vapor Density (AIR = 1)		Evaporation Rate (Butyl Acetate = 1)		
Solubility in Water				
Appearance and Odor				
Section IV—Fire and Explosion Hazard Data				
Flash Point (Method Used)	Flammable Limits	LEL	UEL	
Extinguishing Media				
Special Firefighting Procedures				
Unusual Fire and Explosion Hazards				
Section V—Reactivity Data				
Stability	Unstable	Stable	Conditions to Avoid	
Incompatibility *(Materials to Avoid)*				
Hazardous Decomposition or By-products				
Hazardous Polymerization	May Occur	Will Not Occur	Conditions to Avoid	
Section VI—Health Hazard Data				
Route(s) of Entry:	Inhalation?	Skin?	Ingestion?	
Health Hazards *(Acute and Chronic)*				
Carcinogenicity:	NTP?	IARC Monographs?	OSHA Regulated?	
Signs and Symptoms of Exposure				
Medical Conditions Generally Aggravated by Exposure				
Emergency and First Aid Procedures				
Section VII—Precautions for Safe Handling and Use				
Steps to Be Taken in Case Material is Released or Spilled				
Waste Disposal Method				

(Continues)

FIGURE 8-1   (Continued)

Precautions to Be Taken in Handling and Storing		
Other Precautions		
Section VIII—Control Measures		
Respiratory Protection *(Specify Type)*		
Ventilation	Local Exhaust	Special
	Mechanical *(General)*	Other
Protective Gloves		Eye Protection
Other Protective Clothing or Equipment		
Work/Hygienic Practices		

- Transport information
- Regulatory information
- Other information

There is much variation in the physical environments of workplaces for HIM professionals. With this variation, there are also diverse safety concerns about not only the physical aspects of the environment but the overall working conditions, too. Working conditions consist of a combination of the environment in which work is performed (surroundings) and the physical dangers or risks involved in performing the job (hazards). These conditions may include physical hazards, poor positioning of staff members relative to tasks being performed, noise pollution, poor lighting, and a variety of other factors.

Ergonomics
The design of products, processes, and systems to meet the requirements and capacities of those people who use them.

One area of concern with workplace safety is **ergonomics**, which refers to functional design of the work environment in relationship to the employee's use of equipment, layout of workstation, office furniture adaptation, and attention to other aspects of the work environment that may impact prevention of workplace injuries, accommodating the employee's unique physical requirements so as to facilitate efficacy of work functions. Some of the aspects of the HIM work environment that may need to be addressed when assessing ergonomic safety include, but are not limited to:

- Positioning of computer monitor
- Positioning of hands of keyboard
- Left-handed versus right-handed employee needs
- Height of desk and chair
- Glare on computer screen
- Employees wearing bifocals or reading glasses
- Back support or elbow support on chairs
- Excessively tall or short employees
- Frequency of lifting
- Frequency of twisting

- Ability to take breaks
- Training

Specialists in ergonomics are being hired in increasing numbers for their expertise in human factor engineering. Ergonomics is an applied science that is defined as the "design of products, processes, and systems to meet the requirements and capacities of those people who use them" (Foster, 1988). By combining relevant engineering, psychological, and anthropological concepts, ergonomics introduces the relationship of people to their work environment in today's complex society. Using computers and other high-technology equipment causes stress on the human body with resulting workplace injuries. To avoid or minimize these problems, managers take advantage of the expertise ergonomists have to offer when planning to remodel a department or install new equipment.

As professionals interface with computers and other automated equipment, in a technologically intensive environment, attention must be given to layout design and work methods; at the same time new equipment is planned, or lower productivity may result. "Working smarter" is a phrase that managers use as the teams reengineer patterns of activity for the new environment.

Sensitivity to the needs of customers during the planning phase of remodeling can give managers creative ideas. Physicians and other stakeholders may request, for example, that patient care information be at their fingertips—on the first floor of the facility. Entrance doors into the department take on new importance with such requests. Physicians wish quick access to their records, reviewers and auditors wish to interface with the records in a convenient setting, and patients desire ease in finding the department to request information. Other demands for first floor space can make it difficult to place a large HIM department in such a treasured location. In some facilities, the solution is to divide the department so sections interacting with these customers are placed on the first floor and other sections, such as transcription and birth certificate completion, are elsewhere. Transition to the electronic health record (EHR) has somewhat alleviated the need to have the HIM department on the first floor, as the physicians may access their records from most places within the facility.

Attention to individual employee needs is another trend that is gaining importance. Today departments are frequently open 24 hours a day with different shift employees sharing workstations. When they have different physical needs, difficulties arise that managers must resolve. For example, flexible lighting arrangements will allow employees on any shift to work in individualized settings that meet their needs. Flexible workstation heights can also enhance the morale of employees when they share the same environment and have different needs.

Workstations

The physical area where an employee spends his or her time is now assessed. The design of the present section/team area first needs review, and then recommendations can be made for the remodeled or new workstation. This assessment focuses on ergonomic principles involving the height of the workstation, the lighting, present equipment location, accessibility of reference materials, availability of storage space, and the noise factor.

Figures 8-2 and 8-3 contrast the use of a chair with ergonomic enhancements and one that results in poor posture. Using an adjustable chair with the correct height for the employee and with support for the lower back creates an environment where employees can give optimum effort. Footrests should be available for employees who choose to use them, as shown in Figure 8-2.

Environmental factors at the workstation may result in eyestrain. These will also be noted during the assessment; recommendations may include a MONITOR screen with higher resolution and frequent rest periods.

When purchasing furniture for workstations, it is best to select pieces that are able to be adjusted to accommodate employees of different sizes. While some may think that it is best to fit new furniture to the existing employee, it is important to recognize the fact that the existing employee may not always be there, so the furniture needs to be selected to best meet the needs of the position tasks. If the position requires the employee to be seated most of the time, working on a computer, a chair with armrests may be the best choice, while a position that involves more movement may be better served by a chair without armrests.

Desks also must be matched to meet the needs of the tasks involved with each position. If a coder is going to be using a computer for electronic

FIGURE 8-2   Example of Poor Posture

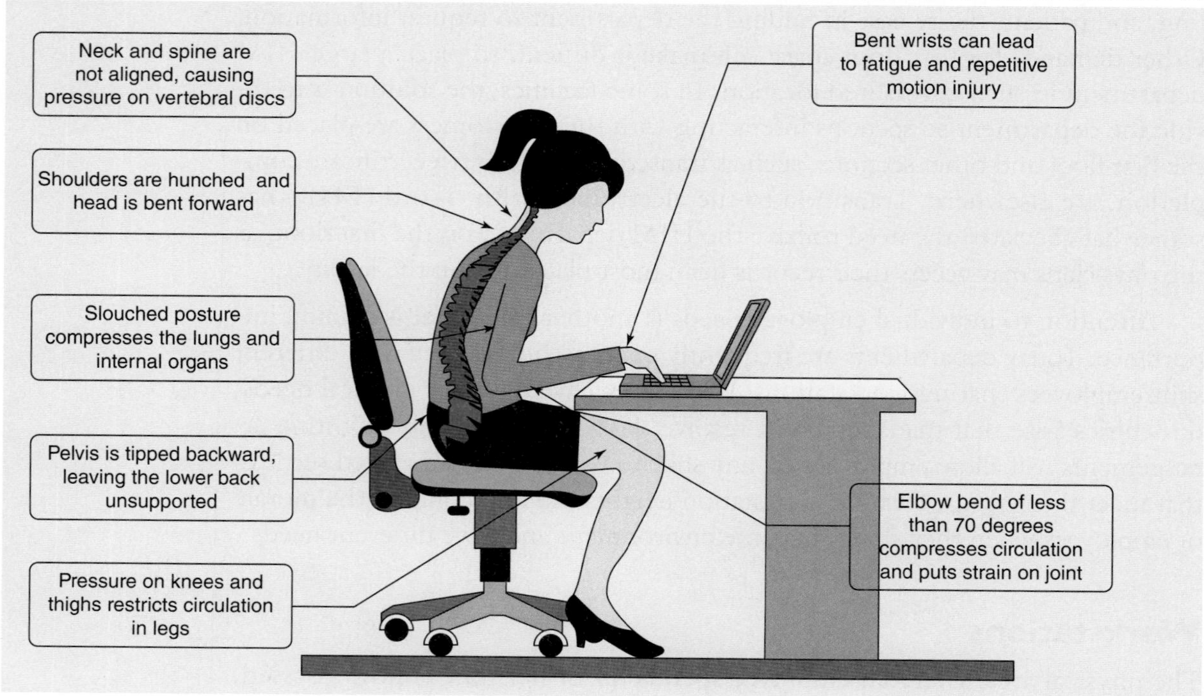

Neck and spine are not aligned, causing pressure on vertebral discs

Shoulders are hunched and head is bent forward

Slouched posture compresses the lungs and internal organs

Pelvis is tipped backward, leaving the lower back unsupported

Pressure on knees and thighs restricts circulation in legs

Bent wrists can lead to fatigue and repetitive motion injury

Elbow bend of less than 70 degrees compresses circulation and puts strain on joint

FIGURE 8-3   Example of Good Posture

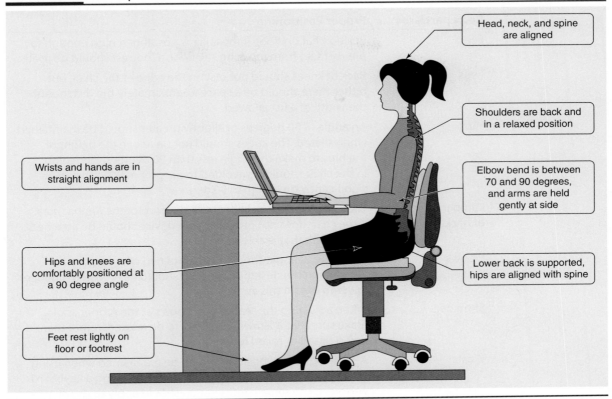

reference, only, then a simple computer workstation desk should fulfill the coder's needs. Monitor position and ability to adjust the keyboard tray are a couple of items to consider when purchasing computer workstation desks. This is another area where options to adjust should be available in order to be ergonomically correct for employees of varied sizes.

Ergonomics training is often included in workplace safety training. In addition to the general items listed above, detailed attention should be focused on ergonomically correct positioning, as HIM professionals often spend a significant amount of the workday sitting at desks. Basic ergonomic principles for individuals working in desk jobs are outlined in Figure 8-4.

With these trends in mind, ergonomic principles are now outlined. These principles apply whether a department is being remodeled or construction of a new department is undertaken. These principles can also be adapted to alternative health care settings.

ERGONOMIC PRINCIPLES

Ultimately, the goal of ergonomics is to increase productivity by creating the best office design for the purpose and for the people. When appropriately

FIGURE 8-4   Basic Ergonomic Principles for Desk Positions

Body part/area	Proper Positioning
Feet	Position flat on floor. If the chair is positioned high enough to prevent feet from reaching the floor, a footrest should be used.
Legs	Back of knees should not rest on the edge of the chair, but rather there should be a space approximately the distance of the width of a fist allowed.
Hips	An angle of 90 degrees or slightly greater should be maintained when seated. The knees should not be above the height of the hips to make the angle less than 90 degrees. Slouching in the chair should be avoided to prevent making the angle significantly greater than 90 degrees.
Lumbar region of back	The chair should have adequate support for the lumbar area. If the chair does not provide this, a device should be attached to the chair that is able to do so.
Elbows	A 90-degree angle should be maintained when typing or working on the desktop. The chair should be adjusted higher or lower to obtain this angle.
Shoulders	When adjusting the seat to put elbows at the proper angle, make sure that it allows shoulders to be relaxed, rather than being raised or rolled forward.
Wrists	A straight, neutral position should be maintained when using the keyboard. This may be accomplished by using a keyboard wrist rest. The same consideration should apply to use of a mouse and can be addressed by use of a mouse pad with a built-in wrist support.
Neck	Position the computer monitor so that the upper portion of the screen is horizontal with the eyes. The monitor should be viewed by looking directly forward, rather than turning neck.
Eyes	Glare protection should be applied to the monitor for employees with desk jobs that require extensive computer use.

designed, there can be job satisfaction and employee comfort. By studying the relationship of people to their work environment, ergonomists match peoples' capabilities and their individual requirements with the equipment and other environmental factors in the workplace. Thus, ergonomics is concerned with the following:

- Noise control
- High-technology equipment
- Lighting
- Heating, ventilation, and air conditioning
- Aesthetics
- Furniture

FIGURE 8-5   General Principles of Ergonomics

1. Select the best worker for the task.
2. Train workers in human factor habits and practices.
3. Analyze and design jobs in order to produce interest, efficiency, and safety.
4. Design equipment that fits human anatomy and physiology.
5. Eliminate stressors that reduce productivity and quality.
6. Design organizational systems that support and involve workers.
7. Build effective organizational communication systems.

Job design includes all of these ergonomic factors. Recommendations are then made to ensure the new design will decrease impediments to high productivity while creating a technologically intensive attractive environment.

Monetary compensation is found to be only one of several motivating factors in employee satisfaction. Therefore, to enhance satisfaction, attention must be given to other factors such as a pleasant work environment and an improved quality of work life. To meld these employee factors into a cost-conscious health care environment, ergonomic principles are increasingly utilized. Seven general principles, outlined by Michael Foster, are listed in Figure 8-5. These principles for the workplace guide the ergonomists as they make recommendations.

Ergonomists use these general principles as a basis for their study when changes are planned. Managers, using the expertise of ergonomists during the planning phase of remodeling, can create a space model for increasing employee satisfaction, comfort, and productivity.

REDESIGN: ASSESSING THE PRESENT DEPARTMENT

An existing department may be remodeled for a variety of reasons. As technological advances have introduced changes, there may be need to get rid of older equipment or filing areas, or there may be a need to accommodate new technology through addition of scanning stations or new computer workstations. When planning a remodel of an existing department, obstacles such as supporting walls or large equipment often require creative solutions to work around. Supporting walls cannot be removed, as they provide physical support for the structure of the building. Large equipment may be permanently wired into the location, so relocation could be time-consuming and costly. In addition, some of the existing departments may have been developed with structures built to accommodate large, older equipment that is being removed, which may present challenges, such as rewiring needs and disposal of old equipment. There are several significant positive points of remodeling an existing department, which include the following:

- Staff may find it refreshing to have a new work environment if it has been a long period of time since previous remodeling.
- Technological advances may have changed processes that impact workflow.
- Morale may improve if staff members are able to play an active role in decisions that make their work areas more pleasant and include changes that facilitate completion of their tasks.

Some of the additional disadvantages of remodeling an existing department may include:

- Resistance to change by staff members who are happy with the current arrangement and may feel like change may disrupt their processes.
- Expense to the organization, which indirectly impacts the HIM department budget.
- Difficulty gaining administrative approvals through justification of need for change.
- Time commitment for planning not only changes to the physical aspects but also any process changes that may result from the project.

Once approval is given to proceed with the plans, assessing the present department design is the first step. Appropriate team members in each section should be involved as this evaluation of their present tasks and workstations takes place. The procedures will show the tasks and workflow for each section or team, so these need to be updated first.

Facility access controls Policies and procedures that limit physical access to authorized staff to the work areas using computers for electronic information systems.

HIPAA Security Rule requirements require **facility access controls** involving policies and procedures that limit physical access to authorized staff to the work areas using computers for electronic information systems are used. Methods to apply this regulation include locked access to offices, strategic positioning of computer monitors so that others are not able to view the display, and use of screen protectors that require the user to be at a direct angle to view the display, minimizing the ability of others to see from a different angle or distance.

Another HIPAA-related concern is protection of information on computer monitors in high-traffic areas. One commonly used method to address this issue is to place screen protectors on the monitors, which limit visibility to the point where the only person who can view the screen is the one directly in front of it.

Workflow The flow of several different processes, handled by more than one person, that are dependent upon each other.

Workflow involves several different processes, handled by more than one person, and dependent upon each other. During an HIM department remodeling project, workflow analysis must be performed, which involves thorough analysis of all contributing processes in order to determine the flow of operations through the entire department. This may be accomplished by doing surveys, questionnaires, time studies, or flow charts of processes performed by

FIGURE 8-6　Workflow Analysis Tools

Workflow Analysis Tool	Example of Use for HIM Department Remodeling
Flow chart	Broad-focus flowchart identifies positions in specific areas of workflow in the department. Narrow-focus flowchart identifies more detailed workflow in each of the areas identified on the full-department flowchart.
Time studies	Release of information staff members can identify the number of customers served according to type of request (walk-in, phone, subpoena, physician office, etc.) in order to determine where more time is spent for response to requests. Physician record assistant can identify amount of time spent helping physicians over the phone, face to face in the department, in physician lounge areas, in patient care areas, or other places.
Survey	Provide open-ended questions to get subjective feedback about potential changes.
Questionnaire	Obtain feedback quickly through offering options from which staff members may choose.

individuals performing each position. Some more specific examples of using these tools for workflow analysis are provided in Figure 8-6.

While management-level HIM professionals may be familiar with best practices for processes, the employees performing the tasks are the most familiar with the details in the organizational processes and are able to provide the most accurate feedback. Actual practice may deviate from what is documented in the organization or department policy and procedure manual, so this is important to identify during workflow analysis with a remodeling project. It is possible that the policy and procedure manuals may be updated as a result of information discovered during the analysis, but manual updates may also be required if processes are changed as a result of the remodeling project, too.

Office design professionals can be contracted to facilitate planning of the physical layout of an HIM department, but there must be active involvement by everyone involved in the department. Office design professionals are not generally familiar with HIM-specific processes and functions that are performed in the area, as their practice is focused on office design for any type of workplace and not just HIM or even health care, so input from those doing the actual work is necessary to determine logical layout of the department. It is also helpful for the staff members to provide information about any special needs, current obstacles, and ideas that may facilitate specific processes.

Another important consideration for management is that communication with front line staff may determine the success or failure of the project. Front line staff members may include employees that include coders, release of information personnel, transcriptionists, physician record assistants, and any other nonmanagement workers in the area. If a remodeling project plan is presented to front line staff members who have not provided any input, there will be anxiety about the unknown of the new workstations, how the changes may impact ability to complete processes, and potential feelings of resentment or anger about lack of communication. As with any change, communication is important to facilitate buy-in for all stakeholders by using the techniques presented in Chapter 3.

Aesthetics Aspects of the workplace that include color schemes, lighting, and other areas that impact the visual appeal of the environment.

Aesthetic aspects of the workplace include color schemes for walls, carpet, and furniture, along with lighting and even sound in the office space. While some may not consider the physical appearance to be very important, there have been numerous studies that have examined the impact of various colors on workers. For example, neutral colors tend to be calming, red tones promote a feeling of warmth, and blues are cooling. It is generally advisable to avoid use of trendy color schemes, as HIM departments are not normally remodeled very frequently and could easily appear outdated relatively quickly.

Interviews and questionnaires can also be used to involve team members. While these interviews and questionnaires combine with procedures to show the workflow, volume of work, bottleneck areas, and interaction with other teams, another aspect should also be assessed. Questions relating to reasons for job satisfaction or dissatisfaction should be asked. Responses relating to ergonomic principles can then be addressed during the assessment.

The Task Itself

With the varied tasks in an HIM department, evaluation of the tasks and the workflow becomes rather complicated. Time must be allowed for a thorough assessment at this point in the planning process.

Next, the physical forces impacting the body and the frequency of each of these tasks is assessed and documented. Carpal tunnel syndrome, musculoskeletal pain, and eye strain can be related to repetitive tasks. These injuries often have a cumulative effect. Professionals showing the greatest number of CTDs in the report are employed in telecommunication and journalism. Clearly, increased use of computers is a major culprit. And, as automated technologies are installed in increasing numbers in HIM departments, the profession is at risk also.

The Employees

During the hiring phase, managers may include ergonomic factors when selecting the best applicant for the tasks within a job description. Technologic requirements for performing the tasks and the individual needs of the applicant can then be compared, reviewed, and assessed. This same type of assessment is needed when remodeling and new equipment installation takes place. The resistance to change is lessened when employees feel their individual needs are being considered in the redesign of their jobs.

The new employee and the employees facing installation of new equipment need effective training. This means more than a quick demonstration of ergonomic principles during orientation. Effective training covers posture, relaxation techniques, rest period spacings, and exercises.

The Department

Physical factors of the total department are also assessed. Factors that are reviewed include the architecture, the workflow through the layout of the department, the humidity and heating, the aesthetics, and the lighting. Documentation will include any other factors that relate to effectiveness and employee safety. As noted earlier, policies and procedures are reviewed.

An inventory of furniture and equipment can be prepared by each team and then combined into one document. Knowing just what is presently in the department is very useful to the manager in negotiations. By emphasizing the need for flexibility in designing workstations that are adjustable for individual comfort, managers can clearly show why specific items of present furniture and equipment will not meet this priority. Just as important is a manager's willingness to use items on hand that can be adapted to the new environment and an inventory reveals these as well.

An automated spreadsheet is effective for documenting the inventory. By including relevant information regarding items such as date of purchase, the spreadsheet can be a very useful document. By updating the inventory as the change progresses, the manager is ready for questions regarding just one piece of equipment or all of the department's furnishings.

The Organization

Corporate culture and its impact on worker health is assessed. The priority given to health and safety, the use of ergonomic devices, and the communication systems are reviewed and documented. The entire assessment is now gathered into a document from which decisions regarding the future can be made.

PLANNING FOR THE NEW DEPARTMENT DESIGN

When the assessment outlined above has been completed with care, any departmental difficulties should be evident. As planning for change gets under way, solutions to the documented difficulties should be worked into the planning. Designing a new HIM department may be necessary when a new facility is opened or if the location of an existing department is relocated within the same facility. When designing a new department, any of the same principles are followed as applied to redesign a department outlined above. Designing a new HIM department as part of a new facility may require the HIM manager to play an active role in provision of input regarding space requirements and appropriate location. There may also be architectural considerations and limitations to be discussed as the facility is planned.

Planning Participants

Ensuring that the project team includes the best participants may not be a task of the department manager, but it should be a concern. The need for an ergonomist has already been mentioned. This expert could come from the human resources department, as one of the experts from a health care consulting firm, or from a firm specializing solely in ergonomics. An architect brings a wealth of helpful information to a project; even a small remodeling project can benefit from such expertise. Health care facilities frequently have an architectural firm they use for remodeling projects. This gives continuity to the planning as a component of the total facility. Or, the architect may come from the same health care consulting firm as the ergonomist. Similarly, an interior design firm may have a contract for planning the design of the entire facility.

Physical plant engineers can bring a wealth of information as planning gets under way. They can answer questions that arise. For example, can the floor bear the weight of file shelving and thousands of patient records? This could be a constraint on the location of the files. They will also supply the architectural drawings and blueprints upon which the remodeling will depend.

Other participants in planning the physical environment include upper-level administration, other department managers who may be impacted by any changes, and the department employees. For large projects, work groups may be selected from among these participants to find recommended solutions to specific problems. As concerns are raised, they can be addressed and solutions documented for all participants. An ongoing challenge is updating each participant as adjustments in the plan occur.

Setting Priorities for Planning the Design

The previous paragraph mentions "adjustments." It is inevitable that some excellent ideas for the department will necessarily be deleted because of scarce resources or other constraints. HIM managers can be ready to negotiate for items on the department's wish list by prioritizing the list, by documenting how each item fits into the total plan, and by preparing valid rationale. This rationale can delineate why an item is essential for:

1. Information systems planning for the facility.
2. Quality patient care.
3. Aesthetic reasons.
4. Other departmental objectives for the future.

As priorities are set, the mission statement and overall objectives of the facility as well as the department must be reviewed, so the planning complements these long-range directional plans. For example, if a facility should plan a shift to increased ambulatory care customers for the next budget period, equipment that will meet the information needs of ambulatory care patients will have high priority.

FUNCTIONAL/PRODUCT FLOW LINES PATTERN

Now that decisions have been made for the redesign of the department or the design of a totally new department, a functional or product flow line is created. First, the present workflow is visualized and then decisions for new workflow patterns are addressed. Blueprints can be copied and used as these decisions are made. Figure 8-7 shows a workflow pattern that exists with traditional paper records and then a revised example with use of an EHR.

Principles for Planning Revised Workflow Patterns

Copies of the blueprint can first be distributed to all section/teams with instructions for visualizing their present workflow pattern. Documentation already completed during the assessment can be utilized for this task. Architectural and flowchart symbols should be used to standardize the blueprints. The managers can then combine the section/team blueprints to create one functional workflow pattern for the department.

Should reengineering of the department be planned, consideration can be given to restructuring around product flow lines. For example, the major products and customers of the department could be considered as:

1. Patient information (patient record) to medical staff and professional staff
2. Statistical patient information from database to business services and other requestors
3. Aggregated statistical information to upper-level management and other requestors
4. Patient information released to attorneys, patients, and other requestors

Using these four product lines in planning the product flow lines pattern forces the managers to consider customers first and thus impact the final blueprint pattern.

As the planning committee reviews the functional/product flow lines blueprint pattern, consideration must be given to new equipment constraints or engineering constraints that could change the placement of a section. When consensus is reached on the pattern, creation of the space model can begin.

FIGURE 8-7   Functional/Product Flow Line Pattern

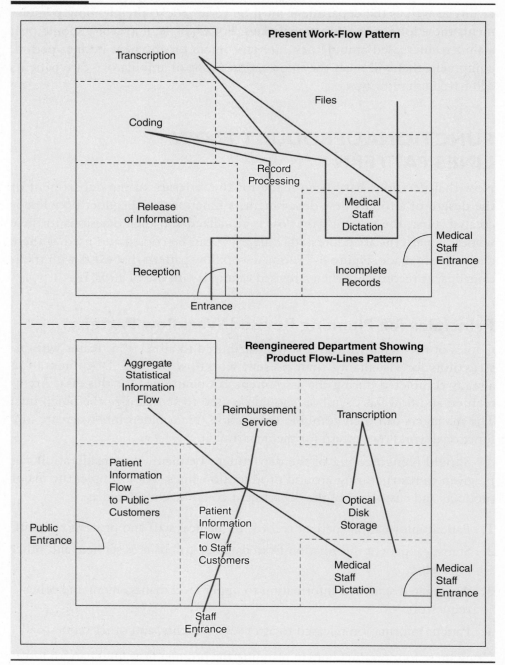

THE SPACE MODEL

The space model or layout brings together all of the planning committee's work and represents the physical space in actual miniaturized detail. Fourteen principles to guide in preparing the space model are outlined in Figure 8-8.

FIGURE 8-8   Principles for Designing the Space Model (Bennett, 1990)

1. Look for equipment vendors who offer efficient use of space for workstations when floor space is at a premium.

2. Place storage and tools for the convenience of employees who will be using them.

3. Arrange the section/team areas in a workflow pattern that minimizes backtracking of record movement and/or team movement.

4. Use present entrance doors or create new ones that will allow customers access to appropriate work areas.

5. Place teams that must share equipment close together, but purchase additional equipment should this principle violate principle 3.

6. Arrange workstations in groups that allow for easy access; where open-area desks are planned, have them facing the same direction.

7. Place team leaders or section managers where employees will be in front of them.

8. Allow natural light to come over the shoulder or the back of the employee, not directly in the face.

9. Ensure adequate ventilation and light when private offices or partially enclosed workstations are created.

10. Provide flexibility at all workstations that will allow for individual adjustments of monitors, desk height, footrest level, and chairs.

11. Provide individual controls for lighting, both for direction of the light and for intensity of the light.

12. Design access to workstations and to the department for accommodating the physically challenged.

13. Provide privacy and record security for customers—patients, families, auditors, reviewers, and, of course, the medical staff.

14. Use L-shaped workstations for employees having to use several materials or resources simultaneously in their activities. Purchase mobile pedestals that can be pushed under workstations when not in use.

Based on Bennett, A. (1990). Methods improvement in hospitals. Topics in Medical Record Management, pp. 20-24.

Many of the principles in Figure 8-8 are self-explanatory; others need comment. Additional comments on the principles are given as space model details are discussed.

Principle I

This principle asks managers to consider space allocation carefully. Facility designers may have already chosen a manufacturer for furniture purchases and managers need to know this information well in advance of the purchase date. This knowledge will enable them to negotiate for appropriate workstations should the manufacturer be unable to supply adequate workstations for HIM use. Modular furniture with privacy panels offers advantages for efficient use of space.

Principle 2

When new systems are installed, teams may need brainstorming sessions to explore the full range of new tools and storage that will be needed. Visits to other facilities can be valuable as ideas are gathered. Decisions such as how many printers should be placed need to be finalized before placement of the equipment and storage of needed materials can be planned.

Planning for storage of present tools can be overlooked since employees are familiar with them. One facility found, after remodeling was completed, that lack of an area to park the rolling carts when not in use was creating problems. In the old department the aisles at the end of the file room had been wide enough to allow space for unused carts. Without that space in the new file room, there was a problem.

One way some facilities handle cart storage is to install a countertop at a height for standing use; then carts can be stored under the counter when they are not in use.

Principle 4

This principle suggests separate doors for customers of the department. It is typical to have a separate entrance into the physicians' work room. However, other customers may be using the same door as employees. Why not have a public entrance separate from a hospital staff entrance? This configuration can give release-of-information teams better control in handling requests. Having a staff entrance also gives employees a less congested reception area for entering and leaving the department, and the reception area can better serve customers.

Another entrance directly into the file room for movement of carts also has advantages. Since carts can damage walls, doors, and furniture, this separate entrance adds to the aesthetics of the other entrances. This file room entrance can have protective covering placed on the walls and door.

These separate entrances have another advantage. The doors for employees and physicians can have keypads installed for authorized entrance only.

Principle 9

Adequate ventilation at each workstation is most important. The architect and engineers need to know the workstation configuration as plans are being developed. Since computers and other equipment generate heat, reviewing this aspect of the layout with these specialists may avoid later problems.

For example, one manager reviewed the ventilation, heating, and air conditioning drawings with the engineers when remodeling a coding area where additional computer terminals and printers were being placed. The manager outlined for the engineers the need for extra ventilation and air conditioning because of the heat generated by the equipment. Despite these precautions by the manager, the engineers did not make the adjustments. As a result, after a grand opening with enthusiastic coders ready to enjoy their new setting, a heat problem soon became evident. In fact, before the end of the second day, the temperature stood at 88 degrees! The engineers had to scramble to adjust the airflow to keep the area usable and then make the permanent changes needed.

Principle 12

Accommodating customers with disabilities is mandated by federal regulation. The concern in this chapter is for the physical layout. Aisle width in the public reception area must accommodate wheelchairs. Since the typical request is to review a record, table height is important. With little added expense, a folding table of wheelchair height can be stored in the reception area, ready for use.

Principle 14

As computers have become the major source of information and data flow, the size of workstations have decreased. This principle holds for departments relying on paper records for the majority of the data flow. Tasks where hard copy references are frequently used need desktop space. Coders have traditionally needed space for records, code books, and reference materials. With EHRs and encoding capabilities there is less space needed, but code books may still be used for complex issues. By allowing the coding team to assess their needs for the future and recommend their own space needs, managers can be assured these technicians have a satisfactory work environment. The use of mobile pedestals that can be pulled out and positioned whenever extra desktop space is needed is one solution used to alleviate space problems in some facilities.

TOOLS FOR LAYOUT DESIGN

Templates, two-dimensional templates, ruled layout paper, rulers, tape measures, and architectural symbols are all tools managers will need during project planning. Office layout templates can be purchased in different scales. One-fourth inch to a foot is a typical scale for a template and ruled layout paper. It is possible to purchase layout paper that is ruled for one-third-inch scale. This size should be avoided, since templates typically come in one-fourth-inch scale.

Templates representing office furniture can also be purchased or cut from card stock. These two-dimensional templates can then be moved around on the space model during brainstorming sessions. They may be backed with an adhesive material that will hold them in place temporarily. It may be helpful to color code these templates by section/team workstations for easy identification. Adhesive tape to represent walls and partitions can also be purchased to save time when creating the layout.

Templates A plastic pattern for drawing scaled layout furniture.

Two-dimensional templates A set of scaled card stock cutouts, representing office furniture, for use in moving around layouts until desired configuration is taped in place.

Architectural Symbols

Working with architects will open a new world of terminology, and learning some of the symbols and terms will be valuable for this interaction. Managers responsible for determining where to place electrical outlets and database access on the layout will want to understand and use these symbols appropriately. The architect or the physical plant engineer can assist HIM managers and the planning team in using symbols effectively. Also, some additional terminology will be heard frequently from architects and engineers as details on spatial requirements are documented. Becoming familiar with this technical language assists HIM managers and teams in making the best decisions.

Vendors can also be valuable resources as space modeling gets underway. They can share success stories from other facilities and share the names of managers who have installed their systems. Networking with these managers and other peers will broaden the scope of ideas for managers and the work groups. Hearing about things that went wrong is just as important to success, so listen to the horror stories as well.

Architectural computer software programs are also used to perform space modeling. Because parameters are integrated into the modeling, managers can test many options without concern that parameters such as aisle width are being violated. Becoming involved with such a computer program can offer managers insight into how other professionals use automated technology.

Eventually, the strenuous effort comes together and the space model is in its final form. A simple space model is shown in Figure 8-9 with the major features of one department on the first floor of a facility.

In this plan, the HIM manager has three section managers reporting to him. With the flattening of the organization levels over the past year, the assistant manager position was eliminated. Now the day-to-day operation of the department lies with the section managers and the team leaders. Frequent meetings of the management team keep all managers involved in the daily activities, and communication takes place by voice mail, e-mail, and written memos. The open-environment setting offers managers room for two-person conferences. In the space model, a conference room is available for larger team meetings.

Two evening team leaders serve as managers for the teams working until midnight. They use the hospital staff reception counter and the record activity team leader's desk during their shift. Management team meetings are held in the conference room at least once a week in the late afternoon and include these two team leaders.

Record Activity Section

Record Activity Section Manager

Glass privacy panels around the top area of the workstation allow the manager of record activity to have privacy. The workstation is at the side of the file area,

FIGURE 8-9   Redesigned Space Model

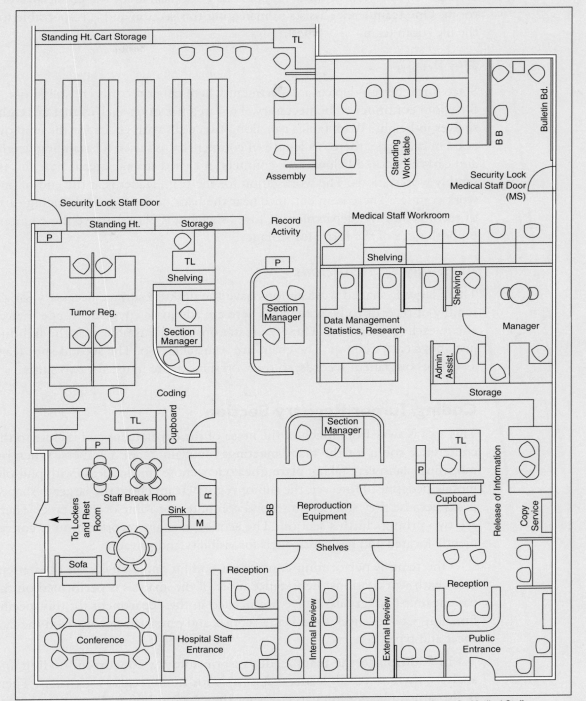

KEY: TL - Team Leader • M - Microwave • Ht - Height • P - Printer • R - Refrigerator • BB - Bulletin Board • MS - Medical Staff

with assembly and filing workstations at the back. This configuration gives the manager an overview of the area. He is also responsible for the physician work room. One team leader assists in managing this section and is responsible for the file room team.

File Room

Since this redesign depicts a department where paper records are still in use, a file room continues to be necessary. This area has open shelves that are eight shelves in height. Work tables run along two walls with chairs for the employees. On each side, there is a length of counter that is raised for standing height and carts are stored below these counters. A closed storage area is near the assembly workstations. The workstation for the team leader is at the end of one work counter. There is an entrance near the back of the files for bringing carts of records into the department. Closed shelving is placed above the counters on both sides of the room for storage.

Assembly Workstations

These large L-shaped workstations have the desktop surface necessary for assembly of records to be scanned. There are adequate covered storage shelves above each workstation. These workstations are adjustable as is the lighting just above each desktop. The chairs are adjustable also. The second-shift team assembles outpatient records, so the workstations are in use for two shifts.

Coding/Tumor Registry Section

This area is away from much of the noise of the department and is close to the conference room for the many meetings involving team members. When remodeling plans were taking place, the coders chose smaller desks with pull-out mobile pedestals. However, the tumor registry team chose the larger L-shaped desks because they still need a second computer for some of their tasks. There are two printers in this section. The section manager workstation is conveniently located and has glass panels for visibility and privacy.

One team is performing concurrent coding and analysis on the patient units with workstations there. Since most of the analysis is performed on the patient units, larger desks were not needed in the department for this specific function. Coders check for missing reports and physician signature on the face sheet and typed reports.

In addition to the team leader responsible for concurrent coding and analysis, there is a team leader responsible for tumor registry activities. There is also a team leader in charge during the evening hours. Team members in this section can work flexible shifts and share workstations. The workstation and lighting components are adjustable to meet the needs of all the team members.

A close relationship exists between concurrent review, quality improvement, utilization review, and social work teams. A physician advisor is available to answer questions from any of these teams during the afternoon.

A conference room for this purpose is available in the medical staff offices across the hall from the department.

Reception/Release-of-Information Section

This section cares for all customers with the exception of physicians entering their work room. The manager's workstation has glass panels and is in the center at the back of the work area. Two large reception counters dominate the area; at least one team member is scheduled for each counter during the day when the public and hospital staff entrance doors are open. During the evening and on weekends, the hospital staff doors are entered by keypad access and one team member staffs this area.

A team leader is in charge of the release-of-information and public reception area. Responsibility includes ensuring confidentiality and privacy for the patients and their families. Two private carrels are provided for them to review records. Auditors, reviewers, and in-house researchers use an audit room between the two reception areas. However, copy service representatives perform their tasks in a separate work area near the team leader's workstation. A cupboard in the audit room holds standard forms frequently needed by auditors and reviewers. In this room, a large work table is provided for internal reviewers working together on a project.

Confidentiality is enhanced with the location of the monitor at each workstation, thus preventing customers from viewing the screen during a database search. Ample seating arrangement for customers allows team members to encourage customers to wait in appropriate areas.

Responsibility for the reproduction equipment room also lies with this section. There is a high-speed copier, a fax machine, and a central printer located here. Space is also planned in this room for future telecommunication technology. A small printer is available for the correspondence software program near the team leader workstation.

Any concerns relating to the conference room, lounge, rest rooms, and locker areas come to this section. There are lunch facilities within the lounge. Adequate lockers for all employees are beyond the lounge. Three lockers are designated for HIM student use, since administration and the managers are committed to providing learning experiences for students in HIM educational programs. Another rest room is located in the main hallway outside the department.

Supplies for this section and some general supplies for the remainder of the department are kept in a large storage area at the back of this section. Supplies for the lounge area are stored under the counter there.

Data Management, Statistics, and Research

The team involved in data management, statistics, and research is in the same area as the manager of the department. The team is directly responsible to him. There is also an administrative assistant in this area who cares for the coordinating activities of the department and scheduling of the float technicians. Being available to assist the manager as needed is also a part of the job description.

There is a printer in this area and a work table for research projects.

Aesthetics of the Department

With this floor plan, the department design enhances the services and information offered. The visual image of the department creates an ambiance of efficiency and competency. The open office landscape minimizes territoriality that is sometimes defined by fixed walls. Thus, employees feel an ownership in the total work environment. By allowing the teams to interact with the interior designer as the aesthetic atmosphere was being planned, managers encouraged a sense of ownership.

Maintaining the Team's Environment

Team members who are allowed to plan the decor within the guidelines of the interior designer tend to increase their commitment to their work space. Wall hangings and plant choices can be a joint effort of the team. Since sharing the workstation environment is a fact of life for many teams, the decor within a workstation may have to be quite mobile. Taking down family photos and other personal items at the end of a workday may need to be done routinely, so the next person can individualize the workstation for his preference. By encouraging open communication and team effort regarding aesthetics in the workstation, managers can increase morale and the satisfaction of each team member.

Maintaining a Clean and Neat Environment

Even though the HIM department is cleaned routinely, there is still a need to encourage employees to keep their work area neat and clean. The team spends a good part of the day in this environment, and when it is kept neat and clean, their self-image is enhanced. The file room is a good example of an area that can look like a battlefield very quickly. Paper may no longer be usable but left scattered, and carts may be left standing where they were last used. Managers can set an expectation of neatness and cleanliness and then walk the talk by keeping their own area orderly.

One way of showing the priority given to aesthetics, neatness, and cleanliness is to plan an in-service education on this topic periodically. Another way is to create a bulletin board display on this subject every now and then. This extra effort helps set the tone for the department.

Looking Forward to Change

Plans are now in place for the actual construction work. At this point, the perception of every employee should be assessed. Any concerns about the changes will need to be addressed. Also, the long-term positive effect of this more technologically intensive environment can be discussed and, hopefully, fears diminished.

When managers verbally reinforce the time and effort taken by the planning committee to see that the workstations are user-friendly and user-created, commitment to the project can be solidified. As the plans are reviewed, the teams can see that these workstations demonstrate that managers respect the emotional and physical needs of employees. Increased interface between professionals and computers can be seen as a challenge for growth. During this transition period, managers will want to be sensitive to these concerns among employees and respond to them.

Changes that will undoubtedly demand new uses for the space just allocated to specific teams are inevitable, but with an open landscape and flexible workstations, changes can be made with minimal expense. Employees are thus encouraged to embrace change by HIM managers who are committed to creating an environment where change is an accepted experience. Teams that see this construction as a step to future changes can be led to think creatively toward those future possibilities.

Managing the Remote Work Environment

There are growing numbers of HIM professionals working from home and other remote locations. These employees are a valuable part of organizations and it is important that HIM managers recognize this by dedicating sufficient attention to their remote office needs. Remote employees are too often neglected as they are not visible to the HIM managers. The manager needs to reach out to the employees to identify any needs they have because some remote employees may not feel comfortable asking for equipment or other items to contribute to a safe and productive work environment. Also, simply being considerate enough to ask if there are any needs demonstrates that the manager cares. Remote employee workspace arrangements must address many issues, including the following:

- HIPAA compliance
- Equipment
- Safety
- Connectivity

Most employers have requirements that a home workspace must be designated for the sole purpose of work activities. Along with this, employees must make provisions to ensure that the workspace will not be used by anyone else. Arranging a home workspace may be approached in a similar manner as a traditional workspace. For example, a computer should be in a location where the screen is not easily viewed by somebody who is entering the space. In addition, the computer settings should include a screensaver with password protection for access. If any hard copy paper documentation is to be kept in the workspace, a locked file cabinet should be used for storage. Similarly, the ability to print from the EHR should be evaluated, and measures should be taken to protect information that is printed. This may include a requirement to shred printed materials. Equipment used in home workspaces should be clearly outlined to identify what will be provided by the organization and what the employee must purchase.

SUMMARY

Providing satisfaction and comfort to employees while increasing productivity of services and information to customers brings challenges to managers. When remodeling is planned for an HIM department, it is inevitable that change will increase the technologically intensive environment in which employees perform their tasks. By careful planning for this new environment, managers can steer the project toward success.

Ergonomics is an applied science that combines engineering, psychological, and anthropologic concepts to create a work environment for today's complex society. Seven general principles of ergonomics are used by ergonomists when assessing the present work flow tasks. Any repetitive activities performed by an employee are especially noted. Changes are then recommended for the remodeled environment.

Managers and teams prepare an inventory of the present furnishings during the next planning phase. An automated spreadsheet is an excellent vehicle for this task. The inventory can be used later for multiple purposes as it should be updated periodically.

Planning for the remodeling can now be accomplished using the information gathered during the assessment. The design participants should be from a wide spectrum of specialists: ergonomists, architects, interior designers, physical plant engineers, top administrators, other department managers, and department employees. When all information has been gathered, the functional/product flow line patterns can be created and space modeling begins. Fiscal constraints may require adjustments, so priorities need to be set by the teams to ensure changes take place in a coordinated fashion.

Principles that can assist the participants in creating an efficient and effective workplace are incorporated in the plan. Many of these are related to employee satisfaction and comfort. These principles include (1) using equipment vendors specializing in efficient use of space; (2) arranging workstations and tools for convenience and a smooth workflow; (3) creating privacy, security, and noise reduction for the records, the customers, and the employees; (4) allowing appropriate access through entrance doors into workstations and customer areas for all employees and customers including the physically challenged; and (5) providing appropriate ventilation, lighting, and work space with the flexibility to give multiple users satisfaction and comfort.

Templates, layout paper, rulers, tape measures, and architectural symbols are some of the tools needed as planning is undertaken. Managers who learn to use these tools find increased confidence and effectiveness as they work with the planning participants. When architectural computer software is available, it is also an excellent tool for creating the model.

As the model is finalized, the aesthetics of the department are considered. Options for individualized work settings may be limited, but by allowing the teams to take advantage of all possible options, managers can increase morale and satisfaction.

During this planning phase, managers can gradually instill the sense of continuous transitional planning among the employees. Because of the changes taking place in the health care environment, HIM professionals who willingly embrace change and make it a part of the culture within their sphere of influence will be ready for future transitions.

The physical aspects of the HIM environment make a great contribution to the ability of employees to complete processes efficiently and effectively. The arrangement and type of furniture in the workspace may not only facilitate or impede the ability to do work but also impact the safety of the work setting. There are regulations that dictate many aspects of the physical work environment. Remote work settings add additional challenges and opportunities for HIM work environment design.

CRITICAL THINKING EXERCISES

1. List several factors you would bring into a remodeling project to give satisfaction and comfort to the team that is facing a change from a manual record-tracking system to an automated system.
2. Define the term *ergonomic principles*.
3. Delineate six factors in job design that concern ergonomists.
4. What does the term *space modeling* mean, and how is it used in a remodeling project?
5. Create a list of several steps a manager would appropriately take in preparing and maintaining an inventory of furnishings and equipment for an HIM department.
6. Explain the role vendors can take in planning the physical layout of an HIM department.
7. What steps would you take in preparing an in-service education for the employees on maintaining a clean, safe, and attractive work setting? Outline your major topics.

APPLICATION OF THEORY EXERCISES

1. Choose an HIM work setting and assess its present environment using the seven general principles of ergonomics. Recommend any major changes you would make to improve the work setting for the employees.
2. Create a simple space model of an HIM department with which you are familiar and show how the work flows through the department. Include the entrance doors on the model and defend your assertion

that they are well placed or poorly placed for efficiency and effectiveness.

3. Prepare two-dimensional templates of workstations for one section of an HIM department and present at least two layout alternative plans that could be used effectively and efficiently for this section.

4. Outline items that you would include in a policy for setting up a remote home office. Address HIPAA compliance, equipment, safety, ergonomics, and communications.

INTERNET ACTIVITY

Search online for regulations at the national and state level that impact management of the physical environment in HIM. Make a table to classify each regulation according to type, such as HIPAA, OSHA, ADA, and fire. Provide at least one example of how each one might be addressed.

CASE STUDY

You are the HIM director for a department that is going to be moved to a new area of the facility. Design a floor plan for the new department. Include the following items:

- Office for HIM director
- Office for HIM assistant director
- Two release of information clerks
- Two scanning stations
- Four inpatient coders
- Six outpatient coders
- One tumor registrar
- Three assembly and analysis clerks
- One physician record assistant
- Four transcriptionists
- One transcription clerk

- Fax machine
- Copy machine
- Small reception area
- Dictation and record completion area for physicians
- Record review area
- Break room with table, sink, microwave, and refrigerator

Create a separate document that describes additional details of the department, including color scheme, ergonomic considerations, type of desks or workstations, chairs, lighting, computers, and anything else you feel is significant to your department design.

REFERENCES

Bennett, A. (1990). Methods improvement in hospitals. *Topics in Medical Record Management*, 20–24.

Foster, M. (1988, September). Ergonomics and the physiotherapist. *Physiotherapy, 74,* 484.

SUGGESTED READINGS

Washington, L. (January 2008). Analyzing Workflow for a Health IT Implementation. *Journal of AHIMA, 79* (1), 64–65.

Organizing to Meet Information Needs of Health Care Facilities

CHAPTER 9

The Process of Organizing Health Information Services

LEARNING OBJECTIVES

After completing this chapter, the learner should be able to:

1. Define the management function of organizing.
2. Describe the three main parts of the basic model for organizational structure.
3. Give the advantages and disadvantages of dividing labor into discrete parts.
4. Demonstrate ways that rules and policies are used in creating a formalized organizational structure.
5. Contrast managerial power with managerial authority.
6. Identify differences between line and staff relationships.
7. List reasons why the span of control varies from one manager to another.
8. Give the four departmentalized organizational structures and an example of each for health care facilities.
9. Explain the advantages of using a contingency management approach in organizing.

INTRODUCTION

Health care professionals who provide care for the human body become knowledgeable about the anatomical structural design of the body and use that knowledge for making treatment decisions. Just as this anatomical structure is a major feature of the body in defining the shape and frame, so an organization has structure that defines its shape. In fact, the root term for organizing is *organism*, meaning an entity with parts so integrated that their relation to one another is governed by their relation to the whole. In this section on the organizing function of management, the integrating role of HIM managers for meeting the organizational objectives is explained.

Dissecting various organizational structures will lead to an understanding of the importance of the organizing function in their success. The inner workings of organizational structure are covered in this chapter and lead to an appreciation of organizational structure and design complexity.

The impact of emerging technologies on managerial planning is mentioned in Section II, during the discussion of SWOT analysis. This impact is also emphasized in Section III on organizing as changes in organizational structure become necessary. In fact, Chapter 11 is devoted to organizing for emerging technologies. Reengineering or redesign of the organizational structure of HIM departments can be an effective response to these changes.

Since the HIM profession is committed to accepting responsibility for quality information throughout health care systems, organizing to best meet this objective, regardless of the setting, is the professional's goal. The basic organizational structure outlined in this chapter can be adapted for use in each of the various health care settings described in Chapter 1.

The need for a contingency approach to organizing HIM departments as change occurs is also discussed. Later chapters in this section examine traditional organizational designs and explore several new designs for organizational structure. By the end of Section III, the foundations of planning and organizing will have form and structure, giving guidance toward the remaining management functions: leading and controlling.

ORGANIZING DEFINED

The definition of the organizing function of management is stated as "the management function that determines what tasks are to be done, who shall do them, the reporting structure, and at what level decisions will be made" (Robbins & Coulter, 2012). This definition lends credence to the crucial role upper-level management has in creating the organizational structure. It is upper-level management that chooses the reporting structure and the level at which decisions affecting the organization will be made. Once these choices are made and responsibility is allocated, managers can organize within designated parameters to meet specific organizational objectives.

As paradigm shifts occur in health care facilities, the board of trustees and the medical staff are given increasing responsibility for assuring stakeholders that an appropriate organizational structure is in place. The board of trustees delegates authority for this assurance to upper-level management. However, perceived community health care needs at present and future projected needs are rightly the concern of board members, mandating that they take an active interest in the structure that will meet the mission and objectives of the facility. Medical staff members are in a unique position to assist in shaping the structure of a facility; they are stakeholders sharing responsibility for success with the board of trustees while making decisions that affect many activities within the organization.

As the decision-making process moves downward, authority is delegated to department managers; thus, HIM professionals organize the department according to the structure outlined by upper-level administration. As the structure takes shape, managers have the opportunity to create levels of decision making within the department that are best suited to the structure and to the activities involved in meeting the objectives.

ORGANIZING TERMS DEFINED

Before turning to a closer look at organizational structure, several terms used as organizing tools must be defined.

Differentiation, Degree of Regulations, and Concentration of Authority

The basic model for organizational structure has three main parts. As each part is dissected and defined, the anatomy of the structure will emerge. These three main parts are:

1. *Differentiation*—one end of the spectrum is simplicity; at the other end is complexity.
2. *Degree of regulations*—with formalization at one end of the spectrum and an informal structure at the other end.
3. *Concentration of authority*—one end of the spectrum is centralization; at the other end is decentralization (Robbins & Coulter, 2012).

Each of these major parts will be brought into later discussions; here definitions, synonyms, and related terms are provided as a foundation to the content.

Differentiation

Specialization of labor An organizing concept where employees specialize in skilled tasks that may then be grouped for efficiency.

Division of labor See specialization of labor.

Differentiation means the **specialization of labor** where each employee specializes in skilled tasks. These tasks may be grouped into a unit for efficiency. Another term for this managerial activity is **division of labor**. When the tasks are few and are quickly learned, they are considered simple. Because of the complex activities inherent in health care settings, differentiation of tasks is found throughout the organization. A wide array of professionals has specific specialties, making the complex specialization of labor crucial to the whole organization. Coordination of the complex activities delegated to the HIM departments within this environment is the exciting task of the HIM managers.

Degree of Regulations

As outlined in Section II, when organizations become larger and more complex, the rules, policies, and regulations increase. Upper-level management then formalizes the structure to standardize activities. This process is called **departmentalization**. Here, employees are grouped together according to their specialized activities. Thus, the HIM department employees perform activities related to health information management to accomplish departmental objectives.

Departmentaliza-tion The process of formalizing the structure by grouping employees together according to their specialized activities.

Formalization The degree to which an organization relies on rules and procedures to direct the actions of employees.

Breaking this **formalization** down further, within the department there may be groups clustered according to specialized tasks. For example, transcription specialists are typically grouped together as a section/team.

To standardize regulations, the rules, policies, and regulations are documented and guide the behavior of employees. In addition to government and accrediting body regulations and policies, each of the various professional associations, whose members are a part of the health care teams, have rules and policies to guide behavior. As a result, employees behave according to their own specialty expectations as well. This creates a formal structure for employees of the health care organization and very little effort may be required by managers in setting policies for those specific behaviors. An example of these expectations is the set of position statements available from the American Health Information Management Association (AHIMA) that covers a wide range of HIM subjects.

There are many examples of government regulations that create formalized behavior for HIM functions. A major set of these government regulations are those mandating specific activities for coding and case-mix management. These regulations lead to a more formalized information structure as managers seek to standardize the activities of the coding section.

Concentration of Authority

Concentration of authority concerns decision making and problem solving. When problems are routinely sent to upper-level management for resolution, there is a high degree of **centralization of authority**. In health care organizations, activities relating to professional specialties are typically decentralized while the organization may be structured toward centralization for other types of authority and decisions. This is additional evidence of the complexity of health care facilities.

Given this complexity within health care organizations and the differences among them, assessing the total structure and gaining a true picture of how these three main parts of the organizational structure operate within a health care organization can be difficult. However, for the HIM functions, there is opportunity to dissect the structure and determine the degree to which each of these parts is scaled.

Since change is expected to continue in health care organizations, in health care professions, in health care regulations, and in health care modalities, managers must become comfortable with creating change as opportunities arise and creating appropriate organizational structures through an integrated model of management.

Managerial Power and Authority

As discussed in Chapter 2, the classical view of managerial thought was that **authority** refers to the rights inherent in the position. For example, an HIM manager has the authority to organize the department and delegate tasks for meeting the objectives. This authority does not relate to the personal characteristics of the manager; it relates to the position (Robbins & Coulter, 2012).

Later management approaches recognized that authority is a subset of the larger concept of **power**. While authority is a right, power refers to an individual's capacity to influence the decision-making process. There are two major categories to identify the type of power a leader possesses: formal power and personal power. *Formal* power is associated with the leader's ability to provide some kind of official response to actions of followers, or a degree of authority to command action from followers. Formal leadership types are coercive, reward, and legitimate. Personal power is expert and referent. It is seen that authority is formal power and may be just one avenue by which an individual affects decisions. However, one may have power without formal authority (Robbins & Coulter, 2012).

For example, the administrative secretary or assistant has a central position within the department and may exert power as the gatekeeper of the department managers. Within the organizational structure, however, the administrative secretary position may lack delegated authority.

Several types of power are used to describe this concept. In contemporary organizations, the following sources of power can be observed in managers and nonmanagers: coercive power, reward power, legitimate power, expert power, and referent power. Each of these sources of power deserves attention.

Centralization of authority The concentration of decision-making authority that lies with upper-level management.

Authority The rights inherent in a managerial position to give orders and expect them to be obeyed.

Power The capacity to influence the decision-making process.

Coercive Power

Coercive power is dependent on fear—fear that negative results could occur from failure to comply. Managers have the authority to suspend employees, assign them to tasks they may find unpleasant, or dismiss them. For example, if an HIM professional is working for a consulting firm, there may be a quota required for obtaining new clients. The vice president of marketing may use coercive power by threatening to cut positions if the quota is not met. Non-managers also possess coercive power; for example, a subordinate may choose to embarrass her manager in public. When nonmanagers use this threat successfully to gain advantage, coercive power is evident.

Reward Power

The opposite approach is taken with reward power, as it is focused on positive reinforcement for desired performance or behaviors. Reward power may be demonstrated by offering a bonus for achieving a goal of reducing the number of unbilled accounts to a predetermined amount. Managers can give rewards that employees value and thus hold power over them. These rewards may be promotions, favorable performance appraisals, enjoyable tasks, requested work shifts, or money. Again, nonmanagers also have reward power such as acceptance, praise, friendliness, and gifts. By comparing these rewards with the coercive power threats listed above, the contrast is obvious. Power to remove something of value is the opposite of giving something of value.

Legitimate Power

Legitimate power is easiest for most to comprehend, as it is the power that is associated with a specific leadership position title, such as supervisor, manager, director, or vice president. This power is synonymous with authority and represents power based on position in the formal organizational structure. Followers recognize individuals with these titles as leaders because they perceive these titles to be attained by professionals with experience, skills, and other leadership traits. However, this is not always the case.

Legitimate power still requires acceptance of the manager on the part of others. Acceptance must come from subordinates as well as other members of the organization.

Personal power is that which does not come from any formal designation or authority but rather has a great deal of the traits explored earlier in this chapter. There are many opportunities in the HIM arena to demonstrate leadership through personal power. If an HIM professional is interested in leadership but does not have any immediately available formal leadership positions within reach, this does not mean that development of leadership skills is impossible.

Expert Power

Experts in their specialty areas are an increasing power source in health care facilities. An example is in technical knowledge. As expertise in health information for the information superhighway becomes increasingly sought after, expert power in this area will become very visible. This expertise will gain importance to the degree the users of the information lack the knowledge to access it. Data capture, analysis, integration, and dissemination are critical power bases for the HIM profession.

Some HIM professionals may have worked for an extensive amount of time in a particular area or may have specialized training that is recognized in the career field. These individuals have expert power, which is based on knowledge or skills. An HIM professional giving a presentation or serving on a panel at an educational meeting has expert power, as does somebody who may have written or contributed to articles in the Journal of AHIMA or other professional publications. Another HIM example of expert power occurred when the AHIMA Academy for ICD-10 prepared trainers to teach other coders the new coding system. AHIMA published the list of approved ICD-10 trainers who were perceived by the membership as expert leaders.

Referent Power

An individual is considered to have referent power if trust and respect have been developed among professional peers. This may be the result of consistent demonstration of a combination of other leadership traits. Referent power is not usually apparent until a significant amount of time has passed for the individual to demonstrate traits respected by professional peers. A similar leadership style, competency-based leadership, considers an individual to be a leader because of a demonstration of competence, assuming that the individual may lead by example, based solely on competency in completing specific tasks or processes. HIM professionals possessing a high degree of competency-based leadership often develop a passion for sharing their skills and knowledge with others in the career field through presentations at educational meetings or in-services.

The base of referent power lies in a desire for resources or personal traits that are attractive. Charismatic leadership power does not have any basis on position title or skills, but rather it is completely based on the individual's presentation to others. Charismatic leaders convey a sense of confidence, set high goals, engage followers by sharing anecdotes, and stating viewpoints that the leader anticipates the audience wants to hear. Caution must be exercised when followers look up to a charismatic leader, simply to verify that the individual should be followed, as it is possible that the charismatic presentation may be so good that it may hide the fact that the individual may have a complete lack of true leadership traits. However, a true leader may also possess charismatic leadership power along with other leadership traits.

Charismatic managers have influence because others are attracted to them, and their behavior and attitudes are modeled. Nonmanagers may also have traits that give them referent power to influence their peers, their superiors, and others in the organization (Robbins & Coulter, 2012).

Resources

In this discussion on power, little mention has been made of the value of resources. However, there are several reasons why resources can relate to a manager's power. Certainly information is one reason—the expert with information valued by others has power. Another reason relates to resources that may be available only through a staff person. For example, final approval for expansion of an HIM department into an adjoining space may depend on the feasibility study prepared by an administrative assistant who holds a staff position in the organization.

Unity of Command

Unity of command The principle that an employee should have one and only one manager to whom he or she is directly responsible.

Management theories describe the **unity of command** principle when outlining the concepts of the division of labor. This principle states that an employee has one and only one immediate manager. This clear separation was considered crucial to a smooth work flow with the absence of conflicting priorities. It is further stated that when this principle of unity of command must be broken, a clear separation of activities and responsibilities should be documented. This concept is important, as there are many adverse issues that may arise if an employee were to directly report to two or more managers. If both managers assigned different tasks with instructions to make the tasks number one priority, a conflict situation may arise between both managers and the employee would be unclear of which task really should be of higher priority. This principle complements the granting of authority principle described above. When carried to the extreme, the concept leads to a chain of command where each action must painfully progress through each link of the chain. To make this unwieldy activity reasonable, management experts state that, when there is confidence and loyalty among the organization members, shortcuts are appropriate. The key is that the shortcuts are not done in a deceitful or secretive manner.

As the authority and responsibility delegated to managers are detailed, this organizational structure can be shown visually as an organizational model. A traditional model is shown in Figure 9-1. It depicts a visual description of the chain of command for an HIM department in a community hospital and demonstrates the unit of command principle. It shows line authority flowing from the HIM manager down to the supervisors of the sections and then to the team members. Line authority is authority delegated to managers, entitling them to direct the work of subordinates.

FIGURE 9-1   A Traditional Organizational Model

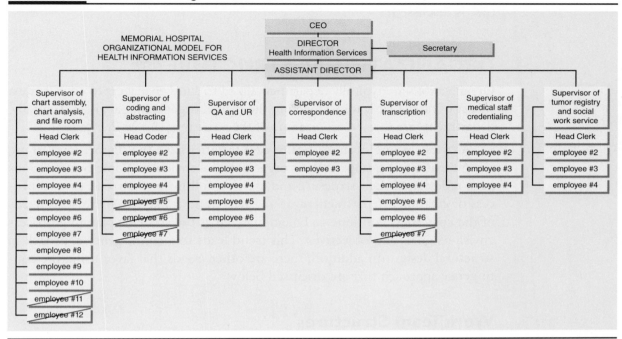

In Figure 9-1, the position of secretary or assistant is shown as a separate line box. This position is one of **staff authority** where the secretary supports, assists, and enables managers in line authority to perform their tasks. Other examples of staff authority are the technical experts who may be employed to implement and train employees when new information systems are installed. These technical experts have no supervisory duties.

Staff authority Authority that supports, assists, and advises managers of line authority.

Span of Control

Closely related to unity of command is the principle called **span of control**. This phrase refers to the number of employees a manager directs efficiently and effectively. Figure 9-1 shows the number of employees under the director's **span of management** and then the number of employees under the span of control for each supervisor. Several factors are responsible for the appropriate managerial span of control (Longest, 1990).

For example, the number of employees changes as contingency variables change. Managers with responsibility for professionals with experience and advanced education are able to have a wider span of control. Other variables include the use of standardized procedures, the physical proximity of the team, and the complexity and variability of the tasks being performed. A crucial factor in an appropriate span of control is the information system available to managers for quality improvement. Another factor is the organizational culture that may dictate status quo. In Chapter 10, several of these

Span of control The number of employees a manager can direct with efficiency and effectiveness.

Span of management The number of employees a manager can direct efficiently and effectively. See also span of control.

factors are discussed further as the design of a matrix organizational structure is discussed.

ORGANIZATIONAL STRUCTURE

Organizations are typically departmentalized to allow managers to coordinate a subset of tasks that leads to meeting the overall organizational goals. Typically, departments are formed around one of the structures shown in Figure 9-2.

As these examples show, health care facilities have the opportunity to use a combination of groups in their organizational structure. Some organizations have redesigned their structure and are now following the trend toward process or customer departmentalization. This trend is likely to increase as needs of the customers continue to be emphasized as the strategic planning process envisions goals and objectives. This trend leads to a contingency approach in structural design. In addition, there are other trends that favor using the contingency approach that are discussed below.

Work Team Structures

As health care facilities seek to become more efficient, they cannot overlook the advantages offered by flexible, self-disciplined, multiskilled work teams given responsibility for performing services. These services may involve all of the work processes, such as the teams created to manage the patient-focused care unit. The multiskilled work teams created for patient-focused care units are grouped for process departmentalization. Under this concept, the admissions, utilization review, testing, therapy, nursing care, concurrent review, and coding are the responsibility of the team. This creates a matrix organization structure that is detailed in Chapter 10.

FIGURE 9-2   Department Structures

1. *Functional departmentalization:* Activities are grouped into like functions such as admitting, accounting, or health information services.

2. *Customer departmentalization:* Customers with common problems are grouped to allow activities for meeting their needs effectively. Intensive care is an example where like customers are grouped together for treatment.

3. *Product departmentalization:* Similar products are grouped into departments where activities relating to them can be accomplished efficiently. In health care facilities, radiation therapy and clinical laboratory departments each have similar activities.

4. *Process departmentalization:* Grouping of activities is based on the flow of the product or service to meet the needs of customers. Insurance validation and other steps in the admission process may be grouped in a facility to enhance the flow of patient admissions.

FIGURE 9-3 Self-Directed Work Team Characteristics (Based on information from Wellins, 1991)

1. *Empowerment:* authority and responsibility to share in managerial functions.
2. *Goals and objectives:* a vision created for the team within the overall goals and objectives of the facility.
3. *Budget resources:* sharing in the budgeting process that allocates resources for meeting the objectives.
4. *Materials:* ordering supplies and approved equipment.
5. *Planning:* organizing the work processes and creating team schedules.
6. *Training and in-service:* coordinating and implementing training and in-service needs.
7. *Hiring:* sharing in hiring decisions.
8. *Quality improvement:* monitoring the quality of services and initiating improvements.
9. *Discipline:* taking responsibility for disciplinary action.
10. *Performance appraisal:* completing periodic appraisals and recommending wage adjustments.
11. *Leadership:* rotating the team leader or choosing a permanent one to act as spokesperson, internal facilitator, and to perform other managing functions.

Self-Directed Teams

Permanent self-directed work teams have unique features, but several characteristics are typical; these are outlined in Figure 9-3.

Shared Leadership Teams

Shared leadership teams can also be created that enable managers to empower employees and give a sense of ownership and control in the workplace. The shared leadership teams may be empowered to perform many of the activities listed in Figure 9-3; those typically not assigned to the team are discipline, budgeting, and performance appraisals. Within HIM departments, the shared leadership team concept is found frequently, but there is no "common" team concept. The empowerment continuum differs depending on the unique circumstances. HIM managers can develop the organizational structure that will best meet the needs of the department and the organization.

Temporary Work Teams

Temporary work teams are created to meet specific needs and may utilize multiskilled employees. An example of a temporary work team is the work group gathered to plan and implement an information system. The members of a temporary work team may be assigned to the team for a specific number of hours per week and continue performing other activities during the remainder of the week. Empowerment varies and typically authority and responsibility rest mainly with the technical aspects of the task assigned to the team.

Other aspects of work teams are discussed in Section IV, where the leading function of management emphasizes the changing role of managers.

Informal Organizational Structure

The planned organizational structure of an HIM department outlined in Figure 9-1 shows a deliberate process of patterned relationships for accomplishing activities. The model emphasizes line and staff authority positions. Within all departments, there is a second structure that emphasizes people and their relationships. This informal organization is not under the control of managers but must be recognized by them. Several factors relating to informal organizations are outlined in Figure 9-4.

Since formal authority is not bestowed on informal groups, the leader exerts power over the group through one or more of the types of power already discussed. Referent power is frequently seen as charismatic employees naturally take the leadership role in informal groups. However, expert, reward, and coercive power are also seen.

Not all members of an informal group have similar needs. One person may become a member of the group to satisfy social needs, another person may be seeking advancement, and a third person may want to obtain information. The group members change frequently and may include employees outside the department.

Managers can take advantage of the informal organization when they understand it. As an additional channel of information, the group can be given information by managers who can then determine employee feelings and attitudes about issues. Being sensitive to these feelings and attitudes allows managers to integrate the interests of informal groups into those of the formal organization. This provides strength and stability toward the accomplishment of department objectives.

FIGURE 9-4   Informal Organizational Factors

1. *Small groups:* Small groups come into being to satisfy individual needs that cannot be fully met by the formal organizational structure.
2. *Leaders:* Members choose leaders they perceive as important for satisfying their needs.
3. *Informal groups:* Informal groups are inevitable within HIM departments.
4. *Positive aspects:* Informal groups can complement the formal organizations and provide stability to work teams.
5. *Negative aspects:* Role conflicts can occur when goals of the groups are not compatible with the goals and objectives of the formal organization.

Organizational Culture

Organizational culture is established by a variety of factors. Figure 9-5 illustrates factors that contribute to organizational culture. A large health care organization is likely to have a more formal and structured organizational culture, while something smaller, such as a physician office may be more relaxed with less structure. The type of services provided has an impact on the culture, too, as a children's hospital would have a much different culture than an addiction treatment facility or a long-term care facility specializing in dementia. Organizational ownership or religious affiliations may also impact the culture of the organization. For example, some organizations with strong religious affiliations may incorporate religious values into various aspects of the organization, such as prayer at the start of meetings. The community served by the organization also has an impact, as employees may need to be provided with **cultural competence** training in some cases to develop an awareness of cultural differences and practices specific to cultural groups within the community. This may include cultural aspects such as nationality, race, language, religious beliefs, socioeconomic factors, or community-specific facets of culture.

Cultural competence An awareness of cultural differences and practices specific to cultural groups.

The organizational culture should be clearly reflected in the mission statement, which is a written statement that sets forth the core purpose and philosophies of an organization or group. The mission statement provides a concise statement that defines the organization or group's general purpose for

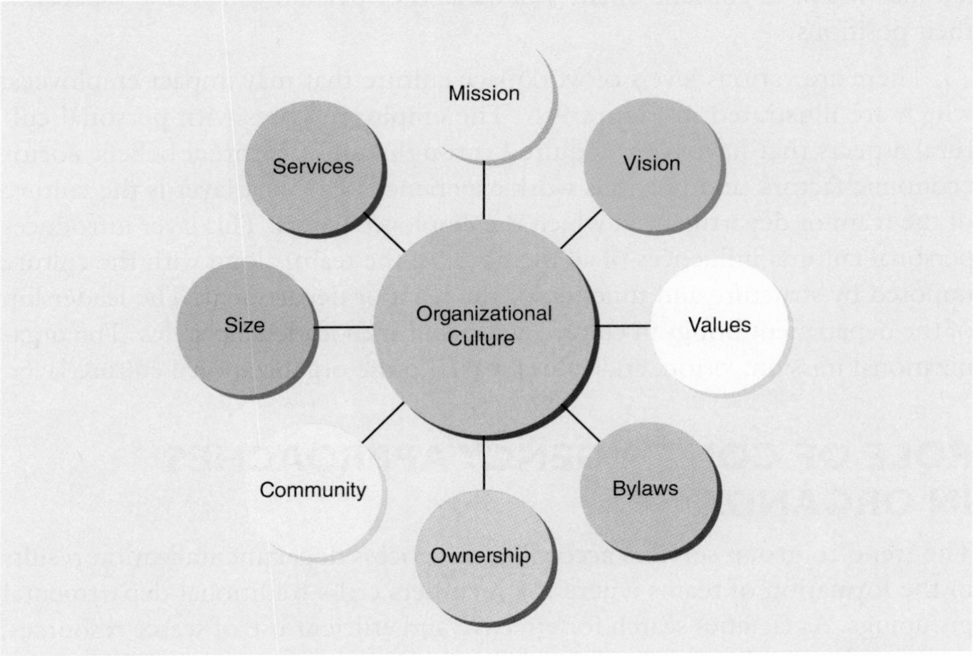

FIGURE 9-5 Contributing Factors to Organizational Culture

existing. An organizational mission statement is rarely changed unless a significant change occurs. The mission statement should drive the establishment of goals during strategic planning activities, as well as the routine daily activities performed in the organization. This mission statement should concisely state the organization's purpose, service population, and what makes the organization unique in comparison to other competitors.

Along with the mission statement, organizations may also have vision and value statements. A vision statement is a short description of an organization's ideal future state. The vision statement may include a list of broad goals. The tone should be positive, realistic, achievable, and aligned with the mission, values, and other organizational cultural aspects. **Values statements** communicate an organization's social and cultural belief system. These may be stated as a single sentence or a list of several statements. Ethical principles followed by the organization should be reflected in the values statements. The philosophy of the organization is presented as fundamental ideologies. The values statements of organizations are to be adopted by all individuals in order to reflect employee or volunteer support of the values.

Bylaws are established as guidelines for issues that may arise in operations, definition of responsibility for roles in the organization, disciplinary processes, and general rules and regulations for the organization. In health care organizations, the bylaws may define the composition of the board of directors, committee structures, financial structure, practitioner credential requirements, and accountability relationships. HIM employees not only serving in management positions, but also in other various roles in the organization, should be familiar with the content of the bylaws as they pertain to specific aspects of their positions.

There are various levels of workplace culture that may impact employees, which are illustrated in Figure 9-6. The employee starts with personal cultural aspects that have been acquired through family, spiritual beliefs, socioeconomic factors, and previous work experience. The next layer is the culture of the team or department in which the employee works. This layer introduces personal cultural influences of all members of the team, along with the culture imposed by structure and function of the team or department. The leadership of the department brings in culture associated with leadership styles. The organizational mission, vision, and values make up the organizational culture layer.

ROLE OF CONTINGENCY APPROACHES IN ORGANIZING

The trend to group services according to process departmentalization results in the formation of teams where the members cross traditional departmental groupings. As facilities search for effective and efficient use of scarce resources, the use of teams that combine the skills of various health care professionals on

Values statement Communicate an organization's social and cultural belief system.

Bylaws Guidelines established by an organization for issues that may arise.

FIGURE 9-6   Layers of Workplace Culture

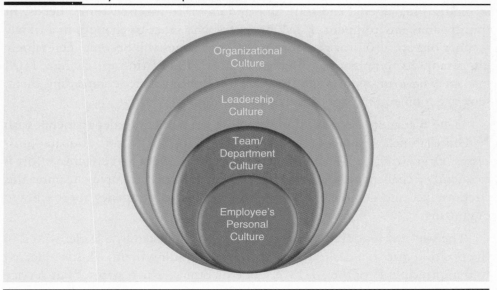

the patient care units is expected to increase. As mentioned earlier, this new structure is called patient-centered care units or patient-focused care units, when the change involves direct patient care. As these trends show, organizational structure changes in response to the vision of upper-level management as the strategic planning process takes place. The changes are likely to be in response to planning function activities such as a SWOT analysis.

The contingency model of leadership is based on the concept that the success of any of the previously discussed leadership models is dependent upon other variables. This model suggests that leadership models do not always fit all situations equally. Relationships between the leader and team members, the organizational structure, organizational culture, and actual position power impact how leadership should actually approach a situation.

The size of an organization also affects its structure in a variety of ways that demand a contingency approach. A community home health care agency, for example, will have an organization structured around a high degree of collaboration and adaptation among the team members. This contrasts with a large hospital where there will tend to be high formalization and structured activities. As the home health care agency experiences growth, however, its structure will naturally increase in formalization. Again the managers will benefit from use of contingency approaches as decisions are made.

During the strategic planning process, health care organizations may choose an objective that will increase information technology capabilities. This objective will then be embraced by the HIM department and a contingency approach to structural changes must be addressed. With appropriate adjustments, the department can keep pace with data capture capabilities that can result in reduced managerial and staff time and effort to meet customer needs. In this dynamic environment, HIM managers who react to changes in a timely manner but are also proactive in suggesting changes will become increasingly important. As the planning function creates a foundation for change, HIM managers have an opportunity to review the contingencies confronting them, seize the momentum, and organize accordingly.

HIM managers frequently find themselves managing departments with systems that include a mix of high-technology capabilities and antiquated processes. Organizing the work flow and teams for efficient and effective effort is frequently a challenge they face. The following practice example illustrates this circumstance and demonstrates how managers use contingency approaches in organizing.

Servant leadership model An approach taken by a leader who is in the position due to a desire to serve others by leading them.

The **servant leadership model** is an approach taken by a leader who is in the position due to a desire to serve others by leading them. This is reflected well in principle II of the AHIMA Code of Ethics, which states, "Put service and the health and welfare of persons before self-interest and conduct oneself in the practice of the profession so as to bring honor to oneself, peers, and to the health information management profession." The HIM profession appreciates the many volunteers who apply this approach when serving in leadership positions for the numerous board positions, practice councils, workgroups, and other opportunities that exist to serve the membership by leading. Attributes of leaders using the servant leadership model are listening, empathy, healing, awareness, persuasion, conceptualization, foresight, stewardship, commitment to growth of people, and building community.

The attribute of listening demonstrates respect for others. It identifies the importance of hearing others in order to effectively serve them. A person in an HIM professional situation demonstrates servant leadership through attentive listening, allowing the follower to share the complete message to ensure effectiveness of the communication. Empathy involves a projection of self-consciousness onto that of others, accepting others for who they are, and trying to understand the feelings and perspective of situations faced by followers. It is impossible to completely understand what it is like to be in somebody else's shoes, but a servant leader does so as much as possible. A servant leader acknowledges that a follower is not able to function at their fullest potential if they are not well beyond the physical sense, but also emotionally and spiritually. Listening to the follower and being empathetic, the servant leader is better able to recognize what the follower may need for healing in these senses. While servant leaders focus on serving the needs of their followers, it is also important to develop an awareness of self. In order to better serve others, an understanding of personal values, feelings, strengths, and weaknesses is necessary. If leader does not recognize any of these, the followers may receive inconsistent messages.

The ability of somebody as a servant leader is based on the ability to use personal skills for persuasion of followers, rather than using position power. Servant leaders possess the trait of conceptualization, providing the ability to identify solutions to potential problems before they occur. For example, an HIM professional identifies potential issues that may arise if the facility has to respond in case of a disaster. Plans are documented regarding roles that each position would assume, such as HIM staff reporting to a staging area to assist with documenting patient identification information and nonclinical information. Foresight is a somewhat related attribute of servant leaders. This attribute involves insightfulness to possible future situations. This attribute is extremely important in the highly dynamic HIM career field.

The attribute of stewardship extends beyond the focus on the followers but rather approaches leadership from a broader perspective of the whole organization. As the future of the HIM career field continues to evolve and overlap with other career fields, such as information technology and nursing, organization leaders acting according to the servant leader model would apply this attribute by addressing actions and plans as related to AHIMA. Current AHIMA initiatives are strong in this area through areas that include clinical documentation improvement (CDI) and health care consumer engagement with personal health records (PHRs). Stewardship is also practiced through displaying a positive image of the organization reflected through actions of leadership.

Servant leaders have a commitment to the growth of people. AHIMA and CAHIIM both promote this attribute for members through their support for both entry-level HIM education and continuing education. This is even addressed in the AHIMA Code of Ethics principle V, "Advance health information management knowledge and practice through continuing education, research, publications, and presentations" and VI, "Recruit and mentor students, staff, peers, and colleagues to develop and strengthen professional workforce." Building community is the final attribute of servant leaders. AHIMA, component state associations (CSAs), and other professional organizations provide a wide variety of options for HIM professionals to build community.

Management theorists, Robert Blake and Jane Mouton collaborated to develop a leadership grid that was separated into five styles of leadership, identified according to the level of concern about people and production. The grid plots values from one to nine, identifying the level of concern that a leader has for production and people. Production values are plotted on the x-axis of the grid and people values are plotted on the y-axis (see Figure 9-7).

Figure 9-8 illustrates the leadership styles that are associated with the five areas of the leadership grid. Leaders possessing lower levels of concern about both people and productivity have an impoverished leadership style. This is a very conservative type of leader, who generally avoid change that could improve productivity, because their concern is about avoiding potential failure

FIGURE 9-7   Leadership Grid

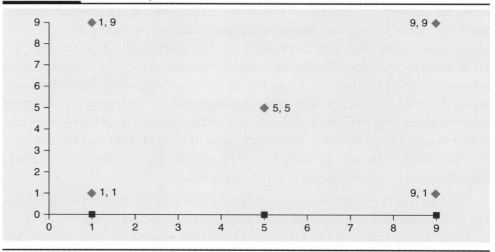

FIGURE 9-8   Leadership Styles Associated with Leadership Grid

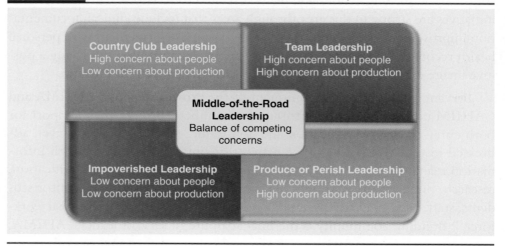

that could impact their own positions, even if it might mean improved processes for their employees. Produce or perish leadership style is focused on improving production for the organization without concern for the employees involved in any associated changes. Country club leadership has a focus on employee satisfaction but neglects the importance of productivity. Team leadership is an ambitious approach that has a high degree of value for employee satisfaction alongside the need for higher levels of productivity. Empowerment of employees to have active roles in contributing to changes that result in increased productivity occurs with this leadership approach. This should not be confused with the middle-of-the-road leadership, which has a balance of concern for employees and productivity, but through compromise, rather than focus on improving both areas.

As previously stated, leadership does not only apply to managerial job titles. Because of this, HIM professionals should explore their own personal traits to identify potential leadership opportunities. Leadership is not the desire of everybody, so another aspect to be considered by followers is development of an understanding of the leaders they are following. There are three categories of managerial skills that are possessed by top, middle, and supervisory managers. These are conceptual, interpersonal, and technical skills. **Conceptual skills** require higher-level intellect to be applied to planning, decision making, and problem solving; **technical skills** focus on operational activities; and **interpersonal skills** are used to communicate effectively with each other, subordinates, and superiors. Figure 9-9 illustrates the skill set used by most top managers. Top managers use higher level conceptual skills in strategic planning activities and directing significant changes within their areas. Lower management positions use more technical skills and direct most of their efforts toward operational details. This would be demonstrated in the HIM career field through positions such as coding or transcription supervisors. This is illustrated in Figure 9-10. While upper- and lower-level managerial positions focus on the technical and conceptual extremes, middle managers tend to maintain a relatively equal balance of conceptual, technical, and interpersonal skills, as illustrated in Figure 9-11. This is because of the flexible nature of their positions that may require serving on administrative level committees, while still maintaining a focus on technical aspects. It is important to note that the interpersonal skills are relatively equally distributed for all managerial levels. Communication with others in a variety of internal and external positions is required for all managers, so this is a valuable skill across the board.

Conceptual skills Skills that require higher-level intellect to be applied to planning, decision making, and problem solving.

Technical skills Skills focused on operational activities.

Interpersonal skills Skills used to communicate effectively with each other.

FIGURE 9-9 Upper-Level Management Skills

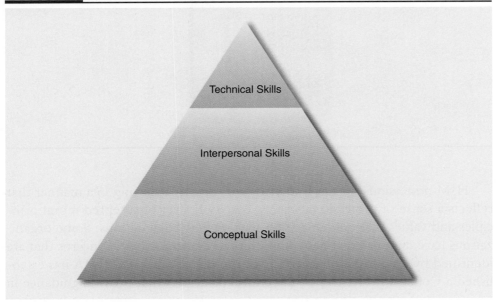

FIGURE 9-10 Lower-Level Management Skills

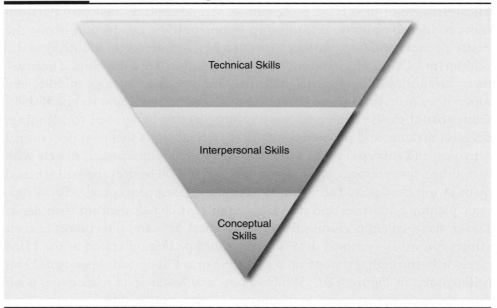

FIGURE 9-11 Middle Management Skills

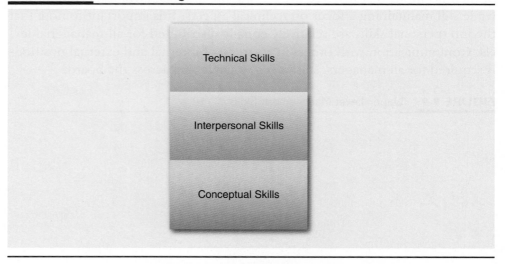

HIM professionals act as leaders by consistently behaving in a manner that reflects a sense of professional ethics, based on a set of accepted moral principles and values that guide decision making and other actions. Some organizations have designated ethics committees to evaluate ethical concerns that are identified by employees or members of the organization. AHIMA has established a Code of Ethics to provide ethical principles that provide guidance in performance of HIM activities and professional behavior. HIM professionals, both managerial and nonmanagerial, should become familiar with the AHIMA Code of Ethics, which includes guidelines for how to interpret each principle in the code, along with activities that HIM professionals should do and what they should refrain from doing. AHIMA has also published Standards of Ethical Coding, which specifically address ethical dilemmas for coders.

Many organizations have a corporate code of conduct included in their corporate compliance plans to present the commitment of the organization to ethical behavior. The development of the corporate code of conduct requires consideration of many perspectives. One of the most important of these is addressing legal aspects impacting health care management and other associated practices. When creating the corporate code of conduct, some organizations may even contract with an ethicist, who is trained in the practice of applying ethical principles to complex situations that involve contrasting perspectives and values. When making ethical decisions, it is important to recognize the fact that the decision may not be consistent with administrative directions. HIM professionals may find themselves in difficult positions that involve decision making between an administrative order and a legal or ethical directive.

Delegation is a leadership skill that should be used at various levels to distribute tasks and decision-making authority to others. Position descriptions are one method used to communicate delegation of tasks that are associated with specific positions. Special projects for workplace teams also involve delegation at a couple of levels. First, the team leader or team as a whole is delegated the assigned purpose for the desired outcome of the group, but second, as the group starts planning for the project, associated contributing tasks will be delegated to group members.

Mentoring is an important application of leadership skills for HIM professionals. It involves sharing knowledge, teaching skills, networking, and encouraging students, new HIM professionals, or existing HIM professionals considering change or professional growth within the career field. The AHIMA Code of Ethics supports mentoring through principle VI, Recruit and mentor students, peers and colleagues to develop and strengthen professional workforce. Within this principle, the guidelines for interpretation state that "Health information management professionals shall…6.3 Be a mentor for students, peers, and new health information management professionals to develop and strengthen skills and 6.4. Provide directed practice opportunities for students." Mentoring is not limited to teaching at educational institutions, but also includes activities such as hosting students for professional practice experience, provision of job shadowing opportunities, participating in interviews with students or others interested in the HIM career field, or grooming an employee for transition to a new position.

Delegation
Distribution of tasks and decision-making authority to others.

Mentoring
Sharing knowledge, teaching skills, and encouraging others to promote professional growth.

The hospital in this example is unusual in that a clinical information system was installed in the 1970s to support physicians, nurses, and allied health professionals in patient care. In that time period, it was typical for the first automated systems to support the billing process. In contrast with that early start toward an EHR, however, several health information services are still performed manually. Figure 9-12 details the automated systems and the manual systems in the department at present.

A review of the systems that are still manual indicates that record management is still very much a paperwork environment. The department is organized into work teams with extensive cross-training. The work teams are led by team leaders; the teams choose whether they prefer permanent team leaders or rotating ones. A temporary work team has been involved in developing the automated systems for the EHR, leading to regional longitudinal health records, and this team will continue this effort for at least another 10 months. This multidisciplinary team has three health information services members; they devote 50 percent of their time to this responsibility and the remainder to their routine activities. Part-time staffers were hired and trained to keep the work current while these team members are out of the department.

FIGURE 9-12   Automated and Manual Systems in Health Information Services

Automated Systems

1. *Record storage:* Longitudinal health records are in the developmental stage with patient information stored on the computer indefinitely; portions of the records remain on hard copy, however. This requires dual storage systems—automated and paper. At present, the longitudinal health record covers patient care within the network of medical staff offices and ambulatory care settings only.

2. *Transcription:* Delivered directly to PCs from outside transcription; can be printed out in hard copy as needed.

3. *Network:* Fiber optic network links workstations, working toward total linkage to the clinical system.

4. *Coding and DRG assignment:* Computerized billing information flows directly to billing services.

5. *Release of information:* PC software is specifically designed for correspondence with attorneys, insurance companies, and other customers.

6. *Statistical information:* Integration of clinical systems data allows for dissemination of aggregate statistics, some medical staff activity, and decision-support systems.

7. *Completion of automated portion of the health record:* Medical staff and nursing staff have responsibility for completing the clinical record with the exception of dictated reports; these are tracked by health information services staff.

FIGURE 9-12 *(continued)*

Manual Systems

1. *Record storage:* Open-shelf filing, until recently the computerized portion of the records were printed out totally for hard copy storage. Now both hard copy and computerized portions of the longitudinal record exist.

2. *Analysis and incomplete record activity:* Analysis has been streamlined; however, cards are used to track completion and manual counting for delinquent records. Physician notification is manual.

3. *In-house transcription:* Transcriptionists use computers linked to the longitudinal record.

4. *Departmental continuous quality improvement:* Data capture and monitoring are possible for some of the work teams; manual tracking continues for other teams.

The teams are responsible for ensuring that each team member is familiar with computer capabilities within his or her work environment and for training when new systems are installed. They are also responsible for quality improvement. The monitoring tools vary, depending on whether the task is automated, with data capture for review or whether the task is manual, with handwritten tallies.

Organizing efficiently and effectively for hybrid systems in the department has challenged the management team, and reorganizing takes place periodically as additional automated capabilities come online. The department's 5-year strategic plan includes the following:

1. Totally automated for the incomplete record system.
2. Automated record tracking for all hard copy record activity.
3. Quality improvement activities increasingly automated as systems are installed that offer monitoring capabilities.

Complete EHRAs these objectives are realized, organizational change will continue to occur. The managers are committed to a contingency approach to organizing and will perform periodic SWOT analysis. The teams are becoming comfortable with redesign of their activities, since the gradual implementation of the EHR began in the mid-1970s. Because of the gradual process, the HIM managers anticipate the changes will not require a total reengineering of the work process.

SUMMARY

This chapter begins a discussion of the management function called organizing. Organizing is described as the function that determines what tasks are to be done, who shall do them, the reporting structure, and at what level decisions will be made. Upper-level management creates the reporting structure and then managers organize within the delegated parameters.

An organizing structure has three main parts: (1) differentiation leading from simplicity to complexity; (2) degree of regulation leading from the informal to the formal; and (3) concentration of authority leading from centralization to decentralization. Specialization or division of labor is frequently seen in health care facilities where differentiation is commonplace because of professional specialties.

A variety of factors, including size, type of services, community, ownership, bylaws, mission, vision, and values, impact the overall culture of an organization. HIM managers must be aware that organizational culture, leadership culture, team culture, and individual personal culture all have an impact on how each employee or team member fits into the structure of each level of the organizational culture.

Managerial power refers to an individual's capacity to influence the decision-making process with authority inherent in the position, not the personal characteristics of a manager. Employees may have power without formal authority.

Coercive power depends on fear, reward power is giving something of value, and legitimate power is synonymous with authority. Expert power is frequently evident in health care and will become increasingly important as the information superhighway is developed. Charismatic managers have influence called referent power.

The unity of command principle holds that an employee has one and only one immediate manager. A traditional organization model demonstrates this principle and shows line and staff positions.

Organizations must choose the best structure for coordinating the tasks that meet their goals. Four departmentalization structures are functional, customer, product, and process. A combination of these structures is seen in complex health care organizations. A contingency management approach assists managers in creating an organizational structure best suited to their needs.

CRITICAL THINKING EXERCISES

1. Describe the organizing function and give several reasons for organizing.
2. Relate how a manager integrates the planning process into the organizing function.
3. How is power and authority given to an HIM department manager?
4. Describe several aspects of an informal organization that differ from those of a formal organization.

5. What is the organizing phrase used to describe the structure when the coding specialists are organized into a team that works independently, making most of the decisions regarding coding activities?
6. Which of the four departmentalizations would be used to best advantage in an HIM department? Defend your answer.

APPLICATION OF THEORY EXERCISES

1. 1. Identify at least two individuals you have encountered or observed as a leader. Compare the traits you noticed about each person. Did the individual have formal or personal leadership power? What leadership models did each seem to follow and what activities or behaviors reflected their leadership styles?

2. Give examples of the five types of power you have seen while interacting with employees in a health care setting.
3. Show how automating several record tasks can lead to a change in the span of control for the managers.

INTERNET ACTIVITY

There are several Internet sites that provide free Myers–Briggs Type Indicator testing. Locate one of the sites and complete the test to identify your personality type. Were your results the same or different than what you anticipated?

CASE STUDY

You are a coding supervisor for large physician group practice. The lead physician in the group insists that you instruct your coding staff members to code all office visits across the board as the highest level code so that they get higher reimbursement. You inform the physician that coding must be based on documentation, but the physician responds, "all of the physicians in this practice perform high-level office visits, but they just do not have time to document everything." Following this conversation with the physician, the practice manager calls you in to reinforce the message with an implied message that your job security may depend on cooperation with the physician's directions. The practice manager also reminds you that you should never question anything that the physicians tell you to do since they are the ones providing your paycheck. Outline your options in this situation and discuss the one you would choose, providing rationale for your decision.

REFERENCES

Longest, B. (1990). *Management Practices for the Health Professional* (4th ed.). Norwalk, CT: Appleton & Lange.

Robbins, S., & Coulter, M. (2012). *Management* (11th ed.). Upper Saddle River, NJ: Pearson.

Wellins, R. (1991). *Empowered Teams*. San Francisco, CA: Jossey-Bass.

SUGGESTED READINGS

AHIMA Code of Ethics. http://library.ahima.org/xpedio/groups/public/documents/ahima/bok1_024277.hcsp?dDocName=bok1_024277.

AHIMA guidelines for ethical coding.

CHAPTER 10

The Organizational Model

LEARNING OBJECTIVES

After completing this chapter, the learner should be able to:

1. Outline factors that contribute to organizational culture.
2. Describe mechanistic structural design and state how functional departmentalization becomes a part of this design.
3. Create organizational charts for the health care environment.
4. Describe critical factors involved as health care facilities choose reengineering the organizational structure in an effort to solve problems.
5. Give examples of reengineering activities that can appropriately belong to HIM professionals.
6. Explain the major features involved in the three phases of reengineering.
7. Describe positions in the C-suite in the health care environment.

INTRODUCTION

Chapter 9 discusses the background for developing organizational models to document the structure of health care firms. From the mission statement and objectives for new organizations come the ideas that translate into decisions regarding the three main parts of the organizational structure and the type of structure to be created. The objective setting process begins with the strategic planning process, which results from the vision of the planners.

As typical organizational models are developed in this chapter, size of the firm is an important variable. Examples of models for complex hospital HIM departments are discussed as are entrepreneurial firms that begin with a flat organizational structure. Since smaller organizations, such as local transcription firms, home health care centers, urgent care centers, and consulting firms, have diverse models, examples from these organizations give insights into their structural design. A major feature of these smaller organizational models is the flat or simple structure where task responsibilities can be quite straightforward. Formal communication flows easily in such a model.

On the other hand, many HIM managers work in complex facilities where organizational models are large and the formal lines of communication tend to traverse upward through several layers. Preparing organizational models for HIM departments in this setting offers creative options. Managers can transform a traditional department structure into a contemporary model by using the steps already outlined for the management functions of planning and organizing. Contemporary examples are:

- Team approaches
- Matrix structure
- Network structure

Each of these structures offers opportunities for HIM professionals to create change. In this chapter, these models are examined and examples are documented.

First, the two major structural designs—mechanistic and organic—are discussed and several additional organizing terms are defined.

MECHANISTIC STRUCTURAL DESIGNS

Mechanistic design A structure that is high in complexity, formalization, and centralization.

When speaking of **mechanistic design**, organizers are referring to a bureaucracy. In this design, the structure is highly complex and formalized, with authority remaining centralized. The larger an organization, the greater the tendency toward a mechanistic structural design (Robbins & Coulter, 2012). In health care facilities tending toward a mechanistic design, **functional departmentalization** predominates over other departmentalization options. As described in Chapter 9, functional departmentalization refers to organizing groups of similar or related occupational specialties into departments. Departmental examples are physical therapy, radiation therapy, and health information management.

An **organizational chart** is a graphic representation of an organization's formal reporting structure. The organizational chart provides a map of authority and reporting relationships for hierarchy structure organizations. Structure is necessary to provide guidance, governance, and distribution of work. The authoritarian organizational structure in which each member is assigned a specific rank that reflects his or her level of decision-making authority within the organization is referred to as a hierarchy. A hierarchy is considered to be part of a bureaucracy, which is a highly formalized organizational structure with strict lines of authority and procedures with little to no flexibility related to decision making.

A traditional organizational chart generally has several different levels, while a flat organizational chart has fewer levels of management. Traditional organizational charts are often pyramid shaped, with the president or chief executive officer (CEO) at the top and a broad base of employees in staff positions at the bottom. Vice presidential positions report to the CEO and have managerial-level positions reporting to them. Managers are generally over departments and have supervisors overseeing activities of employees. Inclusion of all members of the organization in the organizational chart structure, which assigns authority and responsibility to everybody according to a defined chain of command is referred to as a scalar chain. Figure 10-1 illustrates a traditional organizational chart structure.

Functional departmentalization
The grouping of activities by functions performed.

Organizational chart A graphic representation of an organization's formal reporting structure.

FIGURE 10-1 Traditional Organizational Chart Structure

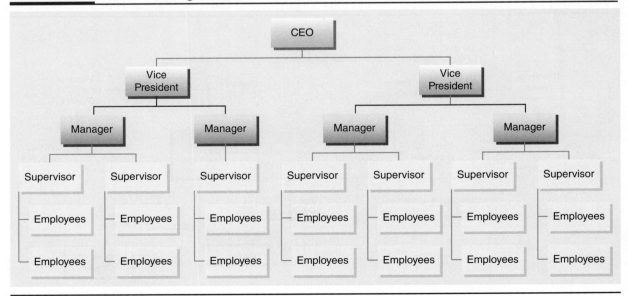

At the top of most organizational charts is the **board of directors**, which is an elected or appointed group of officials who bear ultimate responsibility for the successful operation of a health care organization. The board of directors may also be referred to as the board of governors or board of trustees. The board of directors is often composed of business leaders in the community and other significant stakeholders with an interest in the success of the organization.

There are generally three major categories of managerial leadership represented in an organizational chart. The top level is executive management, which is primarily responsible for setting the organization's future direction and establishing its strategic plan while maintaining the organization's mission and vision. An executive manager is a senior manager who oversees a broad functional area or group of departments or services, sets the organization's future direction, and monitors the organization's operations in those areas. Executive managers include the chief level positions, vice presidents, and directors.

Middle management is the management level in an organization that is concerned primarily with facilitating the work performed by supervisory- and staff-level personnel as well as by executive leaders. Middle managers oversee the operation of a broad scope of functions at the departmental level or who oversee defined product or service lines. Examples of middle managers are assistant directors, supervisors, and lead positions.

Figure 10-2 illustrates a section of a traditional organizational chart with the HIM department highlighted. In this example, the director of HIM

FIGURE 10-2   Section of Traditional Health Care Organizational Chart Highlighting HIM

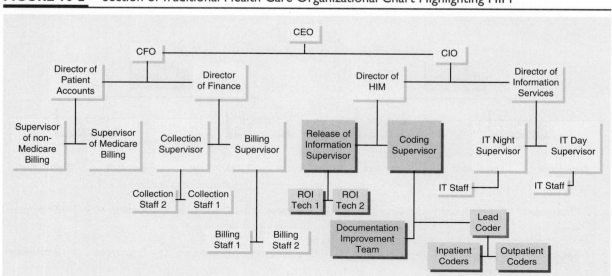

reports to the chief information officer (CIO). Reporting to the director of HIM are the release of information supervisor and coding supervisor. There are release of information technicians reporting to the release of information supervisor. The coding supervisor has a more complex reporting relationship represented on this organizational chart. The orange box represents a Documentation Improvement Team, which is a self-directed work team. The purple box is a lead coder, which is a lower level of leadership position that reports to the coding supervisor yet also has two sets of coders reporting to the position. Note that for the consideration of space in this text, this example does not reflect all positions that would appear in an HIM department.

Traditionally, this structure was seen as enhancing the organization's economies of scale. For example, when all of the coding specialists are responsible to one manager, scheduling for efficiency is possible. Also, the cost of resources is minimized since sharing is feasible. Another advantage in functional departmentalization is that employees are comfortable and satisfied working

PRACTICE EXAMPLE

The complex HIM department shown in Figure 10-3 has a mix of supervisory responsibilities with two locations. Three assistant directors care for the operations of the departments with supervisors and charge technicians serving in managerial positions. The assistant director at the satellite is responsible for managing the department, meeting with upper-level management, and solving routine problems interdepartmentally. Frequent meetings of the managers keep the two departments functioning smoothly.

The transcription department resides at the satellite facility with one transcriptionist at the main location to receive online reports and resolve difficulties. The evening transcriptionists are supervised by the second-shift supervisor with a broken line showing the coordination by the transcription supervisor.

Because the coding technicians are unable to transfer billing information directly, second-shift technicians abstract the information. The strategic plan includes a new information system that links the facilities and enhances the workflow. Efficiencies in the process can be realized when the capability to transfer coding and DRG assignment directly becomes a reality with this system. Coding technicians can then efficiently abstract information from the record that is not already online in the new system. The managers are planning organizational change and **reengineering** of the workflow as installation of the new system occurs.

Analysis or deficiency checking and reanalysis activities involve seven technicians under the assistant director for operations. Traditionally, this facility has performed detailed deficiency checking at the request of the medical staff. The managers have discussed the possibility of streamlining this activity. With less time devoted to record analysis, the technicians will have additional time to assist in medical staff activities that have been a limited part of their responsibility. Positions could also be eliminated or changed during reengineering

Reengineering
The process of changing business practices to maintain quality, reduce costs, and improve performance that involves fundamental rethinking and redesigning processes.

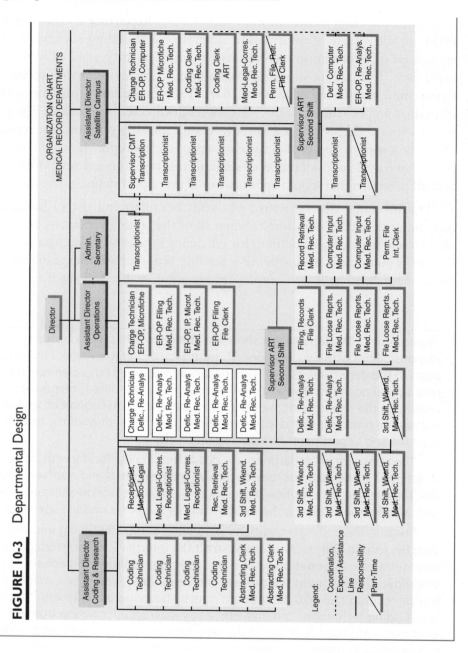

FIGURE 10-3   Departmental Design

with peers who "speak the same language." Figure 10-3 depicts an HIM department design using traditional functional departmentalization.

As the example indicates, technicians such as coding specialists are insulated from the activities of other employees. Record activity technicians performing deficiency review or reanalysis activities may have a limited understanding of the tasks performed by the legal correspondence team. In such an environment, can the technicians lose sight of the objectives of the total department? Of the facility? "Yes," is the response from an increasing number of organizational experts who turn to an **organic design** for appropriate parts of the organizational structure in health care facilities (Hyde & Fottler, 1992). HIM professionals can redesign the workflow and create a more organic design where possible. This change can not only enhance efficiency and effectiveness in the workplace but also create a team environment where job enrichment can be translated to job satisfaction.

Organic design
A structure that is low in complexity, formalization, and centralization.

ORGANIC STRUCTURAL DESIGNS

In contrast to the mechanistic design, an organic structure is an **adhocracy** where complexity is low, formalized design is low, and there is decentralized authority. In this adaptive structure, a facility or a department within a facility can change more easily when operating in a dynamic and uncertain environment. Several options are available when designing organic structures. These include the simple, matrix, network, task force, and committee structures. A review of each of these shows how they may be a desirable option for appropriate applications within health care (Robbins & Coulter, 2012).

Adhocracy See organic design.

The Simple Structure

The size of an organization is a major determining factor in whether a simple organizational structure is feasible. The simple structural option minimizes organizational complexity. Managers of smaller health care organizations will find advantages in using this simple structure, including organizations started by HIM entrepreneurs for the purpose of contracting specialized services.

With this simple structure, there is a flat organization with authority centralized in a single person with two or three vertical levels. Typically, the decision-making authority is centralized in the owner/entrepreneur. The strength of this design lies in its flexibility and low maintenance cost. A flat organizational chart does not have as many levels as a traditional organizational chart. There may be fewer upper-level administrative positions, such as the chief officers and vice presidents. There are also fewer lower-level management positions, such as supervisory and lead positions. An example of a flat organizational chart with the HIM positions highlighted is illustrated in Figure 10-4. Note that this example only has a director of HIM, reporting to the CEO, and all coding, release of information, and transcription staff reports directly to the director of HIM.

One major weakness of the simple structure becomes evident when the size of the organization increases to the point where decision making becomes too slow for effectiveness. Of course, a second weakness is that everything depends on just one person. A major illness can literally destroy the organization at the center (Robbins & Coulter, 2012).

FIGURE 10-4 Flat Organizational Chart

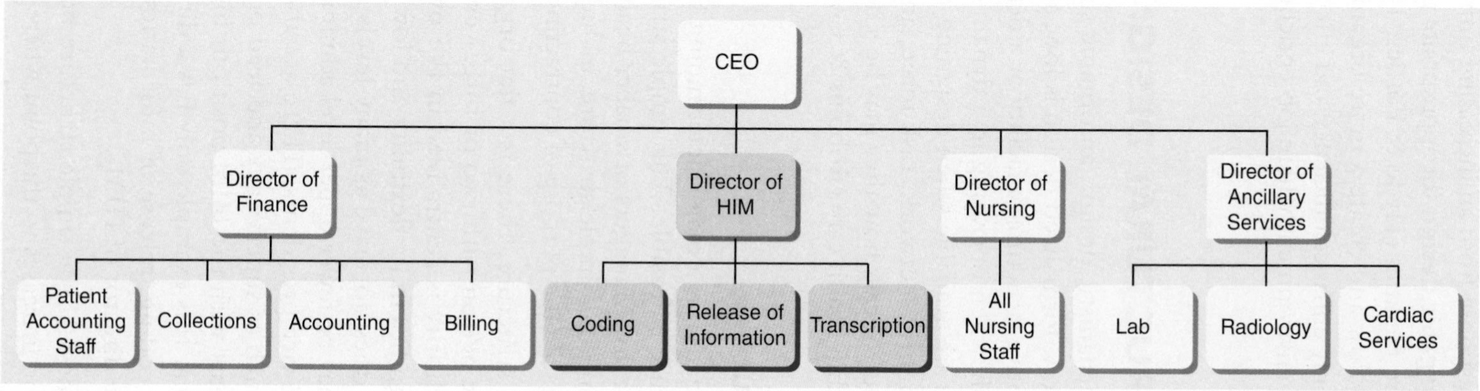

The Modified Simple Structure

While the complexity of acute care facilities usually demands a mechanistic structural design, departments within a facility can develop a modified simple design where the levels of management are kept to a minimum. The modified simple structure includes the team concept where the position of assistant director is deleted and team leaders and team members themselves are empowered with managerial responsibilities.

The Matrix Structure

A more contemporary organizational structure is a matrix organizational chart, which reflects work teams. These teams have employees from different traditional departments working together to accomplish a set of functions that are closely related. This type of organizational structure is able to more efficiently serve customers in various areas of health care organizations, as it eliminates the need to visit multiple departments or wait for staff from different departments to respond since they are generally physically located in the same areas. The matrix structure has the advantage of assigning various professionals to work teams to care for patients or customers in a product-oriented manner. It combines the advantages of functional specialization with the focus and accountability of product departmentalization since professionals from various functional departments are assigned to work together on a specific project or in a patient-focused care center. By creating this structure, managers transform the traditional unity of command principle into a shared responsibility. An example of a matrix organizational chart is illustrated in Figure 10-5.

FIGURE 10-5   Matrix Organizational Chart

Patient Care	Information Technology	Finance	Public Relations	Human Resources	Legal
Nursing Staff	HIM-EHR Trainer	HIM – Coders	Marketing	HIPAA Trainer	HIM – Privacy Officer
Respiratory	Programmers	Patient Financial Services	HIM Community Education	Quality Improvement Trainer	HIM – Compliance Officer
Laboratory	Help Desk	Accounting	Community Outreach		HIM – Risk Management
HIM – Documentation Improvement Specialist					

Unique projects of a specified duration may have professionals from several specialties organized with a project coordinator to whom they are responsible for the duration. This situation can occur when major information systems are being created and installed and the expertise of various professions is demanded. This is the more common form of matrix design (Robbins & Coulter, 2012).

With the trend toward patient-focused care centers, where all activities and care are rendered to patients in the center, matrix configurations will take form in various ways. Such a change demands reengineering efforts, which are discussed later in this chapter. A major difference is that in the patient-focused care centers, the matrix structure is permanent. Having this matrix design for customer services increases the complexity of the organization, so special effort must be made for effective communication across teams and departments.

Multiskilled health professional
A person cross-trained to provide more than one function, often in more than one discipline.

To increase the complexity of the design for patient-focused care centers even further, the team members are cross-trained and become **multiskilled health professionals**. For example, team members are trained in laboratory services such as specimen collection and cardiac testing. HIM professionals are cross-trained to ensure that information systems are flowing properly and to perform administrative functions such as utilization management (Hyde & Fottler, 1992). Futurists predict an increase in this dual chain of command structure (Hyde & Fottler, 1992).

As already mentioned, the unity of command principle is broken with the matrix design. This demands that authority and responsibility be clearly defined and understood by the managers and team members. Quality improvement techniques that include periodic evaluations need careful construction, especially when promotion and pay scale are involved.

Periodic analysis of the design needs to be undertaken to assure there is no confusion or ambiguity. These disadvantages of the matrix structure can result in power struggles.

The appropriateness of department's current work assignments and job content can be determined by performing a work distribution analysis. A similar determination of the most efficient and cost-effective staff mix can be performed through a staffing analysis. One tool that is often used when performing these analyses is a matrix called a work distribution chart that depicts the work being done in a particular workgroup in terms of specific tasks and activities, time spent on tasks, and the employees performing the tasks. These analyses ensure that reporting relationships are appropriate, along with department classifications. As organizations have started to shift to matrix organizational structure, work distribution and staffing analysis have become more complex, as it is necessary to consider factors and relationships outside of the traditional departments. Along with this change has come a shift of

FIGURE 10-6   Organizational Model: Network Structure

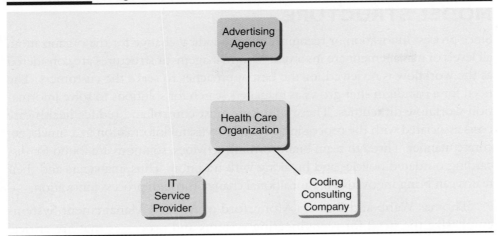

decision-making authority and responsibility to lower levels of the organization, referred to as decentralization.

The Network Structure

The **network structure** is designed to take advantage of the expertise another organization has, rather than build that expertise within one's own organization. This structure is typically seen in small centralized organizations that choose to rely on other organizations to perform a part of the business functions on a contract basis (Robbins & Coulter, 2012). In Figure 10-6, a network structure illustrates how a health care organization supplements its existing structure by consulting with an advertising agency, an IT service provider, and a coding consulting company.

HIM professionals use network structure when they share expertise by performing contract functions for organizations such as physician practice offices. Also, entrepreneurial professionals may choose to outsource the financial aspects or the human resource management aspects of their businesses. Another example of a network design in health care is the urgent care center that contracts with a group of emergency medicine professionals to serve its customers.

Task Forces and Committees

A **task force** is a temporary structure created to perform specific, well-defined, usually complex tasks using professionals from various organizational departments. In contrast, a **committee structure** brings together individuals from various departments to solve problems. Effective use of committees is detailed in Chapter 18.

Network structure An organization that chooses to rely on other organizations to perform some basic business functions on a contract basis.

Task force A temporary structure created to perform specific, well-defined, usually complex tasks using members from various organizational departments.

Committee structure A structure that brings together a range of individuals from across functional lines to solve problems or develop proactive alternatives before problems exist.

REENGINEERING AND CONTEMPORARY MODEL STRUCTURE

Since process innovation or reengineering is a radical change for the organization, all levels of management are involved. New management structures are considered as the workflow is reviewed for the best approaches to serve the customers. The need for a paradigm shift grows as managers search for solutions to solve information workflow difficulties. These solutions must control and reduce health care costs associated with the processing of data into useful information in a timely, accurate manner. Through team brainstorming activities, solutions are found for discarding outdated policies and breaking with tradition. Thus, managers and their teams can bring innovative organizational change through process innovation.

Thomas Webb and Barbara Mountford of Applied Management Systems emphasize the need for reengineering systems and processes that are critical to the delivery of patient care. Their past efforts in reengineering show a 20–30 percent reduction in operation costs. At the same time, the facilities involved in this reengineering increased direct care to the customers by 60 percent (Webb & Mountford, 1994). Webb and Mountford lead facilities toward a goal of transforming the organization into a high-performance hospital that meets or exceeds the expectations of its stakeholders. This transformation goal is led by "a vision that reflects both a responsiveness to the market and a commitment to operational excellence" (Webb & Mountford, 1994).

In their consulting activities, Webb and Mountford (1994) have found that the framework for the reengineering process of restructuring health care facilities must include the following:

1. Upper-level managers define the new organizational culture and lead in its implementation.
2. Department managers commit key staff time and resources to the process.
3. Department managers and team members commit to becoming knowledgeable by reading, thinking, and performing research into the reengineering process.
4. Upper-level and department managers develop an awareness of the "culture shock" that the facility will experience during this process.

Reengineering requires a dedicated project coordinator devoting full-time effort to the process. By creating an environment that nurtures staff, entrusts the teams with patient care, and provides them with necessary resources, the project coordinator successfully leads the task forces in redesign of the systems.

During reengineering of the department, HIM managers will expend extra effort in communication and reassurance. Positions will change, informal relationships will be broken, and stress becomes evident. The opportunities to create a new work environment, focusing on the customers, can enthuse employees. As managers emphasize the need for change and these opportunities, employees are encouraged to grow, learn, become valued team members for the department, and bring reality to the facility's vision.

THE C SUITE

In accordance with initiatives to encourage HIM professionals to pursue higher degrees, upon attaining the higher level of education at the master's degree level, AHIMA also advocates for these professionals to seek positions at higher levels in its organizations. One of the areas of focus is the executive administration level positions that are often referred to as the "C suite," as these are the chief positions that have abbreviations for the titles that start with the letter "C." Examples of C suite positions are outlined in Figure 10-7.

FIGURE 10-7   C Suite Positions

Position Title	Description
Chief executive officer (CEO)	The senior manager appointed by a governing board to direct an organization's overall long-term strategic management
Chief financial officer (CFO)	The senior manager responsible for the fiscal management of an organization
Chief information officer (CIO)	The senior manager responsible for the overall management of information resources in an organization
Chief information security officer (CISO)	IT leadership role responsible for overseeing the development, implementation, and enforcement of a health care organization's security program; role has grown as a direct result of the HIPAA security regulations
Chief information technology officer (CITO)	IT leadership role that guides an organization's decisions related to technical architecture and evaluates the latest technology developments and their applicability or potential use in the organization
Chief knowledge officer (CKO)	Oversees the entire knowledge acquisition, storage, and dissemination process and that identifies subject matter experts to help capture and organize the organization's knowledge assets
Chief medical informatics officer (CMIO)	An emerging position, typically a physician with medical informatics training, that provides physician leadership and direction in the deployment of clinical applications in health care organizations
Chief nursing officer (CNO)	The senior manager responsible for administering patient care services. This is usually a registered nurse with advanced education and extensive experience.
Chief of staff	The physician designated as leader of a health care organization's medical staff
Chief operating officer (COO)	An executive-level role responsible at a high level for day-to-day operations of an organization
Chief privacy officer	Oversees activities related to the development, implementation, and maintenance of, and adherence to, organizational policies and procedures regarding the privacy of and access to patient-specific information and ensures compliance with federal and state laws and regulations and accrediting body standards concerning the confidentiality and privacy of health-related information
Chief security officer (CSO)	The senior manager responsible for overseeing all aspects of an organization's security plan

SUMMARY

Mechanistic structural designs are complex and formalized. They resemble a bureaucracy. Functional departmentalization around occupational specialties is typically seen in health care facilities with mechanistic design. Economies of scale are an advantage of this design.

In organic structural design, the complexity and formalization are low. Redesign can be accomplished with relative speed in a dynamic environment. Structures in organic design include simple, matrix, network, task force, and committee.

Entrepreneurs typically organize using a simple structure with two or three vertical levels. The simple structure must be abandoned when growth brings a halt to effective decision making.

Matrix structure breaks the unity of command principle and consequently demands careful organizing. Matrix structures can be used permanently for bringing various professionals together in work teams or temporarily for special projects.

Network structures build on the expertise of organizations outside the facility. By contracting with a firm offering expert services, an organization can organize for efficiency and effectiveness.

Reengineering or process innovation is occurring with increased frequency in health care facilities as the search to contain costs and increase productivity continues. Reengineering is a radical departure for organizations and requires a commitment from all levels of the organization. By integrating data into information for decision making, HIM professionals play a key role in reengineering as task forces are developed for the process phase of the effort.

The framework for reengineering includes four factors: (1) upper-level management defines and leads the process, (2) commitment of key staff time and resources, (3) individual commitment to learning on their own, and (4) awareness that culture shock will be experienced.

The three phases of reengineering are discovery, vision, and the process itself. A project coordinator is needed to lead the task forces in process innovation and into a new structure where patient-focused care centers and attention to stakeholders' needs predominate.

As HIM professionals are obtaining higher levels of education and more diverse experience, they are achieving high levels of management in the C-suite, which supports the AHIMA Vision 2016 initiative.

CRITICAL THINKING EXERCISES

1. Obtain an organization model presently in use at an HIM department and review it before answering the following questions:
   a. Does the model tend toward a mechanistic or organic structure?
   b. Are the sections within the department organized by functional, customer, product, or process departmentalization?
   c. Are the line relationships clearly drawn?

2. Now create a revised model that uses one or more organic structural designs after making assumptions about reengineering the workflow.

3. As an HIM department manager, choose to use a network structure to meet departmental objectives by contracting with several firms for departmental services. List several types of firms you would choose for this and the expertise you would expect from each of them.

APPLICATION OF THEORY EXERCISES

1. Discuss what type of additional education or experience you might need if you were to pursue one of the C-suite positions.
2. You have made a decision that immediately after graduation you will find employment, for 6–9 months, as a transcriptionist. During that time, you will explore opportunities for starting a transcription service in an underserved area. Develop an organizational model for use during the first 3 years your new company is in operation; then redesign it for an expanded business beginning in the fourth year.

INTERNET ACTIVITY

Search the Internet for information about health care organizations that have experienced a merger with another organization. Summarize the details, including the reason for the merger, leadership changes, the impact on existing employees in both organizations, and other unique details.

CASE STUDY

You have been contracted as a management consultant for a health care organization that is planning to change from a traditional organizational structure to a matrix organizational chart structure. What steps would you recommend to effectively accomplish this task?

REFERENCES

Hyde, J., & Fottler, M. (1992). Application of the multiskilled staffing innovation to the health information management professional. *Journal of AHIMA, 63* (11), 54–60.

Robbins, S., & Coulter, M. (2012). *Management* (11th ed.). Upper Saddle River, NJ: Pearson.

Webb, T., & Mountford, B. (1994). *Organizational Model for Re-Engineering Healthcare*. Burlington, MA: Applied Management Systems.

CASE STUDY

Community Hospital is licensed for 200 beds and has a medical staff of 45. The health information services is responsible to the CFO, and the department manager has the following employees:

1. QI specialist involved in projects and medical staff meetings.
2. Team leader for transcription with three full-time transcriptionists, two part-time transcriptionists, and one part-time courier.
3. Team leader for reimbursement (coding, case management) with four full-time coders, one part-time case management statistician, one full-time tumor registry specialist, and two part-time on-call coders.
4. Team leader for record activity with one full-time second-shift team leader,

two full-time record activity team members, two part-time record activity team members, and one full-time physician liaison.

5. Team leader for customer services, which includes information management, two full-time receptionists/legal correspondence team members, and one full-time correspondence team member.

6. One part-time resource registered record administrator cross-trained to perform many tasks; performs orientation and training activities. The department is open from 7 A.M. to 11 P.M.

7. Develop an organizational design for the health information services using one of the designs discussed in this chapter.

8. Use an organizational design software package, if possible.

CHAPTER 11

Organizing Position Designs for Employees

LEARNING OBJECTIVES

After completing this chapter, the learner should be able to:

1. Outline processes involved in recruiting, interviewing, and hiring.
2. Compare aspects of salary and benefits.
3. Develop training materials for new staff orientation and ongoing routine training.
4. Give a historical description of job design and explain how specialization has been especially important in health care organizations.
5. Explain the value of position analysis and methods used in this analysis.
6. Outline the major components of position descriptions.
7. Assess employee performance using performance evaluation tools.
8. Interpret laws impacting human resources.
9. Identify advantages of job rotation; then give possible drawbacks to its use in health care settings.
10. Contrast job enlargement with job enrichment.
11. Describe the use of work teams and how self-managed teams can increase employee productivity and morale.
12. Summarize the advantages of flexible work schedules.

INTRODUCTION

Once the design of the organization is envisioned through strategic planning efforts, department managers begin the task of organizing to achieve specific objectives. The organizing function plays a key role in the integrated model of management. As new organizations are created and planned, the HIM department managers have an opportunity to plan, organize, and purchase the latest technology and equipment. At this point, it is possible to begin an analysis of each position needed to accomplish the objectives. In this ideal environment, when the new organization begins operation, the HIM information systems in place can make it possible to operate efficiently and effectively. This ideal department will be, in reality, possible for only a few HIM managers.

More typically, the challenge is to redesign or reengineer an existing department to provide timely and accurate access to health care information as organizations become involved in reengineering efforts. And, these changes must occur while the rush of everyday activities continues. These routine activities are performed by employees hired for specific tasks to accomplish objectives. As redesign of a department begins, the tasks performed by each employee and the skills needed to accomplish them will also need review and revision.

RECRUITING, INTERVIEWING, HIRING, AND TRAINING

Recruitment
The process of finding, soliciting, and attracting employees

The process of finding, soliciting, and attracting employees is known as **recruitment**. Recruiting is performed using a variety of methods. The use of classified advertisements in newspapers has significantly decreased in recent years, while Internet career search site postings have increased. Professional networking is a commonly used method of informal recruiting in the HIM career field. Bulletin boards for posting announcements are often available in registration areas of national, state, and regional association meetings. AHIMA also has resources that facilitate recruiting efforts. AHIMA Career Assist is an online resource that provides an area for HIM employers to post jobs and HIM job seekers to post resumes for employers and recruiters to search. An employer may contract with a professional recruiter to seek qualified professionals, too.

When an employer posts information about an available position, information that is generally provided may include the following items:

- Company/institution name
- Position title

- Brief description of the position
- Required or preferred education
- Desired credentials or certifications
- Preferred years of experience

Sometimes, incentives are offered to help recruit for difficult to fill positions. Evening, night, and weekend coverage shifts are generally the most challenging. Many health care institutions offer a **shift differential**, which is an increased wage paid to employees who work less desirable shifts. Another method used to attract applicants is offering a **sign-on bonus**, which is a monetary incentive used by a facility to encourage a candidate to accept employment. A sign-on bonus may range from a relatively small amount of $50 to larger amounts upward from $10,000. Depending on the organization and nature of the position to be filled, relocation expenses may also partially or fully covered.

The application process is handled in a variety of methods. Traditionally, applicants would complete a paper application on-site in the human resources department. Another method of application involves submitting either a resume or curriculum vitae (CV). Some organizations only allow online applications. These may or may not include an option to upload a resume or CV. A resume, which is more commonly used in a traditional work setting, provides information about an applicant's education and employment history. See Figure 11-1 for a sample resume. *Curriculum vitae* is a Latin term meaning "course of life." As the term reflects, a CV provides significantly more detail than a resume. A CV is used more often in academic, research, and publication settings. See Figure 11-2 for a sample CV.

Once applications and resumes have been reviewed, the employer narrows the search by selecting those with the most appropriate qualifications for the position and formal interviews are scheduled for the applicants and potential employer. The Human Resources department may perform an initial review of applicants and apply specific criteria to identify the applicant pool. An initial screening interview may be performed by telephone, online conferencing, or face-to-face. Some organizations have an interview guide that provides a list of written questions to be asked during an interview. When this is done, it is usually part of a structured interview, which is an interview format that uses a set of standardized questions that are asked of all applicants. This provides a means for equal assessment of all applicants so that they all have an equal opportunity to provide information on the same topics. The number of individuals included in the interview varies by employer. Some employers may even hold a panel interview, in which the applicant is interviewed by several interviewers at the same time.

Following the interview process, reference checks may be done for the best applicants. This involves contacting individuals that a prospective employee has listed to provide a favorable account of his or her work performance or personal attributes. Finally, the best applicant is selected and an offer is made. Once

Shift differential An increased wage paid to employees who work less desirable shifts.

Sign-on bonus A monetary incentive used by a facility to encourage a candidate to accept employment.

FIGURE 11-1   Sample Resume

Elizabeth Brown, RHIA, CCS
1234 S. First Street
Anytown, IL 54321
(123)555-1212
E-mail: ebrown@email.com

WORK EXPERIENCE

February 20XX
to present

Best Home Care, Anytown, IL: Supervisor of Health Information.
Duties included: Supervision of 7–9 office employees, preparation of
monthly statistics, and knowledge of Medicare, Medicaid, and other
third-party billing regulations.

September 20XX
to February 20XX

General Hospital, Anytown, IL: Coder. Duties included: Coding and
abstracting inpatient charts and outpatient diagnostic records using ICD-
10-CM codes, coding ER, and outpatient surgery records using ICD-10-CM
and CPT-4 codes, use of 3M encoder, use of optical imaging system for
outpatient records, participation on many quality improvement teams,
and instructing employee training sessions for Quality Leadership Process
and Service Excellence.

March 20XX to
September 20XX

Memorial Medical Center, Anytown, IL: Coder. Duties included coding and
abstracting inpatient and outpatient records using ICD-10-CM, CPT, and
HCPCS codes.

EDUCATION

August 20XX to
May 20XX

State University, Anytown, IL:
Bachelor of Science in Health Information Administration.

FIGURE 11-2   Sample Curriculum Vitae

Elizabeth Brown, RHIA, CCS
1234 S. First Street
Anytown, IL 54321
(123)555-1212
E-mail: ebrown@email.com

EDUCATION

University of State, City, IL
M.S. Health Information Management   20XX

State College, Anytown, IL
Bachelor of Science, Health Information Administration   20XX

CERTIFICATION

Fellow of American Health Information Management Association   20XX
Registered Health Information Administrator (No. xxxxx)   20XX
Certified Coding Specialist (No. xxxxx)   20XX

FIGURE 11-2   *(continued)*

AWARDS
American Health Information Management Association Foundation Scholarship   20XX
Who's Who Among Students in American Colleges   20XX
Dean's List, State, Anytown, IL   20XX

TEACHING EXPERIENCE
State College, Anytown, IL
Adjunct Instructor   20XX–20XX
HIM 205, Introduction to CPT Coding

Upstate University, Collegetown, IL
Adjunct Instructor   20XX–20XX
HI300, Health Care Statistics

RELATED EXPERIENCE
Best Home Care, Anytown, IL
Supervisor of Health Information Services
Supervised 8–10 Health Information Services employees, prepared monthly statistical reports, performed coding audits and coding education, ensured record maintenance and coding compliance according to Medicare, Medicaid, and other third-party billing regulations

University Hospital, Anytown, IL
Coder
Assigned ICD-10-CM, CPT, and HCPCS codes for inpatient, outpatient, skilled nursing, and addiction recovery accounts

CONSULTING
XYZ Publishing, Medical Coding Textbook reviewer
Upstate University, Collegetown, IL. Coding and documentation audits

PUBLICATIONS AND PAPERS
"Best Practices for Teaching ICD-10-PCS"
Journal of XXXXX, no. 10 (October 20xx)

"Transition from HIM Practitioner to Educator"
Journal of XXXXX, no. 3 (March 20xx)

INVITED PRESENTATIONS
"Teaching ICD-10-PCS"
American Health Information Management Association Assembly on Education   20XX
Chicago, IL

OFFICES HELD AND COMMITTEE APPOINTMENTS
President, State Health Information Management Association   20XX
Chairman of annual meeting planning committee, State Health Information
Management Association   20XX

accepted, the organization will likely perform a background check. Some states have adopted stricter requirements relating to criminal history for health care professionals. In most cases, health care organizations will not hire applicants with any kind of felony offence, which includes serious crimes such as murder, larceny, rape, or assault for which punishment is usually severe. A misdemeanor crime that is less serious than a felony may be tolerated, although some organizations may have specific limitations. Health care employers are also required to check the National Practitioner Data Bank (NPDB), which was established by the federal government through the 1986 Health Care Quality Improvement Act. The NPDB contains information on professional review actions taken against physicians and other licensed health care practitioners that health care organizations are required to verify as part of the credentialing process.

Outsourcing
Contracting with a company that enters into a contract with a health care organization to perform services.

It can be difficult to fill some HIM positions that require higher levels of education, experience, or specialized training. Sometimes, alternatives must be explored to cover a vacant position with a temporary solution until a permanent employee is hired. This may be accomplished through **outsourcing**, which involves contracting with a company that enters into a contract with a health care organization to perform services such as clinical coding or transcription. Outsourcing may be used to perform a function either on-site or off-site. One method of outsourcing, which is often a controversial topic, is offshoring, or outsourcing jobs to countries overseas, wherein local employees abroad perform jobs that domestic employees previously performed. Offshoring may sometimes be less costly than outsourcing through a domestic company. However, there are concerns frequently expressed by HIM professionals regarding offshoring that range from asking why jobs are sent overseas when unemployment exists in our nation, to controlling security of protected health information outside of the United States borders.

Another temporary option may be using a domestic or even local consulting agency outside the health care organization to provide contract services for the facility, such as transcription, coding, or copying. A contract coder may also be hired as an independent contractor on a temporary basis to assist with coding backlog. Whether the contract services are performed by an offshore company, national domestic company, local agency, or an independent consultant, a contract must be agreed upon and signed by both parties in order to have a binding, legally enforceable agreement that addresses all aspects of the service.

SALARY, BENEFITS, AND OTHER ASPECTS OF HUMAN RESOURCES

The employees of an organization, or human resources, are often the most valuable resources and can be the most difficult to manage. Hiring an employee involves engaging the services of an individual in return for compensation. This not only includes the wages to be earned by the employee, but also benefit packages. **Compensation** includes all direct and indirect pay, including wages, mandatory benefits, and benefits such as medical insurance, life insurance, child care, elder care, retirement plans, and longevity pay.

Minimum wage and overtime payment regulations are set through federal legislation of the Fair Labor Standards Act of 1938 (FLSA). Federal legislation also requires equal pay for men and women who perform substantially the same work under the federal legislation of the Equal Pay Act of 1963 (EPA). All groups of employees covered by the provisions of the Fair Labor Standards Act are referred to as nonexempt employees. These employees generally work 40 or fewer hours per week and must be appropriately compensated for overtime. They are often referred to more commonly as "hourly" employees. Exempt employees, often referred to as "salaried" employees, are identified as not being covered by some or all of the provisions of the Fair Labor Standards Act. Professionals in management and administrative level positions are often designated as exempt employees, as they frequently work well over 40 hours a week as an expectation of the positions, so overtime is basically absorbed in the generally higher pay rates that are provided to these employees.

The new hire will be asked to sign an employment contract, which is a legal and binding agreement of terms related to an individual's work, such as hours, pay, or benefits. It is important for new employees to thoroughly read the employment contract prior to signing. If any of the details are not clear, the individual should ask questions. Some contracts may include a statement about **employment at will**, which is a concept that employees can be fired at any time and for almost any reason based on the idea that employees can quit at any time and for any reason. Another item that may be included on the contract is a **noncompete clause**, which could include restrictions regarding employment following termination from the employer. A noncompete clause may restrict the employee from seeking employment with a competitor, vendor, or client for a specified period of time. Noncompete clauses are not legal in all states, so the specific state Department of Labor should be referenced to find out if this is allowed. Employees may also be required to sign a nondisclosure agreement that relates to the confidentiality and privacy of patient information as a condition of employment.

The contract not only includes details of compensation, but also the designation of the employee status. A new hire may only be a temporary employee, who is employed for a temporary, definite period of time, such as to complete a specific project or to fill in for a permanent employee on vacation or other leave; or a person who is employed for an indefinite period of time but who receives none of the fringe benefits offered to permanent employees. A permanent employee is a person who is employed for an indefinite, ongoing period of time, typically long term. Another designation of employee status is related to how many hours the employee is contracted to work. An employee who works 40 hours per week, 80 hours per 2-week period, or 8 hours per day is generally

Compensation
All direct and indirect pay, including wages, mandatory benefits, and benefits such as medical insurance, life insurance, child care, elder care, retirement plans, and longevity pay.

Employment at will A concept that employees can be fired at any time and for almost any reason based on the idea that employees can quit at any time and for any reason.

Noncompete clause A clause in an employment contract that may restrict the employee from seeking employment with a competitor, vendor, or client.

considered to be a full-time employee. Likewise, a part-time employee is an employee who works less than the full-time standard of 40 hours per week, 80 hours per 2-week period, or 8 hours per day. If benefits are provided by the organization, part-time employees often do not qualify for insurance, vacation, and retirement plans. Many organizations have different definitions of what is considered to be full time or part time. As economic changes have occurred, some employers went through periods of downsizing to reduce the cost of labor and streamline the organization by laying off portions of the workforce. However, others have simply reduced the number of hours required for employees to be considered full time for the purpose of qualifying for benefits. For example, some organizations may have employees working 32 hours a week but still designate them as full time so that they can have insurance. On March 20, 2010, the Affordable Care Act was signed into law. This reformed affordability, quality, and availability of health insurance for both public and private health insurance companies in each department.

Organizations may have budget approvals for a certain number of full-time equivalents (FTEs). This is different than a simple count of full-time employees. It is a statistic representing the number of full-time employees as calculated by the reported number of hours worked by all employees, including part-time and temporary, during a specific time period. For example, in an organization that considers an FTE to represent 40 hours per week, two part-time employees who each work 20 hours would be counted as a 0.5 plus another 0.5 to equal 1.0 FTE.

One of the employee benefits that is of great value to many is group health insurance through a prepaid medical plan that covers the health care expenses of an organization's full-time, and in some cases, part-time, employees. Most organizations contract with other companies for provision of employee health insurance. However, some administer employer-based self-insurance, which is funded directly by the employers to provide coverage for their employees exclusively in which employers establish accounts to cover their employees' medical expenses and retain control over the funds but bear the risk of paying claims greater than their estimates. Whether health insurance is provided through a group or through the employer-based policy, the employee must provide evidence of insurability, which is a statement or proof of a health status necessary to obtain health care insurance, especially private health care insurance. If an employee is transferring from one insurance provider to another, then the first provider will provide a statement of continuous coverage to reflect that there is no gap in coverage at the time of transfer. Sometimes, evidence of insurability may require completion of a health history questionnaire and physical examination.

Some variation does exist among organizations regarding coverage options for dependents, which may include an insured's spouse and unmarried children, claimed on income tax. The maximum age of dependent children varies by policy. A common ceiling is 19 years of age, with continuation to age 26 provided the child is a full-time student at an accredited school, is primarily dependent upon the covered employee for support and maintenance, and is unmarried. Some health care insurance policies also allow same-sex domestic partners to be listed as dependents.

TRAINING

Upon hire or transfer to a new position, employees require training for the set of activities and materials that provide the opportunity to acquire job-related skills, knowledge, and abilities. An HIM professional may need to serve as a trainer to provide instruction to new employees, or **trainees**, for tasks or skills required for the position. Employee orientation is generally required at most health care organizations as a process in which employees are introduced to their jobs, the organization, and its work culture. Orientation for HIM professionals may occur over multiple days. One part of the orientation may involve massed training, which is an educational technique that requires learning a large amount of material at one time.

Trainees New employees.

Train-the-trainer is a commonly used method of training that involves training of certain individuals who, in turn, will be responsible for training others on a task or skill. HIM professionals may be trained to train others in the department, or other departments, to use the electronic health record. Train-the-trainer method works well for training of a large number of employees.

Train-the-trainer A commonly used method of training that involves training of certain individuals who, in turn, will be responsible for training others on a task or skill.

Some training needs may be served through self-directed learning, which is an instructional method that allows students to control their learning and progress at their own pace. This may involve computer-based training that is delivered partially or completely using a computer. Self-directed and computer-based learning are commonly used for routine mandatory education modules for current employees, too. There is a growing number of HIM professionals working in remote positions, so computer-based training may even be performed through web-based training to provide instruction via the Internet, enabling individuals to learn in a structure that is self-paced and self-directed while interacting and collaborating with other students and the instructor via a conferencing system.

Diversity training Training that facilitates an environment that fosters tolerance and appreciation of individual differences within the organization's workforce and strives to create a more harmonious working environment.

As the health care workforce not only employs staff from varied backgrounds, it is important to also consider the customers being served in the health care environment. This is not limited to patient care providers, so it is important to HIM professionals, who are becoming increasingly present to patients and community members. Because of this, some organizations include **diversity training** in orientation. This is a type of training that facilitates an environment that fosters tolerance and appreciation of individual differences within the organization's workforce and strives to create a more harmonious working environment. The term **diversity** refers to differences among people, such as age, race, nationality, gender, sexual orientation, or tenure with the organization or position. While it may be relatively simple to recognize physical

Diversity Differences among people, such as age, race, nationality, gender, sexual orientation, or tenure with the organization or position.

differences in those from various cultural groups, it may not be as easy to identify the aspects that are not always visible. Because of this, employees in health care may be trained in cultural competence to help them become more aware, with a greater ability to understand and accept beliefs and values of the people that are different than one's own.

Occasionally, in-service education is necessary to provide training that teaches employees specific skills required to maintain or improve performance, usually internal to an organization. Sometimes, this method includes role playing in which participants are required to act out roles that address various situations that may be encountered as part of their daily work. Examples of role playing as a training tool for HIM professionals may involve playing roles in scenarios related to individuals requesting release of information or scenarios that involve interpersonal communication with physicians, other clinicians, and other departments.

Following completion of general organizational training, the new employee will receive on-the-job training in the department where the employee will be working. This method of training provides the ability for an employee to learn necessary skills and processes by performing the functions of his or her position. Upon arrival in the department, the new employee will likely receive a tour that includes introductions to co-workers. Some organizations will even have the new employee spend a specified amount of time observing each area of the department in order to provide an overview of the workflow.

Once overall department orientation and introductions have been completed, the new employee will be required to review a manual of job procedures, which is a structured list of activities required to complete a task or solve problems that may be encountered as part of a position. A mentor may be assigned to the new employee to serve as a trusted advisor or counselor. The mentor is an experienced individual who educates and trains another individual within an occupational setting.

Position design See job design.

Job design The way in which tasks are combined to form a complete position.

Position description See job description.

Job description The written statement summarizing what an employee does, how it is done, and why it is done.

Whether managers are grouping activities to organize a new department or reviewing activities during the redesign or reengineering of a department, the activities and skills needed must be documented. This activity is defined as **position design** or **job design** and leads to full-time position allotments by separating specific tasks, methods, and organizational relationships. The resulting documentation for each is called a **position description** or **job description**. A position description provides documentation of the education requirements, skill requirements, expectations, and activities that are performed by the position. Many positions in health care have job specifications that require skills and competencies that have been acquired either through formal education or previous work experience.

In this section, key components of position descriptions are identified and analyzed. Steps in documentation are discussed and options to the design offer variety. Self-directed teams may rotate leadership positions; therefore, documenting position descriptions for teams is discussed separately. Examples of position descriptions are brought into the discussion.

Identification of pay scale structure varies from one organization to another. Some use the approach of job ranking, arranging jobs in a hierarchy on the basis of each job's importance to the organization, with the most important jobs listed at the top of the hierarchy and the least important jobs listed at the bottom. Another similar approach, which is used for positions associated with federal government organizations, is the job classification method. This method of job evaluation compares a written position description with the written descriptions of various classification grades.

The job description serves many purposes. It should be shared during the interview process in order for the applicant to review to determine if the position is truly appropriate. Upon hire, the position description is used for training purposes so that the new employee may check off each task and be aware of what will be used for performance evaluation. When supervisors complete performance evaluations, the job description also provides details of items to be evaluated and the measurable criteria for comparison.

ANALYSIS AND DESIGN OF POSITION DESCRIPTIONS

Analysis of position descriptions begins with the documented activities that have been identified and grouped. When redesign or reengineering is occurring, all employees will ideally be involved in documenting the activities. Empowering employees to share in developing documentation of the activities that will be a part of the position design gives them a sense of ownership.

Managers will find it helpful to network with the human resources department during the analysis process. Copies of position descriptions are ultimately utilized by the human resources staff for hiring and assigning wage scales to each position. Managers will want to create documents that clearly show the knowledge and skills needed for each position and then use them as tools for defending the requested level of salary.

Figure 11-3 outlines specific items that are typically a part of position descriptions, regardless of the activities to be performed. These details need to be considered during analysis, so decisions can be made as the design is developed. Position descriptions are then created following this analysis. These should clarify the responsibilities, authority, relationships, and accountability expected for the position.

During the analysis and design or redesign of positions, most of the effort will be expended on items 6–9 from Figure 11-3. Item 6 includes the major

FIGURE 11-3   Position Description Content

1. Title of the position
2. Name of the department, position number for human resources use, salary range (optional)
3. Title of the person to whom this position is accountable
4. Status—that is, permanent/temporary, work hours, flextime option
5. Position purpose or mission, may be titled the position summary
6. Major responsibilities of the position—these should be specific to the point that performance can be measured
7. Specifications or minimum knowledge, skills, experience, and abilities required; credentials, if required
8. Working conditions
9. Approvals, dates, revision dates

responsibilities designed for the position and documents the decisions of how activities are grouped. Technical positions, especially, should have measurable expectations for the responsibilities. These expectations give managers interviewing prospective employees an opportunity to bring expectations, knowledge, skills, and experience together.

An example of a position description for an outpatient coder is shown in Figure 11-4.

Other elements of the position description that need mention are the signature of the manager with responsibility for the position and the date of latest revision. Because of the multiple uses for position descriptions, accountability for the content is needed.

Once these elements are in place, a position description will provide a complete understanding of the responsibilities of each position in the department and the qualities best suited in the applicant for each position. Further, they describe relationships, authority, and accountability. Each position on the organizational model developed in Chapter 9 will have a position description that corresponds with the graphic relationship.

DOCUMENTING POSITION DESCRIPTIONS

Once the design or redesign and analysis are completed, the formal documentation of each position description can begin. First, it is helpful to list the multiple uses of a position description to emphasize the importance of keeping it current and accurate. These uses are shown in Figure 11-5.

FIGURE 11-4   Sample Position Description

Position: Outpatient Coder

Number: HIM020

Salary Range: $17–22/hour, based on qualifications

Status: Full-time, permanent

Department: Health Information Management

Reports to: Director of Health Information Management

Objective: Codes medical records and inputs abstracted record data into hospital computer system on a timely basis and according to established standards and practices.

DUTIES:

- Access records using electronic health record system.
- Assign ICD-10-CM diagnosis codes and CPT/HCPCS procedure codes.
- Code records for outpatient diagnostic, emergency department, and outpatient surgery.
- Perform physician queries when appropriate.
- Communicate with billing department when necessary.

QUALIFICATIONS

Required:

- RHIA, RHIT, CCS, CCA, CPC, and/or working knowledge of CPT, HCPCS, and ICD-10-CM coding systems.
- Working knowledge of medical anatomy and physiology.
- 1–2 years recent coding experience in an acute care hospital setting or successful completion of the coding curriculum in an approved RHIA/RHIT program.

Preferred:

- RHIA, RHIT, CCS, CCS-P and/or CCA.
- 3–5 years recent coding experience in an acute care hospital setting.

FIGURE 11-5   Position Description Uses

1. Assist in clarifying relationships between jobs and teams, avoiding overlaps or gaps in responsibility.
2. Enable managers to prepare position orientation materials and procedures.
3. Establish the basis for a just and fair salary within the compensation structure.
4. Create one tool for use in performance appraisals.
5. Establish a base for position analysis and further redesign in the future.
6. Assist manager in position interviews with prospective employees.
7. Create base for benchmark comparison with positions in other health care facilities and with regional compensation reports.
8. Help with strategic planning and budget review.

POSITION DESCRIPTION OPTIONS

This section explores several opportunities managers have to be innovative as they organize for change. During times of change, the challenge of creating an environment that provides motivation for employees and increases job satisfaction becomes even greater. Empowering employees to be a part of the decision-making team has already been mentioned and Chapter 13 offers broad motivational theories. Special mention of motivation as a part of organizing is made here to provide continuity.

Job Characteristics Model

Job character-istics model A framework for analyzing and designing jobs that identifies five primary job characteristics, their interrelationships, and impact on outcome variables.

One approach to position description redesign options is found in the **job characteristics model**. This is a framework for analyzing and designing jobs around five major qualities and their impact on outcome variables. Figure 11-6 identifies these five core dimensions and defines them (Robbins & Coulter, 2012).

As individual tasks are grouped together to form positions within a team, within a section, and then for the total HIM services, managers become aware of the complexity facing them. Some groupings have tasks that are quite standardized and repetitive; at the other end of the spectrum are individualized tasks that may be most effective when performed independently. Awareness of this diversity is one key to organizing success for HIM managers. Each position developed is crucial to the success of the organization, so as employees are hired and trained, whether within a team or independently, the departmental culture plays a major role in having employees accept their place within the department, and the managers create the culture for this acceptance.

Exploring the advantages of various position designs brings an awareness of the need to guard against overspecialization of tasks. As the division of labor became popular in the early 1900s, tasks were separated into minute divisions

FIGURE 11-6   Job Characteristics Model

1. *Skill variety*—the degree to which a position requires a variety of activities, enabling the employee to use a number of different skills and talents.

2. *Task identity*—the degree to which a position requires completion of a whole and identifiable task.

3. *Task significance*—the degree to which a position has a substantial impact on the lives or work of people.

4. *Autonomy*—the degree to which a position offers substantial freedom, independence, and discretion to the employee for scheduling the tasks and determining the procedures for accomplishing them.

5. *Feedback*—the degree to which accomplishing the tasks results in the employee obtaining direct and clear information on the effectiveness of the performance.

with repetitive work done day after day by employees. As discussed earlier, this can lead to boredom and frustration. The designs outlined next recognize this problem and offer solutions.

PERFORMANCE EVALUATION TOOLS

When an employee is hired, an employee record is created and maintained by the human resources department. This record contains information about job performance and other pertinent information relating to the employee's employment history with the organization. Upon hire, the record creation starts with application, resume, copies of certifications, and contract information that contains information about the terms of employment and the starting salary. If immunizations or other physical examination is completed as part of the employment requirements, those are generally maintained by the occupational health department. When the employee completes initial orientation, documentation is maintained of that as well. Following general orientation, larger organizations also have department-specific training that must be documented. Throughout the employee's employment, additional training and continuing education should also be documented, including proof of credential maintenance for HIM professionals with RHIT, RHIA, CCS, or other certifications. Additional documents are created during the course of employment, including performance evaluations, changes in pay, and possibly disciplinary action. When employment is terminated, whether voluntary or involuntary, that paperwork is added to the file, which is then archived. HIM employee records may include the following items:

- Application for employment
- Resume
- Contract
- Copy of job description
- Documentation of orientation and other training
- Copies of college transcripts
- Copies of RHIT, RHIA, CCS, etc. certificates
- Proof of continuing education
- Performance evaluation
- Pay increase documentation
- Disciplinary action documentation
- Documentation of recognition and awards
- Termination documents

Most employers have a **probationary period** of anywhere from the first 30 days of employment to the first 6 months of employment, during which the quality of work and competence are evaluated prior to assuming regular

Probationary period A period of time during which the quality of work and competence are evaluated prior to assuming regular employment with the organization.

employment with the organization. During this period, the employer may make the decision to terminate the employee immediately at any point due to dissatisfaction with the employee's performance. At the end of the probationary period, the employer may do a performance evaluation (some employers may also use the performance review) to provide performance counseling to give the new employee feedback regarding observations of the quality of work and competence during the probationary period. Some of the feedback may include tips about how to improve performance.

Another type of **performance evaluation** is that done on a routine basis, such as annually for the purpose of providing feedback to the employee regarding quality of work during the period since the previous evaluation and review progress on any goals that the employee may have set during the previous evaluation. The performance evaluation should be based on **performance standards**, which are clearly stated in the position description, along with measurable criteria that is deemed acceptable regarding quality and productivity standards for each function performed in the position. When the employee receives a copy of the job description during orientation, the employee should be informed that these standards will be the basis of evaluation.

Three methods of evaluation that may be used include the point method, Hay method, and 360-degree evaluation. The **point method** of performance evaluation involves placing specified weights on each of the standards to be assessed. Sometimes, an evaluation may be associated with a pay increase. This is often referred to as a **merit raise**. If the point method is used for evaluation associated with a merit raise, the amount or percentage of pay increase is determined by the number of points in specified ranges.

The Hay method of performance evaluation is based on the similar principles as the point method, but the evaluating factors are categorized as accountability, know-how, and problem solving. These three factors are assigned percentages to weight the categories according to the proportions appropriate to the position. For example, an HIM position with a need for greater technical skills, such as coding, would have a higher percentage assigned to the know-how category, while somebody in a risk management position would have a higher percentage assigned to the problem-solving category.

Self-evaluation may also be a component of performance evaluation. This involves the employee critiquing him- or herself against the performance standards and then reviewing the self-evaluation with the supervisor. Self-evaluation is often difficult to complete. Some employees tend to be their own greatest critic and may rate their performance too low, while others may approach it from a greed perspective if the evaluation is associated with a merit raise. A 360-degree evaluation provides a well-rounded evaluation using self-evaluation, along with the employee's supervisor, co-worker peers, customers, and subordinates perspectives.

Performance evaluation Provision of feedback to an employee regarding quality of work.

Performance standards Measurable criteria that is deemed acceptable regarding quality and productivity standards for each function performed in the position.

Point method A method of determining the amount or percentage of pay increase by the number of points in specified ranges on a performance evaluation.

Merit raise A pay increase based on positive employee performance.

Self-evaluation An employee's critique of him- or herself against performance standards.

Performance evaluations occasionally occur as part of a disciplinary action as a means to address a behavior issue or unsatisfactory performance. Organizations have varied approaches to how disciplinary action is handled. Whatever approach is used should be clearly outlined in the employee handbook and the human resources policy and procedure manual. Some organizations use a method called progressive discipline, which involves four steps. The first step is a verbal warning that includes coaching to review the reason for discipline and provide advice regarding changes that need to be made. The second step is a written warning, which involves formal documentation of the offense. If the unsatisfactory performance or behavior continues after the written warning, the third step is a suspension for a defined period of time, during which the employee is not allowed to come to the workplace and does not receive any compensation. Finally, if the situation does not resolve after the employee returns to work, involuntary termination of employment occurs.

When termination of employment occurs, whether voluntary or involuntary, access to health information must be discontinued as well. Organizations generally have documented policies and procedures regarding voluntary termination of employment. Most organizations require nonmanagement staff members to provide a notice of at least 2 weeks. Policies and procedures for voluntary termination notice for management positions or other key positions vary by organization. Some may require notice of at least 4 weeks or more, while others may accept the notice as an immediate resignation, especially for positions with access to critical information that may be at risk of loss of integrity if the individual is allowed to remain beyond giving notice. Organizations also have varied policies and procedures related to exit interviews, which serve purpose of providing the employee an opportunity to share suggestions for improvement, additional reasons for leaving, and even positive comments regarding the organization. Some employers have a policy that employees have to request an exit interview at the termination of their employment, while other organizations have the exit interview as a standard step in the termination processes.

JOB DESIGN OPTIONS

As the multitude of tasks under the responsibility of HIM managers are grouped for team effort, options to meet specific department demands and employee needs are available. This section describes several options that can create a cost-effective design for the department. These options include the following:

- Position enrichment
- Position enlargement
- Position rotation
- Work sharing
- Compressed work week

Position Enrichment

Position enrichment The practice of enriching positions by expanding the tasks vertically, usually with planning and evaluating responsibilities.

Position depth A practice where employees are given an increased degree of control over their tasks.

As tasks are grouped, managers can effectively look for opportunities to enrich positions by expanding the positions vertically. Two areas typically added are planning and evaluating responsibilities, thus giving **position enrichment**. A component of this enrichment is an increase in **position depth** where the employees are given an increased degree of control over their work.

The team involved in utilization management, for example, can be trained to prepare the computer-enhanced reports of their activities. Each team member could have responsibility for presenting the results to a facility committee and working directly with the committee members on concerns and suggestions. This procedure gives HIM professionals increased control over their monthly activities and adds planning for the reports as an enriched opportunity. Lastly, evaluation activities could be the result of computer reports, committee member comments, or other performance standards where employees can have increased input in their position design.

Position Enlargement

Position enlargement A practice that offers employees horizontal expansion of activities and an increase in scope.

Job scope The variety of activities within a position description and the frequency with which each activity is repeated.

While position enrichment gives vertical expansion, **position enlargement** offers a horizontal expansion of activities and an increase in job scope. As might be expected, employees can easily feel that enlargement really means additional tasks to complete every day. Because of this effect, managers should combine enlargement with automation or other enhancement that gives added value to the tasks. **Job scope** relates to the number of different tasks required in a position and the frequency with which the task cycle is repeated. As there is an increase in the different tasks to be performed, the cycle may be lengthened if the way in which the tasks are performed stays approximately the same.

For example, as HIM services revise discharge analysis tasks to keep pace with AHIMA professional standards of practice recommendations, the hours allotted to analysis will be lessened. Employees can be given the opportunity to enlarge their positions with other tasks added; thus, the cycle for discharge analysis is shortened while the position is enlarged with other tasks. With specialized tasks, such as record analysis, other task cycles can be added toward the end of the week when discharge activities are current.

Position Rotation

Position rotation The practice of lateral transfers of employees among jobs involving different tasks.

Position rotation, as an organizing design option, can be effective in reducing the monotony or boredom associated with repetitive tasks. By scheduling employees to rotate among different tasks every 2–3 months, managers broaden each employee's knowledge and increase skills and flexibility in addition to reducing boredom or monotony. Teams organized around position rotation increase individual responsibility among the group and thus offer team members a greater sense of ownership.

Training time can be increased with position rotation, however, since each employee is being taught a variety of tasks. Another possible negative is that productivity may fall as rotation occurs and the learning curve slumps until employees are back to full productivity again. The complexity of the tasks must be a factor when considering this organization option.

Rotating activities is best utilized on a voluntary basis since some employees, who are typically highly motivated, may resent forced task change. Within a team's assigned activities, there are typically some tasks that are perceived as undesirable. By suggesting position rotation in a fair and consistent manner as a voluntary option, team leaders can increase satisfaction and overall productivity. Also, the advantages of employees who maintain their skills with such cross-training can maintain productivity when absenteeism occurs. Lastly, position rotation option is most effective in a stable environment where employees are not facing change pressures from other sources.

Job Sharing

Health care professionals such as physicians and nurses are accustomed to job sharing where commitment and continuity are given. Physicians with family responsibilities may choose specific office hours that are less than a full-time schedule and share the office workload in this way. The 24-hour patient care setting in hospitals demands that nurses share in caring for patients, regardless of the hours they work. Communication, verbal and written, is vital to the success of job sharing for health care professionals and patient records reflect the written communication.

When HIM services are available during second and third shifts, continuity of information and work flow are also important to quality patient care. By organizing the change of responsibilities and dissemination of information as team members come and go, managers can maintain effective communication networks for continuity. Position descriptions will reflect this continuity by emphasizing excellent communication skills. This type of job sharing is commonplace.

Figure 11-7 gives advantages and disadvantages the employees and the management team discovered as they implemented and evaluated job sharing.

Other Design Options

Several other position designs deserve mention. One is the **compressed work week** where employees may work four 10-hour days. This concept is fairly common among other health care professionals and shows mixed results. Initially, employees maintain productivity and enjoy the option; however, studies show that over time, fatigue can become a negative factor. Also, over time, employees with families tend to have increased stress.

When faced with the need to downsize or rightsize departments, managers may choose to offer employees the option of **work sharing.** This option

Compressed work week
A schedule where employees work four 10-hour days.

Work sharing
A practice where work is shared across all shifts, or where one full-time position is shared by two part-time employees.

FIGURE 11-7   Advantages and Disadvantages of Job Sharing

Advantages

1. Skilled HIM professionals can continue as valuable employees in a department.

2. Flexible scheduling is possible since two people share the same position. Time management is enhanced as team members cover for one another during vacations or illnesses.

3. Permanent employment as a part-time employee is possible because the full-time position is permanent.

4. Professionals can maintain their current status in health information management.

5. Quality and quantity of work increase, stress and fatigue decrease.

Disadvantages

1. Part-time benefits may not meet the needs of both employees.

2. There is an increase in administrative paperwork, which is more expensive. Position design may require two descriptions.

3. Communication breakdown creates loss of continuity.

4. Perception may develop that part-time employees have a lower commitment to the organization.

can avoid layoffs since work sharing means that employees temporarily reduce work hours and/or salary. The priority tasks are shared as redesign of the workflow occurs. Position descriptions are temporarily revised during this period. An advantage is that the workforce can be reduced through attrition, thus avoiding layoffs, when the change becomes permanent.

The advantages of the flextime option have already been mentioned. When flextime is routinely used in a department, managers may wish to document the possibility of flextime in specific position descriptions. When flextime is a popular option in an organization, prospective employees should be aware of those positions where flextime is not an option.

SUMMARY

HIM managers work closely with the human resources department to recruit employees who are the best fit for positions in the organization. This includes processes of posting the positions strategically so that potential applicants may find them through a variety of methods, including online, hard copy, and word-of-mouth routes. Applicants are interviewed and

the individual who is the best fit for the position and the organization is hired. The job description is a valuable tool that is used during the interview, training, and performance evaluation to provide clear documentation of the performance standards for each position. The hiring process, along with other aspects of employment, has many federal and state regulations guiding decisions and processes. The organization should maintain current information about these laws and have a process in place to ensure all involved are compliant.

The first step in designing position descriptions or redesigning them is to analyze the position. Employees performing the activities should ideally be empowered to share in the analysis and resulting documentation.

Content of position descriptions varies, depending on the facility. Major components of position descriptions include the following:

- Title of the position
- Department name
- Person to whom the position is responsible
- Position summary
- Major responsibilities of the position
- Specification requirements
- Space for approvals and revision dates

This documentation is then reviewed and revised periodically for multiple users.

Current position descriptions are useful for clarifying relationships among team members and within the department, for preparing orientation and procedure documentation, for assessing compensation structure and performance appraisals, and in position interviews.

A job characteristics model is useful in designing HIM department positions where education and skills vary from position to position. This model identifies five core dimensions:

1. Skill variety
2. Task identity
3. Task significance
4. Autonomy
5. Feedback

Using these characteristics, managers can give value to each task and the team member performing it.

Position enrichment is used effectively to expand employee positions vertically. Position depth can be increased at the same time, giving the team members additional control over their activities.

Position enlargement offers horizontal expansion of responsibilities and increases job scope. When position enlargement is coupled with new tools such as automated systems, employees are accepting of the added tasks.

Job sharing is seen frequently in health care and is becoming useful in HIM departments where professionals wish to work part-time in responsible positions. Disadvantages are that communication breakdowns can create difficulties and administrative paperwork will likely increase. However, the time management advantages, such as coverage for vacations or illnesses, can offset the disadvantages when valuable employees are retained through this option.

Work sharing is one option when right-sizing occurs. By reducing work hours temporarily, layoffs are avoided and the work force can be reduced gradually through attrition.

CRITICAL THINKING EXERCISES

1. Describe the two major components in the content of a position description.
2. Briefly explain the major uses of position descriptions.
3. Explain how the job characteristics model assists managers in redesigning position descriptions.
4. Give five options to traditional job designs that assist managers in better meeting employee needs.

APPLICATION OF THEORY EXERCISES

1. Interview an HIM professional and document major responsibilities. Develop a position description for the professional.
2. Redesign the work schedules for an HIM department staff of 16 where rightsizing plans call for an FTE budget for 14. Choose among the position design options.
3. Create position descriptions for two employees who share one full-time position—that of team leader for the coding and reimbursement team.
4. Construct a position description for a release of information specialist that includes all of the elements discussed in the chapter.

INTERNET ACTIVITY

Search online for positions in the HIM field. Use the AHIMA Career Assist and at least one other job search engine, such as Monster or Career Builder. Document the requirements or preferred skill sets for at least five of the positions that are discovered in your search.

CASE STUDIES

1. You are the director of HIM for a 600-bed hospital and need to hire somebody to fill the position of coding supervisor in your department. There are eight outpatient coders and seven inpatient coders. Compile a list of questions that you might ask during the interview.
2. You are being interviewed by the director of HIM for a 600-bed hospital as an applicant for the position of coding supervisor. There are eight outpatient coders and seven inpatient coders. Compile a list of questions that you might ask the HIM director during the interview.

REFERENCES

Robbins, S., & Coulter, M. (2012). *Management* (11th ed.). Upper Saddle River, NJ: Pearson.

Schein, J. (1993). Saying "I do" to job sharing. *For the Record*, 5 (7), 9.

Stine, S. (1993). Take this job and share it. *For the Record*, 5 (7), 6.

Managing with Evolving Technology

After completing this chapter, the learner should be able to:

1. Discuss considerations of HIM managers related to new technology.
2. Identify new technology being used in HIM.
3. Outline the importance of backup systems for technology.

INTRODUCTION

As this chapter unfolds, a vision of how HIM professionals will continue to plan, organize, redesign, and reengineer for the future demands attention. Before this vision becomes focused, there must be a critical look at present organizational design. By creatively exploring alternative design structures, managers can open new vistas for organizing models and embrace new technologies that will focus on meeting the information needs of various customers. By melding new technologies and organizational change, HIM professionals can offer information and services of value in all health care settings. These two factors—new technologies and organizational change—will continue to challenge and excite HIM professionals during the twenty-first century and beyond.

Examples of present and emerging technologies that generate the impetus toward a paradigm shift are included in this chapter. Organizational changes can then lead to opportunities for redesigning the structure or for a complete reengineering of the department. As defined in Chapter 10, reengineering involves radical change in business processes to achieve breakthrough results that increase productivity and decrease costs. The examples where reengineering is appropriate will contrast with examples where redesign is adequate for changing the organizational structure and will provide efficiency and effectiveness. Redesign is less radical than reengineering and practice examples give redesign options that are appropriate for some new technology applications.

Since the focus of this section is on the organizing function in the integrated model of management, the emphasis in this chapter continues to be on structural redesign and reengineering as new technologies are embraced. The behavioral aspects of change and meeting the challenges of managing these aspects are explored in Chapter 20.

ORGANIZATIONAL PROBLEMS WITH NEW TECHNOLOGIES

As new technologies are incorporated into the strategic plan of facilities, one goal may be to solve specific problems. However, at the same time, other unfocused problems may be left unresolved. Or, in other situations, funds may be allocated for only partial solutions to problems and thus new sets of problems can arise, such as when one new automated system is planned for an HIM department, but other systems remain manual. Accountable Care Organizations have introduced new challenges for Health Information technology, as they require the use of technology for sharing information between and among physicians, patients, the hospital, affiliated clinics, pharmacies, and other service providers.

EVOLUTION OF AUTOMATION OF TRADITIONAL HIM FUNCTIONS

Automation of previously manual processes has been an area of evolving technology that has been occurring over the years. The **master patient index (MPI)**, which is a database of the name and unique identification number of every patient who has ever received services at the health care provider organization, has been maintained electronically for many years. This system was extremely cumbersome and nearly impossible to accurately identify duplicates or similar entries when kept manually. Another system that evolving technology improved was **chart tracking**, which includes the process of signing out records and tracking them as they are transferred from one location to another. This process had previously been performed manually by inserting outguides with documentation of the initial chart checkout information to hold the place of the record in the filing area. The problem with initial automation of this process was that the documentation was not consistently updated if the file was taken to another location. This problem was addressed through further evolution of the automated process. Bar code technology was introduced and chart sign-out was performed with a bar code scanner, much like what is used in grocery stores or libraries. If the chart was transferred to another location, it was scanned again to update the system.

Chart deficiency tracking has also been automated for many years. HIM professionals review records to identify documentation deficiencies, such as missing signatures or dictated reports. The deficiency tracking system allows the physician record assistant to run reports to identify what each physician must complete and how long the records have been deficient. As the transition to electronic health records (EHRs) has occurred, the tracking mechanism remains relatively similar. Physicians are also able to log in and obtain their lists of deficient records to complete. Digital signature management technology is used with the EHR to validate the identity of the individual completing deficiencies in records with an electronic signature for authentication of documentation.

Transcription has evolved from use of handheld cassette recorders to recording of sounds using digital dictation to convert to formats able to be stored on computers for random access. That transition allowed physicians to dictate reports remotely and eliminated the need for maintaining a library of cassette tapes. The next step in transcription evolution was speech recognition, which uses technology to provide instant documentation of dictated reports using a digital dictation system, rather than waiting for a transcriptionist to

Master patient index (MPI) A database of the name and unique identification number of every patient who has ever received services at the health care provider organization.

Chart tracking The process of signing out records and tracking them as they are transferred from one location to another.

type the report after it has been dictated. Speech recognition systems can be trained to recognize individual voices and accents. However, speech recognition does not completely eliminate the need for the human element, which has posed some challenges for HIM professionals. The role of the transcriptionist has changed in response to industry needs related to speech recognition. Some transcriptionists have assumed the role of editor, reviewing reports produced by speech recognition to identify obvious errors in computer translation of the spoken words. From a managerial perspective, the experience requirements may be slightly different when hiring an editor versus traditional transcriptionist, as the need is not necessarily as focused on keyboarding speed but rather on ability to recognize grammar and spelling errors. Another change in the role of the transcriptionist is that some providers hire them for the evolving position of scribe, which is an individual who follows a physician with a tablet computer to do real-time transcription into the EHR.

Coding professionals have experienced a variety of technological changes over the years. In the 1990s, encoder software was introduced to allow coders to assign diagnosis and procedure codes using the computer. Encoder software was able to interface with the abstracting system to automatically transfer codes into the abstracting system. Computer-assisted coding (CAC) is a more recent development in coding technology that extracts data that have been entered into the EHR and translates the data into codes. HIM professionals must be familiar with the limitations of CAC, as it is not appropriate at this time to consider the software as a complete replacement for the human element of coding. HIM professionals should advocate the importance of coders with health care providers in all settings, as many interpret CAC as a means to perform coding functions without trained coding professionals.

ELECTRONIC HEALTH RECORD

Traditional paper health records are being replaced with the EHR that provides the ability to create and manage health information in a format that allows for analysis of data in the records and concurrent use by multiple users in different locations. This technological advance presents numerous challenges for HIM professionals. Since the introduction of the EHR, it has become necessary for HIM professionals to gain an understanding of computer technology in order to effectively collaborate with information technology (IT) professionals for development and implementation. Another challenge presented to HIM professionals is the rapidly increasing number of regulations and standards related to management of health information in electronic format.

On April 27, 2004, President Bush signed Executive Order 13335, which called for all health care providers to implement EHRs by the year 2014. Through this Executive Order, the position of Office of the National Coordinator for Health Information Technology (ONC) was also established to become the principal federal entity charged with task of coordinating nation-wide efforts to implement the most advanced health IT and perform electronic exchange of health information. The ONC was legislatively mandated in the Health Information Technology for Economic and Clinical Health Act (HITECH Act) of 2009.

Public Law 111-5, which is more commonly known as the American Recovery and Reinvestment Act (ARRA), was signed into law by President Barack Obama on February 17, 2009. Title XIII of ARRA is known to HIM professionals as the Health Information Technology for Economic and Clinical Health Act (HITECH). The HITECH Act involved $19.2 billion in stimulus funding dedicated to facilitating EHR adoption by health care providers. The decision to provide this funding as part of ARRA was in response to Executive Order 13335.

Although HITECH and ARRA provide funding for health care providers to implement the EHR, there are some strings attached. In 2011, the Centers for Medicare & Medicaid Services (CMS) established requirements that must be met by providers in order to receive funding. These requirements are referred to as "Meaningful Use." The simple explanation of Meaningful Use is that a health care provider cannot just implement an EHR for the sake of having it to be considered "compliant," but rather the provider must also use the EHR in a meaningful manner to the greatest capacity possible in order to justify receiving Federal funding through ARRA and HITECH. Stage 1 of Meaningful Use involved requirements for health care providers to make health information available to patients through a variety of electronic methods. Stage 2 of Meaningful Use took things further, requiring providers to arrange for patients to have access to their health information online, as well as download and transmit their health information within 4 business days of when the provider has the information available. Stage 3 of Meaningful Use is focused on improved outcomes. There are eight objectives of Meaningful Use Stage 3:

1. Protect patient information
2. e-Prescribing
3. Clinical decision support
4. Computerized provider order entry
5. Patient electronic access to their data
6. Coordination of care through patient engagement
7. Health information exchange
8. Public health reporting

Not only is implementation of an EHR a significant financial investment, but time is also an issue. The transition from paper records to hybrid records and finally to a true EHR requires training for physicians and all staff members. Training time creates normal processes to fall behind, as employees are focused on training and do not have time to keep up their work. As with any other new process, there is also a learning curve with EHR implementation, so processes will not be completed as quickly while employees are adjusting to the new system.

Implementation of a complete EHR requires development that meets applicable criteria for certification that has been established by the secretary of HHS. This is not an overnight process, but rather involves several steps to reach a fully functional EHR to meet those criteria. During the transition, health care providers use **hybrid health records**, which have a combination of both paper documents and EHRs. The ratio of paper versus electronic documentation in the records does not impact the designation as a hybrid health record. As long as some paper-based component remains, no matter how insignificant it may seem, the record is still considered hybrid. One major implication of hybrid health records for HIM managers is how the organization will define its legal health record

Hybrid health records Health records that consist of a combination of paper and electronic documentation.

One of the long-term goals of EHR implementation is the National Health Information Infrastructure (NHII) initiative, which will result in the development of a comprehensive knowledge-based network that connects health care providers, public health agencies, and personal health records. This network may contribute to improved effectiveness, efficiency, and overall quality of the health care delivery system in the United States. The Nationwide Health Information Network (NHIN) will facilitate the process of obtaining health records from other providers, which would improve decision making by making health information available without the need to wait for additional communication among providers. Secure health information exchange (HIE) over the Internet is enabled through the standards, services, and policies of the NHIN, which provides a foundation for the electronic exchange of health information across all provider types nationwide to help achieve the goals of the HITECH Act. Development of HIE organizations have already made a significant contribution toward the NHII, as these are regionally administered organizations that support electronic exchange of electronic protected health information (ePHI) among participating providers.

In order to effectively accomplish the NHIN, different information systems and software applications must be developed to be interoperable in order to accomplish communication and data exchange. An independent body within AHIMA has been created to address this important aspect of EHR. The Commission on Certification for Health Informatics and Information Management (CCHIIM) is responsible for establishment and enforcing of standards that were developed as the basis to grant and maintain certification of health informatics and information management professionals.

Health Level Seven International (HL7) An international standard development organization that provides standards that ensure the ability of EHR systems to be compatible for integration of components and exchange of information.

Interoperability of EHR systems and components must comply with standards set by **Health Level Seven International (HL7)**, which is an international standard development organization that provides standards that

FIGURE 12-1   Factors Impacting the EHR

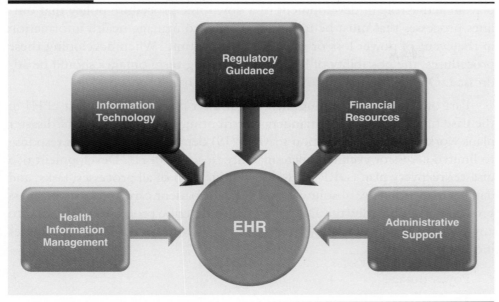

ensure the ability of EHR systems to be compatible for integration of components and exchange of information. Recommendations to the National Coordinator of Health IT regarding implementation, certification criteria, and other standards are generated by the Health Information Technology Standards Committee.

Processes involved in eHIM are still relatively new for many seasoned HIM managers, plus a need for provider support has been identified. Because of this, HITECH developed Health Information Technology Regional Extension Centers (HITREC or REC) for the purpose of providing assistance and guidance in adoption, implementation, and use of EHR technology. These programs are funded by ARRA grants and support providers in becoming compliant with the Meaningful Use requirements. In addition, the RECs are supported by provision of information about the most effective practices that have been developed through applied HIT research. This research is provided by Health Information Technology Research Centers (HITRC), which are also resulting from the HITECH Act, as information is gathered about effective practices through collaboration of the RECs and relevant stakeholders, identifying best practices. See Figure 12-1 for factors impacting the EHR.

DOWNTIME AND RECOVERY PLANNING

While technological advances have provided opportunities for managing health information, there are also some potential obstacles that may be faced. Computer technology use may be impaired in the case of power outage or unexpected downtime of the system. Because of this, HIM professionals must play an active role in development of a downtime procedure policy that outlines processes that must be followed in order to manage health information in the event of power loss or unexpected downtime. When developing these procedures, the possibility of both brief and long-term outages should be addressed. One method that is often used is cloud-based backup.

Part of downtime planning includes disaster planning to protect ePHI in the case of a disaster. HIM mangers contributing to development of disaster plans work with the information services (IS) department to address response to limited access or even complete inability to access ePHI. Development of a disaster recovery plan (DRP) includes identification of all processes, tasks, and data elements that are absolutely necessary for patient care and basic business processes. Additionally, the DRP should also describe processes to respond to any type of disaster that may be experienced by the facility. Some examples include:

- Power outage
- Fire
- Flood
- Tornado
- Hurricane
- Earthquake
- Tsunami
- Terrorist attack
- Internet outage
- Computer virus

Some of these circumstances may just present temporary downtime that does not pose any threat of data integrity loss, while others may cause destruction of data or long-term inability to access ePHI. One strategy for disaster recovery related to EHR is planned redundancy, which involves duplication of all EHR functions and data at another location. Selection of a location for planned redundancy must be done with attention to protection of ePHI at the other location, so caution should be exercised if considering a location that may be at risk for any of the examples listed above.

Redundant systems should be tested on a routine basis to verify reliability. The HIM manager should identify key staff members from each area of the department to test the system so that all of the functions performed by each may be tested using processes performed by each, using processes that are current. Testing should occur in a part of the system that has been set up with fictional patients and data, as real patient information should not be compromised by testing the system. Redundant systems are generally set up to run a few minutes behind the real system so that there is minimal data loss.

HEALTH CARE INFORMATICS

The EHR has presented additional opportunities for HIM professionals beyond the traditional record management functions. One area of practice that has evolved in the HIM industry is health care informatics, which focuses on all elements of health data, including use of technology to perform data analysis functions that may contribute to further developments in health care management. HIM professionals in management positions related to health care informatics often have master's degree level education. Professional guidance for HIM managers in informatics may appreciate the benefits of Healthcare Information and Management Systems Society (HIMSS) membership, which provides guidance for leaders responsible for management of health information through the use of technology.

Introduction of New Processes Using Technology

Registration for patients presenting for health care services may be performed by using an information kiosk that involves a computer-based station for use by patients. The kiosk may streamline the registration processes by allowing the patient to enter demographic information and even basic health history. This practice presents additional new opportunities for HIM professionals to be employed in a leadership capacity, as patient education and training is necessary for the success of this technology.

TELEMEDICINE

Telemedicine is increasing in the health care arena as technology has introduced methods that make this method often more feasible than having professionals on-site at all times. Telemedicine uses technology, such as digital imaging, to communicate information to health care providers remotely for purposes of consultation. One application of telemedicine is using a remote service for reading radiology tests during shifts that are difficult to cover, in order to avoid delays in waiting for a local radiologist to read the tests in emergency situations.

MHEALTH

Another area of recent technology-based growth in the HIM environment is mHealth. This involves the practice of managing health information using mobile devices. mHealth is an issue of pertinence for providers, HIM professionals, and the general public. While the number of mHealth applications is rapidly increasing, there is a need for professionals to provide education to the users, who are making decisions about which applications to use and what information they will share through these applications.

SUMMARY

Technological advances over the years have contributed to automation of processes across the scope of HIM practice. Many of these changes have paved the way for introduction of the EHR. Implementation of the EHR is mandated by the federal government with strict standards that address the extent of use.

Provision of patient care activities may be challenging if a disaster occurs, so the HIM manager may need to develop creative approaches to plan for disaster preparedness and recovery. As technology continues to evolve in the HIM industry, so do the opportunities for managers of health information.

CRITICAL THINKING EXERCISES

1. Choose an automated application for HIM services and explain its impact on organizational design.
2. Identify three avenues that HIM professionals can use in becoming knowledgeable about new technologies.

3. Describe how HIM professionals can enhance strategic planning decisions within an organization.

APPLICATION OF THEORY EXERCISE

1. Discuss considerations of HIM managers assisting with implementation of CAC.

INTERNET ACTIVITY

Visit the HIMSS website, and write a summary of how HIM managers may benefit from joining this organization to supplement AHIMA membership.

CASE STUDY

You are the EHR coordinator for a 1,000-bed acute care hospital with a level one trauma center and high-risk pregnancy unit with neonatal intensive care services. As you are developing policies and procedures for EHR management, one of the tasks you must complete is selection of the location for planned redundancy of the EHR system. The table below provides the locations that have been proposed for maintaining a redundant system. Identify the pros and cons for each site and identify two other locations that may be considered, along with their pros and cons. After evaluating the pros and cons of each location, provide your recommendation for the site you would select and justify your selection.

Location	Pros	Cons
Rural Oklahoma		
New York, NY		
New Orleans, LA		
Small town in Colorado		
Another location in the same city		
An adjacent city 50 miles away		
Canada		
India		
Additional location 1:		
Additional location 2:		

SUGGESTED READINGS

www.hl7.org
www.healthit.gov

www.himss.org

SECTION IV

Leading to Meet Information Needs of Health Care Facilities

CHAPTER 13

Leading: The Interpersonal Aspects of Management

LEARNING OBJECTIVES

After completing this chapter, the learner should be able to:

1. List synonyms for the term *leading,* and state how their meanings differ in emphasis.
2. Describe how leaders use power within organizations to accomplish objectives.
3. Contrast the traits of leaders with the traits of managers.
4. Give the three components of attitudes, and state how attitudes can predict employee behavior.
5. Describe how HIM managers can identify appropriate personality traits for specific positions in a hospital HIM department.
6. Define formal and informal groups within the organization and the role HIM managers have in each.
7. Give advantages of using the team approach for accomplishing objectives in the HIM workplace.
8. Define followership, and outline the role managers have as followers.

INTRODUCTION

It could be said that the management functions of planning and organizing are a preparation that sets the stage for the interpersonal aspect of management—leading. The leading function takes a manager into what may be considered the most complex aspect of management. And, with the demands on HIM managers to increase efficiency and effectiveness, leading the teams that perform the multifaceted activities encompassing the entire HIM field gives added meaning to the term *complex*.

Again, it is important to emphasize the interwoven nature of the management functions. None is undertaken in isolation. There is rarely an opportunity to complete the planning cycle, create the department's organizational design, and then say, "Now it is time to begin hiring and leading the teams that are performing the activities outlined in planning and delegated in organizing." Hence, the complexity increases as the planning vision becomes ongoing reality through the leading function.

LEADING DEFINED

Leading is defined as "the management function involved in motivating employees, directing others, resolving conflicts, and selecting effective communication channels" (Robbins & Coulter, 2012). These interpersonal facets of leading are evidence of the crucial nature of this management function. The purpose of leading is, of course, to accomplish the objectives of the facility through the teams delegated to perform specific activities. This chapter begins by defining terms frequently used in Section IV.

Directing A component of the leading function of management that emphasizes giving assignments and instructions, guiding employees, and overseeing activities.

Also, at times, authors choose the term *directing* to describe the leading function. Leading gives emphasis to the manager's role in setting the tone for the department and in encouraging the teams by example. In contrast, **directing** refers to the giving of assignments and instructions, the guidance of employees, and the overseeing of those activities. Leading and directing are used interchangeably in this text, depending on whether the topic is discussing the interpersonal aspects of an activity or the functional component of an activity.

The interpersonal aspects of managing require HIM professionals to address the need for an understanding of why humans behave as they do within their teams and with others in the organization. Section IV explores human behavior in the workplace and includes examples of individual behavioral response. There is no such thing as an "average" employee. Each one has individual differences.

This chapter focuses on individual and group behavior. Chapter 14 explores the motivational aspects of leading and has a section on conflict and its effects. At times, conflict is seen as the result of faulty communication. Communicating with skill in the workplace is the topic of Chapter 15.

LEADERSHIP POWER AND AUTHORITY

Leadership is the ability to inspire and influence others and, as such, is the process of influencing the behavior of group members in accomplishing the planned objectives. Thus, the leader is the person who has a central role in group activity. By this definition, there can be two types of leaders: the formal or appointed leader and the **informal leader** chosen by the group. The HIM department manager is the **formal leader** of the department, appointed by upper-level management, and thus has the leadership authority. But, does this mean the manager is automatically the informal leader? Since the group chooses the informal leader, the manager may or may not have ownership of both roles. Is this situation a deterrent to the successful performance of the tasks to meet departmental objectives? The section on group behavior offers some conclusions to this question.

In Chapter 9 the discussion on power and authority showed how appointed authority is a subset of power as the formal lines of organization are drawn. Mature, self-controlled leaders will use this appointed authority wisely for influencing teams. The power inherent in their position can be used positively. This power is necessary, not for personal aggrandizement, but to accomplish the goals and thus enhance quality patient care. Effective leaders use the right combination of power and authority appropriate for their group of employees. As stated earlier, there is no "average" employee; the managerial challenge is to know the employees, know their strengths and weaknesses, and then utilize the most effective methods for accomplishing the delegated tasks.

Leadership The ability to inspire and influence attitudes and behaviors of group members in accomplishing objectives.

Informal leader The leader chosen by members of the group to lead the group in certain attitudes and behaviors.

Formal leader The manager appointed to lead an entity and have responsibility for the activities within that entity.

Leaders Versus Managers

Abraham Zaleznik, writing in the *Harvard Business Review* (2004), explains that managers and leaders typically have different personalities, attitudes toward goals, perceptions about work, and relationships with others. These different characteristics lead to situational differences where leaders prefer to make improvements in even successful policies. Managers, on the other hand, tend to be guided by rationality, control, and an impersonal approach toward goals. This tendency may lead to avoidance behavior when making changes in policies that are presently effective.

Reviewing these major differences, it could be concluded that an HIM professional, who tends toward leadership personality traits, will be monitoring trends for the future and then planning possible changes toward a total electronic health record (EHR) as technology advances. In the continuum between these personality traits, however, lies a broad range of characteristics with ample room for variation in managerial styles. Successful professionals are those who acknowledge their personality traits, develop those they desire, and with enthusiasm perform well into the twenty-first century.

Trait approach
A leadership approach based on the premise that leaders possess a set of traits of qualities, setting them apart from nonleaders.

When discussing leadership, some use the **trait approach**, which is based on the premise that leaders possess a set of traits or qualities, setting them apart from nonleaders. There are many traits that may be associated with effective leaders. Some of these include the following:

- Accountable
- Ambitious
- Assertive
- Balanced
- Caring
- Competent
- Confident
- Courteous
- Ethical
- Experienced
- Fair
- Focused
- Helpful

- Honest
- Humble
- Insightful
- Inspiring
- Knowledgeable
- Open-minded
- Patient
- Reliable
- Respectful
- Supportive
- Trustworthy
- Visionary

Almost as crucial to success is the environment in which a leader operates. Successful leadership is also dependent on the followers—the teams within the department—and on the goals and objectives planned for the department and for the total organization. The conclusion is that the successful manager is not a blind adherent to any one particular leadership style, but rather chooses the style considered most appropriate for a given situation (Robbins & Coulter, 2012).

Leadership traits can be learned, and effective managers have learned to develop the skills they desire through effort and practice. By giving diligence and constant attention to the practices outlined in Figure 13-1, new managers can become enthusiastic leaders.

By keeping this list of leadership practices for frequent review, new managers can be diligent in honing their leading skills, conquering their fears, understanding their strengths and weaknesses, and becoming the visionary, competent leaders desired. By taking a long-term view of strategic planning and creating a clear and abiding mission within the organizational structure, leaders guide the team in selecting desirable outcomes and then focus on the goals for success.

ATTITUDES AS PREDICTORS OF BEHAVIOR

Attitudes are evaluative statements that reflect how an individual feels about something. Obviously, the concern here relates to job attitudes and how to explain or predict behavior that is in response to one or more of the three components of attitude:

> *Cognitive attitude component:* This component covers the knowledge, opinions, and belief system held by the employee. "Refusing to code diagnoses based on the highest reimbursement" illustrates a cognition.
>
> *Affective attitude component:* Emotions and feelings are addressed in this component. "I feel uncomfortable surrounded with this bright new wall color at my workstation" reflects the affective component of attitudes.
>
> *Behavior attitude component:* Action takes place with this component. Re-painting the wall because of negative feelings about it puts action into the attitude.

Typically, when an employee attitude is mentioned, the reference is to the affective component, since awareness of feelings is usually most evident. Awareness of attitudes in the HIM workplace is crucial to managerial success, especially as change occurs. One useful managerial goal is to strive for employee job satisfaction and ongoing commitment to the department. When teams participate in planning and organizing their own activities, as emphasized in Figure 13-1, each member can identify with the team goals and increase job satisfaction. As a result, the attitudes of the team members should reflect this involvement. Researchers find that people seek consistency between their attitudes and behavior. When the team members feel the planned change is good for them and for the department, their behavior will reflect this positive attitude and result in **consistency perception** (Robbins & Coulter, 2012).

Cognitive dissonance is the opposite of consistency perception. Incompatibility between the hope an employee has and the behavior that leads toward realization of that hope creates cognitive dissonance. When team members exhibit a positive behavior toward planned changes, for example, and then become frustrated with some aspects of implementation, their affective component is inconsistent with their behavior and leads to a sense of discomfort. Researchers have shown that employees will seek to reduce this dissonance and thus the discomfort.

For example, a team leader who has just given an in-service program on the importance of accurate data in quality reviews, and then is told that the figures released yesterday to a medical staff committee are incorrect, will have dissonance. This will lead her to (1) admit the mistake and submit corrected figures or (2) convince herself that the figures are not so far off and really not that important. Thus, by reducing the dissonance, she has reduced the discomfort and is back to consistency perception (Robbins & Coulter, 2012).

Attitudes Evaluative statements that reflect how an individual feels about objectives, events, or people.

Consistency perception The process of organizing and interpreting sensory impressions in order to give consistency and meaning to the environment.

Cognitive dissonance An incompatibility between two or more attitudes or between behavior and attitudes.

FIGURE 13-1   Leadership Practices

1. Empower and motivate others: Consciously involve those performing the tasks in the planning, when possible. Enlist their assistance and support in creating change and improving the workplace. Get to know strengths and weaknesses of the team members and build on their strengths. Delegate and then ensure they have the tools to accomplish the tasks.

2. Recognize valuable ideas: Give ideas a try even though it means challenging tradition. Empower the teams to offer ideas; give them authority to implement the feasible ones. Challenge them to become part of solutions. Give encouragement, feedback, and praise when appropriate.

3. Serve as a symbol of the work group's identity: Have a winning philosophy that includes professional ethics and a value system.

4. Create a vision: Take time to plan for the long-range future of the department; share the planning and the goals; share the overarching vision; explain the facility mission; and be passionate, intense, and inspirational as the vision takes shape. As new issues arise and policies are developed, communicate and negotiate.

5. Renew the tangible (including people) and intangible resources: Manage them for the future well-being of the facility.

6. Network externally to promote data/information dissemination to customers: Show a willingness to negotiate.

7. Demonstrate credibility to maintain trust: Credibility encompasses candor, integrity, self-control, professional ethics, and moral conviction.

8. Listen, listen, and listen: Keep in touch internally and externally; the best method for developing a sensitivity to employees' needs is to listen. Understand their dreams, their sense of values, and what rewards them. Let them know you care. But, be willing to take a courageous stand on an issue when necessary.

9. Maintain a standard of excellence: Expect excellence, reward excellence, and live excellence.

With this knowledge of attitudes, managers can listen, observe, and take steps to reduce dissonance in the work setting. This may involve something as simple as making sure team members are aware of why change is taking place, why tasks are performed in a specific way, how they can assist in making decisions about tasks, or how external pressures affect their tasks. In the example given above, the manager has the opportunity to use several of the leadership practices in Figure 13-1.

PERSONALITY TRAITS AS PREDICTORS OF BEHAVIOR

Some organizations use personality testing, such as Myers-Briggs Type Indicator (MBTI), to identify various combinations of personality traits to better understand individuals and leaders (The Myers & Briggs Foundation, 2014). This tool examines four dichotomies of introversion (I) versus extroversion (E), sensing (S) versus intuition (N), thinking (T) versus feeling (F), and judging (J) versus perceiving (P). The results are identified through the use of the four letters that represent the individual's preferences for each of the dichotomies. For example, somebody results of extroversion, sensing, thinking, and judging would be reflected as ESTJ. There are 16 different personality types that can be reflected through Myers-Briggs. If an HIM professional mentors a student to help determine what type of HIM specialization, this could be applied by matching the combination of dichotomy preferences. Somebody with the combination of INTF would probably work better as a coder or position that has less contact with others, while somebody with the ESTJ combination would be a good fit for a position involving interaction with others, such as a patient advocate.

Personality traits were mentioned in the previous section as they relate to managerial styles. Knowing the major traits that are predictors of employee behavior is also useful. Stephen Robbins and Mary Coulter (2012) reports on research findings that describe several major personality traits appearing to affect behavior in organizations. Some of these traits have a strong relationship to various cultures and, with our increasingly multicultural work force, an understanding of how these traits affect employee behavior enhances managerial insight.

A leadership style that incorporates traits of both laissez-faire and autocratic leaders is **democratic leadership**. These leaders maintain control of decision making but encourage followers to provide input and reflect that the input plays a valuable role in decisions that are made. AHIMA's organizational structure and bylaws reflect democratic leadership. Decisions are made by the elected and appointed leaders, but input from members is actively solicited. The AHIMA House of Delegates provides input toward decisions made that impact the organization and members. The input of the House of Delegates is the result of the delegates soliciting input from members in their respective component state associations, so their votes are representative of the input of the members.

Bureaucratic leaders are interested in the needs and concerns of followers, yet they maintain complete control in decision making. Bureaucratic leaders have a high value for following rules. HIM professionals working in positions focused on regulatory compliance are generally bureaucratic leaders.

Individuals have unique sets of personal traits, which cause different people to have differing styles of leadership. **Laissez-faire** is a French term that translates literally to "let it do its own thing," This management approach has a low level of involvement by the leader, allowing the followers to function on their own. This leadership style is well suited for an HIM manager who is overseeing a department of self-directed work teams.

The extreme opposite of somebody with laissez-faire leadership traits is an **autocratic leader**, who are stern, rigid, controlling, and do not welcome input from followers. Some also refer to this leadership style as **authoritarian leadership**. Autocratic leaders contribute to efficiency and timeliness for followers.

Democratic leadership A leadership style that maintains control of decision making but encourages followers to provide input and reflect that input plays a valuable role in decisions that are made.

Bureaucratic leader A leadership style that is interested in the needs and concerns of followers, yet they maintain complete control in decision making.

Laissez-faire A management approach that has a low level of involvement by the leader, allowing followers to function on their own.

Autocratic leader A leadership style that is stern, rigid, controlling, and does not welcome input from followers.

Authoritarian leadership The measure of a person's belief in status and power differences among people in organizations.

However, some followers may resist this type of leader due to resentment of traits exhibited by an autocratic leader. HIM professionals with an autocratic leadership style who work in management positions may pose problems in organizations that encourage employee involvement in contributing to performance improvement activities, as the employees may interpret the controlling nature as a manager who does not want input from the employees. This could mean that the employees would refrain from submitting potentially useful performance improvement suggestions to contribute to the performance improvement program of the organization. Persons with high authoritarian personalities perform well in structured jobs where rigid rules and policies define work parameters. Authoritarianism is a measure of a person's belief in status and power differences among people in organizations. When assigning tasks, team members should be chosen carefully for the type of position needed and the interaction involved. When the position demands sensitivity, tact, and adaptation, applicants with low authoritarianism should be chosen.

Machiavellianism is a measure of the degree to which people believe that ends can justify means. This trait is named after the sixteenth-century writer who articulated how to manipulate and gain power. Persons high in this trait do well in positions that require bargaining skills. They should not be chosen for positions where ethical implications are high or for those lacking well-documented standards of performance.

Self-esteem is defined as an individual's degree of like or dislike for himself or herself. Research has shown that people with high self-esteem are more willing to take unpopular stands and are willing to take risks. Also, it is found that employees who tend toward high self-esteem have greater job satisfaction.

Locus of control is a trait with two components. The first is internal, where people believe they control their own fate. The second is external, where the belief is that people are pawns of fate. It has been demonstrated that employees with high externality are less satisfied with their jobs. In addition, they tend to blame others for problems such as blaming their team leader for a poor performance evaluation. Employees who believe in internal locus of control, on the other hand, tend to explain events in terms of their own actions (Robbins & Coulter, 2012).

Robbins and Coulter mention another personality trait that has recently been acknowledged for study. Called **self-monitoring**, it refers to an individual's ability to adjust behavior to situational factors. Initial studies show employees with a high degree of self-monitoring are capable of presenting themselves differently, depending on the situation. In other words, they have different faces depending on the audience. One characteristic of high self-monitoring useful for HIM managers is that employees with this trait tend to observe the behavior of others and adapt accordingly. When hiring employees who will be working with the patients and their families, this trait could be a strength (Robbins & Coulter, 2012).

Machiavellianism A measure of the degree to which people are pragmatic, maintain emotional distance, and believe that ends justify means.

Self-esteem An individual's degree of like or dislike for him or herself.

Locus of control A personality trait with two components; internal, where people believe they control their own fate and external, where people believe they are pawns of fate.

Self-monitoring A personality trait that measures an individual's ability to adjust his or her behavior to external situational factors.

The effort to match personalities and attitudes with the work environment for effective behavioral response is an ongoing challenge for HIM managers. When consideration can be given to matching personality types with compatible work environments, the result offers efficient performance, greater job satisfaction, and effective teams.

PERCEPTIONS AS PREDICTORS OF BEHAVIOR

The discussion of attitudes and personality traits as behavior predictors may give the impression that HIM managers can conduct several applicant interviews, assess the strengths and weaknesses of each applicant, and choose the one with the best match of traits for the work environment. Of course, it is not that simple. Education and experience are also considerations. Another consideration is **perception**, which is the process of organizing and interpreting sensory impressions so as to give meaning to the environment. Research gives credence to the axiom that individuals looking at the same thing perceive it quite differently (Robbins & Coulter, 2012). The practice example illustrates this point.

Perception
The process of organizing and interpreting sensory impressions in order to give meaning to the environment.

	PRACTICE EXAMPLE

Jeanne, the record-processing team leader, verbalizes in a management meeting that she is finding it difficult to obtain timely data she needs from Gwen, a disorganized medical staff relations coordinator. In negative terms, Jeanne states that when data are not available on the due date, Gwen explains to her that because the information must be verified before release, it is often not ready by the tenth of the month. By asking if other team leaders are having difficulty working with the medical staff relations coordinator, Jim, the manager, opens the floor for discussion. "I find Gwen very easy to work with," responds the statistical specialist, Hal. "I am aware the monthly data are reviewed and verified by the medical director and, because of the thoughtful, deliberate actions of Gwen in verifying and releasing accurate data, I never have to question the validity of the information."

In this illustration, there are several factors that operate to shape or distort perception. One factor is the perceiver. Both Jeanne and Hal are perceivers. Their personal characteristics influence the interpretation they make of the target being perceived—the medical staff relations coordinator, Gwen. These personal characteristics include attitudes, personality, motives, expectations, and past experiences. Here it appears that expectation plays a major role in the perceptions. Jim asked questions of Jeanne and Hal and thus discovered the underlying problem. Jeanne needs the data from Gwen by the tenth of the month, whereas Hal can allow Gwen two additional days because his data are due on the twelfth of the month. By asking questions and unearthing the expectation differences, Jim is using problem-solving steps for changing interpersonal perceptions.

To solve the problem, Jim changes the deadlines for submission of the data from Gwen. Thus, the medical staff information is now needed at the same time by both the team leader and the statistics specialist. But, will Jeanne continue to perceive Gwen as disorganized? This perception is not likely to change immediately. Jim can take every opportunity to offer positive reinforcement to Gwen when the data are submitted on time and do this in the presence of Jeanne and Hal. It is likely that a series of interactions where Jeanne perceives Gwen in a positive light will need to take place in order for that negative perception to diminish significantly.

How Managers Can Shape Behavior

In the practice example, the actions taken by the HIM manager are an attempt to mold or shape future attitudes and behavior. This shaping in successive steps toward behavior that benefits the total department is a managerial tool for learning. As positive reinforcement in this fashion results in learning, so appropriate negative reinforcement shapes behavior also. For example, during meetings, managers may ignore employees who tend to frequently raise their hands and speak. In response to this negative reinforcement, these employees will tend to weaken the hand-raising behavior until it falls to acceptable levels.

Another reinforcement tool is punishment, which can result in a different type of learning. It too weakens behavior, but over time other problems may surface. HIM professionals can best use punishment as a reinforcement tool with caution.

LEADERSHIP AND GROUP BEHAVIOR

Employees, in most instances, are assigned to some type of group activity in HIM departments. This predominantly interpersonal activity increases the need for leaders to understand how personality traits and attitudes affect employee behavior. This section looks at how managers use the leadership skills already discussed to effectively lead teams in reaching their objectives. Formal sections or teams are organized to perform specific tasks within the HIM department and are detailed in the organizational design model. Not listed on the model, however, are the informal groupings. Many employees join informal groups because they find informal groups meet their social needs for security, status, and self-esteem. These informal groups within the HIM department create nonstructured social alliances that affect the attitudes, behavior, and even the productivity of the sections and their individual members (Robbins & Coulter, 2012).

A third grouping of employees consists of voluntary members who typically work together solving specific problems. These groups may be called quality circles or task forces.

Formal Group Structure

Formal groups are created by managers to perform tasks that lead to the accomplishment of departmental goals. HIM departments may have several formal groups or sections performing the major assigned activities. These groupings typically revolve around similar tasks such as transcription, coding and reimbursement, record processing, and confidentiality and release of information. Cross-functional teams, focusing on process innovation, formed within the department or across departmental lines, are becoming more common.

A department's organizational design details each team and the tasks of the members. Relationships across the teams can also be detailed but may be more easily seen from the procedures that show interactions among team members. As the groups perform the manager-assigned tasks, they develop team objectives compatible with the strategic plan for the department. While these details are performed at the department level, the cultural change process is the responsibility of upper-level management. Planning teams should involve people at all levels of the organization with education and information sharing major priorities. Enthusiasm and commitment for a self-directed work environment, with opportunity to participate in decisions and learn other job skills, can be the result of well-planned empowerment.

Education begins first with the managers. Self-directed teams demand mentors, facilitators, coaches, visionaries, and communicators. Leaders must develop the skill to assist others in leading themselves. As responsibilities change, leaders need new roles, and role-clarity sessions assist in communicating details.

To illustrate how perceptions affect group behavior, the interactions within a transcription section are examined. The section has six transcriptionists working the first shift and five working the evening shift. With this organization, the section will typically have a transcription supervisor and an evening lead transcriptionist. There may also be a secretary, depending on the level of automation. Each member of the section brings a valuable resource to the group—his or her ability to perform medical language specialist activities effectively. Members also bring their personality traits, attitudes, and perceptions. When these tend to be positive, there is a positive influence working within the section, resulting in job satisfaction and high productivity. When negative forces predominate, dissatisfaction results and lower productivity follows.

During organizational change, turning this transcription section into two effective teams may be just a change in terms, but when a name change combines with a change in leadership style, it can also build esprit de corps through cooperation and morale enhancement. As change was initiated, the transcription section was empowered to reorganize and chose to form two teams—one for the day shift and one for the evening shift. Team leaders were then chosen by the team members themselves. Empowering these teams to solve problems, develop

FIGURE 13-2   Behavioral Advantages of Team Building

The team-building steps lead managers to:

1. Understand employees and know the strengths and weaknesses of each.
2. Manage by negotiation and dialogue with a mentoring stance.
3. Build a sense of ownership that leads to continuous quality improvement.
4. Flatten the organizational structure and reduce costs.
5. Develop department teams that become self-directed groups, operating efficiently in the absence of the manager.

work schedules, choose in-service topics, and be a part of the decision making in choosing new equipment requires leadership skills from the HIM manager.

HIM managers, who can build successful teams as they lead them through goal setting and team building, may choose to employ a facilitator skilled in reengineering to ensure all the tools necessary for this effort are in place. Figure 13-2 lists the behavioral advantages of work teams.

Once a pattern of behavior is established within a team, it is called a norm. The norm is an agreement among the team members as to what constitutes appropriate behavior. Once a norm is in place, the team may pressure members to conform. A team member with low self-esteem is more likely to conform than one with high self-esteem. As team leaders are taught group behavior concepts, they will find that norms can enhance team effectiveness.

Dynamic Teams: Quality Improvement and Quality Circles

The evolution toward the team concept has been enhanced by QI concepts. Empowering employees within a team toward decision making and independent activity has led to a strengthening of the team concept. Chapter 18 details quality improvement concepts for HIM managers. With continued emphasis on quality improvement in the Joint Commission standards, this trend toward excellence will only increase.

Quality Circles

The value of quality circles in solving problems lies in the commitment of each member of the work group to solve the problem at hand. Work group members meet regularly to discuss problems within their area of responsibility, select those problems appropriate for the quality circle, and recommend a solution. Although some quality circle problems can be solved at the team level, those that cannot are referred to the department managers for further review. Team members typically rotate membership in the quality circle work group (Robbins & Coulter, 2012).

LEADERSHIP AND INFORMAL GROUPS

Embedded within formal organizations are informal groups, created by employees to meet their needs for personal security, recognition, and other needs that cannot be met by the formal structure. Participants in informal groups typically share similar values and enjoy social interaction. Members value the communication channel or grapevine afforded by the informal group. The informal setting also offers leadership possibilities and some may join for this reason.

While informal groups are not officially recognized, they offer opportunities for HIM leaders to build stronger departments through cooperative efforts. Destructive informal groups also exist and cannot be ignored. Some positive aspects of informal groups deserve consideration first.

Positive Informal Group Elements

HIM professionals have an opportunity to turn informal groups into a positive force within the workplace. Figure 13-3 lists several positive factors available to managers.

Negative Informal Group Elements

It is inevitable that informal groups will at times work at cross purposes to the objectives of the formal organization. What is best for employees is not always in the best interest of the facility. A role conflict results. Since organizational change may be viewed as a threat to informal groups, managers can approach change with the informal group values and interests in mind.

By integrating the interests of the informal groups with those of the formal departmental objectives, HIM managers can maintain a strong leadership role where understanding and acceptance are valued. Figure 13-4 lists several negative factors for informal groups.

FIGURE 13-3   Positive Informal Group Factors

1. *Simplifies management's role:* When managers understand the informal organization groups within the department and know the leaders of the informal groups, delegating tasks and initiating change can be instituted in a way that is complemented by the informal group values.

2. *Complements the formal structure:* Generates flexibility and spontaneity that cuts across formal barriers to accomplish activities.

3. *Provides social stability:* Employees gain a sense of belonging and self-worth as part of an informal group; the group meets human needs and offers acceptance.

4. *Offers a channel of communication:* Experience can give managers the ability to use the informal grapevine to determine feelings and attitudes of employees on specific issues; informal leaders communicate information shared by the managers and offer feedback when positive controls are present.

FIGURE 13-4   Negative Factors of Informal Groups

1. Objectives of the group may not be consistent with organizational or departmental objectives.
2. Roles in the informal group may conflict with roles in formal groups.
3. The group may feel threatened by organizational change and will cease being an effective group.
4. Gossip may get started through the informal nature of communication within the group.

LEADERSHIP AND FOLLOWERSHIP

Robert Kelley has authored a book on the flip side of leadership: *Followership-Leadership-Partnership* (1992). Dr. Kelley brings to our attention the total picture of one's role in a work setting. Explore the activities of several managers for a week and it quickly becomes evident that more time is spent being a follower of leaders up the organization than in leading those down the organization. Dr. Kelley suggests that more attention be paid to this **followership** role. He outlines six areas of outstanding skills exemplary followers have developed:

Followership
The theory that managers spend more time following leaders up the organization than in leading those down the organization.

Attending to self-management

Caring and commitment

Building confidence

Learning how to contribute

Building credibility

Having a courageous conscience

Followers with these exemplary skills consider themselves as just having a different role than their leaders, not as inferiors. At the other end of the spectrum are people who are alienated as followers. They lack the team spirit that leads to developing the exemplary skills outlined above.

In the middle of the spectrum are the majority of followers, according to Dr. Kelley. These followers tend to let others do the thinking and planning for them. They also prefer to figure out which way the wind is blowing and then react accordingly.

Leaders, who have developed the leadership practices outlined earlier and have developed exemplary followership skills, will gain an understanding of their employees and predict their behavior. With this knowledge, they are positioned to encourage the exemplary followers, develop the mainstream and alienated followers, and motivate followers toward reaching full potential. Motivation is the focus of Chapter 14.

SUMMARY

Leading is defined as the management function involved in motivating employees, directing others, resolving conflicts, and selecting effective communication channels. Understanding why humans behave as they do assists managers in this effort.

Leadership power is delegated by upper-level management. Through appropriate use of this power, HIM managers lead employees as they develop their personality traits through effort and practice.

The major predictors of behavior are attitudes, personality traits, and perceptions.

Managers shape behavior by understanding these predictors and shaping behavior appropriately.

The team approach to organization design results in group behavior that is enhanced by empowerment and increased responsibility. Informal groups also exhibit behavior in the workplace with positive or negative elements.

Followership skills help managers understand employees and predict their behavior. As exemplary followers, HIM managers can assist employees in reaching their full potential.

CRITICAL THINKING EXERCISES

1. Develop a profile of personality traits that an HIM professional beginning her own transcription firm would value.
2. Assess the attitudes of employees you have observed recently and categorize them into three attitudes as predictions of behavior.
3. Relate a personal experience with cognitive dissonance and the action you took to return to consistency perception.
4. Document the informal groups to which you belong and state the value you find in membership.
5. Identify three reinforcement tools of value to managers.
6. Describe how formal groups are structured in the workplace and how they differ from informal groups.
7. Give five behavioral steps in team building.

APPLICATION OF THEORY EXERCISES

1. Using the personality traits identified in this chapter, develop a list of the traits best adapted for various positions in an HIM work setting.
2. Interview two HIM professionals by asking questions about their skills in followership. Be prepared to discuss the results of this survey in class.

INTERNET ACTIVITY

Find an online personality test similar to Myers-Briggs, and take it. Were your results what you expected?

REFERENCES

Kelley, R. (1992). *Followership-Leadership-Partnership*. New York, NY: Doubleday.
Robbins, S., & Coulter, M. (2012). *Management* (11th ed.). Upper Saddle River, NJ: Pearson.

The Myers & Briggs Foundation. (2014). MBTI® Basics http://www.myersbriggs.org/my-mbti-personality-type/mbti-basics/
Zaleznik, A. (2004). Managers and leaders: Are they different? January 2004 issue. *Harvard Business Review*.

SUGGESTED READINGS

Rollins, G.. (2010, January). Leading: What it means in HIM. *Journal of AHIMA, 81* (1), 30–33.

Sheridan, P.T., & Smith, L.B. (2009, Summer). Redefining HIM leadership: Toward an HIM leadership framework: A commentary on HIM leadership. *Perspectives in HIM, 6.*

CASE STUDY

Sara has worked for 10 years as a scanning clerk for Memorial Hospital, which is a union organization. Her previous experience includes a variety of positions in the organization over a period of 8 years. Her father serves on the facility's governing board.

Over the years, Sara had been subject of many different disciplinary actions related to attendance, poor performance, and conduct. Rumor had it that Sara had threatened physical harm to supervisors over the years, so her behavior and performance problems were overlooked by management.

Sara also had a history of work-related injuries, and she was on medical leave when Rhonda was hired as Sara's new supervisor. Upon hire, Rhonda reviewed the duties of all in the department and developed new performance standards. Upon Sara's return, she was provided with training on the new performance standards and requirements to submit daily work logs. Sara did not submit her daily logs and had to be reminded several times by Rhonda to do so. Rhonda performed random audits of work reported and found the following:

1. Loose reports were logged as being scanned but were found hidden at a later date.
2. Information had been requested for billing, but documentation was never sent, which resulted in jeopardizing insurance payments.
3. Sara had been caught multiple times making personal phone calls, including ordering a pizza during a time that was not a scheduled break period.

When Rhonda confronted Sara about these issues, Sara raised her voice so that the entire department could hear and accused Rhonda of targeting her as an individual. The following day, Rhonda met with Sara first thing in the morning to provide a task list for the day and helped her set priorities. Through positive reinforcement and continued daily coaching, Rhonda attempted to motivate Sara to complete required tasks in a professional manner. After 2 weeks of this daily process, Sara continued to have performance issues, including a significant incident that resulted in a $60,000 billing loss. Rhonda had submitted all of the issues to the department director, Abigail, who forwarded them to administration for further discussion. Abigail and Rhonda were told to approach the situation carefully, as administration feared that Sara and her father may start a legal battle since her father had already voiced concerned to administration that Sara was being treated unfairly. Additionally, others in the department had complained to Rhonda regarding Sara's unprofessional behaviors and poor performance issues. Some of the employees were so discouraged that they were considering transfer to other departments to escape the issue.

How should Rhonda proceed with the situation in a manner that addresses all areas of concern? Share the rationale for your decision.

CHAPTER 14

Motivating for Leadership in the Health Care Environment

LEARNING OBJECTIVES

After completing this chapter, the learner should be able to:

1. Relate motivational theories to HIM situations.
2. Apply motivational methods to improve productivity.
3. Describe the three major views of conflict and the differences among them.
4. Explain the role of the HIM manager in conflict resolution when self-directed teams perform departmental activities.
5. Suggest strategies for motivating difficult employees.
6. Define stress, and suggest methods HIM managers can use to keep stressors from disrupting departmental activities.

INTRODUCTION

HIM leaders who develop motivational strategies and apply them consistently can see increased productivity, higher levels of quality, and creative solutions to team problems. This chapter explains how leaders can utilize motivational theories in developing strategies that will make a difference.

The last section of this chapter leads into a discussion of conflict and stress—factors that can thwart the best manager's efforts toward motivating the teams. Professional and highly skilled employees in health care are particularly susceptible to stressors that detract from goal attainment.

MOTIVATIONAL CONTENT THEORIES

Motivation, the term commonly used to refer to an individual's level of ambition to do something, is a topic that has been a constant concern of managers. Motivation may be generated through intrinsic or extrinsic factors. **Intrinsic motivation** is performance of a task because it is personally enjoyable or personal value is seen in a certain behavior. For example, many people find intrinsic motivation to pursue a career in the health care field because they enjoy helping others. Coders often feel intrinsic motivation about their work because they enjoy the challenge of searching for details. A common statement by HIM professionals is that their passion about pursuit of career growth field comes from enjoyment of learning new things. This is also intrinsic motivation. **Extrinsic motivation** is performance of a task because of a potential reward or penalty. Employees are extrinsically motivated to be at work on time every day to avoid punishment or getting fired. Students are extrinsically motivated to put effort into writing research papers or studying for exams, trying to get good grades.

Both intrinsic and extrinsic motivation are based on the concept of doing something in order to obtain an outcome that is positive or avoiding an outcome that is negative. A theory that follows similar principle is the **expectancy theory of motivation**, which is based on the belief that an action will result in an outcome that is desired or expected. An example is that an employee will attend a training seminar with the expectancy of learning new skills that will be valuable on the job.

A series of studies were performed in the 1920s at the Western Electric Hawthorne facility to examine the effects of lighting on productivity of workers. However, an unexpected result emerged through analysis. It was

Motivation A willingness to exert high levels of effort to reach departmental goals, conditioned by the ability to satisfy some employee need.

Intrinsic motivation Performance of a task because it is personally enjoyable or personal value is seen in a certain behavior.

Extrinsic motivation Performance of a task because of a potential reward or penalty.

Expectancy theory of motivation A motivational theory based on the belief that an action will result in an outcome that is desired or expected.

determined that workers were more productive when they knew that they were being observed and less productive when they were not. Further study was performed to confirm this phenomenon, which was named the **Hawthorne effect** because of the location where the discovery was made.

Hawthorne effect
Workers are more productive when they know they are being observed.

Since the early 1900s, when Frederick W. Taylor, considered the father of scientific management, increased productivity and earnings at Bethlehem Steel, researchers have explored motivational theories in the workplace. The findings have only emphasized the complexity of motivational factors facing leaders regardless of the activities. There is consensus that motivated behavior is goal directed. Taylor showed that the goal of increased earnings changed behavior (Robbins & Coulter, 2012).

Later researchers focused on *what* motivates employees (content theories) and *how* the process takes place (process theories). To summarize their findings, the best motivator is a challenging position that offers advancement, growth, a feeling of achievement and responsibility, and earned recognition (Longest, 1990).

Maslow's Hierarchy of Needs Theory

Abraham Maslow's hierarchy of needs theory is among the best known of the motivation theories. Abraham Maslow was a psychologist who believed that all people are motivated to develop an awareness of their greatest capabilities. Maslow referred to this awareness as "self-actualization," and he outlined a hierarchy of needs that must be met prior to being able to attain the realization of self-actualization. Maslow's hierarchy of needs is useful for managers to help identify behaviors of employees trying to attain various levels within the hierarchy that need to be met prior to being able to reach the level of greatest potential. He believed that within every human being needs exist in a hierarchical fashion. His pyramid of needs is as follows: (1) physiological, (2) safety, (3) social, (4) esteem, and (5) self-actualization. He stressed that the higher needs become dominant after the lower needs are satisfied (Longest, 1990). A graphic depiction of this hierarchy of needs is found in Figure 14-1.

The base of the pyramid is physiological needs, such as breathing, nourishment, hydration, elimination, and sex for reproductive purposes. If these are not met, it may prevent the ability to meet needs of higher levels. For example, if an individual is not breathing, the higher levels do not even matter. The second level is safety. This addresses the sense of need for security in a variety of aspects of life, including employment security, safety of personal property, safety of family, and safety from a health perspective. Once the individual feels that applicable safety needs have been met, love and belonging needs may be reached. This includes a sense of belonging within the family unit and circles of friends. Sexual needs at this level are able to be met at a level of intimacy rather than simply to reproduce for species survival. After a sense of

FIGURE 14-1   Maslow's Hierarchy of Needs

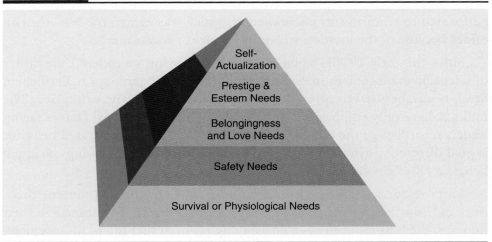

Source: Adaptation based on Maslow's Hierarchy of Needs.

belonging has been established, esteem needs may be realized. Esteem needs not only include self-esteem but also a sense of self-confidence, respect by others, the ability to respect others, and a sense of achievement. Once esteem needs have been met, self-actualization may be realized. Individuals who have achieved self-actualization are able to accept facts and lack prejudice. Self-actualization allows individuals to act spontaneously, express creativity, and adhere to a sense of morality.

The two major premises to Maslow's theory emphasize that (1) needs not yet fulfilled will motivate behavior, and (2) when one need is fulfilled, another emerges to be fulfilled. In truth, the needs in Maslow's hierarchy interact together within an individual and the lower needs recur again and again. Within this interaction, it is found that people are motivated by what they seek more than by what they already possess. Also, a person's needs are not fully satisfied; new needs are generated through life's experiences (Robbins & Coulter, 2012).

Developing situations in the HIM department that permit employees to satisfy their needs is the ongoing challenge for managers. To further complicate the picture, an action that may meet one employee's needs may not meet another's needs. This situation can lead to frustration for the employees and for the manager. Even more crucial, what will motivate the team as a whole may frustrate one or more of the team members. The following practice example shares the experience of a leader facing such a frustration.

Herzberg's Two-Factor Theory

The two-factor theory by Frederick Herzberg has been used frequently to explain job satisfaction and motivation. Despite criticisms of Herzberg's research methodology, his theories on job enrichment have been used widely

Pam, the HIM manager, had enjoyed the networking involved in developing a matrix team for the patient-focused unit reorganized recently. Two employees from the coding and reimbursement team were reassigned to the matrix team and spent most of their time on the unit. They were joined by an employee from admissions who had a coding background. The three of them were assigned responsibility for admissions, reimbursement screening, concurrent record completion, and coding. At the second meeting of the team with its managers, nursing team members suggested that care on the unit would be enhanced if the three team members rotated work hours so the early evening hours were covered. Since physicians are often on the unit during the late afternoon and evening, completing records and solving coding questions could be efficiently and effectively cared for by them. The three voiced negative feelings about a schedule change, so the HIM manager suggested that the proposal be put on hold until the next meeting, while those involved explored the various alternatives.

The cross-functional team and its success can be considered the "big picture" here. Pam and the admissions manager met to discuss the best approach for their upcoming meeting with the three team members. First, they reviewed their knowledge of the employees and discussed what would motivate them and satisfy their needs. They developed several options to offer at the meeting. Next, they made a decision to hold their options until the team members offered a plan.

At the meeting, several team members presented a plan for rotating the schedule to ensure that a team member was on the unit with knowledge in record completion and coding during the evening hours. One of the team members offered to be cross-trained for these tasks and wanted evening hours twice weekly. It was a win-win situation since the other three employees were happy to rotate their work hours for the remaining shifts. The managers withheld their recommendations and commended the team for developing a resolution.

(Longest, 1990). According to Herzberg, the factors that lead employees toward job satisfaction are distinct from those leading to job dissatisfaction. He explained that employers who work toward eliminating the dissatisfactory *maintenance* factors may end dissatisfaction, but not necessarily motivate employees. Herzberg suggests emphasizing motivating factors. Figure 14-2 lists the maintenance and motivating factors promoted by Herzberg and his followers (Longest, 1990).

A review of the differences between the two sets of factors reveals that the maintenance factors tend to be related to the external environment of work whereas the motivating factors relate directly to the job itself and the person's performance. When compared to Maslow's hierarchy of needs, the two-factor theory shows similarities. A major difference is that Herzberg carried motivation into more detail, showing that it derives mostly from the work itself (Longest, 1990).

FIGURE 14-2 Herzberg's Maintenance and Motivating Factors (Based on Robbins, 1994; and Longest, 1990)

Maintenance Factors

1. Company policy and administration
2. Technical supervision
3. Interpersonal relations with supervisor
4. Interpersonal relations with peers
5. Interpersonal relations with subordinates
6. Salary
7. Job security
8. Personal life
9. Work conditions
10. Status

Motivational Factors

1. Achievement
2. Recognition
3. Advancement
4. The work itself
5. The possibility of personal growth
6. Responsibility

Now consider the process theories of motivation and how they can assist HIM managers in their motivational efforts. First is expectancy theory, developed by Victor Vroom. It states that an individual will exert effort at a certain level to achieve the performance that will result in attractive rewards. Three primary variables surface as follows:

1. *Choice:* the degree to which an employee perceives he or she can select from different performance behaviors; the individual has freedom.

2. *Expectancy:* the degree to which an employee believes that a particular behavior will lead to success.

3. *Preferences:* the value or importance an employee attaches to potential outcomes or rewards (Donnelly, Gibson, & Ivancevich, 1987).

The vital role that perception plays in motivating employees is emphasized in expectancy theory. The importance of perceptual differences among employees is emphasized in this theory, which then gives importance to selecting employees with not only skills and abilities for specific activities but also motivational factors. Of course, once the team is in place, the manager has the opportunity to offer leadership support and encouragement by utilizing the leadership practices outlined in Chapter 12.

Since people do not work in a vacuum, equity theories have been developed to address motivation in terms of whether an employee perceives the reward he is receiving for his effort is fair. Three referents are suggested by J. Stacey Adams. He suggests employees compare their reward with others, with the system, and with their own past experiences (Longest, 1990).

To illustrate, an HIM professional has exerted great effort in leading his employees toward thinking of data and information as resources the department makes available to its customers. A new software system was installed that required extra effort from an employee, who perceived his programming skills were of value in fine-tuning the system. Suddenly, he surprised the HIM professional and his fellow employees when he angrily announced his resignation. The catalyst? He discovered the programmers in the information systems department were making significantly more than his salary.

Seldom, however, is the equity theory seen in isolation. The motivation theories discussed in this chapter cannot be viewed independently. The underlying ideas are complementary, and only by integrating them together does the full picture emerge. HIM managers can have the insight to use the very best option for the specific situation. To review, predicting employee behavior assists HIM leaders in reaching objectives; thus, taking an active role in motivating that behavior is important. By integrating motivation theories into a knowledge base and by reviewing new research studies on motivation as they come into print, HIM professionals can take advantage of the benefits offered by motivation theories.

Theory X and Theory Y

Douglas McGregor of the MIT Sloan School of Management developed two theories based on Maslow's hierarchy of needs in relation to the employee's needs toward the ability to achieve self-actualization being facilitated by the workplace environment. The first of these was **Theory X**, which is based on the assumption by managers that employees are not motivated by doing work, but rather by monetary results of a paycheck to meet personal needs. The other theory, which is more positive in nature, **Theory Y**, is based on the assumption by management that employees are intrinsically motivated by the work that they do, and that provision of optimal working conditions, including interpersonal relationships within the workplace, will enhance that motivation. Management assumptions and motivational approaches commonly based on Theory X and Theory Y are outlined in Figure 14-3.

INTEGRATING MOTIVATION THEORIES

By now, the high priority that needs to be given to the human side of management should be evident. And, motivation strategy is the catalyst leading to results. Over time, satisfied, productive employees cannot be legislated,

Theory X
The assumption by managers that employees are not motivated by doing work but rather by monetary results of a paycheck to meet personal needs.

Theory Y
The assumption by management that employees are intrinsically motivated by the work that they do and that the provision of optimal working conditions, including interpersonal relationships within the workplace, will enhance that motivation.

FIGURE 14-3   Assumptions and Approaches Based on Theory X and Theory Y

	Management Assumptions	**Motivational Approach**
Theory X	• Employees dislike work • Employees are lazy • Employees only care about their own well-being • Employees only care about getting a paycheck	• Strict supervision • Use job security and monetary compensation as coercion to get employees to do work
Theory Y	• Employees love their jobs or careers • Employees gain increased sense of satisfaction by work	• Broaden scope of position • All participation in decisions • Allow employees to set their own goals for part of performance evaluations

manipulated, mandated, or ordered. Each individual has unique, specific motivators operating within her value system. Managers can unlock this potential by following the leadership practices discussed in Chapter 12, especially those relating to participative management, such as self-directed teams and motivational theories. Some specific contemporary recommendations for motivating employees are listed in Figure 14-4.

FIGURE 14-4   Recommendations for Motivating Employees

1. Offer challenging positions that lead to a feeling of achievement. Employees must perceive the position is challenging.

2. Outline in clear language the objectives and purposes for the task. Be sure your understanding is clear before sharing with employees.

3. Match the needs and wants of the employee with the interests of the department and assign work accordingly. Empathize with employees, especially during the training period.

4. Ensure that objectives are perceived as attainable and that increased efforts will lead to rewards.

5. Remove any obstacles between the employee and the task; see that equipment and other tools are workable; ensure adequate work area; ensure adequate training period.

6. Individualize rewards and link them to performance.

7. Use communication techniques, especially listening skills. Share the "big picture" frequently.

8. Develop each team member's potential while coordinating teamwork among the group. Plan growth for individual employees, but only when it is in the best interest of the entire team.

9. Check for equity in the system periodically. Adding this task to the budget process ensures it is updated on a schedule.

It is risky for managers to suppose their personal work motivators can be transferred to employees and will predict productive behavior on the part of the total team. Each team member has strengths, weaknesses, and behavior patterns that influence motivation factors. Only by asking questions and listening can managers become acquainted with these factors. By encouraging employees to visualize the benefits and rewards of a productive team, the desire to achieve will grow. So too will the satisfaction when success follows the participative effort and the benefits are realized.

The majority of people continue to enjoy opportunities to be creative and imaginative. When tangible and measurable benefits are also derived, the motivation level increases. There is an impetus toward greater interest in continuing and accelerating the process even further. An added benefit is the carryover of enthusiasm to other employees and departments. The groundwork is then laid to increase the momentum of enthusiasm and motivation.

Motivational Methods to Improve Productivity

As managers focus on balancing efficiency and effectiveness in the workplace, the topic of productivity is a key contributor. **Productivity** is a measure of the amount of work completed in a specified amount of time. In the HIM career field, accuracy and quality of work are extremely important. Because of this, productivity standards are developed that not only define the expectation for the amount of work to be completed in a defined period of time, but also the quality expectation. For example, a productivity standard for coding emergency department records may be stated as 120 records in an 8-hour workday with at least 95 percent accuracy. Measurement of coding quantity for productivity purposes is relatively easy in most health care setting, as a report may be generated to list the accounts completed by each employee, based on login information. However, there are other areas of HIM that may be a bit more difficult to assess productivity.

Productivity
The overall output of products and services produced per employee hour that meet the established levels of quality.

Sometimes, employees may need motivation to help encourage them to meet productivity standards. There may even be times when it is necessary for employees to try to exceed productivity standards, such as at the end of a fiscal year or during a time of excessive backlog due to vacated positions waiting to be filled. Employees may be better encouraged to apply greater effort by offering an incentive. This may be financial in nature, or other incentives may be offered. Incentive pay may be provided as a productivity bonus that will be rewarded to employees meeting specific goals within a defined amount of time.

Everybody has different motivating factors. Managers should get to know their employees to identify what may motivate each one. For example, an employee who is a single parent in a lower paying position may find a monetary incentive to be motivating. However, another employee may have a wealthy spouse, works simply because she loves the HIM career field, but perhaps has low self-esteem and feels her work is not truly appreciated. This employee may find recognition for her work to be more motivating than something financial. Another employee may have been working a lot of overtime hours to accomplish a big goal, so she is exhausted by the time the goal is met. This employee may appreciate a paid day off as a productivity bonus.

MANAGING CONFLICT AND STRESS

Conflict
The perceived incompatible differences that result in interference or opposition.

Managing **conflict** is one of the most important skills that leaders can possess. Results of research studies by John Graves (1989) showed that the leadership skill most positively related to managerial success was that of handling conflict. Conflict is defined as the perceived incompatible differences between parties that result in interference or opposition (Robbins & Coulter, 2012). The term *perceived* is used to emphasize that whether or not the differences are real is irrelevant; the manager must respond to the conflict.

Figure 14-5 explains three differing views of conflict in organizations that have evolved over time. Because of the complexity of health care organizations, and the diversity of the employees and staff, conflict is fairly high and sometimes breaks over into public view through news media (Longest, 1990). HIM managers find the skills for conflict resolution are among the most valuable assets they can possess.

Functional and Dysfunctional Conflict

As difficulties arise in interpersonal relationships, HIM managers are challenged with deciding whether a conflict falls into the functional or dysfunctional category. A healthy disagreement over the objectives being prioritized for a team

FIGURE 14-5   Views of Conflict (Based on Longest, 1990)

1. *Traditional view:* Conflict is destructive and managers should work toward eliminating conflict from the organization.

2. *Human relations view:* Conflict is inevitable and a natural consequence of human interaction in organizations. Humanist philosophers observed that conflict can be a positive force for organizational performance.

3. *Interactionist view:* Some conflict is necessary for survival of organizations. Lack of conflict can result in inadequate decisions and stagnant thinking. This current view encourages a minimum level of conflict to keep teams viable and self-critical. Creativity is perceived as a response to conflict.
   a. *Functional conflict:* conflicts that are constructive and support the goals of an organization.
   b. *Dysfunctional conflict:* conflicts that result in destructive behavior and prevent organizations from achieving goals.

can lead to discussions that offer additional alternatives in the decision-making process. In this way, conflict can be a positive force in the department. On the other hand, if the team members have an underlying personal conflict that has erupted during objective-setting meetings, the destructive forces could delay action (Robbins & Coulter, 2012).

A functional conflict may arise when the coding technicians from the clinical data management team are under pressure to have records coded within 3 days of discharge and the patient-focused care center team desires to hold discharged records an extra 24 hours for a project. This conflict is relatively independent of the individuals involved, so personal conflict can be at a minimum. This allows the managers to focus on the conflict and its resolution rather than on personality differences.

Conflict Resolution

Managers respond to conflicts by assessing the situation first, determining whether to intervene, and then taking appropriate steps for conflict resolution. Not every conflict situation can be resolved effectively, but, by following the steps outlined in Figure 14-6, HIM managers can develop effective conflict resolution skills.

Guidelines that are helpful during **conflict resolution** include (1) avoidance of personal attacks or sarcastic comments, (2) no interrupting other participants, and (3) use of specific examples. It is the manager who sets the tone of the meeting, builds rapport, and establishes an atmosphere of respect and willingness to compromise. As a facilitator or mediator, the manager ensures that all participants have shared their feelings and understand the issues.

> **Conflict resolution** An action by managers to resolve conflicts through accommodation, force, compromise, or collaboration.

Managing Difficult People Amid Conflicts

Personality conflicts seem to follow some employees, and managers skilled in conflict resolution understand the need to evaluate situations involving these employees and take action. Negative team members can erode morale and disrupt the effectiveness of the team. Connie Podesta, of Communicare in Mandeville, Louisiana, offers several suggestions for managers of these difficult people:

1. Be assertive and positive. Use short answers in response to negative comments or questions.
2. Give choices; ask them to be part of the team and perform their tasks. Complaining is not a choice.
3. Refuse to listen to gossip—from the negative employees or others; bring the individual who is the subject of the gossip into the discussion of the problem.

FIGURE 14-6 Steps Toward Conflict Resolution (Based on Robbins, 1994; and Cecil, 1994)

1. Take time to review the issue and past actions before making the decision to intervene. Understand the participants, their values, personalities, and resources. *Assess* the true source of the conflict, categorized as follows:

   a. *Communication differences:* Misunication misunderstandings and cultural differences can create communication difficulties. However, personalities and value system differences may be creating the communication problem.

   b. *Structural differences:* Conflict over objectives, alternatives in procedures, and performance criteria are rooted in the structure of the organization itself. The root problem could be ambiguous policies, position descriptions, and procedures.

   c. *Personal differences:* Chemistry between the participants can cause conflict.

2. Understand your preferred style for conflict resolution. Contingency management calls for action in response to the review in step 1 and may call for changing your preferred style in a specific situation.

3. Choose whether to intervene and to what extent. Delegating discipline to self-directed teams can lead managers to serve as referees and not interfere with the team's responsibility to resolve the conflict. By keeping the participants focused on the issues, the manager acts as the facilitator in conflict resolution.

4. Know conflict resolution options and choose among them, either as a direct participant or as a facilitator.

   a. *Accommodation:* Encourage participants to place another individual's concerns and needs above their own.

   b. *Force:* Use when quick action is demanded; one participant's needs are satisfied at the expense of the other.

   c. *Compromise:* Encourage each participant to relinquish something of value. This is effective when a temporary solution is needed while the problem is reviewed for a permanent solution.

   d. *Collaboration:* Win-win solution where all participants gain advantage; time-consuming resolutions as alternatives are reviewed.

   e. *Avoidance:* Conflict may be trivial or emotions are high and a cooling-off period is needed; also of value when insufficient information makes open discussion of minimal value. Future date for discussion should be scheduled.

4. Empower the team and challenge negative team members with job enrichment activities.

5. Use an anonymous questionnaire to solicit information from each team member.

6. Take a tough line with difficult people; do not allow them to dominate the team. Be a tough facilitator in conflict resolution (Scott, 1993).

Managers may need to document unacceptable behavior for the personnel file, which can help employees recognize how disturbing negative behavior is to the team and the department. Specific examples of the behavior need to be a part of the documentation.

Managing Stress

Stress has both positive and negative aspects in an organization and can contribute to productivity of the teams and the HIM department as a whole. A formal definition of stress can be stated as a dynamic condition in which an individual is confronted with opportunities, constraints, or demands related to something desirable but perceived as unattainable (Robbins & Coulter, 2012).

Employees who have a desire to earn a promotion will have stress before a performance review. However, when employees have the abilities outlined in a position description, are capable of performing well, and have a high level of self-esteem, the stress is lessened.

Another stress factor is the personality trait of employees. Studies show that type A personalities have higher levels of stress under the same conditions compared to type B personalities. Type A personalities have a sense of urgency and strong competitive drive. In contrast, type B personalities tend to be relaxed and noncompetitive. Understanding these differences in personalities helps HIM managers respond to symptoms of stress (Robbins & Coulter, 2012).

Employee counseling through the human resources department is one alternative when employees exhibit dysfunctional symptoms of stress. Biofeedback, exercise, proper diet, and relaxation techniques are strategies for reducing stress and avoiding burnout.

In *Working Woman*, Kathryn Stechert (1988) offers several suggestions for lowering stress to acceptable levels:

1. Avoid work overload—this includes too much work, too little time to perform tasks, having necessary skills for the position, and having the tools to perform effectively.

2. Make it possible for people to succeed and then let them know they are doing a good job.

3. Give employees a sense of involvement and control by empowering them in decision making.

4. Offer employees information and feedback. Let them know what is happening in the department and the facility. Let them know how they are performing on a routine basis.

5. Admit mistakes honestly and grow from them.

Stress A dynamic condition in which an individual is confronted with an opportunity, constraint, or demand related to what he or she desires for which the outcome is perceived to be both uncertain and important.

SUMMARY

Motivation content theories include Maslow's hierarchy of needs and Herzberg's two-factor theory. These theories emphasize the complex nature of motivation.

Victor Vroom developed a process theory called expectancy. This theory states that employees are motivated by choice, expectancy, and preferences. Each of these relates to the perception employees have about the work environment.

Recommendations for motivating HIM department employees include (1) challenging positions with clear objectives, (2) matching needs and wants of employees with the tasks, (3) ensuring that objectives are attainable and rewards are given for increased effort, (4) removing obstacles to success in performance and checking for equity in the system, (5) communicating effectively, and (6) developing employees to their potential in a coordinated team effort.

Managing conflict is a major leader's task. The current view of conflict is interactionist, where conflict is considered necessary and to be encouraged at a minimum level to keep teams viable and self-critical. Functional conflict occurs when teams have conflicting priorities and may be resolved without the personal chemistry difference prevalent in dysfunctional conflicts.

Stress is a dynamic condition that confronts employees when opportunities, constraints, or demands related to something desirable are perceived as unattainable. HIM managers can reduce their stress and the stress in the workplace by avoiding work overload and allowing people to succeed with a sense of involvement and control. In the complex health care environment, managers of health information may have role overload from the sheer volume of demands placed upon them.

CRITICAL THINKING EXERCISES

1. Identify two major motivational theories and contrast their premises.
2. Choose two contemporary motivating factors that especially appeal to you and give reasons for their value in the workplace.
3. Explain how managers respond to functional conflicts versus dysfunctional conflicts.
4. List four steps that lead to conflict resolution.
5. Offer five options managers have for lowering stress in their activities.

APPLICATION OF THEORY EXERCISES

Individuals have unique priorities in life that provide motivation. Do you know what your life priorities are and what motivates you the most? Review the following list and rank them according to how you see them as personal priorities, starting with your highest priority and ending with your lowest priority. Compare your rankings with your classmates or even family members. Write a brief analysis of why your priorities are ranked the way they are and why you think others from your comparisons are different.

_____ Career   _____ Money

_____ Family   _____ Relaxation

_____ Friends   _____ Spirituality

_____ Health

INTERNET ACTIVITY

Sometimes managers need to think beyond traditional methods to motivate employees and improve morale in the workplace. Do an Internet search to find creative ideas for employee motivation and increasing morale. Summarize your findings and share why you think ideas you found may be effective or not.

CASE STUDY

You are the director of Health Information Management at a 100-bed acute care hospital. The community is experiencing economic changes due to a large factory shutting down, which has impacted some of your employees and their families. Administration has informed you that you must eliminate one full-time equivalent from your staff and pay rates have been frozen, so raises will not be awarded this year. Because of these changes, morale in your department has decreased slightly. Your department is composed of long-term employees who are generally satisfied with the work environment, so you want to do what you can to retain them and keep them motivated to continue to working in your area. Sarah is a coder who lives an hour away from work and is concerned with increasing cost of gasoline, especially since her husband lost his job with the factory closure. The release of information coordinator, David, is an RHIT, who is in school pursuing a bachelor's degree so he can become an RHIA, but the classes in the upcoming semester are scheduled when he works. Janet and Ellen are full-time scanning quality reviewers, who both have young children in day care and have expressed an interest in cutting their hours to spend more time home with their children and save money on day care. The facility has finally made the transition from hybrid records that are mostly scanned documents to an electronic health record with a small hybrid component of few scanned documents. Write a plan for how to address the employee needs, changes in tasks, administrative changes, and decreased morale related to the economy and pay rate freeze.

REFERENCES

Cecil, C. (1994). Talking through trouble. *Advance for Health Information Professionals, 4*(9), 10.

Donnelly, J., Gibson, J., & Ivancevich, J. (1987). *Fundamentals of Management* (6th ed.). Plano, TX: Business Publications.

Graves, J. (1989). Successful management and organizational mugging. *New Directions in Human Resource Management*. Englewood Cliffs, NJ: Prentice Hall.

Longest, B. (1990). *Management Practices for the Health Professional* (4th ed.). Norwalk, CT: Appleton & Lange.

Robbins, S., & Coulter, M. (2012). *Management* (11th ed.). Upper Saddle River, NJ: Pearson.

Scott, F. (1993). Empowerment: The secret to staff motivation. *Advance for Health Information Professionals, 3*(21), 22.

Stechert, K. (1988). Your best defense against office stress. *Working Woman*, August, pp. 61–64.

SUGGESTED READINGS

http://www.ncbi.nlm.nih.gov/pmc/articles/PMC3725246 /The effectiveness of managerial leadership development programs: A meta-analysis of studies from 1982 to 2001.

Doris B. Collins and Elwood F. Holton III. Article first published online: 1 JUN 2004, DOI: 10.1002/hrdq.1099.

CHAPTER 15

Communicating in the Health Care Environment

LEARNING OBJECTIVES

After completing this chapter, the learner should be able to:

1. Describe the process of communication as the message flows from the sender to the receiver.

2. List several barriers to effective communication and steps managers can take to reduce these barriers.

3. Create the outline for a training session involving a new process in the HIM department.

4. Develop and document a speech for an in-service education meeting.

5. Suggest positive uses for the grapevine communication network.

6. Describe the use of communication skills when interacting with HIM department customers.

INTRODUCTION

Ideas, policies, reports, requests, and visions—these managerial items are communicated up, down, and across a facility's channels as necessary communicating functions of leaders. It is too often assumed that senders of information and receivers of that information understand one another through these **communications**. Since understanding is the key to communicating, its definition can best be stated as the transferring and understanding of meanings (Robbins & Coulter, 2012).

Communication is critical in all aspects of health information management (HIM). HIM professionals communicate with people in their department, in other departments, and with people outside of the organization. Consider all of these stakeholders, individuals or entities impacted by or having an impact on HIM processes, and issues that may need to be communicated with each person involved in each process. Examples of stakeholder communication with HIM professionals are outlined in Figure 15-1.

Because of the amount of communication that occurs between HIM professionals and all of the stakeholders identified in Figure 15-1, it is important to be aware of processes involved in communication. It is also necessary to develop an understanding of other variables impacting communication, including type of communication and how to overcome obstacles that may interfere with communication.

Communicating involves the mental, psychological, and emotional characteristics of both individuals. Further, communicating is undertaken in various mediums, and the technical characteristics of the medium used are also involved in the process.

Communication
The transferring and understanding of meaning.

FIGURE 15-1   Communication Needs for Stakeholders

Stakeholder	Examples of Communication
Co-workers	Asking for assistance Training
Physicians	Physician queries for coding
Other departments	Coders communicating with patient accounting or billing departments
Patients	Request for release of information
Vendors	Requesting information and identification of needs for electronic health records

The process of communicating is the first focus of this chapter; then, since the leading function is especially dependent on communication, group dynamics and leading are discussed. Communicating with the customers using HIM information is covered in the final section.

THE PROCESS OF COMMUNICATION

Managers use several media or channels for communicating. The basic communication process is cyclical in nature, involving a series of messages exchanged between a sender and receiver, as illustrated in Figure 15-2.

These include oral interaction, written communications, nonverbal communications, and electronic media. In the process, the purpose for the communication or the **message** passes from the sender to the receiver. It is converted to symbolic form called **encoding**. Figure 15-2 traces the path of the message through the medium or **channel** and through **decoding**, or interpretation of the message by the receiver. Thus, an HIM manager conveys her message through this process.

As Figure 15-2 depicts, the employee sends a message by **feedback** to the manager. But, throughout the process, lightning bolts depict the **noise** that can create barriers to effective communication. These barriers may be illegible writing, garbled speech, telephone static, inattention, cultural differences, attitudes, or knowledge. Nonverbal communication, such as tone of voice and body language, also creates barriers (Robbins & Coulter, 2012).

Message
A purpose to be conveyed.

Encoding The converting of a message into symbols.

Channel The medium by which a message travels from a sender to a receiver.

Decoding
The retranslating of a sender's message.

Feedback A process for determining whether the receiver of a message understood it.

Noise Disturbances that interfere with the transmission of messages.

FIGURE 15-2   The Communication Process

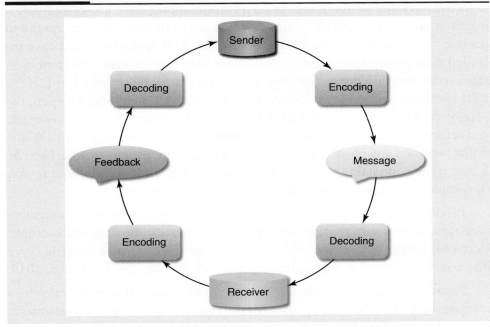

Communication starts with a sender, who initiates a message directed to a receiver. For example, a release of information (ROI) specialist in the HIM department communicates with a patient who wishes to obtain a copy of his or her health record. The patient tells the ROI specialist, "I am here to get a copy of my health record." In this instance, the patient is the sender and the ROI specialist is the receiver. The sender identifies the most appropriate media and format to convey a message to a receiver. Examples of media include writing, speaking, nonverbal, and electronic methods. Once the media is identified, the sender encodes the message into a format that best fits the needs of the media being used to convey the message. In this situation, the patient orally requests information. Written and spoken media may require the sender to assess the needs of the receiver to determine if the message needs to be encoded into a different language or into simplified terms. In the example above, the patient identified spoken communication as the appropriate media for the message and it was encoded into spoken words.

Upon receipt of the message, the receiver must decode the message in order to interpret the intended message. Upon receiving the message, "I am here to get a copy of my health record," the ROI specialist decodes the meaning of the question and provides feedback with the message, "I need you to fill out this form," while handing the patient a clipboard with the ROI authorization form. The cycle continues with the patient's feedback, which is the oral response "okay."

Considerations for Message Delivery

Effective message delivery is dependent upon appropriate use of nonverbal media in order to ensure the ability of the receiver to accurately interpret and decode the message. In the ROI scenario, the ROI specialist could have included nonverbal communication that could have sent two very different messages to accompany the instructions for the patient to fill out the form. If the ROI specialist would have provided the form without a clipboard or pen, the patient could decode that the ROI form should be taken home to complete and return, rather than complete in the waiting area. However, if the ROI specialist provided a clipboard and pen, plus directed the patient to an area to be seated while completing the form, the patient would understand that it is okay to complete and return during that visit to the department

Electronic media may have special formatting requirements for encoding messages, such as specifications for types of data that can be sent. For example, electronic billing may require specific formatting of a date to be mm/dd/yyyy. The computer system would understand the code 07/08/2014 as July 8, 2014.

Password protection is another example of encoding. If a sender encodes a message by locking it with a password, the receiver must use that password as part of the decoding process to access the message.

Medical coding may also be considered a type of encoding for electronic billing. The coder encodes the message by entering a procedure code into the computer, and the insurance company decodes the message with software that adds the description of the diagnosis to the alphanumeric code that was entered by the coder.

TYPES OF COMMUNICATION

HIM professionals use a wide variety of communication methods. These methods may be classified into major categories of verbal, written, and electronic. It is important to note that there may be some overlap with these categories, as electronic communication may involve written messages in the form of electronic mail.

Verbal Communication

Verbal (oral) communication may occur face-to-face, over the phone, or via the Internet. One benefit of verbal communication is the ability to emphasize meaning through tone of voice. Additionally, if verbal communication occurs in person, nonverbal cues enhance the message. Listening is the most important communication skill and is enhanced through active listening, which involves not just hearing the message sent, but also restatement of the message by the receiver in order to verify that the correct message was received. Oral communication may have limited effectiveness if there are language barriers, speech or hearing impairment, if there is a lot of background noise, or limited time for the exchange. If a verbal message needs to be shared with others, there is a possibility that the original message may be unintentionally altered when shared with the next recipient because the first recipient forgot important details.

Verbal communication is generally informal and permanent records of the exact messages are not retained on a regular basis. However, there are some exceptions. Voicemail is a verbal message that is recorded and maintained until the recipient deletes the message. It may be replayed and forwarded to additional recipients. Health care provider dictation of reports, such as consultations, operative reports, or discharge summaries, is another method of recorded verbal communication. In these cases, the recipient is the medical transcriptionist. Technology has played a significant role in the use of this method of communication for transcriptionists, as voice recognition and recording have been adopted by many organizations. This change has not completely eliminated the medical transcriptionist position, but it has caused significant change for a focus on editing and verification of quality in the final resulting document.

Written Communication

Written communication allows a message to be shared with others in a manner that allows the original message to be unchanged. Written communication in health records and other areas of HIM may be admissible as evidence in court and is one reason why documentation of this communication media must be carefully constructed to ensure accuracy and clarity of the intended message. Important uses of written communication in HIM are documentation of medical care using electronic health records (EHRs) and e-mail, and capturing communication among health care providers and professionals.

Electronic Communication

Electronic communications may be accomplished through the use of common software applications such as spreadsheets, databases, word processing, graphics, presentation, and e-mail. EHR systems and components of EHR systems communicate electronically with each to share information. Technological advances related to electronic communication have introduced many opportunities to improve communication, but this has also been accompanied with some challenges.

Positives of Electronic Communication

Communication via technology, the Internet, and mobile devices is increasing in HIM in a variety of ways. Many organizations have employees working remotely, using electronic communication to complete procedures. Some of the challenges with remote employment that are related to this (other challenges will be addressed in future chapters) include the barrier of lack of face-to-face interaction between employees and managers, technical support not immediately available in-person, compatibility issues between personal computers and health care software, and unexpected outage of power or Internet service without institutional backup power.

Electronic communications, also used as a means of consultation between health care professionals located in different areas, allow for easier access to health records by remotely located specialists for complex conditions and present an opportunity to fill needs for overnight shifts. For example, some institutions contract with services that are associated with radiologists located in countries on the other side of the globe in order to keep 24-hour staff for such purposes as reading digital radiology imaging.

Challenges with Electronic Communication

Along with the inability to observe nonverbal cues, electronic communication does not contain voice inflections that may supplement verbal, non-face-to-face communication. For these reasons, it is important to ensure that adequate detail is included in electronic messages on both ends, paying careful attention to ensure that the recipient understands the terminology. As electronic communications have expanded to involve communication with patients, this is even more critical, as there is no human in the communication process to identify nonverbal cues that reflect that the patient does not thoroughly comprehend the instructions or content of the messages.

Electronic Communication Standards

When electronic communications are used for any purpose in health care, it is important for the entities involved to strictly adhere to standards that are in place to ensure compatibility among devices that communicate with each other. Communication standards address settings within the EHR systems, formats used in fields, and interoperability. For example, if a laboratory result processing system does not meet communication standards for interoperability, there may be a chance that laboratory results will not import properly into the EHR. HIM professionals directly involved in working with vendors and the information technology (IT) department for EHR components should make certain that all components in an information system are certified by the **Certification Commission for Healthcare Information Technology (CCHIT)**. CCHIT is an independent, voluntary, private sector initiative organized as a limited liability corporation, which was awarded a contract by the United States Department of Health and Human Services (HHS) to develop, create prototypes for, and evaluate the certification criteria and inspection process for EHR products. CCHIT certification of EHR components ensures that they are compatible with other CCHIT-certified components and that communication standards are met. Incompatible EHR components can result in a break in the electronic communication process at one or more points.

Certification Commission for Healthcare Information Technology (CCHIT) An independent, voluntary, private sector initiative organized as a limited liability corporation, which was awarded a contract by the United States Department of Health and Human Services (HHS) to develop, create prototypes for, and evaluate the certification criteria and inspection process for EHR products.

BARRIERS IN THE COMMUNICATION PROCESS

The steps in the communication process have many points where barriers may occur. Some of these barriers are unique to specific types of communication, while others exist for all methods. For example, a power outage might only interfere with electronic communication, but a language barrier could be a problem in verbal and written communication.

Distortion is possible at any step of the communication process through the noise factors that occur. But there are other barriers as well, such as filters, selective perception, time constraints, language, emotions, and nonverbal cues.

The communication process is far from perfect. It is often prone to noise, or, interferences with various aspects of the process. Verbal communication may be disrupted by volume control issues or excessive background noise. Written communication may be illegible, or the receiver may have literacy issues. Technical complications may interfere with electronic communications; if there is an interruption in Internet service, e-mail communication will not be available until service is restored. A break in communication due to non-CCHIT-certified components falls into the category of noise interference. Encoding and decoding obstacles may include language barriers, use of medical

FIGURE 15-3   Noise in the Communication Process

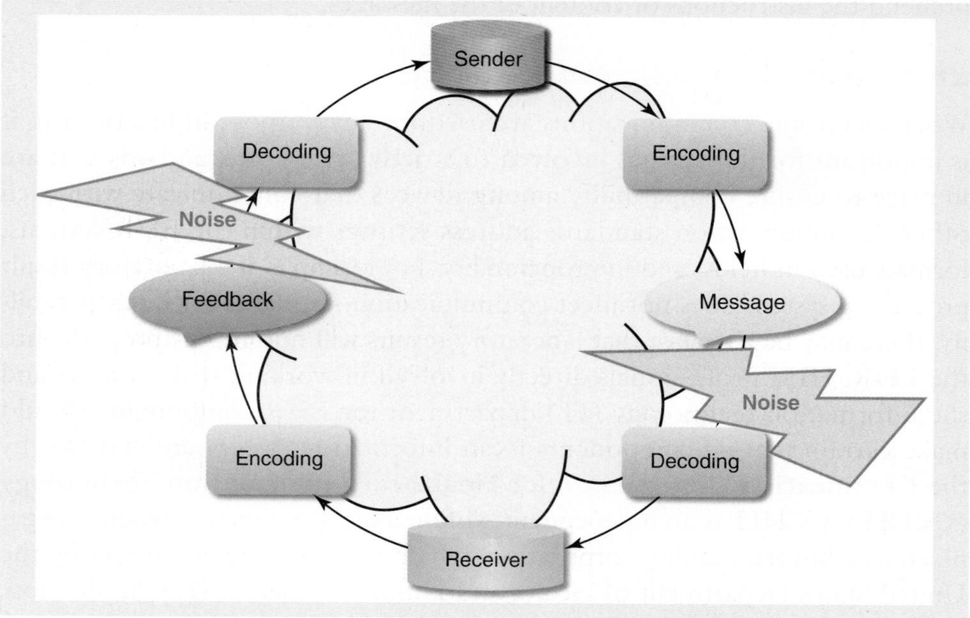

jargon, or speech, hearing, or vision impairment. The sender may try to communicate too much information at one time, send conflicting messages, omit pertinent information, or send the incorrect message. Figure 15-3 adds noise barriers to the illustration of the communication process and demonstrates how noise may impact any or all parts of the process.

Filtering

By manipulating information, the sender can make the message appear more favorable to the receiver. This may be more common as information flows upward in an organization but can also occur when upper-level management sends a message downward through several levels. Organizational culture can discourage filtering by rewarding openness (Robbins & Coulter, 2012).

Selective Perception

Past experiences, expectations, motivations, and other personal characteristics distort the perception of messages. For example, an HIM team leader interviewing a prospective coder may expect the person to put family problems ahead of work responsibilities when the prospective coder begins discussing her husband's health problems. The team leader has this expectation, having recently reprimanded a coder who was habitually late because of family illness (Donnelly, Gibson, & Ivancevich, 1987).

JOHARI Window

It is important to recognize that the sender and receiver may have different interpretations of the same word. For example, vague terms referencing size or quantity, such as a request for a large box for paper documents being retained in off-site storage following scanning. The sender knows that the box being requested is a long banker's box, which allows folders with records to fit perfectly for storage, but the receiver may be looking at two boxes and simply select the larger of the two, which may be smaller than what the sender requested or not a box that would be appropriate size for record storage. A sender may also say something to the receiver, which could be perceived as sarcasm, rather than the serious meaning intended by the sender. One tool that may be used to gain an understanding of this is called a JOHARI Window. This tool was developed in 1955 by Joseph Luft and Harrington Ingham, who created the name from a combination of their first names, Joe and Harry (Joe + Harry = JoHari).

As an example of how the JOHARI Window may be applied in an HIM department, see Figure 15-4, The JOHARI Window, which represents the situation where a coding supervisor instructs a newly hired coder to abstract all pertinent information from a record set. The new employee performed this same task at a previous employer, and the new employee assumes that the procedure is the same at the new facility. However, when the trainer reviews the work, there were a few issues: the new employee missed one item that the facility collects, and the new employee attempted to abstract an item that was collected by the previous employer, but not by the new employer. In the JOHARI Window for this scenario, the open area would reflect that the supervisor and coder both understand what is involved in abstracting information. The blind area is a list of items that are considered pertinent by the institution but were not previously shared with the new employee. The hidden area is the abstracting procedure from the new employee's previous employer, which is different than the new workplace. The unknown area is procedures performed in other

FIGURE 15-4   The JOHARI Window

	Known to Self	**Not Known to Self**
Known to Others	**Open Area** (What is known by both yourself and others) • A general understanding of abstracting a record set	**Blind Area** (What others know, but you do not) • New employer's abstracting policy
Not Known to Others	**Hidden Area** (What you know, but others do not) • Employee's previous employer's abstracting policy	**Unknown Area** (Unknown to yourself and others) • Abstracting policies for other organizations

facilities. The JOHARI Window tool helps the manager and new employee to recognize similarities and differences in perspectives, identifying common areas, and presenting potential for exploration of unknown areas.

Time Constraints

Short circuiting occurs when time pressures do not allow every team member to be a part of the communication process. Time pressures also cause distorted perceptions when the receiver rushes through the decoding process (Donnelly, Gibson, & Ivancevich, 1987).

Language

Differences in word meanings create major barriers to communication, especially when age, education, and cultural differences are present. In health care settings, technical jargon is commonplace and can distort communication because the sender may not be aware of modifications made to word meanings by the receiver (Robbins & Coulter, 2012).

Emotions

Feelings enter into how an individual receives a message; managers can avoid some distortions by considering how employees, in general, feel at certain times, such as during the afternoon hours at the end of the workweek or the week before a major holiday.

Nonverbal Cues

When nonverbal cues are inconsistent with oral communication, confusion results and the intent of the message becomes distorted. For example, when the HIM manager invites a team leader to have a chair while explaining a changed procedure, and then goes through the day's mail while listening, inconsistency reigns (Robbins & Coulter, 2012).

OVERCOMING BARRIERS IN COMMUNICATION

The list of barriers to communication seems formidable, but the following steps can make the process effective: Utilize feedback skills, empathy, listening skills, and language simplification.

Feedback Skills

By asking questions relating to the communication, managers can lessen misunderstandings. The questions should include more than "yes" and "no" answers and should be specific to the intended communication (Robbins & Coulter, 2012).

Empathy Skills

By becoming receiver oriented, managers can anticipate how a message is likely to be decoded and respond accordingly. When the education or culture gap is great, empathy is a very important tool for effective communication (Donnelly, Gibson, & Ivancevich, 1987).

Listening Skills

Listening is difficult, but managers who develop active listening skills enhance their communication ability. Active listening is defined as listening for full meaning without making premature judgments or interpretations (Robbins & Coulter, 2012).

Language Simplification

Using appropriate language for the receiver is one way managers can facilitate understanding. Jargon is acceptable when the audience understands the meaning. Regardless of the channel used for communicating, the language used should be clear and concise (Robbins & Coulter, 2012).

APPLICATIONS OF THE COMMUNICATION PROCESS

This section presents scenarios in which communication theories and techniques are applied by HIM professionals. These examples are representative of some very basic situations that may be encountered with HIM-related communication. The diversity of positions held by HIM professionals and the increased communication with others external to the HIM department provide countless variables that may impact communication. The customers of HIM departments expect excellence in-service as their information needs are met. These expectations are enhanced when effective communication is practiced by managers and team members.

Patient Seeking Health Care Services

The communication process can be applied to a scenario involving a patient seeking health care services. A patient calls a physician office to set up an appointment. During that phone conversation, the patient is the sender of information to the person from the office who answers the phone. When the message is received from the patient, feedback occurs as suggested appointment times or additional questions regarding the patient's needs. The sender and receiver roles are passed back and forth until the appointment is set. When the patient arrives for the appointment, the patient provides a written message by signing the appointment check in sheet at the front desk. When the provider is ready for the patient, a nurse or medical assistant calls the patient name in the waiting area, which prompts the patient to walk to the exam room. Communication in the exam room involves alternating roles as sender and receiver between the nurse or medical assistant and the patient, and the physician and the patient.

When the medical provider communicates with the patient, it is very important for the provider to be alert to both verbal and nonverbal messages in order to be consistent. After the encounter, the documentation is reviewed by the medical coder. Coding professionals contribute to the communication process when messages are prepared to be sent for billing with narrative information encoded into a language that will be understood by the computer on the payer's receiving end. Electronic communication occurs when the bill is submitted through an electronic billing system. Feedback from this communication may involve payment or a message that outlines items that are not eligible for reimbursement.

Data Collection

E-HIM Management of health information through the use of electronic technology.

Health information exchange (HIE) The electronic transmission or exchange of health information between health care providers, payers, and others, such as labs and pharmacies in order to facilitate coordination of care and provision of more efficient health care services.

HIM professionals may also be involved in processes that contribute to implementation and management of technology that is used for the purpose of collecting and storing data and for reporting information. This reporting is considered to be an electronic form of communication, as data are being communicated electronically to different agencies, third-party payers, other providers, government officials, and other users of information. Projects involving HIM professionals may include the development of networks, including intranet and Internet applications to facilitate the EHR, personal health records (PHRs), public health, and other administrative applications. Contributions of HIM professionals to technological implementation processes require communication with IT professionals to provide guidance for HIM principles that may impact or be impacted by new or changed policies or processes.

Evolving HIM Communication

Management of health information through the use of electronic technology is referred to as **e-HIM**, which includes communications in the form of electronic billing or **health information exchanges (HIEs)**. An HIE is the electronic transmission or exchange of health information between health care providers, payers, and others, such as labs and pharmacies in order to facilitate coordination of care and provision of more efficient health care services.

Communication arising from these information exchanges requires accuracy and compliance with electronic communication standards. An example of evolving HIM communication related to e-HIM is use of **patient portals**, which are websites that provide the ability for patients to access to information about test results and other personal health information without a health care professional needing to be available to answer questions or explain findings. For this reason, HIM professionals are now in a position of providing consumer education regarding reliable sources for additional information and **health literacy**, which is the ability to understand basic health information and make decisions related to personal health care management. Health literacy has become an important focus of consumer education communication provided by HIM professionals. Education was not previously a traditional HIM function, but these examples demonstrate how technology has introduced a new kind of need for HIM professionals to communicate with others outside of the more traditional communication within the HIM department, such as ROI requests.

Patient portal
A website that provides the ability for patients to access to information about test results and other personal health information without a health care professional needing to be available to answer questions or explain findings

Health literacy
The ability to understand basic health information and make decisions related to personal health care management.

GROUP DYNAMICS AND LEADING

Attending and participating in meetings is one of the responsibilities HIM managers have in health care facilities. For some managers, the hours in meetings take their toll and this drain provides the impetus for creating meetings where agendas are prepared and distributed beforehand, and other steps are taken to keep meetings short. Committee meeting agendas, minutes, and steps that increase the likelihood of effective meetings are discussed in Chapter 18. This section focuses on meetings held for training sessions and in-service seminars.

Training Sessions and In-Service Seminars

Planning a training session to introduce new techniques or processes in the department gives HIM managers an opportunity to develop meetings with a specific focus. Because of the specific focus and the interest of the team members in learning how to perform new tasks, training sessions are among the easiest types of meetings to plan. However, even though the training materials seem straightforward and the participants will be interested, leaders should prepare the presentation with care, document what they hope to accomplish, and follow public speaking guidelines.

In-service seminar planning needs the same attention to details; however, guest speakers can be invited to speak on topics of interest. Encouraging the employees to offer ideas for in-service seminars can create interest in a current topic. Both training sessions and in-service seminars need to be held periodically and documented for accrediting or licensing agencies. Making them interesting and informative for the participants gives HIM professionals experience in planning meetings and in public speaking. Chapter 18 discusses communicating effectively through committee meetings and department meetings.

Teleconferences and videos are also excellent tools for sharing up-to-date information. As employees become involved in the planning of seminars, they can become enthusiastic about learning new ideas, new technologies, and medical science. Another benefit is that change becomes a pattern of thought as team members visualize possibilities that are open to them.

Grapevine Communications

Grapevine The informal communication network.

Informal social groups have a communication network that is referred to as the **grapevine**. Even the health care facility that boasts excellent communication tools through formal structural lines is unable to disclose all the information that is available on the grapevine. Managers can use the grapevine to advantage, as already mentioned; however, distortions can lead to false conclusions and bad decisions, so care must be taken. The grapevine is best used as a barometer of opinions, attitudes, and concerns.

SUMMARY

As the scope of the HIM profession continues to expand, so do the participants of HIM communications. The basics of the communication cycle may be applied to all methods of communication. HIM professionals must be mindful of selecting the most appropriate communication media to meet the needs of the message content and recipient. The process of communicating effectively offers managers opportunity for success. The process travels in steps from the sender, where encoding takes place and selection of the channel or medium for transmission is made. The channel may be face-to-face communications, written communications, telephone, group meetings, or electronic mail. Nonverbal media also communicates. As the message reaches the receiver, it is decoded or interpreted and then feedback completes the loop.

Noise such as filters, selective perception, time constraints, language, and emotions can be barriers to effective communication.

Managers can overcome these barriers by being aware of them and utilizing feedback, empathy, listening skills, and language simplification.

Technological developments have already introduced a variety of new options for communication over a distance and new methods are likely to continue to be developed in the future, related to e-HIM and remote access to health information.

Managers communicate through leading in training sessions and in-service seminars. Through careful planning, HIM professionals can enthuse employees and assist in their learning process through periodic meetings.

The grapevine is a communication network involving informal social groups. This network cannot be eradicated and managers can use it to advantage for communication. There are frequent distortions in messages on the grapevine, which must be expected. By keeping documentation updated and using effective communication skills, HIM leaders can employ both formal and informal lines of communication to advantage.

Being of service to HIM customers includes excellence in communication skills.

Conflict resolution takes place as communication is increased. Teams within the department also benefit from effective communication when their activities are dependent on one another.

CRITICAL THINKING EXERCISES

1. Answer "yes" or "no" to the following communication questions; be prepared to discuss them in class.
   a. I choose to use face-to-face communication when talking with a friend about a sensitive topic.
   b. My writing is clear, reasonably concise, and free of cliches.
   c. When I am talking with other people, I am an active listener by keeping their points of view in mind without being judgmental.
   d. When I am talking with others about problems or opinions, I listen and ask questions, rather than offer lectures.
   e. I keep alert for nonverbal communication when interacting with others.
   f. I ask my friends for feedback on my communication skills.
   g. I keep my eyes on the speaker as much as I can.
   h. I use open-ended questions that encourage another person to share more freely.
   i. I let the other person finish her own sentence, even when pauses seem quite lengthy.

2. Outline six steps in communicating and describe each step briefly.

3. Explain how the communication process can be distorted by barriers.

4. What are the major disadvantages to grapevine communications?

APPLICATION OF THEORY EXERCISES

1. Prepare an outline for an in-service education talk on a topic of your choice.
2. Examine the roles of the following stakeholders involved in HIM processes and relate them to the most effective methods of communication that should be used. More than one may be used and each role may involve communication of different methods with different people.
   - Coder
   - ROI specialist
   - Director of HIM
   - Physician
   - Risk manager
   - Health care consumer

INTERNET ACTIVITY

Remote work settings and professional communications with colleagues in different geographic locations have presented new communication needs. Search online for information about different technology options that facilitate communicating over a distance, using electronic communications that allow sharing computer screens and providing the ability to video conference.

CASE STUDY

You are the HIM director for a 500-bed acute care hospital, which is part of a health care network that includes four other hospitals and 30 physician office practices. You have been asked to help develop a communication policy that addresses selection of appropriate media and guidelines for use of each type of communication media. List suggestions that you might make for the guidelines.

REFERENCES

Breske, S. (1993). Communication is key to being a good supervisor. *Advance for Health Information Professionals, 3* (25), 10.

Donnelly, J., Gibson, J., & Ivancevich, J. (1987). *Fundamentals of Management* (6th ed.). Plano, TX: Business Publications.

Luft, J., & Ingham, H. (1955). *The Johari Window, a Graphic Model of Interpersonal Awareness.* Proceedings of the western training laboratory in group development. Los Angeles: University of California.

Robbins, S., & Coulter, M. (2012). *Management* (11th ed.). Upper Saddle River, NJ: Pearson.

Terry, G., & Franklin, S. (1982). *Principles of management* (8th ed.). Homewood, IL: Richard D. Irwin.

SUGGESTED READINGS

http://myphr.com/HealthLiteracy/

http://www.healthit.gov/providers-professionals/ehr-interoperability

SECTION V

Controlling to Meet Information Needs of Health Care Facilities

CHAPTER 16

The Focus of Control in Health Information Management

LEARNING OBJECTIVES

After completing this chapter, the learner should be able to:

1. Define controlling, and explain the relationship to the other management functions.
2. Describe ways management information systems (MISs) assist HIM managers in quality improvement (QI) activities.
3. List the four major steps involved in the control process.
4. Give several methods managers can use to obtain subjective monitoring information.
5. Identify steps that will ensure integrated information systems for obtaining valid monitoring data.

INTRODUCTION

The controlling function of management is the final link in the managerial chain. Not isolated, it is a valuable link in the continuous chain of the integrated model of management. HIM managers delegate processing activities to employees and empower them to perform these activities, which then require monitoring and modification. This chapter begins with a discussion of the controlling function within an integrated management approach. Chapter 17 emphasizes quality improvement (QI) concepts and the growing importance that continuous monitoring for improvement is having in service industries throughout the country, and specifically in health care facilities.

Monitoring

A process of taking the action necessary to be aware of the quality and quantity of employee activities that may be performed by manual or electronic means.

Monitoring and improving quality using QI concepts and tools use management information systems (MISs) to collect raw data, analyze the data, and integrate these data into information that can be assessed and disseminated. Systems provide needed information to all departments in the facility as computer hardware and software enhancements are crucial to obtaining reliable data for implementing QI. HIM professionals must have input into the purchase decisions to ensure the data captured in the MIS will meet internal customer needs for strategic information in controlling and making decisions that best serve the facility and its customers.

In Chapter 19, specific controlling tools for measuring productivity are detailed. They include work sampling and the work standards that are given broad measurable identities in the planning and organizing functions of management. The last chapter in this section is devoted to several human resource management aspects of controlling.

CONTROLLING DEFINED

Controlling has traditionally been the fourth function of managers in the process approach continuum. In this traditional sense, controlling ensures that plans are accomplished through monitoring employee activities and then through remedial action to correct significant variations (Robbins & Coulter, 2012). Once plans are approved in accordance with the vision/mission of the facility, and organization of the department's resources is in place, the activities performed are evaluated for efficiency and effectiveness. In today's health care environment, it is essential that departments monitor and document processing factors of production through controlling activities.

There is no need to think of controlling as a sinister activity involving surveillance, correction, or even reproach. Rather, it can be normal, positive, future oriented, and dynamic. Through automated, continuous monitoring of processes and activities, managers are able to focus objectively on problem avoidance or correction. Improving the systems to better meet the needs of customers then becomes the focus of the controlling function.

SETTING STANDARDS AND MONITORING PERFORMANCE

Continuing with an integrative theory of management, this section melds systems, behavioral approaches, and contingency approaches in a cohesive pattern to give controlling the continuity of a total process approach. Integrating the best of these approaches seems particularly applicable with the QI model where the customers' changing needs, wants, and expectations are a major focus. Using MIS to meet increasing information demands helps HIM managers to refashion department functions to meet the opportunities of the future.

Of course, health care facilities across the country are not increasing their MIS capabilities in a uniform manner. Flexible management approaches are needed by HIM managers as their personal vision may be quite divergent from the vision of any particular health care facility. As the HIM manager attends meetings, reads the literature, and enthusiastically endorses and shares knowledge about effective and efficient methods for QI through new technologies, all levels of management can join in and "catch the spirit" that quality health care comes through quality information. However, the HIM manager may need to actively promote change and encourage the need for tools that can offer continuous monitoring and, as a result, continuous improvement.

For example, knowing that the Joint Commission is planning an agenda for change that includes a performance improvement (PI) focus or awareness that the Centers for Medicare and Medicaid Services (CMS) has published an intent to require additional billing data, gives the HIM manager powerful motivation to promote change. Negotiating for the budget necessary to capture and analyze the data is also enhanced with this knowledge.

As upper-level management commits to implementation of PI initiatives and the cultural changes involved, the HIM manager is positioned to be a leader in improving the interrelated processes that support the revised mission of the facility. By taking the initiative in PI tools and techniques in problem-solving situations, the HIM manager will be ready to share success stories throughout the facility.

Through preparation, the HIM manager is also ready should the facility choose to move into a major **work transformation** or reengineering effort which, in reality, may focus on the human side of health care. The long-range objectives for reengineering, productivity standard setting, redesigning of systems, or PI must include a stable, financially sound organization that emphasizes quality for the customers and enhances employee work life.

Work transformation See reengineering.

Setting Standards

One of the recommendations from the 1990 Institute of Medicine study is that information in the electronic health record (EHR) be designed to "manage and evaluate quality and cost of the data within the system" (IOM, 1991). Data in the EHR and related information assist in evaluating QI activities. The HIM manager can be an information innovator and can participate in the development of an MIS that will access required data across the network for use in making these QI decisions for measuring and modifying processes in the pursuit of excellence.

Looking for valid monitoring data within the department's present systems is one of the challenges of the management team as QI tools are first used. With increasing capabilities of MISs, the capture of meaningful data can frequently be incorporated into the routine activities for setting performance standards with minimal extra cost.

Reviewing the literature, visiting with vendors, and interacting with peers are excellent activities for keeping managers aware of capabilities and enhancements to MISs and for monitoring productivity. Sharing this knowledge with the department managers and team members will assist in discussions of the most useful applications for continuous monitoring of specific HIM activities.

Tools for Standard Setting

Section II emphasized the role of the manager in establishing standards for the total department and for each section. In this chapter, these standards are explored in greater detail. Four steps are typically involved:

1. Capturing data to measure actual activity
2. Analyzing the data into integrated information for comparison with the standard
3. Determining whether variations are significant
4. Taking team and managerial action

Just as objectives prepared during planning are to be measurable, so the systems implemented to monitor activities must be measurable. Not all relevant data can best be captured electronically; managers and teams can expect to use more subjective methods also. Questionnaires, survey forms, or work sheets can be used effectively. Each has particular strengths and weaknesses, so these materials should be used in combination for reliable information.

Questionnaires

Questionnaires can be tedious to respondents, so only pertinent vital information should be requested. For example, physicians complete numerous questionnaires and are familiar with them. By explaining a questionnaire's value in maintaining or enhancing service for physicians, a manager can gain their cooperation; most will gladly share their comments in a short questionnaire.

Surveys

A popular survey method is a follow-up telephone call to recent customers. For example, this monitoring tool could be used to evaluate the service provided to those who request records or patient information from the department. Not only do the customers feel valued by the call but they willingly cooperate by responding to questions that can then become part of a monitoring process. Questions on the survey form used by the interviewer should include nonverbal communication also, such as "Was the customer's response spontaneous and positive in tone?"

Within health information services, surveys that include personal observations can generate a negative response to questions that are subjective, without careful planning. The surveyor can overcome this problem by assuming a questioning attitude, not a critical one. Several factors combine to create an activity, and any one of these factors, or a combination of some, could be a reason why variations from negative to positive may be significant. Employee interaction may be only one of the factors in the total process. By first encouraging a team spirit, a manager can defuse signs of negativism and uncover the reason for it.

One reason why it is important to use several methods and several types of data to monitor the effectiveness of a section is the importance the team will place on the criteria chosen for review. What is measured determines, to a great extent, where the team will choose to excel. Thus, a broad approach to auditing the processes builds consensus for excellence across activities within the team.

History of Total Quality Management for Monitoring Quality

The terminology used to describe the controlling function, especially as it relates to quality, is revised periodically. The term **total quality management (TQM)** was the standard for some time, notably in industry. Many articles, books, and manuals are available to assist in becoming familiar with TQM concepts and tools. This chapter gives an overview of TQM and includes a list of suggested readings for further study.

Total quality management (TQM) A management philosophy that recognizes employee involvement in meeting customer needs and expectations.

Several Americans introduced initial TQM theories; among these were W. Edwards Deming, Walter Shewhart, and Joseph Juran. AT&T initiated early efforts toward quality control. As the Japanese began sharing their success stories, corporate America listened and responded. Deming was invited to consult with several major corporations, some of which significantly raised the quality of their products and lowered production costs. By the mid-1980s, articles appeared on the successes of these companies. Most of them were in the manufacturing sector of the economy (Robbins & Coulter, 2012).

The health care industry has watched this quality movement with interest, and seminars on Japanese-style quality circles, one component of the Japanese TQM system, slowly began to emerge by 1990. The quality assurance component of monitoring patient care retrospectively had been in place since the 1970s, with structure and form outlined by the Joint Commission.

FIGURE 16-1   DAT Model for Total Quality Management

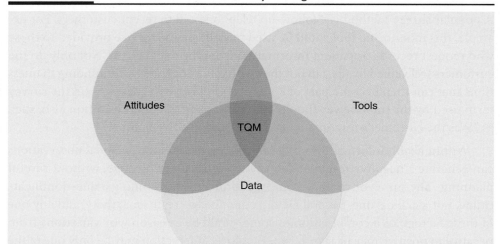

A significant study was published in 1990 by the National Demonstration Project (NDP) on Quality Improvement in Health Care that showed that the TQM model can be applied successfully in health care institutions. In its 1992 *Accreditation Manual for Hospitals* (AMH), the Joint Commission stated it is "beginning a carefully planned transition to standards that emphasize continuous quality improvement." The Joint Commission had chosen to use the phrase *continuous quality improvement* in 1992 as it initiated a transition from the term *quality assurance.* These factors gave impetus for HIM professionals to gain a working knowledge of continuous QI and share that knowledge as outlined in Chapter 17 (JCAHO, 1992). In its 1996 manual, the phrase used to describe all aspects of improvement is *performance improvement.* One model for capturing TQM concepts is the DAT Model, which represents the interrelationship among data, attitudes, and tools (Figure 16-1).

Quality management in health care has continued to evolve since the introduction of TQM. In 2001, guidelines were published for implementation of ISO 9000 quality management systems in health care. ISO 9000 considers the needs of all stakeholders, along with regulatory requirements that are related to a product or line of service. ISO 9000 was introduced into the health care sector by way of the automotive industry, as three of the major automotive companies had an interest in provision of health care services for their employees. The automotive company employers perceived implementation of ISO 9000 in health care as a means of establishing a client-supplier relationship as a component of QI and cost containment for employee health care services. ISO 9000 not only evaluates the needs of a specific industry, but also addresses needs of societal stakeholders related to that industry. ISO is based on eight quality management principles which are outlined in Figure 16-2 (ISO Central Secretariat, 2012).

FIGURE 16-2   ISO 9000 Principles

Principle 1	Customer Focus	Organizations must focus on customer needs because the organization is dependent upon their customers.
Principle 2	Leadership	Leaders set the direction and must encourage an environment that allows employees to become involved.
Principle 3	Involvement of People	Employee involvement encourages use of their abilities to benefit the organization.
Principle 4	Process Approach	Establishment of a process facilitates efficiency in achievement of results.
Principle 5	System Approach to Management	Objectives may be more efficiently and effectively be met when the system is understood through interrelated processes.
Principle 6	Continual Improvement	The organization should have continual improvement as a permanent objective.
Principle 7	Factual Approach to Decision Making	Data and information analysis leads to effective decision making.
Principle 8	Mutually Beneficial Supplier Relationships	Interdependence of the organization and suppliers may create a mutually beneficial relationship for increased value on both sides.

Terminology and Integrated Information Management

Continuous QI has been used in the health care industry to describe the continuous nature of QI where the process maintains a focus on customers and employees. However, the generic term *PI* best describes the philosophy of providing customers with better services, ideas, and products, and it is used interchangeably in this section.

INFORMATION SYSTEMS FOR CONTROL

Theoretically, an MIS can be manual or computer based. Historically, managers relied on manual systems for the information to monitor the functions under their span of control until computer capabilities offered the opportunity to build systems based on computer-supported management applications. This is not to say that manual systems are no longer needed; they continue to be a component of the monitoring activity as discussed earlier.

A look at data as raw facts emphasizes the need for **integrated systems** to develop a true MIS. Data can be a collection of, for instance, listings showing the number of records coded for the week and the number of patients for whom billing data were sent to the billing department. Also available might be a record of the dates of discharges, the dates the bills were sent for payment, and the amounts of the bills. These bits of data can be listed in various activity reports. But, these discrete data are not useful to the manager for performance monitoring until they have been analyzed and processed. To reiterate, data are raw facts,

Integrated systems A system where data and information on separate automated applications are integrated to allow invisible transfer of information among them.

numbers, dates, or quantities until they are analyzed, processed, and presented as information. Thus, an appropriate MIS system for HIM managers collects data, manipulates data, and turns them into meaningful information. Today, it is possible to integrate information on interactive network systems that can become powerful tools for managerial decision making with outcomes that can then re-fashion the process.

The challenge of integrating data from the various systems throughout the facility creates an opportunity for HIM managers to be information innovators and strategic information resource professionals. As such, HIM professionals can maintain a vital role in the development of an MIS that will create efficient and effective systems monitoring productivity not only for health information services but for other departments as well.

To reach the goal of integrated data to serve the MIS customers, HIM managers and their staff should participate in the steps outlined in Figure 16-3, as the strategic plan relating to productivity is defined.

As the integrated systems are in the development phase, HIM managers and other customers should be able to say, "These are the key operating statistics my team leaders and I need to see every morning at 8 A.M. We want them presented in this format." They should feel assured that once the systems are in place, these performance tools will be online for monitoring operations.

Today's managers can then anticipate or identify problems almost as they occur using real-time decision support systems. No long delays will hamper their getting the needed information; alternatives can be identified quickly; what-if questions can be asked; and selection of the best alternative can be made efficiently.

As integration of data from the various facility systems progresses, it is likely there will be data islands where incompatible formats make integration impossible. HIM managers have the qualifications to participate on the team that resolves such difficulties and creates a control system that meets the needs of health care facilities in the future.

FIGURE 16-3   Steps for Integrating Information Systems

1. Evaluate present flow of data and the points where decisions are made.
2. Determine source of the information needed at the points of decision making.
3. Analyze information requirements at these decision points.
4. Aggregate the decision needs and ensure needed data are collected only once.
5. Develop uniform data definitions.
6. Standardize documentation.
7. Ensure quality improvement data are available for analysis.
8. Assist in designing the integrated system; know what vendors have to offer and be a strategic resource in the decisions.

SUMMARY

Controlling is defined as ensuring that plans are accomplished through monitoring employee activities and then through remedial action to correct significant variations. Controlling can be considered normal, positive, future oriented, and dynamic.

To monitor performance continuously, managers use QI concepts that take advantage of MISs that have integrated system capabilities. As standards are set by managers and the teams, adjustments as MIS enhancements are brought online will become necessary. Increased information will mean that performance monitoring can become increasingly automated.

Four major steps set the stage for monitoring: (1) capturing data for measurement, (2) analyzing the data for comparison with the standard, (3) determining whether variations are significant, and (4) taking team/managerial action.

Subjective tools for monitoring include questionnaires, surveys of external customers, and surveys within a department.

Japanese firms have been successful in TQM activities, and health care facilities in the United States are incorporating continuous quality monitoring in increasing numbers. The major elements in TQM are data, attitudes, and tools. The Joint Commission is using the term performance to describe the TQM process.

Integrated information systems are needed for developing the CPR as well as for monitoring quality activities. As HIM brokers disseminate meaningful information for these and other uses, they become the strategic information resource professionals of the future.

CRITICAL THINKING EXERCISES

1. Outline the history of TQM, describing its adoption globally and the modifications that increase its value in health care settings today.
2. Describe how an integrated MIS assists in the controlling function and list eight steps in integrating data for performance measurement.
3. List three subjective monitoring methods and give one example of how each of these methods is best used.

APPLICATION OF THEORY EXERCISE

Identify activities that would represent each of the ISO 9000 principles.

CASE STUDY

Outline how ISO standards may be specifically applied to a situation in health information management.

INTERNET ACTIVITY

Search online to find recent updates to the Information Management standards in the Joint Commission manual.

REFERENCES

Institute of Medicine. (1991). *Report of Committee on Computer-Based Patient Records*. Washington, DC: National Academy Press.

ISO Central Secretariat. (2012). *Quality Management Principles*. Geneva, Switzerland: ISO. http://www.iso.org/iso/qmp_2012.pdf.

Joint Commission on Accreditation of Healthcare Organizations. (1992). *Accreditation Manual for Hospitals*. Oakbrook Terrace, IL: JCAHO.

Robbins, S., & Coulter, M. (2012). *Management* (11th ed.). Upper Saddle River, NJ: Pearson.

SUGGESTED READINGS

AHIMA. (2011, August). HIM functions in healthcare quality and patient safety. *Journal of AHIMA, 82* (8), 42–45.

Dimick, C. (2012, February). Calling HIM quality experts: NQF seeking HIM input on quality measures. *Journal of AHIMA, 83* (2): 48–49.

Viola, A., & Kallem, C. (2011, April). Guide to US quality measurement organizations. *Journal of AHIMA, 82* (4), 40–42.

CHAPTER 17

Quality and Performance Improvement

LEARNING OBJECTIVES

After completing this chapter, the learner should be able to:

1. List the results HIM managers can achieve when the model for integrated QI management is implemented in the department.

2. Identify changes in the culture of an HIM department when customers become the focus of activities.

3. Explain the value of a facilitator when educating HIM teams in QI concepts.

4. Give examples of the value of benchmarking as a tool for QI management.

5. Suggest appropriate rewards for employees and the reasons why managers may choose different rewards.

INTRODUCTION

There are certain expectations that health care consumers have when they seek health care services. These expectations go beyond simply having tests and receiving treatment. Health care consumers expect **quality**, or a degree to which an activity produces a product or service that meets the standards set for that activity. Quality expectations for health care services are not only defined by patients, but also by payers, government regulations, and accrediting organizations.

Adjectives used by board members, upper-level and middle management staff, and team members to describe their experience with quality improvement range from fantastic to frustrating. Why are some facilities so successful in adjusting their culture and why do others fail in their first attempt? These are questions this chapter explores as specific steps for success are outlined. But the major focus of the chapter is giving managers appropriate tools for success. Success is achievable for this paradigm shift as management and leadership styles are adjusted to meld **quality improvement** (QI) concepts with the best of the integrated management approaches of the past for managing into the twenty-first century.

References from several experts in quality improvement are listed at the end of this chapter; they offer information on specific QI skills. The references also include articles from current literature that will assist in understanding current thought as managers make this paradigm shift. This chapter discusses a manager's overall role in the process of quality improvement and gives broad managerial concepts for success, not details for implementing programs.

Use of standards developed by other entities to evaluate health care quality is known as quality management. Health care organizations need to do more than provide quality services. There is a constantly growing expectation of how quality is defined, especially in a competitive health care environment where consumers are able to access outcome quality information and make more informed decisions about where they may receive services.

Health care consumers in today's society are more quality-focused than ever before. In addition, health care consumers also have easy access to information that reflects quality of health care providers. The Joint Commission, AHRQ, and NCQA all provide information on their websites that are consumer-friendly in order to not only provide quality health care information for patients, but also to provide educational information so that health care consumers know what quality indicators they should be aware of. Because of this, health care providers must maintain a competitive edge related to the delivery of quality services.

Quality The degree to which an activity produces a product or service that meets the standards set for that activity.

Quality improvement The philosophy that processes, management, and employees all benefit from efforts to provide better service, products, and ideas focusing on the customer.

By focusing on the process or the system and using statistical quality control techniques, HIM managers can develop strategic plans that increase efficiency and effectiveness of the systems under their span of control. QI concepts emphasize that the employee, the physician, or the "other" department is not targeted for blame. People are considered only one element in the process—the procedures, the equipment, the materials, the resources—are all emphasized as being a part of the system's input. The outcome is influenced by appropriate changes and these are undertaken following statistical quality control steps. These changes create improvement because people have joined together to work on the process and make it happen.

Figure 17-1 gives a model for integrated QI management. As this figure shows, the emphasis is on **statistical modeling**. When a project is undertaken by a team, the results should include standardization of the procedures, elimination of non-value-added steps, and reduction of unnecessary variation—a tall order, but the following example illustrates the success stories.

Statistical modeling A model that uses information systems data as a base for quality improvement management.

FIGURE 17-1   Managing in the Integrated Quality Improvement Environment

1. Become familiar with QI management concepts through formal courses, seminars, review of literature.
   1.1 Network with peers.
   1.2 Share enthusiasm for integrated QI management models.

2. Use facility vision/mission plan and strategies to develop quality improvement strategies for department activities.
   2.1. Involve yourself in facility steering committees and information systems needs for the future.
   2.2. Standardize functions in the department to the extent possible for each section.
   2.3. Assist and empower management team and employees in each section to develop a quality improvement plan relating to their functions.

3. Identify department customers—internal and external.
   3.1. Document internal and external customers, their needs, wants, and expectations, for the total department with assistance from the management team.
   3.2. Assist management team in documenting the customer needs, wants, and expectations for each section with assistance from each section team.
   3.3. Begin documenting perceived problem areas as teams discuss customers, information flow, timeliness, and present complaints.

4. Share QI management concepts with the management team and section teams during activities listed above and continuously as change is undertaken.
   4.1. Develop in-service programs for all levels of employees.
   4.2. Emphasize the long-range nature of the changes.
   4.3. Monitor reactions for resistance and defuse concerns.
   4.4. Empower employees to initiate ideas for quality improvement projects and steps for implementation.
   4.5. Separate formal training/quality improvement sessions from routine department activities.

(*continues*)

FIGURE 17-1 *(continued)*

5. Encourage team spirit among employees at all levels.
   5.1. Empower employees by giving increasing responsibility for their work environment.
   5.2. Change position titles and activity titles as ideas are generated by the teams.
   5.3. Coach the management team and section teams as needed.
   5.4. Prioritize quality improvement projects using input from the teams; choose initial ones carefully.
   5.5. Use an expert in quality improvement tools as the **facilitator** of project teams; use just-in-time training.
   5.6. Ensure that new employees have thorough initiation to process.
   5.7. Encourage interdepartmental and interdisciplinary interaction.

6. Ensure that information systems are in place for accurate data capture for use in statistical control techniques leading to validity in data dissemination.
   6.1. Review present systems used for clinical care, for interdepartmental and external customers, and for intradepartmental activities.
   6.2. Encourage brainstorming and nominal technique sessions to anticipate information system needs for changing customer expectations.
   6.3. Document future plans for information systems needed to meet data requirements for the future and present to administration.

7. Assure tools and release time for team members as they analyze data, retrieve data, and prepare presentations.

8. Network for effective benchmarking efforts.

9. Disseminate results of projects.
   9.1. Encourage the management team and team members to share in presenting results of projects.
   9.2. Share the learning experience and results throughout the facility as appropriate.
   9.3. Share results of projects with internal or external customers as appropriate.

10. Reward achievement and extra effort.

11. Monitor activities and adjust process as necessary.

QUALITY IMPROVEMENT

Quality assurance (QA) involves activities that measure performance and compare with standards to determine how well that service or outcome meets criteria associated with the specific standards. The difference between approved standards, criteria, or expectations in any type of process and actual results is known as a quality gap. This quality gap presents an opportunity for the health care organization to analyze processes to identify areas of deficiency that must be addressed to make changes that facilitate meeting or exceeding quality indicators (also known as performance indicators) used for measurement of key characteristics. Quality improvement activities involve acting on quality gaps by implementing quality improvements, then following up by measurement to determine effectiveness with a goal of improved health care outcomes.

Quality is an aspect of health care that has become a focal point over the years. In the HIM profession, this started in 1918, when the American College of Surgeons (ACS) established the Hospital Standardization Program. This program identified quality of documentation as an important contribution to quality of care. Physicians were more concerned with patient care than documentation, so the ACS documentation quality standards were determined to be best managed by medical records professionals. The importance of the medical record professional in relation to quality documentation management eventually led to the establishment of the Association of Record Librarians of North America (ARLNA) in 1928. The original objective of the ARLNA was to elevate the standards of clinical recordkeeping in hospitals, dispensaries, and other health care facilities. In 1944, the ARLNA became the American Association of Medical Record Librarians (AAMRL), followed by a change to the American Medical Record Association (AMRA) in 1970, which evolved to the American Health Information Management Association (AHIMA), which exists today. AHIMA is the professional organization for health information management professionals, which also provides certification, accreditation, and education.

The United States Department of Health and Human Services Agency for Healthcare Research and Quality (AHRQ) is the branch of the United States Department of Health and Human Services that is focused on improving safety, quality, accessibility, and affordability of health care. AHRQ focuses on safety, quality, effectiveness, and efficiency of care. Its work provides information for health care consumers to make decisions about health care services. Health care policymakers at federal, state, and local levels depend on the research findings of AHRQ in order to develop new policies that are appropriate. Health care providers depend on AHRQ findings to ensure that they are providing the highest quality of care possible. HIM managers apply AHRQ guidelines to establish criteria for review of health record documentation in order to ensure compliance.

ADJUSTING TO MANAGING THE QI PROCESS

Education is one of the keys to success as managers begin using QI concepts. A seasoned manager has the advantage of a peer network within the facility and in the professional community and can learn from the experiences of others. These experiences lend credence to the theory being learned in formal courses or seminars. Current professional journals are also excellent sources for both theory and experiences of others.

As students gain the formal knowledge of QI tools and anticipate using them in the work environment, they gain practical knowledge through professional practice experience and affiliations. Here they become acquainted with clinical practitioners and begin the networking that will hopefully continue throughout their professional careers.

In their first positions, new graduates will need time to become knowledgeable in the terminology and methodology used in their particular facility. By integrating the theory, the practical knowledge, and the facility-specific culture, terms, and techniques, new managers gradually unlock their full potential and they will gain confidence as experts.

Enthusiasm is known to be contagious. Some managers may hesitate to become enthusiastic for the integrated QI management model when they read that it takes more time. Look more closely at the success stories. Yes, the project takes longer from start to solution implementation, but there are trade-offs that can free a manager's time. As the move progresses toward sharing leadership tasks and empowering the team to find areas for improvement, managers are released from traditional managerial activities and are ready to be challenged in other areas.

Initially, managers may spend time developing strategies for the mission of the facility and in choosing global projects. These projects can then be narrowed to priorities at the departmental level. Other challenging tasks can include assisting the staff in making cultural adjustments, defining the department's customers, and prioritizing projects. But, once the teams are functioning smoothly with the team leader, managers can resist the temptation to micromanage and allow the process to work. By consciously concentrating managerial energies elsewhere, HIM professionals can enjoy job enrichment. Adapting the QI team approach to the unique features of the department and watching the teams meet their goals, managers can become advocates, sharing their enthusiasm for the process.

Accreditation

Accreditation
Voluntary process that involves assessment of an organization's performance against established standards to evaluate the quality of operations and outcomes.

Accreditation is a voluntary process that involves assessment of an organization's performance against established standards to evaluate the quality of operations and outcomes. The accreditation process generally involves an on-site survey, during which representatives of the accrediting organization visit to view evidence of performance and interview individuals in the organization. This is a method of demonstrating that a health care entity has met standards that reflect quality health care services.

Joint Commission

The Joint Commission is a private, voluntary, not-for-profit accreditation organization that grants accreditation to health care organizations. Joint Commission was formerly known as the Joint Commission on Accreditation of Health Care Organizations or JCAHO. This organization not only has performance measurement standards that must be met in order to maintain accreditation, but also has a significant focus on quality and safety of health care.

The accreditation manual published by the Joint Commission is called the Comprehensive Accreditation Manual. The chapters of the Joint Commission's

Comprehensive Accreditation Manual most pertinent to HIM professionals are the Management of Information (IM) chapter and Record of Care, Treatment, and Services (RC). The comprehensive accreditation manual is published annually for the following settings:

- Ambulatory care
- Behavioral health care
- Critical access hospital
- Home care
- Hospital
- Laboratory
- Nursing and rehabilitation (formerly long-term care)
- Office-based surgery

ORYX Initiative

One example of a standardized performance improvement (PI) measure is the Joint Commission's ORYX initiative, which supports the integration of outcomes accreditation process on key patient care, treatment, and service issues data and other performance measurement data into the accreditation process, often referred to as ORYX. While the focus of ORYX is clinical care and outcomes, documentation must be maintained to provide a means for evaluation. HIM professionals may play a significant role in the health care institution as a documentation quality reviewer, comparing documentation against established criteria to identify areas that may need to be brought to committee for review in order to make improvements in care delivery and documentation of elements of the core measure set related to the following areas:

- Venous thromboembolism
- Heart failure
- Emergency department
- Surgical care improvement project
- Substance use
- Tobacco treatment
- Pneumonia measures
- Immunization
- Acute myocardial infarction
- Children's asthma care
- Hospital-based inpatient psychiatric services
- Perinatal care
- Stroke
- Hospital outpatient department

Tracer Methodology

The Joint Commission uses a tracer methodology during the on-site survey to follow individual patients through the processes within the health care organization in the order that patients experience the various services from the point of admission through discharge. The tracer methodology allows surveyors to take a systems approach to tracing the organization's experiences of specific patients to assess patient care quality. Patients are usually selected based on complexity of services provided, tracing the effectiveness, efficiency, and quality of delivering multiple services during the admission.

Intracycle Monitoring

On January 1, 2013, the Joint Commission intracycle monitoring (ICM) process was introduced. This process includes a Focused Standards Assessment (FSA), which serves as a replacement for the periodic performance review, to facilitate risk identification and management. The FSA should be incorporated into the organization's compliance activities as they relate to maintaining accreditation standards. The ICM process and FSA tool provide the ability to report information during the accreditation cycle and report performance measure data with a reduced need for costly on-site surveys.

Utilization Management

Managed care and financial limitations require health care providers to become more mindful of the cost of providing health care services. Because of this, utilization management has become a necessary component across the health care delivery system to incorporate policies and processes that ensure treatment and diagnostic testing are provided for patients when they are justified to be necessary, but also maintain a balance that prohibits excessive use of services that are not medically necessary. This is accomplished through careful evaluation, based on established guidelines that are intended to limit excessive use of services without compromising quality of care. Utilization review positions have been established by providers and payers for the purpose of evaluation of medical necessity against preestablished criteria at various points in delivery of health care services. **Prospective review** is required by some payers in order to authorize services before they are provided. This type of review prevents overutilization, which in turn prevents the provider from incurring expenses for which they will not be reimbursed or that the patient may be required to pay out of their own pockets. If a patient is receiving inpatient services, **concurrent review** may be performed in order to determine necessity of continuation of services. This is often a cooperative effort involving utilization review professionals for the payer and at the provider facility. Concurrent review provides a degree of control of the services being provided along the

Prospective review Review of records prior to delivery of services.

Concurrent review Review of records while the patient is still receiving services.

way, evaluating what has been provided and approving continuation of care for specified time frames. **Retrospective review** may also be performed following discharge and billing. This process involves thorough audit of the health record to review documentation of services provided to identify if medical necessity truly existed. Utilization review positions have traditionally been held by registered nurses, but this career has expanded to include HIM professionals. Nurses have clinical experience and training that enable them to understand the patient care perspective of utilization review. However, the growing shortage of nursing professionals has created an opportunity for HIM professionals to pursue this career option. While HIM professionals do not have hands-on clinical experience, the increased rigor of HIM education includes pathophysiology, pharmacology, and reimbursement methodologies, which provide adequate preparation for performing utilization review activities.

Retrospective review Review of records following delivery of services.

THEORIES RELATING TO QUALITY IMPROVEMENT AND PERFORMANCE IMPROVEMENT

In order to increase the likelihood of achievement of desired health care delivery outcomes, health care organizations do PI activities to continuously study and adapt functions and processes. PI processes may be applied to an organization as a whole, specific departments, processes within departments, or even individuals. The goal of PI is focused on a predetermined desired outcome that is measurable in a result-oriented system.

Total Quality Management

The concept of total quality improvement (TQM) was introduced briefly in Chapter 2. Edward Deming popularized the concept of TQM in the 1980s. His theory addressed all activities in an entire (total) organization with a specific focus on the needs of **customers**, recognizing both internal and external customers. Through this process, efficiency and full potential of each area are ensured through a continuous cycle that produces quality products or outcomes. The concept of external customers is often easier for employees to understand than internal employees. Internal customers may be easier to identify as a "next process" customer. One HIM-related example that examines the relationship of three processes starts with the process of coding, which is dependent upon timely completion of record analysis, so this makes the coders the next process customers for the record analysis team. If there are delays, errors, or other issues in coding processes, then the next process customers in the billing department will be impacted. Figure 17-2 illustrates this example of next process customers as a series of gears, in which one is dependent upon the next in order for movement to occur. Consider what would happen if something

Customers Those persons who use the services provided or have a stake in the success of an organization.

FIGURE 17-2   Next process customers

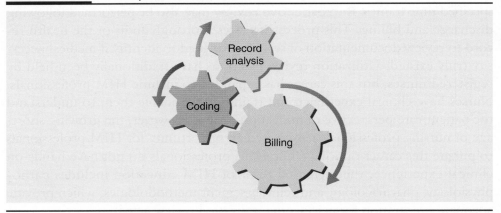

were to interrupt the process of record analysis. That would cause the record analysis gear to slow, which in turn would slow the coding gear, and subsequently, the billing gear.

As a system of processes is analyzed in an organization, it may be easy to identify that worker performance may not be the problem, but rather process issues or faults in the system that interfere with transitions to the next process customers. One of the TQM facets is the **eighty-five/fifteen (85/15) rule**, which assumes that faults in the system are the cause of 85 percent of problems, and worker performance is only responsible for 15 percent (see Figure 17-3).

Eighty-five/ fifteen (85/15) rule Assumption that faults in the system are the cause of 85 percent of problems, and worker performance is only responsible for 15 percent.

Continuous Quality Improvement

One management philosophy, continuous quality improvement (CQI) has an emphasis on the necessity of anticipating expectations of customers and reduction of process variation. This is accomplished through data collection and analysis to produce knowledge applicable to process improvement. CQI

FIGURE 17-3   85/15 Rule

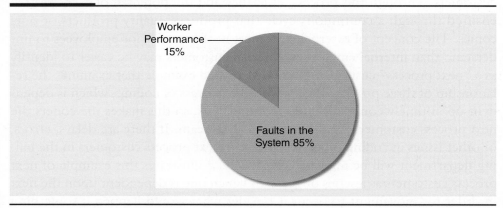

FIGURE 17-4   Continuous Quality Improvement

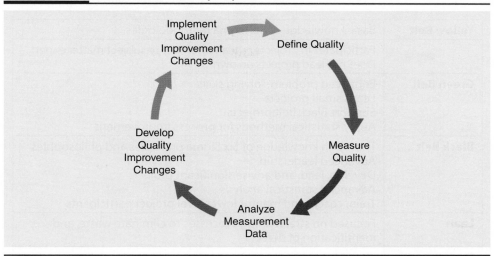

activities are based on the PDCA cycle, which was introduced in Chapter 2. Figure 17-4 illustrates the processes involved in CQI. Quality must first be defined, usually based on accreditation standards, regulatory guidelines, or other aspects of care identified to be important to the organization. This quality definition should include measurable goals, as the next step involves collection of data to measure performance against the defined aspects of quality. These data are analyzed to identify opportunities for improvement. When these opportunities have been identified, changes are developed and implemented, leading to repeat of the cycle to monitor and continuously improve.

Six Sigma

Six Sigma is a highly disciplined and data-driven methodology used for reducing or eliminating defects in any process. Motorola, USA originally developed this business management strategy in 1981 for the purpose of improving the quality of process outputs by addressing defects and defective processes. Six Sigma uses quality management methodology that includes use of statistics. Experts in Six Sigma are referred to as black belts. Levels of Six Sigma are identified in Figure 17-5.

Six Sigma A highly disciplined and data-driven methodology used for reducing or eliminating defects in any process.

PERFORMANCE IMPROVEMENT ACTIVITIES AND TOOLS

In order to perform quality improvement and PI activities, there are a variety of tools available to facilitate the data collection, communication of findings, and data analysis to generate solutions for quality defects and create improved processes that are more efficient and effective for improved outcomes.

FIGURE 17-5 Six Sigma Levels

Yellow Belt	Basic knowledge of Six Sigma methodologies
	Participates in projects as team member or subject matter expert Does not lead projects on own
Green Belt	Enhanced problem-solving skills Leads small projects Support Black Belt projects Apply statistical methods for process improvement
Black Belt	Thorough knowledge of Six Sigma principles and philosophies Advanced leadership Develop, lead, and advise significant projects Advanced statistical analysis Train, coach, and mentor lower level project participants
Lean	Focused on streamlining processes to eliminate waste, and identification of defects
Design for Six Sigma (DFSS)	Designing and redesigning projects and service delivery methods to meet customer expectations

Measurement Tools

In order to develop PI initiatives, it is necessary to start by measuring outcomes of currently existing processes to identify opportunities for improvement. The PI teams administer some of the measurement activities. Other activities are accomplished through measurements by the individuals performing processes.

Time Studies

Time studies examine the amount of time required to complete processes or components of processes in order to determine inefficiencies and develop improvements. There are different methods to approach time studies, which are dependent upon the nature of the process and the level of details required for the study. A basic approach to time study is use of a time ladder form used by employees to document time that they spend on a specific task. A variation of the time ladder, the check sheet, permits the systematic recording of observations of a particular phenomenon so that trends or patterns can be identified. Figure 17-6 illustrates an example of a check sheet used to track the number of telephone and walk-in release of information requests by time of day for the purpose of identifying.

Questionnaires and Surveys

Questionnaires and surveys provide data through self-reporting by subjects of study. Employees may provide details of processes or identify aspects of their work that have issues that need to be addressed. Communication may come from internal and external customers, too. In health care, this is often accomplished

FIGURE 17-6   Checksheet

Hourly Release of Information by Type of Request			
Employee	**Date**		
Time	**Walk-in**	**Telephone**	**Electronic**
7:00–8:00			
8:00–9:00			
9:00–10:00			
10:00–11:00			
11:00–12:00			
12:00–13:00			
13:00–14:00			
14:00–15:00			
15:00–16:00			
16:00–17:00			
17:00–18:00			
18:00–19:00			
19:00–20:00			
20:00–21:00			

through the use of patient satisfaction surveys. Data may be collected through use of open-ended questions, which provide the opportunity for responses that may be more subjective and detailed in nature. Another type of question frequently used on surveys is the Likert scale, which is an ordinal rating technique used to measure attitudes, level of agreement, or level of importance for items. Responses are reported using a progression of categories, usually a five-point scale. An example of a Likert scale is provided in Figure 17-7.

Analysis Tools

Not all aspects of PI are based on ordinal, measurable data elements. Some PI activities require analysis of processes and other inputs. Tools used for this type of analysis sometimes require facilitation of a team member trained in use of PI analysis tools.

Root Cause Analysis

The underlying cause of a problem may be identified by performing a root cause analysis to identify the underlying causes of the problem. The aspects of man, machine, methods, and materials are examined to determine how each may have contributed to the problem and to use the findings to prevent future occurrences of the problem. A root cause analysis is diagrammed in a tool called

FIGURE 17-7   Likert Scale

	Strongly Agree	Agree	Neutral	Disagree	Strongly Disagree
Discharge instructions were easy to understand.					
I will recommend services at this facility to others.					
I will return to this facility for my personal healthcare needs in the future.					

a fishbone diagram, which is named because of its appearance. Figure 17-8 illustrates use of a fishbone diagram to identify the root cause of the problem of coding backlog. The "man" aspects identified in this example include the physicians with incomplete documentation and coders who have been out sick. "Machine" aspects evaluate computers and software. "Methods" potentially contributing may be related to documented procedures, which may be inaccurate or outdated if not maintained to be consistent with changes associated with EHR. "Materials" possibly impacting the problem may be lack of necessary references or even coding queue not being provided in a timely manner to communicate coding needs to the coders.

SWOT Analysis

SWOT Analysis is a tool used in PI planning to identify the strengths, weaknesses, opportunities, and threats. Strengths are aspects that provide an

FIGURE 17-8   Fishbone Diagram

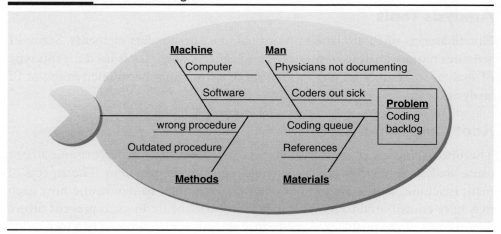

FIGURE 17-9 SWOT Analysis

Strengths	Weaknesses	Opportunities	Threats
• Well-trained coding staff • Administrative support	• Coding staff are not comfortable with EHR	• Community college near hospital with CAHIIM-accredited Health Information Technology degree program	• Two other similar organizations in the area • Coders nearing retirement

advantage over competing organizations. Weaknesses are areas that may require improvement.

Opportunities include untapped resources and new trends. Threats are obstacles to success. When completing a SWOT analysis, items should be identified in basic terms, yet clearly defining the aspects. There may be times when items are identified as more than one category. Figure 17-9 provides an example of a SWOT analysis as part of a PI project in the coding area of a hospital. In this example, the department has well-trained coders and strong administrative support. However, two of the most experienced coders are nearing retirement and the remaining coders are not comfortable with the EHR. Other hospitals in the area have been attempting to recruit coders to fill vacant positions and are offering higher salaries. There is a CAHIIM-accredited health information technology associate degree program at a nearby community college, which has a strong relationship with the hospital and students frequently complete professional practice experience at the hospital.

Process Flow Diagram

Process flow diagrams are useful to illustrate the workflow of all steps within a process to identify areas of potential delays, duplication of effort, or other opportunities for improvement. The diagram will be analyzed to incorporate knowledge gained into process redesign to implement minor changes and provide education or training about the new process. Another use for process flow diagrams is for reengineering, involving significant rethinking and redesign of processes for PIs, such as those that may occur with the transition from paper records to the EHR. Figure 17-10 provides a basic example of a process flow diagram with a broad focus on the coding process.

Force Field analysis

A force field analysis is a tool that identifies driving forces and restraining forces as they relate to a specific aspect of an organization or proposed change within the organization. The exercise is conducted with a group with the issue identified either on a whiteboard or flipchart with a single line down the middle to represent either an issue to be solved or a decision to be made. The

FIGURE 17-10   Process Flow Diagram

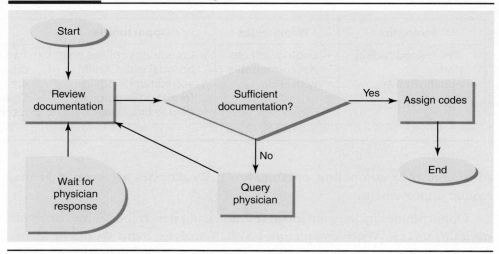

session with the tool works in a similar manner as a brainstorming session with group members sharing their perceptions of the driving and restraining forces. The stronger driving and restraining forces are often represented by longer or wider arrows, while the weaker forces are represented by shorter arrows. Figure 17-11 illustrates use of a force field analysis to analyze the decision to allow coding staff members to work from home rather than on-site.

Data Display Tools

PI activities are communicated to selected stakeholders, based on their role or impact that may be realized by the activities. A general overview of the activities may be reported using a dashboard, which highlights key findings that are

FIGURE 17-11   Force Field Analysis

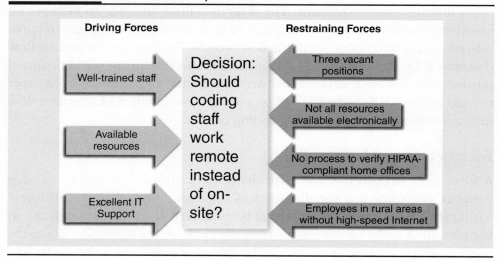

FIGURE 17-12   Graphical Display Techniques

Graphical display technique	Type of data displayed
Bar chart	Pictorial representation of data
Graph	Pictorial representation of data
Histogram	Frequency distribution of continuous data in a series of bars on a chart
Run chart	Data collection over a period of time to identify trends or patterns
Control chart	Run chart with upper and lower control limits to identify degrees of variation in processes over a period of time
Pareto chart	Bar graph arranged in descending order to prioritize issues
Pie chart	Proportions of data displayed as portions of a circle like pieces of pie, comparing relationships of each portion to the whole

pertinent to the audience to which the information is presented. The concept of a dashboard is most often compared to a car dashboard, which provides the driver the ability to take a quick glimpse to see if the vehicle is functioning properly or if attention is needed from a simple warning light. In health care PI activities, the dashboard may provide that same convenience through a highlighted report finding of an extended wait time for physicians to respond to coding queries or high number of release of information requests counted at a certain time of day.

While a dashboard provides a concise report of findings and PI activities, a storyboard may be used to provide a visual or graphic display to communicate details. A storyboard may be used to display summarized findings of time studies and surveys, root cause analysis diagrams, SWOT analysis findings, process flow diagrams, and force field analyses. There are a variety of graphical display options to display data from time studies and surveys, which are outlined in Figure 17-12.

QI PLANNING STRATEGIES

An enthusiastic HIM manager can impact implementation of quality improvement in the entire facility. By becoming knowledgeable through review of the literature, through seminars, and through formal courses, the manager can be an advocate and share the vision in meetings and in discussions with the management team. Offering to be a part of the steering committee is an excellent way to be involved personally and to have department involvement from the beginning. A background in systems, in data capture and analysis, and in statistical techniques gives HIM managers the expertise that will be of value for generating ideas and implementing change.

The first step in having measurable data for decision making is to update and standardize present procedures. Electronic exchange of information mandates the standardization of terms and techniques across all teams in the department. Standardized terms will be needed among all users in the facility. This will be an ongoing process as implementation takes place. At the same time, HIM managers can empower employees in each team to use unique and team-specific terms and techniques where feasible as they take increased responsibility for their work environment.

Using the facility-wide projects and the department projects, the teams can develop their strategic plan and prioritize projects. By assisting the teams in understanding how their projects enhance the department and facility-wide projects, managers can increase the sense of ownership employees feel toward their team. This enhances the success of the quality improvement effort.

Customer-Driven Attitudes

An exciting, appropriate, and pervading principle of quality improvement is the focus on the customers—their wants, needs, and expectations. As an HIM manager attends quality improvement seminars or a student learns techniques in a quality improvement course, customers of the department will become a major focus. Internal customers and their changing wants, needs, and expectations may be viewed differently. For instance, an employee may view demands from another department quite differently than a manager. Consider how coding technicians may view the multiple demands made by billing department employees when problems arise with codes and incomplete billing information. Their feelings about interruptions to correct problems may be viewed quite differently from managerial concerns between their manager and the manager of the billing department. In contrast, the billing department employees may perceive the interaction about the problem in another way.

Or, for example, consider students, spending professional practice experience time with employees. They may or may not be impressed with the employees' understanding of the internal and external customers awaiting the product of their work. The view of students may be very different than the view of the employees.

Changing to a customer-driven cultural attitude is exciting, rewarding, and stimulating for employees. It can also be threatening. HIM managers will want to look for positive signs and respond with encouragement and rewards. Cultural change comes gradually and must flow from the top. As upper-level management focuses on customer-driven opportunities, managers at all levels can share enthusiastically with the employees in personal interaction, through in-service seminars, and through a story board. Most importantly, managers must "walk the talk" in their own management style.

By tackling the specific needs of a customer such as described in the previous example, employees will learn teamwork skills interacting with another department. Additional departments may also need to be involved as the source of the problem is uncovered, thus making the project truly interdisciplinary.

Quality improvement techniques call for the manager and the team to meet customer needs and then go beyond that, striving for excellence in performance by doing it better the next time, by anticipating future needs, and by staying one step ahead of customers in the strategic planning process. Inevitably, there will be times when expectations of customers will need to be negotiated or reshaped.

Another aspect of the customer-driven and information-driven systems approach is the increased need for data. Think of the enhanced role of the HIM department in bringing standardized data capture systems to the integrated management effort as the facility moves toward an information-driven approach to excellence. By knowing the capabilities of the systems in-house and in the marketplace, the HIM broker will be able to explore options with customers. When another department requests information about capturing appropriate data for its needs, HIM brokers can offer suggestions.

As the strategic plan for the facility is developed and projects are prioritized, the opportunity to impact the decisions must be seized or it may be lost to others. It is the HIM broker who can take information needs outlined for the next 3 to 5 years and suggest how the present systems capabilities or future systems expansion can provide the needed data.

Exceeding the customers' expectations for information is the goal, and planning systems where staff members are involved in shared leadership can make that goal a reality.

Employee Education Needs

Employees will react differently to the same set of stimuli, making a broad approach necessary as QI concepts are presented to them. Some will be early adopters who will quickly learn the needed skills and embrace the change. Another group will tend to resist change and will require extra encouragement and support from managers as changes occur.

This resistance could be especially evident if the facility has a history of programs that started with fanfare but the commitment was not sustained and eventually the program was dropped. The HIM managers will need to emphasize that QI concepts will be integrated into the culture and activities of the department, and QI will impact their work environment over time and into the future.

A facilitator with the ability to present the tools and techniques in an informative yet interesting way should be on the staff of the facility and available to give in-service programs and special training sessions to teams. An effective learning tool is just-in-time education, where the section or team is instructed in the tools and techniques for a specific task as needed. Confidence in performing the task at hand is thus enhanced, which builds success in small steps.

Peter Drucker's advice to the Japanese in the 1950s continues to be valid today. He strongly recommends holding formal training sessions away from the routine activities. He states the pressure of work activities will detract from the learning experience and lead to failure as daily duties and set routines become the predominant focus. This situation makes clear the need for a budget that includes support staff to perform routine work while the staff members are in training.

Encouraging a Team Spirit

One of the benefits HIM managers can expect as integration takes place and cultural change occurs is an enhanced team spirit among employees. This should be increasingly evident throughout the facility as upper-level management supports the changes and demonstrates that leadership is with the people, not above them.

Coaching the sections as they are giving increased responsibility is also an important aspect of the HIM manager's role. This coaching should begin with upper-level management and flow to the HIM manager, who then educates the teams, thus empowering them to meet customer needs. Deming discusses a threat to empowering employees. That is, when crises occur, there may be times when managers, under pressure, return to making unilateral decisions.

As teams brainstorm and choose initial projects, the HIM manager should guide in the selection of the initial projects. As tools are used for the first time and techniques are being learned, success will be enhanced if the first projects are straightforward. While emphasis is placed on success stories, not all of the projects will culminate in success. What is important, when failure occurs, is a willingness to acknowledge failure honestly. Employees respect an honest admission of failure and a willingness to explore new options for solving a problem. Team members must be allowed to fail as part of the empowering process.

Since quality improvement projects are ongoing, it is inevitable that new employees will be hired for a team during any phase of the project. Human resources management should have monthly orientations for new employees to receive QI information; the HIM manager should assess the extent of involvement the new employee may have in QI activities before the formal orientation. A special session can then be held for the new employee, if warranted. New employees are customers, in a sense, needing information to perform their work effectively.

Despite obstacles to scheduling interdepartmental team meetings, developing such teams is an important facet in building team spirit across the facility. As interdepartmental teams work toward solutions that will benefit customers of the facility, this interaction promotes understanding of other disciplines among all staff members involved.

MANAGING DATA NEEDS WITH QI

As brainstorming sessions create an increased need for data, few HIM managers will be confident that present systems are adequate for capturing and analyzing data to produce the needed information for proposed projects. Because of the importance of correct decisions when enhancing present systems or purchasing new ones, it is imperative that HIM managers update their knowledge in this area.

They must ensure that careful documentation is ongoing and then, through negotiations and with graphic descriptions, the manager can present the pros and cons of system needs to administration. Fortunately, resources are available from AHIMA and other professional organizations that can increase knowledge of software/hardware systems.

A team may find the solution to a problem blocked by a data barrier. In fact, as long as paper records are needed for ongoing patient-care requestors and for administrative requestors, these customers will experience frustrations.

The facilitator is an excellent resource in determining the tools needed for specific data analysis and retrieval. But the responsibility for assuring the availability of these tools rests with the HIM manager. Team members will become frustrated with deadlines should they lack the tools to complete their assignments. Another frustration comes when an assignment is added to a schedule already packed with routine activities. Time must be allocated for assignment completion as well as for meeting attendance.

Using Benchmarking as a QI Tool

Benchmarking is an important comparative data tool in PI efforts. Benchmarking means research for new ideas by networking, reviewing the literature, or attending seminars on organizations and then adopting or modifying the best aspects of those organizations found to have outstanding performance. A definition is offered by author R. C. Camp in his book on benchmarking and this definition focuses on the networking aspects. He defines benchmarking as "the continuous process of measuring products, services, and practices against the toughest competitors or those companies recognized as industry leaders." Benchmarking ideas can improve department operations when incorporated into the quality improvement process (Camp, 1989).

Benchmarking The search for the best practices among like entities or past practices that lead to superior performance.

Internal benchmarking refers to the process of looking for superior performance in other departments within the facility and adapting the best ideas into the HIM department processes. Competitive benchmarking is a form of external research that involves comparing the department's operation with those of competitors.

Networking develops into benchmarking when innovative ideas are exchanged and internalized. Sharing of information about the best practices is mutually beneficial; some health care facilities are forming consortia for specific sharing of information. A new word being formed for this action is *coopetition*, where competitive health care facilities share for the good of the community.

Managing the PDCA Tool

To generate ideas and data for monitoring one aspect of a process, managers can suggest that teams use the QI tool, asking participants to plan, do, check, and act (PDCA). By getting the team members involved and educated in using PDCA, HIM managers empower the team to create solutions to problems and then evaluate effectiveness.

Choosing Rewards for Employees

Knowing the team members, their preferences and interests, assists HIM managers in choosing appropriate rewards at the end of a team project. Rewards are best tailored to the values of the individual. Awards, verbal commendations, publicity in newsletter or bulletin boards, special parking spaces, or dinner tickets are some of the rewards that come to mind. It is usually better to vary the reward, to use creativity and innovation, rather than to plan a standard reward for each project. Many facilities have an "employee of the month," and there might be a "team of the year" special reward involving the whole facility. Rewarding the effort a team expends, even though present results may be less than optimal, is also important.

Communicating Performance Improvement Findings

When communicating findings of PI studies, employees generally respond more favorably if information is presented in a positive manner. For example, the phrase, "opportunity for improvement" is easier for employees to hear than terms like "error, mistake, or problem." It is important for management to allow input and quality improvement suggestions from employees. If this does not happen, employees will quickly feel that management does not want their input and they will stop generating potentially valuable ideas, resulting in missed opportunities.

PRODUCTIVITY MEASUREMENT, PERFORMANCE STANDARDS, AND WORK SAMPLING

The focus on customers and their needs continues to create paradigm shifts in health care organizations in ways that impact all levels of managers and staff. This shift is mandating that HIM managers lessen dependence on carefully designed productivity measurements that tend to highlight the failure of specific employees. Rather, managers envision systems that will assist their self-managed teams in monitoring team effort and continually improving the work processes toward increasing customer satisfaction. As this paradigm shift occurs, team member cooperation toward mutual customer-oriented objectives and increased productivity will be a major focus for HIM managers.

Manufacturing organizations with well-defined inputs and outputs have been ahead of **service organizations** in this customer focus and in the creation of tools to meet increased productivity. Health care facilities are typically labor-intensive organizations and offer products or services that can range from cardiac surgery to a clean room to a well-documented health record.

Too often, productivity is defined simply as the ratio between input and output. This definition considers quantity and efficiency as the baseline factors in determining the level of productivity. But effectiveness is equally important in service organizations, so quality has a shared importance. Quality may be defined as the extent to which outcome standards are met, while quantity is a reflection of a measurable amount of work that is completed in a defined period of time. Productivity incorporates aspects of both quality and quantity to reflect the amount of satisfactory work completed in a defined period of time, such as an hour or a day.

As teams are empowered to create redesigned environments using tools such as CQI to increase customer satisfaction, they are given the responsibility of assisting in development of appropriate performance monitoring systems. These systems may include manual data gathering methods, depending on the application and the setting. Increasingly, however, data are gathered electronically and the needed information is disseminated to the teams in the form they have requested. As HIM managers redesign departments with new equipment, work methods, and performance-measuring systems, increased productivity can become a reality. Empowered employees assist in the redesign and then, as self-managed teams, they create monitoring systems for their unique needs.

Measuring and improving team performance for increased productivity is a part of the controlling function of management. In practice, however, these processes lead back to the planning function, where objectives are developed to give reality to the organization's vision of the future. This chapter outlines steps for measuring performance and setting standards through team

Service organizations Organizations that offer services to their customers in contrast with manufacturing organizations that offer products.

empowerment with a focus on process improvement. As paradigm shifts occur in health care settings, these steps for measuring performance can keep pace with new expectations and systems.

The redesign or reengineering efforts discussed in previous chapters are the building blocks for this chapter. The focus now is on productivity improvement and the tools that can be used effectively to measure productivity once the planning vision efforts have defined the tasks and set the objectives for reaching customer-oriented goals through team effort.

Product Lines and Productivity Improvement Efforts

Before beginning the discussion of measurement efforts that will lead to productivity improvement, it is helpful to assess the direction managers should take in developing HIM product lines or services to meet customer needs. Managers in service organizations such as health care facilities face new challenges as tools are adapted from manufacturing organizations to meet their needs. As redesign changes a department's structure from the traditional functional division to customer-focused services, productivity improvement tools will change also. HIM managers and their teams, who expend effort toward working more productively without working harder or longer, will now be creating services that customers want and will be discarding non-value-added tasks.

Writing in the *Harvard Business Review* in 1991, Peter Drucker outlines four tasks that managers in service organizations must undertake in their efforts at working smarter for productivity improvement. Figure 17-13 lists these tasks.

The use of technology for monitoring activities is also emphasized by Drucker. Involving the teams in developing quality and quantity monitoring with the tools currently available is a starting point for improving productivity

FIGURE 17-13   Managerial Tasks for Productivity Improvement (Based on Drucker, 1991)

1. Focus on defining departmental tasks. Begin with the planning vision, then set objectives for reaching the goals within the guidelines set by upper-level management or regulations. Answer the following questions:
   a. What are the tasks for the department?
   b. What accomplishments can be documented to show completion of tasks?
   c. Why are present tasks being done and should they be done at all or in this way?
2. Concentrate activities on the redefined tasks. Observe work flow, make changes, redesign, and reengineer.
3. Define performance. Work with the team in setting standards and monitoring tools.
4. Empower employees.
   a. Build responsibility for productivity and performance improvement through continuous learning for each team member.
   b. Build responsibility within the team by asking team members to teach others through crosstraining and new employee orientation.

and performance (Drucker, 1991). HIM managers with access to technologies, redesigned work processes, and self-managed diverse teams face opportunities for synthesizing these inputs into the outputs that will provide the best possible service to customers.

Initiating Performance Standards and Productivity Measurement

When performance standards are not in place as the change process begins, managers and team leaders are challenged with creating an environment where team members willingly embrace change and redesign the work processes. Steps for initiating performance standards, as outlined in Figure 17-14, will give direction to this effort. The first steps take managers back to the

FIGURE 17-14   Steps in Initiating Work/Productivity Standards

1. Analyze present work processes and choose appropriate organizational changes as outlined in earlier chapters.
    a. Involve upper-level management.
    b. Include all employees in this process; have them assist in analyzing and documenting present systems.

2. Review present monitoring systems—electronic and manual.
    a. Develop a list of reports available and in use at present for each section/team.
    b. List capabilities of present automated systems for additional monitoring possibilities.

3. Coordinate the departmental changes with any changes occurring throughout the facility.

4. Develop priority list for creating appropriate customer-focused productivity measurements for sections/teams that include quality and quantity monitoring.
    a. Begin the changes with one or two motivated teams, with one where problems of quality and timeliness surface frequently, or with one where measurement can be quite straightforward.
    b. Plan methods for sharing the success stories of these pilot teams and set the pace for implementing performance improvement throughout the department.

5. Document standards for performance measurements that include quality, quantity, and other crucial factors.
    a. Review any productivity standard reports in use and establish present performance levels.
    b. Use benchmarking tools.
    c. Adapt or upgrade monitoring reports and develop new ones as necessary during redesign/reengineering process.

6. Request exception reporting where possible.

7. Use frequent team meetings to monitor progress and develop changes as needed.

8. Implement changes and continue the cycle.

organizing function where the functional activity of the department was developed. Of course, when performance standards are already in place, managers can enter the steps in Figure 17-14 at the point where change is anticipated.

Figure 17-14 mentions quality as well as quantity in giving equal importance to doing the right things right the first time. Increased productivity can result when priority is given to both quality and quantity measurement as standards are developed.

TOOLS FOR PERFORMANCE MEASUREMENT

One of the first measurement tools needing development as productivity monitoring is started as a listing of the terms that will be used in measuring performance with definitions that give every team member a clear picture of what the term means and how it will be used. These terms must be defined as standard units for comparison across teams and, when possible, throughout the facility and in benchmarking tools as well. As automation of data collection increases, this listing will need modification. Automated systems should be flexible enough to add additional collection units as needs arise.

Standardizing terms has benefits in areas where performance standards are often utilized. These terms must be well-defined, measurable, and used consistently when measuring performance. For example, the term "coded charts" lacks specificity for measurement purposes. Better standardized terminologies might be "coded inpatient charts," "coded emergency department charts," and "coded outpatient surgery charts." Similarly, in the release of information area, rather than simply referencing "requests processed," terminologies should specify what type of requests, such as subpoenas, walk-in patients, electronic requests, or phone call requests.

Tools for Documenting Present Work Processes

By using present procedures and observation, teams can prepare documentation of their work process to use in PI activities and productivity measurement. Figure 17-15 is a sample form that can be effective. Initially, emphasis can be given to the areas where monitoring will begin. Those tasks that are repetitive and would lead to the greatest saving of time should be considered first. Another factor initially is data collection and the systems available to collect the needed data efficiently and with little or moderate monitoring effort.

Tools for Documenting Present Monitoring Systems

Knowing what is being monitored in a continuing fashion is the next step. Documenting these tools for each team and then examining the work processes as a total will assist the management team. Figure 17-16 is an example

FIGURE 17-15   Sample Form to Document Work Process

Employee Name:	Sally Jones		Date:	June 2, 20XX
Job Title:	Release of Information Specialist			
Task	**Time spent on task**		**Notes**	
Phone call – fax information to physician office	5 minutes		Electronically faxed from EHR	
Walk-in request for information	10 minutes		Records in archive. Explained 24-hour turnaround time for release. Helped patient complete release form	
Phone call	2 minutes		Simple question about policy for release of information	

of this documentation for coding quality. Based on the findings of coding audits, coding quality for each coder may be calculated. The industry standard for coding is suggested to be 95 percent accuracy. However, individual institutions should establish their own quality standards. These standards should

FIGURE 17-16   Sample Coding Quality Log

Memorial Hospital Coding Quality Audit Log			
Auditor:	Jane Doe	**Date:**	March 7, 20XX
Account Number	**Findings**		**Coder**
1083554	None		SS
1086579	MCC present but not coded		CW
1089482	Incorrect coding of urosepsis; physician query needed		CW
1084468	None		LR
1084597	None		CW
1086527	None		SS
1083461	Inappropriately assigned principal diagnosis		ML
1084893	None		LR

be included in the position description so that the employees will know the expected quality standards they are required to meet.

Tools for Documenting Standard Measurements: Benchmarking

National productivity standards are available to assist HIM managers in benchmarking tasks performed in health information services. Upper-level management may be receiving reports on nationwide or regional productivity standards from organizations that provide benchmarking data on which institutional standards may be based. HIM managers who become informed about what is being used to benchmark productivity within the facility or in the region can utilize these tools also. Using comparative databases for assessing departmental monitoring systems gives managers the opportunity to determine whether their monitoring systems are adequate and comparable.

Tools Used in Creating New Monitoring Systems

Lastly, documentation of the new data collection systems that allow monitoring to occur must be created. Once in place, these tools will have wide usage; not only will the teams use them, but managers can document productivity data for the budget, annual reports, and rationalization of staffing needs. Then the reports showing team performance can be used in appraising the team as a whole or individuals on the team, should individual performance appraisals be a part of the controlling function.

As teams assess their capability to measure performance, emphasis should be focused on monitoring that will provide the greatest payoff. With the technology available to gather data indiscriminately, care must be taken in choosing measurement tools appropriately. For example, the record maintenance team may perceive that there are inefficiencies in the exception reporting for monthly medical staff committee record review. More records are being pulled than needed. Since these are monthly medical staff retrievals, there will be minimal productivity savings by narrowing the exception reports, so fewer records are targeted. Rather, effort spent correcting inefficiencies in the daily retrieval of patient records for scheduled admissions will have greater payoff. Setting priorities according to payoff allows corrections to be made in a consistent manner.

Work Sampling/Exception Reporting

Sampling
The process of measuring productivity by making a series of observations at random.

In automated PI monitoring systems, exception reports are requested as an efficient tool for taking subsequent action. In automated systems, while the data are collected continuously, deviations from the standard are separated out and exception reports are prepared to reveal problem areas. In manual systems, exception reporting is better accomplished through task **sampling** where periodic tracking shows problem areas. Increasingly, HIM managers will use automated exception reporting as an effective and efficient tool in measuring performance.

SUMMARY

Quality improvement concepts are introduced in this chapter as a part of the integrated management approach. For long-term success, upper-level management must lead in the quality improvement effort and cultural change, but there is much the HIM manager can do to promote the process, initiate personal and departmental change, and use appropriate tools as opportunities arise.

As quality and PI are addressed in health care, it is important to consider internal and external stakeholders impacted by all aspects of quality. Government regulations, accreditation standards, and utilization management all contribute to PI activities in which HIM professionals are involved. TQM, CWI, and Six Sigma are commonly used approaches to performance in the health care arena. Through these approaches, several PI tools are available for data collection, data analysis, and communication of findings and activities.

Tools and techniques for implementing specific QI concepts are found in the literature. A facilitator familiar with the use of these tools and techniques is an important member of the team; hopefully, a full-time expert will be hired by the facility for this purpose.

Quality improvement is a customer-driven, information-driven approach to solving problems using statistical control techniques for analyzing and presenting the information. This approach builds team spirit and increases a sense of ownership among staff members. Tools such as PDCA give structure to the approach.

Differing staff member personalities and values create a demand for innovative approaches to learning tools used and rewards given as change is undertaken. Experts in QI concepts can best lead in formal learning sessions that take place away from the work setting.

HIM managers have an opportunity for internalizing and using new leadership skills while integrating QI concepts into their present management styles. As staff members observe this change in their leaders, a sense of ownership for their own work ethic and environment can increase and enhance the team spirit. While coaching and facilitating this change, HIM managers may revert to old management approaches as facts of life impact the workplace. Apology then becomes a growth experience for all participants. Empowered employees need to be given permission to fail.

Increased data needs are to be expected, which increases the need for managers to maintain current knowledge of systems available and their capabilities. Benchmarking assists the managers in suggesting or implementing the best ideas in systems and procedures. Networking contributes to the sense of community.

Monitoring and making adjustments when variations are significant are the last steps in the process and can allow managers to anticipate future problems and avoid them.

HIM managers are changing productivity measurement patterns in tandem with the changes that are occurring throughout the health care industry. Redesign or reengineering department organizations based on a customer-oriented focus leads to the creation of teams responsible for product or service lines.

The emphasis on working smarter to increase productivity demands using new technology and tools for setting performance standards and monitoring results. Productivity is defined as the number of task units produced per employee hour that meet the established levels of quality.

Four major managerial tasks can improve productivity: (1) focusing on defining departmental tasks, (2) concentrating activities on these redefined tasks, (3) defining performance, and (4) empowering employees. HIM managers increasingly use automated tools in performing these tasks.

Initiating productivity standards involves several steps: (1) analyzing present work processes; (2) reviewing present monitoring systems; (3) developing a priority list for productivity measurements including appropriate facility-wide changes; (4) documenting standards for performance measurements that include quality and quantity; (5) upgrading monitoring reports, using exception reporting where possible; and (6) meeting with teams for progress reports, developing changes, and then monitoring the process periodically.

Standardization of terms used for measurement is an important tool as performance monitoring is initiated. This list of terms can be used regionally and nationally for comparison. Regional and national firms provide subscription services to facilities and their benchmarking reports are available for comparative data.

Manual methods of work sampling will continue to be used for specific application.

CRITICAL THINKING EXERCISES

1. Describe the role of a facilitator in QI implementation.
2. Explain how health information services develops a customer-driven attitude.
3. How do managers use the tool known as PDCA?
4. Define productivity and document specific quality and quantity items that the coding and reimbursement team might use in creating performance measurement tools.

APPLICATION OF THEORY EXERCISES

1. Develop a model for encouraging a team spirit among members of the record activity section of health information services in an acute care facility. The coding section is frustrated because the assembly/analysis team within the record activity section is increasingly unable to obtain and complete all discharged records within their procedural guidelines.

    In discussing the problem with the managers on the patient units, the record activity section manager and the assembly/analysis team leader discovered the patient care givers are holding records for completion because of the recent staffing change to 12-hour shifts from 7 A.M. to 7 P.M. They frequently need to complete documentation after 7 P.M. At present, the team members assemble and analyze the available records from 7 P.M. to 10 P.M., ready for coding the next morning.

    Plan a brainstorming session with the team to solve this problem; state who should participate in finding a solution; offer two creative ideas; and then give rationale for using these ideas as tools to build team spirit.

    Select a problem that you have recently experienced and evaluate it using a fishbone diagram.

INTERNET ACTIVITIES

1. New approaches to quality PI are constantly being developed. Search for recent (within the year) information or articles that present innovative approaches to quality and PI. Summarize your findings.

2. Search the Internet to find organizations providing benchmark data for various health information management functions (coding, release of information, transcription, etc.). Summarize your findings in a table format.

CASE STUDIES

1. You have been designated as a PI trainer for an acute care hospital and have been assigned the task of outlining training priorities for the organization. Describe how you would approach this task, including which levels of management and staff must be trained and which tools should be included in initial training.

2. You are the coding supervisor for an acute care facility. Coders will be receiving merit-based wage increases based on productivity and quality using the following criteria:

Average Accounts Coded per Day	Accuracy	Wage Increase
30 or more	99%	5%
30 or more	98%	4%
30 or more	97%	3%
At least 25	99%	4%
At least 25	98%	3%

Average Accounts Coded per Day	Accuracy	Wage Increase
At least 25	97%	2%
At least 20	99%	3%
At least 20	98%	2%
At least 20	97%	1%
Less than 20	Less than 97%	No increase

3. Determine the merit wage increase based on the following coding productivity and quality audit findings:

Coder	Accounts Reviewed	Accounts with Errors	Average Accounts Coded per Day
Jasmin	150	2	23
Ricardo	150	0	28
Aaryn	150	3	32
Annika	150	8	18
Eduardo	150	6	24

REFERENCES

Camp, R.C. (1989). *Benchmarking: The Search for Industry Best Practices That Lead to Superior Performance.* Milwaukee, WI: Quality Press.

SUGGESTED READINGS

AHIMA. (2015, July). Best practices in the art and science of clinical documentation improvement. *Journal of AHIMA, 86* (7), 46–50.

Dougherty, M., Seabold, S., & White, S. E. (2013, July). Study reveals hard facts on CAC. *Journal of AHIMA, 84* (7), 54–56.

Drucker, P. (1991, November–December). The new productivity challenge. *Harvard Business Review.* 69–79.

Stanfill, M. H. (2015, April) A call for additional coding metrics. *Journal of AHIMA, 86* (4), 56–57.

The Joint Commission Survey Activity Guide for Health Care Organizations. http://dicon.medicine.duke.edu/sites/dicon.medicine.duke.edu/files/documents/2013_Organization_SAG%20%282%29--Survey%20Guide.pdf

SECTION VI

Special Issues for Health Information Managers

Project Management in Health Care

After completing this chapter, the learner should be able to:

1. Identify the steps in the project management life cycle.
2. Outline the processes involved in the initiation phase of the project management life cycle.
3. Create a project plan that includes vendor selection or contracted services.
4. Implement the project plan in the execution phase of the project management life cycle.
5. Evaluate and monitor the effectiveness of a project following implementation.

Project management Managing a significant project using a defined set of procedures in order to plan and control all of the associated activities necessary to meet the project goals.

By definition, **project management** is a method of managing a significant project using a defined set of procedures in order to plan and control all of the associated activities necessary to meet the project goals. An example of a project that would use project management principles would be an electronic health record (EHR) implementation project. There are two common approaches to project management; some organizations define it as a temporary process that is linear in nature, while others define it as a continuous cycle.

THE PROJECT MANAGEMENT LIFE CYCLE

Figure 18-1 illustrates project management as a temporary approach, starting with the process of initiating and then coming to a close at the end of the project. This approach may be appropriate for a short-term project. It might also be appropriate for a small project that feeds into a larger project or process that will be continuously monitored for quality.

More commonly, to be consistent with performance improvement activities, the project management life cycle is represented as a continuous process (see Figure 18-2), starting with initiation of the project, continuing through planning, execution, and controlling/monitoring. However, the cycle does not stop with controlling/monitoring, but rather performance improvement activities related to the project will be initiated based on findings in the controlling/monitoring process. While quality outcomes are considered through all steps in the project management life cycle, the controlling/monitoring phase is where the outcome is examined with a more critical eye in order to identify any adjustments that must be made in the process. This does not necessarily have to start immediately but could occur over a period of time spent monitoring outcomes.

Initiation phase

Initiation phase The beginning of the project management life cycle.

The **initiation phase** includes project definition, identifying expectations for all aspects of the project in order to clearly describe what the project is, when it will be finished, and how the project will be completed. Members will be

FIGURE 18-1   Project Management as a Temporary Process

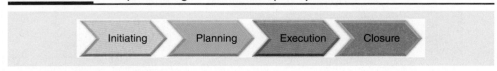

Initiating → Planning → Execution → Closure

FIGURE 18-2 Project Management as a Continuous Process

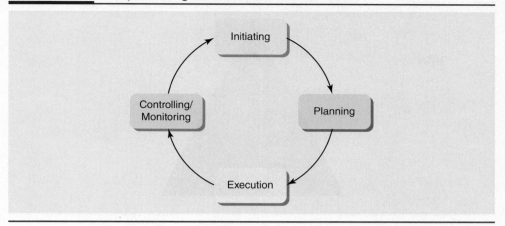

identified for the project team, who will be responsible for various aspects of the remaining phases in the project management life cycle. A **statement of work** (also known as **project charter**) is proposed to pertinent stakeholders to define the broad scope and objectives of the project. The initiation phase should include an impact analysis that involves calculation of a cost-benefit analysis, identifies potential return on investment, and outlines the potential benefits that may be realized through the completion of the project.

Statement of work Definition of the broad scope and objectives of a project.

Project charter See statement of work.

Determination of Need

Prior to planning too much for the project, the project team should conduct a needs assessment to determine that the project truly is necessary. This is generally completed through administering a survey or questionnaire to key stakeholders that collect data for analysis to determine if the current situation presents specific needs, or if stakeholders desire a change. Depending on the extent of the proposed project, a certificate of need (CON) may be required for submission to the state, as some states require detailed plans to be submitted for health care organizations along with justifications for new equipment purchase, new construction, or development of new service offerings requiring cost in excess of a state-specified amount.

Planning Phase

In the **planning phase**, the project plan will be drafted, including a detailed schedule that outlines tasks to be completed for the project as well as start dates and deadlines for each contributing process. The **scope** of the project will be developed to outline all work processes and resources required to complete the project. As the scope, timeline, and costs associated with the project are determined in the project plan, it is important to find the best balance between these three factors that will result in the greatest quality outcome.

Planning phase The second step in the project management life cycle.

Scope All work processes and resources required to complete a project.

FIGURE 18-3 Project Management Triangle

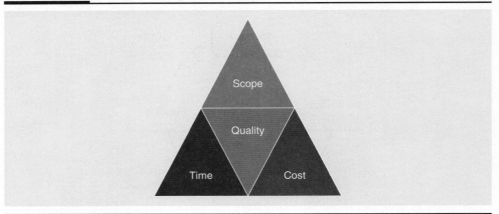

This balance is illustrated in Figure 18-3 in the form of a commonly used project management triangle.

Contracts

HIM professionals are often involved in projects that involve evaluation and management of contracts, which are legally enforceable agreements. Because of this, it is important to develop an awareness of contract law. This is a branch of law that is based on common law that deals with written or oral agreements that are enforceable through the legal system. Most contractual agreements in the HIM environment are documented clearly with comprehensive details. Depending on the nature of the contract and structure of the organization, the HIM professional may work closely with the organization's legal counsel when entering a contractual agreement.

Common activities that require HIM professionals to be involved with contractual agreements are EHR implementation, audits, document storage, scanning, release of information, transcription, and coding. Contract services are entities that provide certain agreed-upon services for the facility, such as transcription, coding, or copying. Contract coders are commonly hired as independent contractors on a temporary basis to assist with coding backlog or temporary coverage for vacations and interim positions while waiting to fill vacant positions.

When seeking contract services, there are several steps that are followed from the point of identifying a need to receiving services. When the decision is made that a contracted service is needed, research is done to determine what is available from different vendors. This is accomplished through sending a **request for information (RFI)**, which is a written document that is sent to a broad list of vendors during the design phase of the systems development life cycle to solicit general information about the products provided by each vendor. The information received is reviewed and the list of vendors is narrowed down for further evaluation. At this point, a **request for proposal (RFP)**

Request for information (RFI) A written document that is sent to a broad list of vendors.

Request for proposal (RFP) A request for specific information about a vendor's product and proposed contract information.

is sent. This is a request for more specific information about the vendor's product and proposed contract information. The RFP is generally sent to a narrowed list of vendors, following review of documentation received from the RFI.

Due Diligence

Once proposals have been received, the process of **due diligence** begins. This is a process that involves taking the time in order to make a fully informed decision, including exploration of potential technical, financial, legal, and other consequences of doing business with each vendor. Figure 18-4 illustrates how a decision matrix may be used in the due diligence process. Consider the process of contracting services for coding. For this example, three vendors will be evaluated against four criteria. Each of the criteria is ranked according to priority with the highest priority item assigned the highest number and the lowest priority item assigned the lowest number.

Vendor C is the most expensive, so a rank of 1 is assigned. Vendor A has the mid-level price, so it is ranked 2. The lowest price is Vendor B, so the highest rank of 3 is assigned to indicate that the price criteria is best met. The ability to provide services quickly with short notice is best met by Vendor A (rank 3), followed by Vendor B (rank 2), and least met by vendor C (rank 1). Since there are only two different responses for the criteria of the coder being able to work on site, the higher rank of 2 is assigned to both Vendor B and Vendor C, both able to meet the criteria, and the lower rank of 1 is assigned to Vendor

Due diligence
Process that involves taking the time in order to make a fully informed decision, including exploration of potential technical, financial, legal, and other consequences of doing business with a vendor.

FIGURE 18-4   Decision Matrix

	Priority Multiplier	Vendor A	Vendor B	Vendor C
Price	2	$100/hour (2)	$50/hour (3)	$100/hour plus travel (1)
Ability to provide services quickly with short notice	4	Coders immediately available at all times (3)	Requires advance notice of 1 week (2)	Requires advance notice of 2 weeks (1)
Coder available to work on-site	3	Remote coding services only (1)	Yes (2)	Yes (2)
Reputable company able to provide several references	1	Established nationwide company with few references (2)	Established local independent contractor with several local references (3)	New nationwide company with no references (1)

FIGURE 18-5   Decision Matrix with Calculations

	Priority Multiplier	Vendor A	Vendor B	Vendor C
Price	2	$2 \times 2 = $**4**	$2 \times 3 = $**6**	$2 \times 1 = $**2**
Ability to provide services quickly with short notice	4	$4 \times 3 = $**12**	$4 \times 2 = $**8**	$4 \times 1 = $**4**
Coder available to work on site	3	$3 \times 1 = $**3**	$3 \times 2 = $**6**	$3 \times 2 = $**6**
Reputable company able to provide several references	1	$1 \times 2 = $**2**	$1 \times 3 = $**3**	$1 \times 1 = $**1**
Total		$4 + 12 + 3 + 2 = $**21**	$6 + 8 + 6 + 3 = $**23**	$2 + 4 + 6 + 1 = $**13**

A, which does not meet the criteria. Vendor C is a new company with no references, so it is assigned the rank of 1 for the criteria of being a reputable company able to provide several references. Vendor A is an established company with few references, so it is assigned a rank of 2 for the criteria of being a reputable company able to provide several references. Vendor B is an established company with several references, so it is assigned the rank of 3 for the criteria of being a reputable company able to provide several references. The next step is to multiply these ranks by the priority multiplier. Once this is completed, the vendor with the highest total is determined to best fit all criteria according to the established priorities. This is illustrated in Figure 18-5.

Once the vendor has been selected, due diligence continues through negotiation of the final contract. Some of the aspects to be addressed with contract negotiation may include terms of payment, support, turnaround time, length of contract, and renewal options.

Project Execution Phase

Execution The phase of the project management life cycle that involves implementation of the plan.

As soon as the project plan has been completely approved, project **execution** may begin. The execution phase involves implementation of the plan in a manner that complies with all defined elements in the plan. Unfortunately, project execution sometimes deviates from the plan. If any area of the project management triangle formed by the balance of time, scope, and cost, is altered, quality of the outcome, or even the ability to achieve the desired outcome, may be compromised. The project management triangle illustration in Figure 18-6 demonstrates the potential result if the corners are not balanced with the

FIGURE 18-6 Project Management Triangle Lacking Dedication of Time

FIGURE 18-7 Project Management Triangle with Scope Too Broad

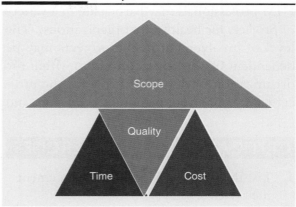

others. If the project team makes a plan to complete the project in a shorter time frame than may be necessary, note how quality falls out of the triangle. This may be the result of the team cutting out critical steps processes or quality assurance activities in order to finish the project sooner.

Another potential planning pitfall may be planning a project scope that is broader than what is realistically able to be completed to ensure a quality outcome. Figure 18-7 illustrates the potential result for this situation. Note that there are areas of scope that extend beyond the planned triangle. This phenomenon of **scope creep** occurs if the initially proposed scope of the project grows beyond previously defined limits. The end result in this case may translate to completion of the project, but not all areas in the altered scope will reflect quality.

Scope creep
Phenomenon that occurs if the initially proposed scope of the project grows beyond previously defined limits.

Evaluation and Monitoring Phase

When it has been determined that the scope of the plan has been achieved, evaluation of the outcomes should be performed to identify if all proposed goals were appropriately met, deadlines were met, and cost of the project was maintained within the budget. Based on the continuous process project management life cycle model, monitoring of the project outcomes will continue beyond the point where completion would have occurred with the temporary project management model. During the monitoring process, elements of the project, defined in the project plan, will be assessed at routine intervals, also defined in the project plan. During these routine assessments, any time areas are identified that quality may be improved through implementation of change, the cycle returns to the initiation phase for planning and implementation for performance improvement.

SUMMARY

HIM professionals may participate in a variety of projects for health care organizations. The level of involvement in the projects may be dependent upon the exact position within the organization or designated role on the project team. Initiation, planning, execution, and evaluation/monitoring activities in the project management life cycle to accomplish successful achievement of project goals, which may lead to initiation of performance improvement changes, starting the entire process back at the initiation phase.

CRITICAL THINKING EXERCISES

1. List the steps in the project management life cycle.

2. Interview an HIM professional involved in planning a project. Document the tools being used in planning the project and in carrying it into implementation.

APPLICATION OF THEORY EXERCISE

You are an HIM professional employed as an education coordinator for the department of public health and want to propose a community health literacy education campaign. Describe the activities that you must complete during the initiation phase, including elements that you might include in a determination of need for the project.

INTERNET ACTIVITY

There is a wide variety of software options available for project management. Search for project management products and compare at least two of them. Evaluate aspects including cost, ease of use, unique features, advantages, and disadvantages of each.

CASE STUDY

You are the HIM director of a 500-bed acute care hospital and have been asked to serve on the planning committee for EHR implementation. Your purpose on the committee is to identify needs from an HIM perspective. Make a list of information that would be useful for you to receive with the RFI, which could help you contribute to the decision-making process. Also make a list of important issues to be addressed during the contract negotiation phase.

SUGGESTED READINGS

Bailey-Woods, L., Dooling, J., Fabian, D., Kuehnast, T., & Luthi-Terry, S. (2014, August). Roles for HIM professionals in HIOs. *Journal of AHIMA*, *85* (8), 46–49.

Butler, M. (2015, February). Mind the gap: HIM rushes to bridge educational and professional gaps caused by a quickly advancing industry. *Journal of AHIMA*, *86* (2), 20–24.

CHAPTER 19

The Effective Committee

LEARNING OBJECTIVES

After completing this chapter, the learner should be able to:

1. List several reasons why managers choose to use committees and meetings for managerial tasks.
2. Weigh the advantages and disadvantages of using committees for decision making.
3. Identify the major techniques for group decision making and suggest appropriate uses for each.
4. Give the major responsibilities of a committee chairperson and committee participants.
5. Describe the components of a meeting agenda and state why each one is necessary.
6. Explain the value of each of the components that are a part of minutes.
7. Identify advantages and disadvantages for using computer technology to create electronic meetings.

INTRODUCTION

In health care organizations, committees and meetings are frequently used to bring together employees of different disciplines to perform managerial tasks. There are a wide variety of meeting types in which HIM professionals may be involved throughout their careers. Some of them are face-to-face, while some may occur as virtual meetings if those attending are not geographically able to attend in person. Meetings may be formal or informal in nature, depending on the organization or purpose of the meeting. Meetings attended by HIM professionals are not always directly related to a position in the workplace but rather may be part of a role being served as a volunteer for a professional organization, such as AHIMA, a CSA, or other organization. Departments also use meetings to share the decision-making tasks with employees. These tasks vary widely, depending on the committee's purpose, but coordination is ideally achieved as the members work toward a common effort. HIM professionals may spend a significant portion of time sharing expertise as members of these various committees and as participants at meetings. In addition, informational meetings are a normal communication tool that managers use for in-service presentations and to keep staff informed. This chapter explores opportunities available to committee members and chairpersons to create efficient productive meeting environments that use this time wisely.

Negative comments are frequently made about committees and meetings, which may indicate they are sometimes used inappropriately. To minimize the negative aspects, the major advantages and disadvantages of choosing the committee method for accomplishing managerial tasks are detailed. A chairperson's role in using committees to fulfill department objectives is outlined. The responsibilities of committee participants are addressed. Members who choose to create a cooperative, effective group of decision makers have an environment where ideas are generated, alternatives are sought, and integrated decisions are made.

Interdisciplinary committees may be considered as a type of matrix structure that can be permanent or temporary. The temporary committee is also called an ad hoc committee. Monitoring the progress of ad hoc committees is the responsibility of the delegating manager who sets deadlines to ensure action, decisions, and/or recommendations. This temporary committee is then disbanded when its purpose ends. The permanent interdisciplinary committee offers opportunities for HIM professionals to be advocates of automated health information systems and other HIM issues.

Preparing and distributing agendas and minutes are covered next. These documents guide the meetings as the chairperson communicates the direction the meeting should take, publicizes decisions made, and then adds action plans to assure delegated responsibilities are clearly known.

TEAM BUILDING

The health care industry implements teams for diverse purposes in all settings and all levels of organizations. Because of this, HIM professionals must have team building skills, which ensure proficiency in the organization, development, and promotion of effective teams. Teams may be formed for a variety of reasons in health care. Some may be long-term in nature, such as a self-directed work team in a specific area of the HIM department. Others may be temporary for the purpose of completing a project or addressing short-term objectives.

Most workforce teams have an executive sponsor, who provides a sense of direction for the team and organizational support. The executive sponsor may be the director of the department if the team is within the same department. Often, teams in health care are cross-functional in nature, including members representing multiple departments, service areas, or specializations. This team composition may present obstacles to members lacking knowledge of the functions of other team members. Depending on the purpose of the team, the level of information required regarding the functions of other members may be basic. However, if a cross-functional workgroup is being formed, there may be a need for cross-training so that members may learn greater detail about processes involved in other positions in order to better understand how the team members may complement each other's work.

Bruce Wayne Tuckman, whose work was focused on educational psychological research, published an article entitled "Developmental Sequence in Small Groups" (Tuckman) in 1965, which introduced a model of team development that uniformly defined four stages of progression in team group dynamics of cautious affiliation, competitiveness, harmonious cohesiveness, and collaborative teamwork. The most commonly referenced model identifies these steps as forming, storming, norming, and performing. These phases are illustrated in Figure 19-1.

Forming is when the team members first meet. The team members may not already know each other and it could also be the first time serving on a cross-functional team, so some team members could be new to teamwork

Forming
The team-building phase when team members first meet.

FIGURE 19-1   Position Description Content

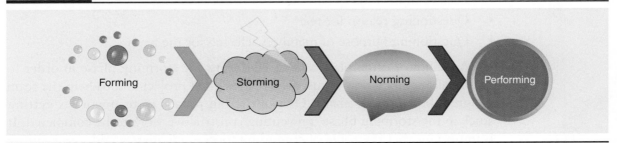

activities in the organization. If a team is created with members who do not know each other, at a minimum, each member should provide an introduction that includes information to identify pertinence on the team. Sometimes, icebreaker activities are performed. Team members should be able to recognize not only interests and knowledge that they may have in common but also diversity that allows each team member to bring unique contributions to the functioning and success of the team as a whole. During the forming phase, the following behaviors may be observed by team members:

- Hesitation
- Silence
- Observing others
- Politeness
- Impersonal
- Questioning purpose of team
- Caution

In order to progress beyond the forming stage, a facilitator may help by providing a sense of direction, provide necessary resources, and define the general expectations. Clear and complete communication should be provided to the team members regarding the reason for assignment to the team and the expectations. Team members should also be provided with opportunities to ask questions and share concerns. A common purpose should be established for the team and accountability should be clarified. When individual team members examine their role within the group, the second step of **storming** begins. This is the result of individual members beginning to realize the extent of the work expected of the team and examining how each member will be able to fulfill the purpose of the team. This may result in a sense of increased anxiety, which could lead to some of the following behaviors:

Storming
The phase of team building when members examine their roles in the group.

- Threatening to leave the group
- Disagreement about purpose of team
- Becoming confrontational with other team members
- Feeling trapped
- Lack of motivation
- Questioning reason for team
- Questioning purpose of members selected for the team

A facilitator often plays a key role during the storming phase in order to ensure all members stay focused on the assigned project and to help the team progress beyond this phase. One of the big pitfalls of teamwork is getting stuck in the storming phase, preventing constructive work to be completed. It is important that the topic of communication is adequately addressed during the storming phase, as lack of effective consistent communication among all team members could compromise the ability of the team to work together to accomplish the goals. Leadership, within the team or as a facilitator, should be alert to identify potential interpersonal issues that may arise during this phase and address them accordingly so that they do not interfere with progression of the team. Another method of overcoming obstacles that are presented with storming is focusing on opportunities to better understand the perspectives of other team members.

Norming is the third of the four steps in forming a functional team, during which each team member comes to understand the roles of all members and how they will fit together to work for a common goal. If the team has a facilitator involved, that individual may begin to back out at this point, as the team is on track to function with less guidance and external support.

Behaviors experienced during the norming phase include:

- Organization
- Setting priorities
- Constructive feedback

A functional team requires the following:

- Common, agreed-upon, measurable goals and outcomes
- Clearly defined roles for each member of the team
- Trust
- Mutual respect
- Effective communication

During the norming phase, the questions, "what," "how," "who," and "when" are answered. The team determines agreement about what objectives will be met by the team, how the objectives will be met, who is responsible for specific tasks, and when deadlines will be met. The details of what and how team objectives will be accomplished may already be defined to an extent when members are assigned to the team, although smaller milestones may be set for steps necessary to accomplish the ultimate goals. These steps will be established when the team members reach an agreement about how the goals will be met. All of these details should be documented for future reference to keep the team on track. A team charter may be created to explain the issues the team was formed to address, outline the team's goal or vision, and list the charter members of the team and their respective departments. A charter includes agreed upon team norms or rules, both explicit and implied, which determine both acceptable and unacceptable behavior for the group. These norms may also include ground rules that address meeting attendance, participation requirements, documentation, and decision making. Depending on the organizational culture, size, and nature of the team, roles may be assigned to team members.

Norming
The team-building step during which each team member comes to understand the roles of all members and how they will fit together to work for a common goal.

The charter specifies key roles of member and may also document which individuals will be serving in those roles. These roles may be filled by individuals through simply volunteering to serve in the position or something more formal, like election by team members. The role of team leader is generally responsible for the overall effectiveness of a team's work. The role of recorder/scribe is responsible for documenting details of a team's activities during meetings, including any documentation required by the organization. The rest of the team members are responsible for actively participating in team meetings, projects, and other activities. A team facilitator may be assigned to the team. The facilitator is responsible for serving in an advisory capacity to ensure that the team maintains focus and all projects pursued by the team run smoothly. The facilitator may also be used as a consultant for suggesting or training team members to use various quality improvement tools and techniques.

Performing
The phase in team building during which each team member is in a position to work toward achieving the team's stated goals.

The fourth step in forming a functional team, at which point each team member is in a position to work toward achieving the team's stated goals is **performing**. When the team reaches this phase, each member has fully embraced assigned roles, all members are contributing to reach common goals, and the members are working together to improve processes within the team. Milestone accomplishments should be celebrated and team members should be appropriately rewarded for their efforts. Some of the behaviors encountered in this phase include:

- Sharing
- Open communication
- Tolerance of diverse opinions

Depending on the nature of the team, there are two directions for the team following achievement of the performing phase. If the team was formed for accomplishing a project with short-term goals, the next step is adjournment. However, if the team is formed to become a long-term group, the performing phase becomes a circular process that involves continual development of improved processes to reach ongoing objectives. Occasionally, the composition of the team may change as a result of members leaving or being added. When this occurs, the group could potentially revert to earlier phases as the new and existing members strive to become a cohesive functional group. Another potential cause of reverting to earlier phases is significant conflict that arises among group members.

CREATING AND PARTICIPATING IN EFFECTIVE MEETINGS

Permanent, regularly scheduled committees are a part of the professional experience of HIM professionals. These meetings may be in health care facilities, professional organizations, community organizations, or regional councils. By sharing in the responsibility for effective meetings, HIM professionals can assist in creating time-saving sessions and can impact the decisions made by the group.

Meetings attended by HIM professionals in the workplace are dependent on the position of the employee. Management and upper-level administration employees often spend a significant amount of time in meetings. These meetings may include meetings for strategic planning, compliance, forms development, EHR planning, and other administrative committees. Meetings attended by nonmanagement employees are less frequent. Department meetings may be held monthly. Specialized areas within departments usually happen on an as-needed basis. Other meetings attended by nonmanagement employees include in-services, specialized training, and sometimes performance improvement focus groups. Outside of the workplace, examples of meetings attended by HIM professionals include meetings for continuing education and meetings for volunteer committees, workgroups, practice councils, board of directors, and various subcommittees for professional organizations.

Determining the frequency and length of meetings are based on a variety of factors. Some committees may meet on a quarterly basis, and some on a monthly basis. If a committee has a time-sensitive project to complete, meetings may be more frequent. If an organization needs to have a one-time only issue addressed or project to complete, the meetings may be held on an **ad hoc** (Latin term meaning "for this"), or as-needed, basis for the purpose of that designated purpose. **Standing committees**, on the other hand, are established for the purpose of oversight of ongoing and sometimes cross-functional issues. Some examples of standing committees on which HIM professionals may serve include:

Ad hoc As needed.

Standing committee A committee established for the purpose of oversight of ongoing and sometimes cross-functional issues.

- Medical staff committee
- Quality steering committee
- Safety committee
- AHIMA practice council
- AHIMA workgroup
- Board of directors for AHIMA, CSA, or other professional organization

It is important to remember that meeting attendance requires all attendees to be away from their work and not completing tasks associated with their positions. This should be considered in terms of the salary expense of attendees who will not be productive in these tasks during meeting time. In addition, work processes may also get behind if employees are away for meetings too much. For this reason, the composition of the group to be meeting should be carefully evaluated to determine how critical each person may be to accomplishing the purpose of the meetings.

The location should be considered when planning meetings. The location should provide sufficient seating to accommodate all attendees. Depending on the purpose of the meeting, table space may be needed for taking notes or completing other tasks. If a meeting is going to be for an extended period of time, such as an entire work day, if attendees will need laptop computers or mobile devices during the meeting, arrangements should be made to provide access to power outlets and availability of Wi-Fi. If the meeting will be in a lecture format for a very large number of attendees, there may be extra expense required to provide power and Wi-Fi.

Guidelines for creating and participating in effective committees and meetings are shown in Figure 19-2. The structure of a temporary committee may be more informal, but the guidelines outlined in Figure 19-2 still apply.

The guidelines in Figure 19-2 suggest responsibilities for the members as well as the chairperson and the recorder. When committee members accept responsibility for effective committee participation, the recommendations and decisions made can often have greater accuracy and offer better solutions than a single individual would make. The disadvantages of committees and meetings are outweighed by the advantages (Longest, 1990). Also, the time and effort spent by HIM professionals and other participants can be satisfying.

FIGURE 19-2   Guidelines for Effective Committees and Meetings

Delegated authority: Formally designated groups receive authority from the person or group with delegating power. This delegation may be for an advisory, informational, decision making, or coordinating committee or meeting. Authority is documented and specific. Ad hoc committees are given a time limit for action. The role and scope of committees is outlined and the membership may be specified.

Membership: Members should be kept as few in number as possible, but must include those with complementary skills and knowledge to effectively accomplish the objectives of the group. Assignment to a committee may be by position. When team members can select someone from among their ranks, that person should have communication skills for adequate group interaction and for sharing information back to the team.

Chairperson: Appointed by position usually but may be chosen from among the members or designated because of expertise. Chairpersons should understand group processes, be able to hold respect, and have ability to set the tone for the meetings. Responsibility includes coordinating efforts toward meeting the objectives delegated to the group and delineated in the agenda. Items on the agenda can be delegated to others as desired.

Agenda: Planned by the chairperson, by the group, or structured according to the objective for that meeting. Prepared in advance, the agenda should have a time frame for each topic with the responsible presenter listed. With the agenda distributed in advance of the meeting, each member can be responsible for coming to the meeting ready to participate as items come before the group.

Recorder and minutes: Assigned to someone with attention to detail and the time to prepare the minutes and action plans for timely distribution. Major points of each meeting, recommendations, decisions, and action plan items need recording. Minutes and action plans are then distributed as soon as possible following the meeting. In this way, activities that need accomplishing before the next meeting are not easily forgotten.

Advantages of Committees and Meetings

Communication and coordination have already been mentioned as major reasons for gathering people into groups for presentations, brainstorming, and decisions. Figure 19-3 details specific advantages for using committees in making organizational decisions.

The advantages listed in Figure 19-3 offer valid reasons for HIM professionals to make committees and meetings an integral part of managing their departments, teams, and interdisciplinary activities. However, the disadvantages of meetings listed in Figure 19-4 are also valid and give reasons for judicious use of the group process.

While the group process disadvantages can be minimized through skillful chairing of meetings, the cost factor is difficult to contain. Keeping the

FIGURE 19-3 Advantages of Using Committees in Decision Making

Group judgment aids in improving the quality of a decision.

Group interaction stimulates creativity.

Interteam and interdepartmental committees coordinate activities toward meeting department objectives.

Committees enhance acceptance of decisions and group cohesion as the pooling of specialized knowledge aids in understanding.

Group decisions divide responsibility and thus can increase commitment and motivation toward goals as knowledge of the problem is enhanced through discussion.

Agendas, minutes, and action plans communicate information and lead to coordinated efforts by the group and then by the departments and/or teams represented by each member.

FIGURE 19-4 Disadvantages of Using Committees in Decision Making

Cost of bringing groups of employees together to make decisions is high—employee salary time is significant.

Committees are time-consuming; decisions may need to be made and implemented in a shorter time frame.

Motivational deadlocks can occur when committee members have conflicts with the objectives; these deadlocks can create unrealistic compromises.

Divided responsibility can also be a disadvantage since members may not feel individual responsibility for decisions or recommendations.

Compromised decisions can be mediocre; therefore, when decisive action must be taken, one person may be better suited to making the decision. Committee recommendations can then be used for information only, not decision making.

Strong-minded, vocal members can control meetings; chairpersons may thus find it difficult to use group process methods effectively to assure everyone has the opportunity for input.

members on a committee to a minimum and keeping within the time schedule for each meeting are two responsibilities the chairperson must accept.

Techniques for Effective Group Decision Making

Managers have an array of techniques for use in group decision making, including consensus, voting, brainstorming, nominal group technique, and Delphi technique. Which technique is best suited to a particular need is the first decision. Then, when a decision is made to have group interaction, the type of group and the individual members must be decided. Decision by vote may be the best method, especially when every member has an equal stake in the action that results. Consensus building may be chosen as the most effective technique when the issue is not controversial and when there are benefits for the whole team, the entire department, or the facility.

Brainstorming, nominal group technique, and Delphi technique each have value in group decision making when a wide array of alternatives need to be evaluated before a final decision is made. These techniques are time-consuming, so the time factor must be considered.

Consensus Building

Managers may choose to use consensus for arriving at a group decision. When a consensus is achieved, each member of the group is accepting of the chosen solution to a problem—each member is able to support the decision and implement any plan of action necessary. The strength of consensus building lies in the participation of all members during the process, the use of sufficient time to resolve any items of disagreement, and the support of every member once the consensus is reached. Figure 19-5 details the basic guidelines for effective use of the consensus-building technique.

When consensus cannot be achieved, the chairperson can choose to ask for a motion, second the motion, and vote on alternatives. If time allows and the

FIGURE 19-5 Guidelines for Effective Consensus Building

Constraints from upper-level management will not prevent acceptance of group decision.

Manager can support and implement group decision.

Each group member has time to present views and alternatives for a solution.

Areas of disagreement are exposed, discussed, and resolved.

Areas of agreement are explored fully.

Use of bargaining or voting is avoided.

Support of decision is possible for all group members.

difficulty is with a lack of complete information on the item, it may be feasible to choose an ad hoc committee to gather the additional material and present it at a future meeting. For example, at an HIM department employees meeting, one agenda item concerns the purchase of a divider to separate the customer reception area to give more privacy to the release-of-information staff. After a description of the proposed divider was presented, two group members had strong objection to it and asked that consideration be given to a divider they had seen in a hospital department in a nearby city. Because of a lack of consensus, the chairperson suggested an ad hoc committee be chosen to visit the other department and report back in 2 weeks. This action plan was approved and implemented. At the next meeting, the chairperson called for a motion, a second, and a vote was taken on which divider to purchase.

Brainstorming

When an informal atmosphere where creativity can be encouraged is an appropriate setting for engendering ideas on a subject or a problem, brainstorming can be effective. Brainstorming generates creative ideas and develops concepts without typical group inhibitions or pressures toward conformity. Thus, it is an idea-generating process that encourages alternative suggestions. Managers have important tasks in preparing for brainstorming sessions, however. These are included in the suggestions outlined in Figure 19-6 for successful sessions.

Brainstorming is a commonly used method and may be structured or unstructured in nature. New strategic goals are often the result of brainstorming, which involves spontaneous generation of sometimes creative ideas from all members of the group. Unstructured brainstorming is a group problem-solving technique wherein the team leader solicits spontaneous ideas for the topic under discussion from members of the team in a free-flowing and non-judgmental manner. Unstructured brainstorming has the advantages of being able to share ideas as they come to mind and other members of the team can easily build on the ideas of others. The disadvantages of unstructured brainstorming are that team members with more dominant personalities may take over the discussion and less assertive members may not feel comfortable speaking up to share ideas. Structured brainstorming is a technique wherein the team leader asks each participant to generate a list of ideas for the topic under discussion and then report them to the group in a nonjudgmental manner. This approach to brainstorming provides all team members equal opportunity to contribute to the discussion. However, the delay in waiting for a turn to contribute in structured brainstorming may allow the opportunity for team members to forget ideas or parts of ideas that they have generated.

Brainstorming sessions should start with stating ground rules for the session. The most important of these should be that all should maintain an open mind and not criticize anybody else's ideas. The reason for this is that it

Brainstorming
Spontaneous generation of sometimes creative ideas.

FIGURE 19-6   Techniques for Successful Brainstorming

Develop a clear understanding of the subject or problem and a set of questions to begin the session.

Gather tools for the session such as flip charts/wall charts and writing supplies for recording ideas.

Ask someone who is not a group member to serve as recorder for the meeting.

Begin the session with an introduction to brainstorming technique and the goals of the meeting. The following points should be covered:

a.   Review the subject or problem to be discussed.

b.   Encourage each member to share ideas, so there is a large quantity of input.

c.   Explain that no idea is considered too outlandish as ideas are generated, no criticism of ideas is allowed, and no value judgments are made.

d.   Explain that no praise of ideas is allowed.

e.   Remind everyone that during this idea-generating phase no discussion of an idea is allowed.

f.   Begin asking the prepared questions and have several ideas to offer that will generate thinking; at least one should be far-fetched.

Exhaust idea generation, making sure each group member contributes.

Cluster the ideas by grouping similar points together and assist the group in looking for patterns of similarity.

Encourage the group to suggest additional improvements from these clusters, refine wording, and develop alternatives for the subject or problem through consensus.

Inform the group of how the developed alternatives will be used.

promotes individuals to share ideas, which they may not otherwise share due to worry about the reaction of the group. Some of the most effective and innovative solutions come from brainstorming that encourages any suggestions, no matter how unconventional they may initially seem. Even if that specific idea is not used, it could potentially be the basis for something greater. Group members should provide enough information to fully explain each idea, yet keep it brief in order to allow time for others to speak. A common practice is to go around the table to allow each team member a chance to speak, continuing to repeat the process around the table until nobody has anything more to contribute, or until a designated time limit is reached.

Brainstorming generally results in a large number of ideas, which could be cumbersome to evaluate if kept in the order they were shared. A commonly used method for organizing ideas from brainstorming sessions is affinity grouping, which categorizes similar ideas together. Sometimes, this may result in combining like ideas, which could reduce the list of ideas. However, a need generally remains to further narrow the selection. One approach to this is the multivoting technique, which may be approached in different ways, depending on the structure of the group. Some groups may post flipchart pages around a room and give each member sticky notes to number 1 to 5, then place their sticky notes on the pages with the ideas to "vote" for them, with 5 being the highest rank. The votes for the ideas are calculated and the ones with the highest totals are selected for the final discussion. The number of finalist decisions is determined by the group prior to voting. Another approach to multivoting is use of electronic means by sending an electronic survey to group members after the brainstorming results have been compiled and organized. The benefit of this method is that it allows a greater sense of anonymity. However, the drawback is that results are not immediately available, as they would be if the process were to be completed at a meeting.

Nominal Group Technique

Another method of generating ideas in a group is the **nominal group technique**, which is somewhat similar to brainstorming but provides anonymity of ideas and allows the team to narrow the choices. Each team member writes ideas and submits them anonymously to the team leader or other designated individual. Once all members have submitted ideas, they are listed for all to review prior to voting. The voting process involves each member ranking their top choices of ideas on the list. The number of choices to be ranked is identified by the team leader. Once all members have ranked their choices, the results are tallied and shared with the group. Benefits of the nominal group technique are that the anonymous nature of the idea submission with the nominal group technique allows members to share ideas that they may have concern may be judged by the other group members, plus this technique helps avoid the phenomenon of groupthink, in which members of the team tend to simply agree with each other in order to maintain a sense of harmony in the group, which in turn reduces fresh, unique idea generation.

Nominal group technique A method of generating ideas that involves anonymous submission of ideas followed by voting to rank the ideas.

The generation of ideas for decision making is the first goal of nominal group technique; however, the group session is highly structured and personal interaction is minimized. The chairperson's role with the nominal group technique is outlined in Figure 19-7 and emphasizes the independent thought of each member during the initial phase of the process.

An advantage of using the nominal group technique is its unbiased approach to decision making. Group members work together without restricting independent thinking. Managers who choose the nominal group technique to enhance decision making must be ready to accept the alternative ranked highest by the group if this was stated as part of the process. On the other hand, managers can use the nominal group technique process to bring forth several alternatives of high ranking that will then be developed further by the management team for a final decision.

Group members need to understand what use will be made of their product to enhance ownership of the eventual decision.

FIGURE 19-7   Steps for Successful Nominal Group Technique Meeting

Develop a clear understanding of the subject or problem and a set of questions to generate creative thinking.

Gather tools for the session such as pads of paper for members, flip charts/wall charts, and writing supplies for recording suggestions and priorities.

Ask someone who is not a group member to serve as recorder for the meeting.

Explain the NGT process to the group. The following points should be covered:

a. Present the subject or problem.

b. Distribute pads of paper and ask each member to silently think about the subject or problem and record ideas for later sharing.

c. Emphasize that no talking is permitted during this phase unless a point of clarification is raised.

d. Explain that during the recording phase each member will read one item at a time, around the group, in sequence, until all ideas are recorded.

e. Encourage unusual ideas, quantity of ideas, and the value of piggybacking on someone else's idea once the list is exhausted.

f. Emphasize that no criticism of ideas is made during this phase.

Begin the silent idea generation phase; allow ample time.

Ask each member, in turn, to read one idea for recording on the flip chart; repeat in sequence until all ideas are recorded.

Cluster ideas and encourage evaluation and discussion of pros and cons.

Assign a letter of the alphabet to each idea or cluster of like ideas.

Ask members to record, on paper, their ranking of the ideas, using the letter assigned, prioritizing by order of importance. No discussion is allowed during this phase.

Pick up papers and record votes on the flip chart next to the corresponding letter. Total them for each idea.

Choose the ideas with the highest ranking (5 to 10 of them) for further discussion, refinement, and improvement.

Inform the group of how the ideas and rankings developed will be used.

Delphi Technique

Delphi technique
A group decision-making technique where members do not meet face to face.

When time constraints are not present and group members are physically separated, a more complex technique can assist in futures planning. The **Delphi technique**, for instance, assists HIM managers employed by multihospital corporations in bringing a degree of standardization to health information activities among the facilities. The major features of the Delphi technique are listed in Figure 19-8.

Assessing the perspective of widely scattered members can also be achieved effectively with the Delphi technique. For example, selected members of a national organization such as AHIMA can be asked to offer ideas on a subject impacting the future of the association. Although the Delphi technique does not offer the advantages of face-to-face interaction as with brainstorming, fresh ideas can surface as expert minds consider alternatives and build consensus over time.

FIGURE 19-8   Characteristics of the Delphi Technique

Identification of the subject or problem occurs and group members are chosen.

Questionnaires are carefully designed to elicit responses from group members toward solving the problem or developing ideas about the subject.

Group members complete this first set of questionnaires and return them for compilation.

Group members receive the compilation and a second questionnaire that will hopefully elicit new alternatives and narrow the options.

Compilation of the second set of questionnaires brings the group closer to consensus and another questionnaire is developed and distributed with the second compilation, if necessary.

Distribution of compiled information and new questionnaires continues until consensus is reached.

Sharing decision-making tasks, when delegated to those responsible for creating proposed changes, offers managers increased ideas and options. Committees can offer the appropriate setting for beginning the change process.

When HIM managers understand the alternative methods available to them for informing, sharing, obtaining ideas, and motivating, they can be effective chairpersons by choosing the most effective technique for the situation.

The Effective Meeting Participants

For truly effective meetings, all participants must understand why they are attending and then conscientiously fulfill their roles. While the chairperson sets the tone of the meeting, he or she cannot create success unless the participants are actively involved in fulfilling the goals for the meeting. This section looks first at the role of the chairperson and then at how the participants can contribute to group effectiveness.

The Chairperson

The manager of an HIM department in an acute care facility participates in many committees and meetings. This section focuses on those meetings where the HIM manager serves as chairperson. These meetings or committees are given various names such as management team meetings, administrative council, team quality improvement group, team planning group, department in-service meeting, or interdisciplinary team meeting. When a new group is formed, the members enjoy naming the committee and this ownership of the name can enhance their commitment to the objectives.

Regularly scheduled meetings can become boring committee sessions unless the chairperson uses creativity to stimulate ideas and present routine information in unusual ways. Figure 19-9 offers suggestions to keep regular meetings focused and positive.

FIGURE 19-9   Planning Committees and Meetings

Regular Meetings Within the Department

Decide whether routine items come before the group or are communicated by another route: newsletter, team leaders to team, e-mail, or bulletin board.

Choose whether a scheduled meeting is needed—cancel unless needed. Schedule short meetings when the full time allotted is not needed.

Encourage each employee to place items on the appropriate agenda. Have the team manager review the item with the employee.

Include items pending from the last meeting: any previous items needing further action.

Special Meetings Within the Department

Announce well in advance.

Plan meetings for second- and third-shift teams as needed.

Define the objectives, role, and scope of the meeting, especially when authority is given for decision making.

Confirm the meeting with guest speakers and other invited guests the day before the meeting.

Interdisciplinary Meeting

Communicate with other department(s) regarding a meeting, structure of the meeting, and agenda items.

Offer to share responsibility for chairing the meeting, preparing the agenda, and distributing background material and minutes.

Encourage teams to suggest agenda items.

Plans Common to All

Separate agenda into categories:

a. Information-only items
b. In-service presentations
c. Decision-making brainstorming to gather list of alternatives
d. Decision-making solution to problem

Chairing the Meeting

Begin the meeting with enthusiasm. State the objectives using action verbs. Repeat specific objectives as necessary for agenda items, changing the tone of the meeting appropriately.

Have material organized by agenda items; have notes of specifics to be mentioned.

Encourage participation by each member; ask for input by name, as needed.

Use active listening skills to gain a clear understanding of ideas.

Use a controlling mechanism to the extent necessary for reinforcing positive behavior or for keeping attention on the subject at hand.

Repeat decisions and motions for the recorder.

Use the consensus approach to decisions when feasible; when necessary, ask for a motion, a second, and call for a vote.

Allow the group to give opinions and suggestions without judgment, domination, sarcasm, or argument.

Be professional at all times but with a sense of humor.

End the meeting on time by staying within the time frame for each agenda item.

The Members

When a committee meeting convenes, the participants bring to the meeting their unique ideas, expertise, personal biases, and concerns. Putting aside personal interest and making decisions in the best interest of the department or the facility can be a challenge for the employees.

A major responsibility for members comes before the meeting itself. Reviewing the minutes of the past meeting and becoming knowledgeable about areas that are less familiar is a first step. Next, the action plan needs to be read as it may serve as a reminder of specific responsibilities with a deadline. By meeting action plan obligations within the time frame, members participate in creating a successful group and, in turn, success in the workplace. The third responsibility comes when the agenda for the upcoming meeting arrives. Reviewing the items, looking for any topics that have background material attached, begins the preparation process for the meeting. This may include networking with experts or reading current journals or books to gain current knowledge on a topic.

An ongoing responsibility for committee members is to actively look throughout the workplace for problems, potential problems, and possible areas needing change to add to future agendas. Being a catalyst for quality improvement and for initiating paradigm shift proposals enhances the value of meetings and offers satisfaction to members.

During the meeting itself, effective members arrive on time, vary seating arrangements to avoid cliques, participate as active listeners, and offer ideas constructively. Each member can guard the time factor by refraining from bringing up issues that have little value for the item being discussed or could more appropriately be resolved in another setting.

HIM professionals desiring to gain experience in meeting leadership can offer to present specific topics or chair the meeting for a specific decision-making agenda item. Managers willing to offer growth experiences to their staff can be rewarded with increased enthusiasm and commitment.

DOCUMENTATION TOOLS FOR COMMITTEES AND MEETINGS

Communication contributes to the success of the group process, and agendas, minutes, and action plans are important communicating components. This section details effective use of these documentation tools.

The Agenda

Prior to a meeting, the person or group in charge of leading the meeting creates an **agenda**, which is a document that provides the order of items to be covered in the meeting. Agendas are distributed to attendees either prior to

Agenda
A document that provides the order of items to be covered in a meeting.

the meeting or at the start of the meeting. It is common practice to provide an agenda with the meeting notice so that those invited may identify topics on which they may need to prepare by gathering information to bring to the meeting or do research to identify any questions or comments regarding the topic for discussion at the meeting.

The value of creating structure for committee meetings through use of agendas was mentioned earlier. By attaching background material to the agenda and distributing it in advance of the meeting, chairpersons add to the ingredients for success. Agendas should be considered communication tools where committee members can both learn the direction the group is taking toward meeting the objectives and share in that move by suggesting agenda items.

Components of an agenda include the following:

- Name of the group or committee that is having the meeting
- Location of the meeting
- Date and time of the meeting
- List of invited attendees
- Start time
- Items or issues to be discussed during the meeting
- Name of the individual who will be presenting each item
- Amount of time allotted for each item
- Adjournment time

The agenda should introduce each topic in a simple sentence, phrase, or even just a few words. If the agenda is for an educational meeting, it may be accompanied by brief paragraphs about the topics and biographical information for the presenters. Educational meetings often require attendees to travel to an unfamiliar location, so directions or a map should be provided as an accompanying document.

A timekeeper may be designated to serve the role of the attendee who is responsible for ensuring that the meetings are kept in line with the agenda and alerting the team of remaining time for each agenda item in order to help the team make satisfactory progress toward meeting and project goals. Sometimes, the items "old business" and "new business" may also be included immediately prior to adjournment of the meeting. "Old business" provides a time to discuss issues that have been addressed at previous meetings but may not yet be resolved. "New business" is a time designated for attendees to present issues that are pertinent to the group and may warrant further discussion or action. An example of an agenda is provided in Figure 19-10.

When creating the agenda, the overall length of the meeting should be evaluated to determine if there is a need for any breaks and how often they should be. This is often the case for meetings that last the entire work day, such as strategic planning, in-services, or educational meetings provided by

FIGURE 19-10   Sample Agenda

**Memorial Hospital
Executive Board
Quarterly Meeting**

Agenda

1.	Call to Order		
2.	Assignment of timekeeper	5 minutes	P. Thompson
3.	Approval of minutes from April 21, 20XX	5 minutes	P. Thompson
4.	Administrative Report	10 minutes	J. Schmidt
5.	Finance Update	10 minutes	R. Johnson
6.	Medical Staff Report	10 minutes	C. Gibson
7.	Committee Reports		
	a. Quality Steering Committee	10 minutes	P. Collins
	b. Compliance Committee	10 minutes	D. Williams
	c. Bylaws Review Committee	10 minutes	B. Spring
8.	New Business	10 Minutes	P. Thompson
9.	Adjournment		

regional, state, and national organizations. The amount of time for each topic should be adequate to cover necessary information but not too long so that attendees do not lose interest or feel their time is being wasted.

Robert's Rules of Order, also referred to as parliamentary procedure, is a commonly used guide for keeping meetings orderly and efficient, addressing everything from the agenda, to reports during the meeting, to the minutes. Robert's Rules of Order were created by Henry Martyn Robert in 1876 when he realized that a need existed to provide structure and order to presiding over meetings. As of 2011, there have been 11 editions published for Robert's Rules of Order, with updates to address expanded roles and more detailed descriptions about processes. The rules were established based on study of parliamentary law. One of the useful topics covered in Robert's Rules of Order is how to handle motions, discussion, and voting on issues for which decisions must be made during meetings.

The Minutes

Most meetings require that **minutes** are taken to provide documentation of key events in the meeting. Taking minutes for a meeting may be approached in a manner similar to taking notes for a class in school. It is not necessary

Minutes
Documentation of key events in a meeting.

to capture every word or every comment in minutes. Documentation of minutes may take a while to master determining what points are necessary for inclusion.

The minutes serve as a record of decisions made and are valuable legal documents showing when policies changed or when other changes occurred. This information is needed for accrediting and licensing bodies and shows the level of effective business practice. A facility may have specific guidelines for writing minutes, especially those involving medical staff attendance. The recorder then follows this format in writing the minutes.

The HIM department will need to maintain minutes of department meetings, showing the attendees and actions taken. Accrediting staff will ask for documentation that in-service programs involved all employees and covered a range of topics. And, of course, minutes complement the agenda as communication tools for the meeting members. When distributed promptly after a meeting, minutes reinforce the decisions made, act as reminders of activities still needed, and give the date of the next meeting.

Minutes are taken in a variety of formats. The format to be used is generally identified by the organization or group for which the minutes are being taken. Some formats commonly used include simple outline or bulleted list, narrative with paragraphs, or a grid that identifies action items to be completed following the meeting (see Figure 19-11) The content of minutes may vary, the format differ, but the major components remain the same. Figure 19-11 shows minutes of a medical record committee meeting, chaired by a physician. Note that absent physicians are listed as excused for medical staff statistics.

The major components of minutes include:

1. Name of meeting, date, time, and location.

2. Those present at the meeting; should also include those absent to assure members unable to attend will receive a copy of the minutes.

3. Items brought before the group, with motions, votes, consensus decisions, actions, deferments; expressed in clear, concise language. Deadlines, persons responsible for future action are included.

4. Substantiating materials are attached to the official minutes such as outlines of in-service presentations, recommendations brought before the group from another committee, or supporting documents.

5. Name and title of the chairperson and of the recorder are indicated. This can be in the list of those present or as the final line of the minutes.

6. The action plans are also attached to the minutes and distributed.

Unless the meeting is quite informal, it is preferable to have a staff member who is not a member of the group as the recorder. Members should be given opportunity to concentrate on the issues, not on recording the actions.

FIGURE 19-11   Sample Minutes

Memorial Hospital Monthly Coding Meeting April 1, 20xx				
Present: • Anna Schmidt • Delores Jones • Victoria Sanders • Ed Davis • Lisa Anderson			**Absent:** • Rhonda Andrews • Jeffrey Fulton	
Topic	**Discussion**	**Action Items**	**Person Responsible**	**Due Date**
1. Approval of minutes from March 20xx meeting	Motion to approve made by Jason S. and second by Martha W. Vote to approve unanimous.	N/A	N/A	N/A
2. Review of audit findings	Overall findings reflected 98% accuracy. Errors identified in coding for new endoscopic approach for cardiac procedures.	Plan continuing education presentation for coding staff to provide information about new cardiac procedures being performed.	Susan C., Coding Supervisor	May 1, 20xx
3. Scheduling	Three coders have maternity leave anticipated to start in June. Coverage options were discussed.	Obtain administrative approval for overtime. Secure contract coder to assist with backlog.	Sandie B., HIM Director	May , 20xx

The Action Plans

Tasks that must be accomplished following the meeting, which are referred to as action items, are documented in the minutes, along with the individual or group designated as being responsible for completion. Action items may also have due dates documented if they are time sensitive for completion. Assignment of due dates for action items provide an effective means for accountability by designated responsible individuals.

A very successful meeting can be held with all the members enthusiastic about the direction of the plans as they leave the meeting. But, success can

Action plan
The document that assists committee members with delegated responsibilities by reminding them of tasks and deadlines; prepared and distributed immediately following committee meetings.

be halted in its tracks if an **action plan** to remind members responsible for follow-up activity is lacking.

Minutes should be completed as soon as possible following a meeting. Some may even take a laptop or tablet device to the meeting so that they may create a rough draft concurrently. Waiting too long following the meeting to complete minutes allows time to forget important details related to notes taken during the meeting. Following the meeting, the draft should be reviewed for accuracy and submitted to the committee chair and members of the committee according to accepted processes of the group. Sometimes, the chair may require initial review of the minutes prior to distribution to the rest of the committee.

Some meeting minutes may need to be retained as official documentation of activities for various purposes. Accreditation-related meetings require documentation of activities and attention to cited deficiencies or performance improvement plans. Meeting minutes may be used as legal documentation of actions by committees. Because of this, accuracy of information documented in minutes is critical. Formal committees generally have review and approval of minutes of the previous meeting as one of the first agenda items.

TECHNOLOGY USE FOR MEETINGS

Technology has provided the ability for HIM employees to work from remote locations, but that has also introduced the challenge of determining logistics for meetings with remote employees. Remote meeting needs also exist for committees that involve members in varied geographic locations that create difficulty in organizing face-to-face meetings. Not only are face-to-face meetings for committees with geographic diversity difficult to coordinate with schedules, but they may also be quite expensive if travel, hotel, and meals need to be provided.

There are several technology-based methods to facilitate and enhance meetings. Some of these are used in face-to-face meetings; others are used to help connect attendees for virtual meetings, and others may be used for both. Face-to-face meetings sometimes involve presentation of information. In the past, this was accomplished through posters or film-based slides. Now, presenters may use PowerPoint to share graphs, photographs, diagrams, and other information. The slides may be easily printed for distribution at the meeting.

Due to expense, time, and logistics, face-to-face meetings may not be the best option for all meetings. Many options are available to facilitate virtual meetings. Conference calls are cost-effective and do not require expensive technology. Conference calls are easily attended by committee members who are not even able to be in their own offices at the time of the call. If a committee member is traveling at the time of a conference call meeting, any phone may be used to dial in to attend the call. Caution should be exercised if attending a conference call when driving. Many states have laws prohibiting mobile phone use while driving without use of hands-free devices, which are easily used with Bluetooth technology. Even if a hands-free device is used, the attendee must ensure that safe driving is the primary focus of attention and refrain from trying to write notes from the call while driving.

Conference calls may not be able to thoroughly meet all of the communication needs during virtual meetings. Presentation of information, such as charts, diagrams, videos, or software demonstrations may require more advanced technology. Many desktop sharing programs are available for the purpose of showing PowerPoint presentations, videos, or other documents over the Internet. These applications often allow attendees to pass desktop sharing ability to other attendees if more than one individual is presenting information.

Scheduling of meeting for large committees, especially those involving representation from different disciplines or different organizations, is often difficult to coordinate. The process of scheduling meetings can often be challenging to approach. The committee chairperson or other individual responsible for planning the meeting may send an e-mail to committee members to gather scheduling suggestions, but this method may result in a large number of messages that could be too cumbersome to realistically and easily handle. Several Internet-based products and services are available to facilitate event or meeting scheduling. The meeting planner can send a notification to committee members with a link to a website that provides a list of proposed dates and times for each member to identify availability during each time slot.

CONFLICT IN GROUPS

All individuals have unique backgrounds, opinions, knowledge, skill sets, and cultural origins. Because of this, situations may arise in teams that generate conflict. Conflict may be constructive or destructive in nature.

It is important to accept the fact that not all conflict results in negative outcomes. Some degree of conflict is actually necessary in order for progress to occur. Conflict may uncover a previously unknown issue that needs to be addressed. For example, conflict regarding a workflow process might bring attention to procedures that should be updated or may even lack formal documentation of procedures.

While most workplace conflict may be relatively easy to resolve with little or no intervention, occasionally, the conflict may be of a magnitude that requires an objective, neutral third party to mediate the situation through constructive confrontation to explore all aspects of the situation. This intervention may involve meeting with all parties involved, as well as performing conflict management on a one-on-one basis, meeting with the individuals to identify solutions that will be acceptable for each, and then meeting again with all parties to evaluate the options and determine a mutually acceptable solution.

Active listening is critical to resolving conflict in teams or anywhere else in the workplace. As a manager or leader using active listening, it is necessary to make sure you first make an accurate assessment of the conflict. When discussing the issue with involved parties, this may be done using active listening techniques of restating what has been said, paraphrasing in your own words to verify that you truly understand the issue, and summarize the scenario so that the full picture of the issue is identified. When gathering information about the conflict, be an empathetic listener, refrain from using "you" statements, and clarify feelings. Once the problem has been clearly identified and agreement has been reached that a problem exists, all parties involved should contribute to brainstorming for solutions, and a solution should be mutually agreed upon.

While complete absence of conflict in teams is not a realistic goal, there are preventative measures that may be taken to reduce the incidence and severity of conflict. Maintaining clear, open communication in team or other group settings provides an atmosphere of trust. This should include active listening techniques. Should conflict arise, the team leader or a neutral facilitator may provide guidance to prevent the situation from escalating. Advice for individuals in conflict situations is outlined in Figure 19-12.

FIGURE 19-12 Conflict Management Tips

Conflict Management	
DO	**DO NOT**
Focus on the process, not the person Respect others, even if you do not agree Encourage others to share their side Listen Maintain an open mind	Blame others Take things personally Focus too much on things that cannot be changed Make assumptions Interrupt

SUMMARY

Teams are widely used in health care organizations and related professional associations. HIM professionals may serve on teams within the HIM department, cross-functional teams involving many departments, or even teams outside of the workplace, such as volunteer committees for professional organizations. The team building process involves challenges that must be overcome as the members progress through the phases of forming, storming, norming, and performing. As the team becomes functional, the composition of the group should be considered when generating ideas and addressing any conflict that may arise.

Meetings and committees are an integral part of the group process within health care, and managers spend a significant portion of their time as members, committee chairs, or participants in informational meetings.

Making meetings effective demands effort on the part of the chairperson and each participant. This effort is worthwhile because the advantages of using committees in decision making outweigh the disadvantages. The advantages include improving the quality of a decision, stimulating creativity, increasing coordination, solidifying group cohesion, and enhancing commitment.

Major disadvantages of using committees for decision making are the cost of bringing groups of employees together, the time factor, motivational deadlocks, lack of individual responsibility for decisions, consensus that may lead to mediocre decisions, and strong-minded members who may control the meeting.

Managers have responsibility for choosing the best technique for group decision making; these techniques include consensus, voting, brainstorming, nominal group technique, and Delphi technique. Chairpersons may change from consensus to a vote when an issue becomes controversial. Informing participants of how the product of their efforts will be used is an important component when the chairperson wishes an array of alternatives for a later decision.

Agendas, minutes, and action plans communicate with group members and serve as legal documents. Agendas include a time limit for each item and are distributed with background material before the meeting. The recorder uses clear, concise language in the minutes to describe the meeting and the actions taken. Items that need further action are documented in an action plan that serves to remind members of later assignments.

Using computer technology for electronic meetings can shorten the time in making a decision and can offer anonymity and honesty. To take advantage of face-to-face discussion, the chairperson may choose to end the meeting with verbal interchange as refinement of alternatives is undertaken.

CRITICAL THINKING EXERCISES

1. What qualities would you like to see in the chairperson of a committee where you are a member?

2. List five techniques managers can use for group decision making. Which technique would the manager of a coding and reimbursement team most likely use for gathering proposed workstation designs for the team's area of the new department? The alternatives are to be submitted to the department manager in 10 days. The final decision will be made by the construction planning team.

3. What is the follow-up document that accompanies the minutes? Who uses this document and why?

4. Obtain copies of the agenda and minutes from a recent meeting and analyze them for effectiveness in serving as communication documents.

5. Attend a committee meeting, take minutes, and prepare the minutes for distribution.

APPLICATION OF THEORY EXERCISES

1. Identify two situations in which you encountered conflict, either in the workplace or another setting—one that was effectively resolved and the other that was not. Describe the conflict situations and explain how each was addressed. Explain what was effective and ineffective with the management of each situation and how each might have been managed to have different results.

2. Summarize your activities from last weekend using one the formats presented for meeting minutes in Figure 19-2. Provide a brief discussion of each activity that is identified as a topic. Identify any action items that emerged, along with a due date and individuals responsible for the items.

INTERNET ACTIVITIES

1. Search online to find creative methods of team building and overcoming obstacles to formation of a functional team. Outline at least five different activities that you found and identify potential situations in which they may be used.

2. Search online to find technology options that are available to facilitate the process of meetings for groups connecting from remote locations. Compare two of the products that you find, including identification of features (such as ability to share computer screens or use computer to call into the meeting), price, and other aspects that you might identify as being significant.

CASE STUDIES

1. You are the manager of a large HIM department that has recently experienced loss of three supervisory positions. You have decided to approach the situation by organizing your department into self-directed teams. Which HIM functions would you combine in teams and which functions would you keep on separate teams and why? How will you explain this change to your staff members? What kind of support or guidance should you be prepared to provide to facilitate the change?

2. You are the HIM director of a 400-bed acute care hospital. The vice president of finance has assigned you with the task of developing a revenue cycle management committee. Create a proposed plan that outlines what key positions from which departments in the organization should be included, frequency of meetings, and standing agenda items.

REFERENCES

Tuckman, B. W. (1965). Developmental sequence in small groups. *Psychological Bulletin, 63* (6), 384–399.

Longest, B. (1990). *Management Practices for the Health Professional* (4th ed.). Norwalk, CT: Appleton & Lange.

Robbins, S., & Coulter, M. (2012). *Management* (11th ed.). Upper Saddle River, NJ: Pearson.

SUGGESTED READINGS

http://www.robertsrules.com/

http://www.rulesonline.com/

CHAPTER 20

Managing Change as a Health Care Professional

LEARNING OBJECTIVES

After completing this chapter, the learner should be able to:

1. List the major forces that are creating a mandate for change in the health care industry.

2. Give three categories where change typically occurs in health care organizations.

3. Identify major challenges that face HIM professionals initiating change in both acute care facilities and ambulatory settings.

4. Define revitalization and explain why change experiences are needed for professional career growth.

5. List four underlying reasons why employees may resist change and explain the rationale for each.

6. Discuss six steps managers can take to reduce resistance to change.

7. Explain the factors that offer value to the role as a broker of health information.

INTRODUCTION

Multiple trends are shaping the health care industry, and most of these trends impact the HIM profession to some extent. From the paradigm shift toward integrated delivery systems to increased ambulatory care, the pressures to obtain accurate, timely health information appear to consistently increase. These shifts to an information-driven health care setting, where communicating health information via technological tools reigns, add to the impetus for HIM professionals to increase analytical, assessment, and evaluation skills. The need to embrace expanded communication roles will also increase. As professional organizations develop contemporary definitions of the profession that emphasize a combination of knowledge in medical science, health data needs, confidentiality and legal issues, systems thinking, and information technology, changing roles will emerge.

Accepting shared responsibility for the development of an integrated longitudinal electronic health record (EHR) that will meet customer needs through integrated networks, HIM professionals can find new opportunity for **revitalization** of their professional vision. HIM professionals can choose to accept responsibility for being change agents in shaping future health care trends, articulating a **new vision** and molding a contemporary definition of the profession that is understood by their customers.

This chapter explores the inevitable changes that are impacting the health care industry and suggests three major categories of change: technical, structural, and employee and interpersonal relationships. Next, the challenges and rewards of embracing change and proactively planning, organizing, and implementing change activities are discussed. Change offers opportunities for career advancement and the next section revisits briefly the opportunities outlined in Chapter 1. This section also shows why HIM professionals need periodic revitalization to stimulate a new vision that can lead to expanded roles, excellence, and excitement in the workplace.

Creating an environment for reducing resistance to change is a crucial skill for change agents. The next section looks at some factors that cause resistance, and methods that managers can use to create a sense of ownership and belonging among employees to lessen the resistance.

The last section of the chapter takes a broad look at managing and brokering health care information into the twenty-first century.

Revitalization
A growth concept where professionals consciously stretch their horizons and gain new visions for the future.

New vision
The creation of new professional career goals as the result of assessment and revitalization efforts.

CHANGE IS INEVITABLE

The strategic planning that consumes a significant portion of managerial time and effort is, more often than not, in response to perceived forces that result in a revised vision, new objectives, and improved customer relations. These forces may be external to the enterprise, or they may come from internal pressures.

External Forces

Government laws and regulations regarding health care are an example of external forces that may be anticipated by managers. Or, the laws and regulations can change quickly, leaving health care managers to react by initiating change. Pending legislation is published in the *Federal Register*, which is also known as the "Daily Journal of the United States Government." This is where public notices, proposed regulations, final rulings on new legislation, and significant documents are published. HIM professionals may keep abreast of *Federal Register* materials by signing up for the listserv to get notifications by e-mail. The American Health Information Management Association also provides an *Advocacy Assistant*, which provides information about pending legislation that impacts the HIM career field. The *Advocacy Assistant* also provides templates for letters to elected officials and information about how to contact the elected officials in specified geographic regions.

Community growth or the actions of other health care institutions may be anticipated—these external forces result in changes that impact how a facility meets the needs of its customers. Notice that the word *anticipation* is used to describe these examples of external forces. If the SWOT analysis is not performed and strategic planning is neglected, the facility will not have an anticipatory, proactive approach to change. Instead, top executives and middle management will be reacting to the imposed changes when the pressures mandate action. The example of government laws and regulations, enacted quickly, shows that despite the SWOT analysis, reactive change is sometimes necessary. However, innovative organizational changes do not take place in a reactive environment.

Internal Forces

Internal forces also create an environment for organizational change. At the extreme, the objectives of the facility can be revised when a new upper-level management team is employed—with resulting vision and cultural changes. Other internal forces that stimulate change for HIM professionals frequently involve technology with new equipment that demands retraining for new skills among the employees. Another internal change that may be faced in times of change in the health care environment is change in the organizational structure or even merger with another organization. Anticipating and planning for such change offers opportunity for revitalization for the HIM managers and the teams involved.

An unfortunate internal force for change involves dissatisfied employees and results in increased stress and behavior problems. Resistance to change causes dissatisfaction and stress; these issues are discussed later in this chapter.

Major Categories of Change

Strategic planning is crucial to managing organizational change from the internal and external forces mentioned above. When organizational change is undertaken, it typically involves one or more of the three major categories of change. These categories are (1) changing the technology, (2) changing the structure, and (3) changing employees and interpersonal relationships. Figure 20-1 briefly describes activities that HIM professionals will perform as these major categories of change are undertaken.

As the details in Figure 20-1 suggest, a balanced approach to creating change includes a combination of appropriate elements from these three categories as managers look for the tools and techniques that will bring successful results. Since internal and external pressures that bring change are inevitable, HIM professionals must continually seek a proactive stance in meeting the challenges. While not possible with every pressure, anticipating and planning in a proactive manner offers rewards as outlined next.

FIGURE 20-1   Major Categories of Change

Changing the Technology

External forces may be the likely reason for new equipment such as laptops, smartphones, and iPads, or for new software. As integrated delivery systems increase with new technologies such as cloud sharing and phone apps, standardization may mandate additional hardware and adaptable software. This will necessitate revised policies, revised procedures, and retraining of employees. On the surface, these changes may not appear to involve any major change in the objectives planned for the department. However, it is likely that technology changes will provide a catalyst for change in the other two categories as well as with organizational redesign and team-building relationship enhancement.

Changing the Structure

As discussed in Chapter 8, organizing the department is not a static process. Innovative organizational changes to flatten the managerial structure, to create self-managed teams, or to decentralize some sections are redesign or reengineering options. Utilizing facets of organizational design best suited to their unique settings, HIM managers can use structural change to create efficiencies and effectiveness that will offer excellence to their customers. Such changes will involve the redesign of positions, of position descriptions, and of the workflow to better meet customer needs. With implementation of these structural changes, attention must be given to the last category—interpersonal relationships.

Changing Employees/Interpersonal Relationships

Changing interpersonal relationships in response to planned technology and structural changes is crucial to success. The redesign of a department where employees are empowered through creation of self-directed teams results in increased responsibility and authority for these teams. With such major changes, the department may need consultants with expertise in **organizational development (OD)**. OD is defined as a focus on techniques to change people and their interpersonal work relationships (Robbins & Coulter, 2012). Consultants in OD can assist in preparing employees for change by offering sensitivity training, team building, and interteam development techniques. Effective communication of the vision, objectives, and benefits of the changes are also needed.

Organizational development (OD) A system of techniques to motivate people and improve the quality of interpersonal work relationships.

CHANGE: THE CHALLENGE AND THE REWARDS

In the preceding sections, several reasons for implementing change activities in an HIM department are offered. The advantages of planning and implementing innovative organizational change where there is anticipation of external or internal factors are then emphasized. When the management team anticipates and then plans strategically, the opportunities for success are enhanced. With success come rewards that can include satisfied customers, motivated employees, recognition for change agent excellence, or personal career advancement.

Within the Department

The principles outlined in Chapter 4 for effective time management are crucial to meeting the challenges facing HIM professionals in anticipating and preparing for change. When the pressures of uncontrolled response time do not allow reflective, creative, periodic thinking and planning time, the challenge of anticipating change and instituting strategic departmental planning can go unrealized. The resulting stress only increases as dependency on crisis management becomes more and more commonplace. Revitalization of the vision cannot take place.

By taking the steps outlined in Chapter 4 and managing time effectively, not only can stress be lowered, but HIM managers can begin to envision rewards as they anticipate, plan, and implement change in their roles as innovators, systems thinkers, and technology-wise brokers of health information. The increasing demand for data capture, analysis, integration, and dissemination will result in a wider distribution of knowledge among employees as they serve the customers of health information. Managers who recognize the advantages of educating and empowering teams with increased knowledge, skills, and responsibilities will be rewarded with visionary teams that give excellence to customers and are motivated to accept the next responsibility.

Within Ambulatory Settings

Mergers, managed care, integrated delivery systems, health maintenance organizations (HMOs), and similar terminologies are used to describe the trend toward the growing networks of health care providers and insurers. Increasingly, the trend is to provide the full spectrum of care for contracted patients. In response to this trend, developers of EHR and related information systems are accelerating the pace of open, interoperable, integrated health care information systems that can lead to a functioning EHR network. As patient care moves increasingly into the ambulatory arena, HIM professionals have the opportunity to build careers within the ambulatory setting. Being part of the teams that shape delivery of health care patterns for the future can be rewarding.

Within Other Settings

Challenge and reward face HIM professionals who choose careers in diverse settings such as those outlined in Chapter 1.

PROFESSIONAL REVITALIZATION AND NEW VISION

To revitalize is to offer enriched opportunities for personal growth that energize people and stimulate them to perform at their optimum. Busy HIM professionals may have difficulty finding the time and expending the effort to scan the environment, think critically, and adjust their vision for the future on a periodic basis. But for personal growth and for collective professional growth, it is essential. Professionals who take the time, at least every 5 years, for this revitalization process, can be the leaders, thinkers, and planners who take the HIM profession into future successes.

To create a new professional vision means to view the future with imagination and clear thinking that can be shared with others. Through leadership, this shared vision brings a community of individuals together, working toward the same objectives. The process of change can then occur.

Specific steps toward revitalization and creation of a new vision are outlined in Figure 20-2. These steps offer professionals an opportunity to develop visionary skills and leadership. Each step is discussed below.

Step 1: Create Time for Planning

Comparing the present vision with accomplishments gives HIM professionals insight into the direction they have taken during the period. While a major revitalization and a new vision is of value every 5 years or so, a yearly assessment

FIGURE 20-2   Steps Toward Revitalization and New Vision

Step 1. Create time for planning: Set aside time to revisit the past and plan for the future.

Step 2. Initiate activities for growth: Initiate professional growth planning such as taking formal courses in leadership, critical thinking, and systems thinking; read current literature; attend seminars and workshops.

Step 3. Practice new thought patterns: Practice using new thought patterns that lead to proactive mode; be information focused.

Step 4. Embrace creative tension: Embrace creative tension that leads to cognitive dissonance; resolve through focus on ultimate vision.

Step 5. Share the new vision: Share the new vision with the management team; articulate and integrate plans into action.

is equally valuable. In fact, Peter Drucker, in *Managing the Non-Profit Organizations,* suggests a yearly self-assessment that focuses on a review of the past year, a comparison with the goals for that past year, and a vision for the future (Drucker, 1990). This evaluation will require setting aside personal time, away from external pressures, and then answering several questions in a search for revitalization. These questions should include the following:

1. What have been my major successes in the past year and have they given my customers, my employees, and myself satisfaction?
2. Have I enriched my position over the past year so that I have added responsibilities and enrichment?
3. What do I want to be remembered for and am I progressing toward that goal? What adjustments do I need to make to remain stimulated to achieve this goal?
4. Have I served as mentor to others as I introduced change over the past year?

By answering these questions, HIM managers can review the direction of their careers, their work environment, and then make the necessary adjustments that keep them focused on the ultimate vision.

Step 2: Initiate Activities for Growth

Lifelong learning activities assist in maintaining the focus of revitalization and offer opportunities to change thinking patterns. Because traditional health information activities have focused on objects such as the physical medical record and its contents, courses in technology and systems thinking have special value.

Step 3: Practice New Thought Patterns

Breaking away from routine thought patterns and reactive modes of behavior can take great effort. HIM managers who make that effort find creating a satisfying and rewarding new vision stimulating. The resulting revitalization has benefits for the HIM professionals, for their work environment, and for the collective profession.

Step 4: Embrace Creative Tension

In Chapter 13, cognitive dissonance was discussed as a sense of uneasiness created by a difference between reality and hopes. HIM professionals can create an environment where creativity takes root and empowered teams envision and build systems that will close the gap between reality and the vision.

Step 5: Share the Vision

Leadership involves visionaries who can motivate others to move toward the vision. By articulating the objectives and vision to the working teams and persuading each employee toward the best effort, the shared vision can become reality.

Shaping the Curve

Each professional has a lifetime career curve and the shape of that curve is the responsibility of the individual. Figure 20-3 depicts a curve that illustrates the career of an individual who chooses to enter the health care industry as an HIM professional and is initially enthused about his or her job and the profession. As the years go by, however, the HIM professional appears to be waiting for someone else to parade the next new vision into his or her professional life. When that does not happen, when the HIM professional does not reach out for revitalization, for growth, nothing happens. Instead, he or she stagnates and the result is the flat curve seen in Figure 20-3. The curve begins normally and then flattens out as there is no stimulation to create a new vision experience.

Revitalizing means continuing education, job enrichment, and increased breadth of experience. For example, a manager who has spent the last 5 years with a fairly stable department chooses to stretch them self and their staff by becoming informed about creating a departmental business venture. Planning with the coding and reimbursement teams, he or she then chooses to develop documentation improvement educational services for physician offices in town. By initiating a plan to become a revenue-producing department in this entrepreneurial manner, the HIM manager can revitalize her own professional spirit and create new vision experiences for the coding and reimbursement teams as well. The curve in Figure 20-4 has a new vision experience just beginning, and this demonstrates the growth of revitalization.

To avoid stagnating, of course, HIM professionals may choose promotion by educating themselves to become CIOs, vice presidents, or managers of ambulatory settings. Advanced education, growth experiences, and

FIGURE 20-3   Lack of New Vision Experience

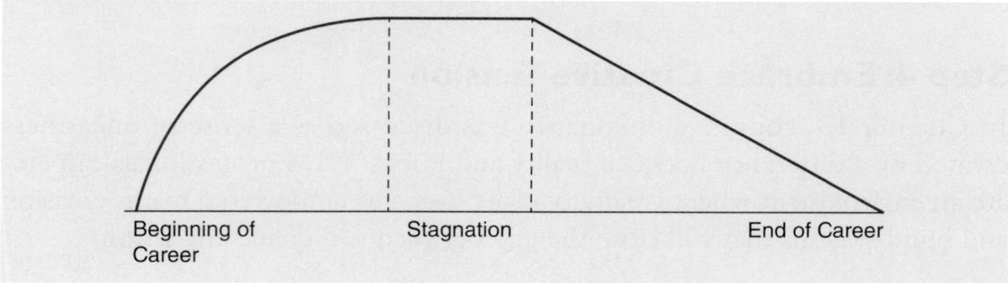

FIGURE 20-4   New Vision Experience

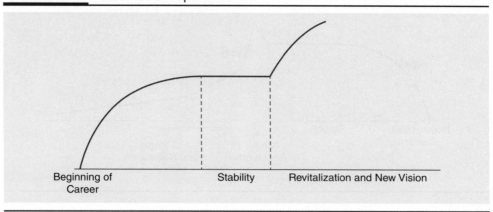

Beginning of Career   Stability   Revitalization and New Vision

FIGURE 20-5   Lifetime New Vision Experiences

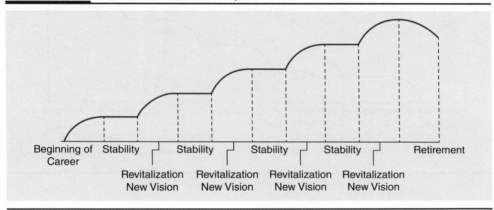

Beginning of Career   Stability   Stability   Stability   Stability   Retirement

Revitalization New Vision   Revitalization New Vision   Revitalization New Vision   Revitalization New Vision

mentoring are three steps that professionals may utilize in the new vision process. Figure 20-5 offers a lifetime glimpse of new visions that can keep HIM professionals excited about their daily activities and revitalized over the life of their professional careers.

Scarring and Self-Protection

Revitalization is not without risks. These factors can be counterproductive to new visions and will be setbacks on the path to continual growth curves for HIM professionals. Negative attitudes can result when professionals reach out for revitalization and are hindered in their plans. For example, after 5 years as regional manager of a copy service firm, an HIM professional chose to grow by returning to school and obtaining a master's degree in business administration. When a position opened within the firm for a vice president on a national level, the regional manager applied for the position, and, after several weeks of infighting and political maneuvering, did not receive the promotion. This experience scarred the manager to the extent that they left the health care

FIGURE 20-6 Scarred Attempt at a New Vision Experience

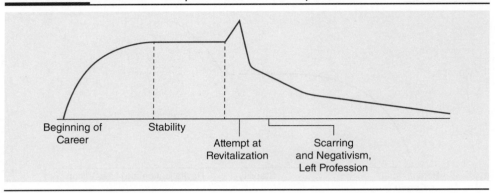

FIGURE 20-7 Scarring and Healing with Mentoring Experience

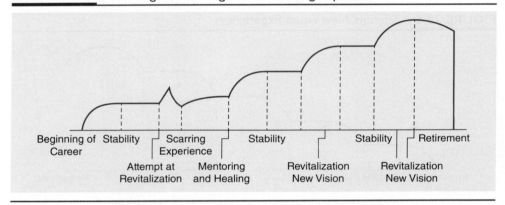

industry and protected them self from further pain by taking a staff position in a stable food product business.

Figure 20-6 offers a pictorial review of this experience. The curve that showed promise has flattened and the scar may prevent further new births. Mentoring can guard against the self-protection that arises following a painful scarring. When a seasoned HIM professional assists in restoring self-confidence to a scarred colleague, new vision experiences can revitalize and renew the spirit. The disjointed curve in Figure 20-7 offers a realistic view of the value that mentoring can have in the life of a scarred professional.

Entrepreneurial HIM professionals can extrapolate these personal growth ideas for their businesses also. Starting a new business that offers services or products in health care can be exhilarating, and when riding the crest of success, entrepreneurs may feel they are on top of the world. This euphoria can lead the professionals to feel their business will stay there by continuing to do things the same way. This is a fallacy; their business will decline unless they have a series of new visions, revitalization, and a dedication to stay on the leading edge of advancing technology. Businesses will have the declining curve of Figure 20-3 without this constant effort for growth.

Emerging Roles for Advancement

As trends in health care continue, new roles emerge that offer opportunities for HIM professionals. Several have already been mentioned, but other possibilities expand the vision. For example, evolution of the EHR has contributed to opportunities in health information exchange. As responsibility for creating databases, maintaining confidentiality, and disseminating meaningful reports becomes focused, HIM professionals can fill the opportunity niches that will emerge for accomplishing these activities. By joining committees, councils, and associations, HIM professionals will stretch their imagination and sharpen their skills for fulfilling future needs.

Standardization efforts as health care networks grow can offer an attractive niche also. From insurance forms to smart card technology, standardization will enhance the speed of change toward the EHR, and HIM professionals can find opportunities for career paths within the vendor community. Developing new tools and techniques to assist in data capture, analysis, integration, and dissemination of health information are also roles that can bring satisfaction to HIM professionals as vendor employees.

As relationships between physicians and hospitals change, there are opportunities to create niches where HIM professionals can carve out their roles. Some hospitals are creating physician support services departments with broader objectives than the typical medical staff office. Especially when these departments are involved in the automatic transfer of patient information, HIM professionals may find fulfilling careers implementing new technologies and managing such departments. As the range of ventures and contracts between physicians, hospitals, and insurance firms continues to expand, additional opportunities for challenging careers are created for HIM professionals with a vision of the future.

The legal profession has captured the hearts of some HIM professionals. With additional legal knowledge, these leaders are now filling key roles within professional associations, the government, and health care facilities. As legal decisions are made regarding national health information networks, confidentiality, or standardization, the direction provided by these experts adds to the esteem of the profession. Participating in legal health care activities offers rewards to many HIM professionals.

Consulting firms attract HIM professionals looking for career changes. The wide range of roles within consulting offers the opportunity to be on the leading edge of health care changes in specialty areas of interest. Some entrepreneurs choose to transition into self-employment by creating new companies while phasing out present positions. Being personally accountable for career advancement and choosing their personal best time for new growth experiences bring rewards to HIM professionals. Those who innovate change for the future and not just react to pressures mandating change are the true visionaries.

REDUCING RESISTANCE TO CHANGE: CREATING AN ENVIRONMENT FOR CHANGE

Employees bring their total past experiences into the work environment and these experiences likely include attitudes about change. To better understand the human element of resistance to change, then, requires that managers know their team members and be environment creators for reducing resistance to change. Implementing more than one change reduction method to meet the needs of individual team members may be necessary.

The most likely reasons for resisting change fall into four major categories. These are outlined in Figure 20-8. As underlying causes of resistance, they must be addressed; if only the symptoms of these causes are addressed, resistance will likely erupt again.

Awareness of the reasons for resistance to change offers advantages to HIM managers. Now they can be masters of the change process, not prisoners of the symptoms prevalent when change is planned. These advantages allow managers to review resistance factors and then take specific steps. These are outlined in Figure 20-9 and can reduce resistance as managers become environmental creators by utilizing steps that are appropriate to the situation.

BECOMING A BROKER OF HEALTH INFORMATION RESOURCES

Responding to the change initiatives outlined in this chapter can leave HIM professionals breathless. Because the health care industry is playing catch-up as it

FIGURE 20-8   Reasons for Resistance to Change

Change creates uncertainty: Uncertainty upsets equilibrium and resistance may continue until there is a return to status quo. For example, when there is concern that team members may lose their jobs, the status quo can return when team members learn jobs will be lost only through attrition.

There is a fear of loss: Employees feel secure in their familiar settings. Change creates a fear they may lose what is already possessed or they may not be able to learn new equipment and new methods.

There is team pressure to resist: When the change is perceived to alter status symbols within the team or break up informal relationships, there can be pressure from some team members to resist. This can create tension for other members who must choose between following friendship pressures or employer initiatives. The price of cooperation may then be perceived as too high.

There is a belief that proposed change is not in the best interest of the department: There could be instances when resistance is valid. When valued employees have rational reasons for resistance, managers who listen to these reasons and review the options may avoid mistakes.

FIGURE 20-9   Steps for Reducing Resistance to Change

Communicate: Reduce uncertainty by communicating the need for change. Schedule meetings to be sure all shifts are covered. Assure that interdepartmental teams impacted by the changes also have the information. Share success experiences of others. Stay positive and enthusiastic. Be as specific as possible. Use all the communication tools available—people learn through different avenues. Use the grapevine judiciously. Be an active listener.

Educate: Insist on adequate training for all involved team members. Have teams share in changing policies and procedures—educate them in the process. Build credibility and trust of all levels of management, if necessary. Share the background reasons for change through in-service. Use vendor knowledge when possible.

Participate: Enlist help from team leaders and informal leaders. Involve those who have negative feelings; make them a part of the change process to facilitate a sense of ownership.

Facilitate team building and interpersonal relationship enhancement: Update the teams involved by offering team building and interpersonal relationship enhancement programs. Incorporate specifics about the changes into these programs.

Negotiate and reward: Offer alternative change options, when feasible, to allow negotiation in decision making. Offer rewards throughout the change period, especially verbal rewards. Offer fun time to release tension and build commitment.

Evaluate and make corrections: Evaluation of the changes must be ongoing; resistance can return quickly when problems erupt. Make necessary corrections, communicate, and stay positive.

moves from the information age into the communication age, change and turmoil will continue. In this turbulence, finding the time to take a deep breath and make time for a personal assessment will demand discipline. Unique confidentiality and legal issues have hampered past change initiatives in health care and will continue to bring stress to HIM managers in their role as change agents.

At the root of change, however, are the familiar terms *efficiency* and *effectiveness*. Vision and objectives may be adjusted as the industry moves into new frontiers, but efficiency and effectiveness remain the energizing goals of managers. With these goals, offering excellence to customers as information is communicated using the latest technology will continue to guide managerial action. Disseminating accurate, timely data and database information by presenting them in a format that meets the expectations of diverse customers remains a goal that will keep HIM professionals focused. This goal translates into having the skill and knowledge to develop health care databases that are flexible, dynamic, and interactive. Moving the health care industry through these change initiatives takes cooperative effort among many professionals, with each one contributing specific skills.

To stay on the leading edge of change, HIM managers must develop anticipatory skills, must be knowledgeable by reading or scanning a wide range of articles and books, and must be familiar with vendor applications. Becoming acquainted with tools, techniques, and systems for the profession requires consistent effort. Developing the EHR and health information exchange opportunities for communicating health care information will challenge the skills and knowledge of health information brokers. Technical tools such as electronic health care applications, Wi-Fi technology, health information exchange and others will become familiar terms. But anticipating and having the technical knowledge are only the beginning.

To be brokers of health information, HIM professionals must also have managerial skills for becoming proactive change agents. As such, they must be willing to take risks, to initiate change, and to develop a sense of destination for themselves and the profession. Using powerful communication tools, knowledge, and skills will allow health information brokers to take part in the exciting future of health care that can lead to lasting wellness for the customers in the community or traveling the globe.

SUMMARY

External forces continue to exert pressure on the health care industry to change. Because of confidentiality and other issues unique to health care, transition from the information age into the communication age has been hampered in the past. HIM professionals must become proactive change agents in solving these issues and be a part of moving the industry forward. Internal pressures also demand change, frequently in step with those demanded by external forces.

The major categories of change are (1) changing technology to meet the needs of integrated delivery systems, (2) changing the structure, with present trends toward flattening the organizational design, and (3) changing employee/interpersonal relationships, which includes responding to such initiatives as team organizational structure and CQI. Organizational development consultants are useful in communicating the vision, objectives, and benefits of change.

The challenges to HIM brokers during these turbulent times are many and varied, but the rewards within acute care departments, within ambulatory settings, and for professional advancement create incentives that make the challenges worthwhile.

New vision experiences keep managers from stagnating. By revitalizing their professional life every 5 to 9 years, HIM professionals renew their spirit and energize themselves and their employees. The broad range of career opportunities in health care offers endless options for professionals seeking career advancement and unique satisfying roles.

Resistance to change can be anticipated. Underlying reasons that lead to resistance include uncertainty, fear, team pressures, or vested interests. Steps that can reduce this resistance include communication, education, participation, team building, rewarding, and ongoing evaluation. Knowledgeable managers can journey successfully through the maze of change with their teams and reengineer their departments into models with systems in place, ready for the communication age and poised for the future.

CRITICAL THINKING EXERCISES

1. Give the five steps that HIM professionals can take toward revitalization.
2. Choose one of the four factors for resistance to change and discuss reasons for the resistance.
3. Choose one of the steps for reducing resistance to change and discuss the rationale for its effectiveness.

APPLICATION OF THEORY EXERCISES

1. Interview an HIM manager who is planning a departmental change. Prepare a table that shows the following:
   a. Planned change—separate the change into subsets showing how a change in one factor of the department will create the need for changes in other factors.
   b. State which of the three major categories of change is involved for each subset of change planned.
   c. List some challenges the manager will face for each of the subsets of change.
   d. Offer some possible reasons why the employees may resist the proposed changes.
   e. Discuss steps the manager can take to reduce the resistance reasons offered above.
2. Interview an HIM professional who has changed career paths at least twice. Prepare a curve line that shows revitalization and any self-protection efforts taken because of scarring experiences.

INTERNET ACTIVITY

Search online for articles about change management. Summarize both a successful and an unsuccessful change management story that you find.

CASE STUDY

Sarah has been working as a coder in the same acute care facility for nearly 20 years. The transition to using EHRs has been difficult for her, and now her organization is starting to discuss adoption of computer-assisted coding. Discuss how her manager might facilitate the change and help Sara accept it better. What might Sarah do herself to reduce the anxiety she is feeling about the change?

REFERENCES

Drucker, P. (1990). *Managing the Non-Profit Organizations.* New York: Truman Talley Books.

Robbins, S., & Coulter, M. (2012). *Management* (11th ed.). Upper Saddle River, NJ: Pearson.

SUGGESTED READINGS

Desai, A. (2015, May). Scanning the HIM environment: AHIMA's 2015 report offers insight on emerging industry trends and challenges. *Journal of AHIMA, 86* (5), 38–43.

Eramo, L. A. (2015, April). Learn more to earn more ... how to further your HIM education, and what it gets you. *Journal of AHIMA, 86* (4), 28–34.

CHAPTER **21**

Personal and Professional Career Management

LEARNING OBJECTIVES

After completing this chapter, the learner should be able to:

1. Describe the content of professional resumes and state four principles that guide in their preparation.

2. Explain four reasons for writing a cover letter that introduces the resume.

3. Identify three major reasons for careful planning prior to a position interview.

4. List 10 major personality organizational types and explain how each type tends to organize personal work.

5. Describe five major tools and techniques for effective personal and office time management.

6. Identify aspects of professionalism that are of concern to health care professionals.

7. Describe opportunities HIM professionals have to enhance personal and professional growth.

Managing professional career goals and personal life with the same enthusiasm that brings success to the workplace is an important HIM activity. This chapter includes six areas of emphasis for personal and professional career management:

Preparing resumes and cover letters

Preparing for interviews

Managing personal time

Planning for positive performance evaluations

Investing personal effort toward professional growth

Maintaining professionalism

Specific rules to guide in these activities are offered with suggestions from practitioners who already have successful careers.

PERSONAL PLANNING FOR A PROFESSIONAL CAREER

This section is devoted to personal planning for a professional position. As you have internalized the management planning principles of this text, you may have discovered some that apply directly to your personal life. Have these concepts been helpful this week in day-to-day experiences? At first it may take conscious thought to develop patterns of planning practice; then it will become a way of life. It is rewarding to develop the skills in using management concepts for planning your professional future. Your first position following graduation will be very important to you. No less important is the position you will hold 5 years later. The strategic planning undertaken now may determine whether you will stretch yourself to reach each plateau at the time interval planned today. Flexibility and contingencies are discussed as important components in organizational strategic planning; they are equally important in your professional planning. Setting attainable goals with alternatives, should change occur, gives reality to long-range personal planning.

Two excellent beginnings for creating a vision for the future are (1) to read a variety of publications on the profession and (2) to network with and learn from successful practitioners. A vision will take shape as you read and listen to the variety of opportunities available. Lock into the one that excites you and become a part of the dynamic future of health care. In this industry devoted to the healing arts, there are options in the future that may be unheard of today. This demonstrates another reason for flexibility in long-range planning.

To create the image you wish to project and to be noticed in the marketplace, take time to prepare a winning resume. This resume and its cover letter introduce you and set the tone for an interview.

Planning a Resume

The application process is handled in a variety of methods. Traditionally, applicants would complete a paper application on-site in the human resources department. Another method of application involves submitting either a resume or curriculum vitae (CV). Some organizations only allow online applications. These may or may not include an option to upload a resume or CV. A **resume**, which is more commonly used in a traditional work setting, provides information about an applicant's education and employment history. See Figure 21-1 for a sample resume. **Curriculum vitae** is a Latin term, meaning "course of life." As the term reflects, a CV provides significantly more detail than a resume. A CV is used more often in academic, research, and publication settings. See Figure 21-2 for a sample CV.

Resume
A summary or brief account of one's background—work experience and education.

Curriculum vitae
A detailed history of work history, education, publications, presentations, awards, and other related activities.

FIGURE 21-1   Sample Resume

Elizabeth Brown, RHIA, CCS
1234 S. First Street
Anytown, IL 54321
(123)555-1212
E-mail: ebrown@email.com

WORK EXPERIENCE

February 20XX to present	Best Home Care, Anytown, IL: Supervisor of Health Information. Duties included: Supervision of 7–9 office employees, preparation of monthly statistics, and knowledge of Medicare, Medicaid, and other third-party billing regulations.
September 20XX to February 20XX	General Hospital, Anytown, IL: Coder. Duties included: Coding and abstracting inpatient charts and outpatient diagnostic records using ICD-10-CM codes, coding ER, and outpatient surgery records using ICD-10-CM and CPT-4 codes, use of 3M encoder, use of optical imaging system for outpatient records, participation on many quality improvement teams, and instructing employee training sessions for Quality Leadership Process and Service Excellence.
March 20XX to September 20XX	Memorial Medical Center, Anytown, IL: Coder. Duties included coding and abstracting inpatient and outpatient records using ICD-10-CM, CPT, and HCPCS codes.

EDUCATION

August 20XX to May 20XX	State University, Anytown, IL Bachelor of Science in Health Information Administration.

FIGURE 21-2   Sample Curriculum Vitae

Elizabeth Brown, RHIA, CCS
1234 S. First Street
Anytown, IL 54321
(123)555-1212
E-mail: ebrown@email.com

EDUCATION
University of State, City, IL
M.S. Health Information Management   20XX

State College, Anytown, IL
Bachelor of Science, Health Information Administration   20XX

CERTIFICATION
Fellow of American Health Information Management Association   20XX
Registered Health Information Administrator (No. xxxxx)   20XX
Certified Coding Specialist (No. xxxxx)   20XX

AWARDS
American Health Information Management Association Foundation Scholarship   20XX
Who's Who Among Students in American Colleges   20XX
Dean's List, State, Anytown, IL   20XX

TEACHING EXPERIENCE
State College, Anytown, IL   20XX–20XX
Adjunct Instructor
HIM 205, Introduction to CPT Coding

Upstate University, Collegetown, IL   20XX–20XX
Adjunct Instructor
HI300, Health Care Statistics

RELATED EXPERIENCE
Best Home Care, Anytown, IL
Supervisor of Health Information Services
Supervised 8–10 Health Information Services employees, prepared monthly statistical reports, performed coding audits and coding education, ensured record maintenance and coding compliance according to Medicare, Medicaid, and other third-party billing regulations

University Hospital, Anytown, IL
Coder
Assigned ICD-10-CM, CPT, and HCPCS codes for inpatient, outpatient, skilled nursing, and addiction recovery accounts

CONSULTING
XYZ Publishing, Medical Coding Textbook reviewer
Upstate University, Collegetown, IL. Coding and documentation audits

FIGURE 21-2 *(continued)*

PUBLICATIONS AND PAPERS

"Best Practices for Teaching ICD-10-PCS"
Journal of XXXXX, no. 10 (October 20xx)

"Transition from HIM Practitioner to Educator"
Journal of XXXXX, no. 3 (March 20xx)

INVITED PRESENTATIONS

"Teaching ICD-10-PCS"
American Health Information Management Association Assembly on Education   20XX
Chicago, IL

OFFICES HELD AND COMMITTEE APPOINTMENTS

President, State Health Information Management Association   20XX
Chairman of annual meeting planning committee, State Health Information   20XX
Management Association

A resume is a summary of your work experience and education. It is an advertisement to create an interest in you. Resumes take careful thought and preparation; they are an introduction to a prospective employer, and yet, by definition, a resume is quite impersonal. A cover letter sent with the resume serves as a bridge between you and the potential employer. Sincerity and honesty, however, can be expressed in both the resume and the cover letter. The following principles will guide in preparing a resume:

Make it interesting enough to secure an interview.

Make it visually attractive.

Make it brief but informative.

Personalize it.

To assist in the creation of a winning resume, the following guidelines offer ideas for taking these principles into action.

Resumes may be in chronological format, functional format, or in a combination approach. The following descriptions of these three formats will facilitate in choosing the best one for you.

Chronological Format

The **chronological resume** is the best known and widely used. It is arranged with the most recent information or experience first and then descends in reverse chronological order and ends with the oldest experience or information. This format makes it easy to review career progress from one step to the next. Obvious gaps in work history can be readily seen.

Chronological resume
A summary of one's work and education experience in reverse date order.

Functional Format

To emphasize overall skills and abilities, the **functional resume** downplays dates. In fact, specific dates are omitted. The work history is defined by specific examples of experience and responsibilities. Previous positions may or may not be included. The focus is on responsibilities and accomplishments.

Combination Format

Combining chronological and functional formats, the combination approach is becoming increasingly popular. Transferable skills or capabilities used in a variety of positions are emphasized. This format pinpoints job titles, dates, and past employers. Its strength is that both career direction and depth of experience can be shown.

Writing Your Resume

The following rules for writing resumes give guidance in documenting your background. Most are listed as positive action, but a few of the guidelines include specific things to avoid:

Rule 1. Heading: Start with your name, address, and telephone number. Place your name on every page. Do not use the words *Resume of ...* Include your business telephone number if appropriate. Check your answering machine message—be sure it is professional in tone.

Rule 2. Career objective: Use a career objective if desired and if your objective will relate to the position for which you are applying. Make it specific and allow it to give focus to the remainder of the resume. The cover letter is an alternate place for the career objective and allows the resume to be used when applying for various positions. The career objective can then be tailored in the letter toward the specific position.

Rule 3. Work experience or education first? Either can come first. When work history is scanty, education is best placed first. List most recent education or work experience first and proceed in reverse chronology.

Rule 4. Main headings: Plan headings that will guide or lead into the information. Headings should catch the eye and be visually compelling. Be conservative rather than gimmicky. Some basic headings are:

Career Objective	Education
Employment Experience	Professional Education
Work History	Certificates and Licenses
Business Experience	Special Skills
Professional Highlights	Technical Skills
Selected Achievements	Relevant Experience
Memberships	Publications

Rule 5. Phrases versus sentences? Be concise; use phrases rather than complete sentences. Avoid use of pronouns such as "I" or use of third person to refer to yourself. Use parallel sentence structure. Make every word count.

Rule 6. Abbreviations: Avoid abbreviations except for degrees such as B.S. Use vocabulary related to the profession.

Rule 7. Action verbs: Use action verbs to describe your responsibilities. Examples are:

administered	delegated	interviewed	reduced
analyzed	designed	lectured	revised
assisted	developed	managed	selected
communicated	directed	monitored	supervised
conducted	evaluated	organized	taught
controlled	formulated	performed	trained
coordinated	implemented	planned	translated
created	initiated	proposed	wrote

Rule 8. Gaps in work history: Avoid obvious gaps by using a functional format. Homemakers can avoid obvious references to time spent at home. Rather, highlight volunteer or unpaid experience in the community or social organizations that can parallel responsibilities in a work environment. For example, "Developed training manual for Girl/Boy Scouts."

Rule 9. Previous employer information: Omit reason for leaving a previous employer. Never include salary requirements or previous salary. Never list name of a supervisor. The formal application will request this type of information.

Rule 10. Accomplishments: Include special awards, superior grade point average, extracurricular activities, and other accomplishments that are relevant.

Rule 11. Publications: List names of publications with information on when and where they were published.

Rule 12. Personal information: Omit information such as birthdate, marital status, hobbies, health status, and a photograph. Employers are looking for valuable employees, not friends, and in most instances this information is not appropriate.

Rule 13. References: Rarely include references in a resume. If you wish to use the term as a line item, state "Available on request." Should the prospective employer have requested references, list them on a separate sheet.

Rule 14. Appearance: Use cream, white, buff, or light gray high-quality paper. Use standard-size paper with no borders. Print on one side only. Use boldface, italics, and underscoring with discretion. Proof-read carefully; have someone else proofread also.

Rule 15. Attachments: Never attach transcripts or letters of recommendation. When these are specifically requested by a prospective employer, include them as separate sheets in the packet of material. Do not place in a report cover. Mail with cover letter.

Rule 16. Individualize for employer: Be prepared to make changes in your resume to create it specifically for a prospective employer.

Preparing the Cover Letter

Cover letter
An introductory document that accompanies a resume sent to a prospective employer.

A well-written **cover letter** introduces you to the prospective employer and neutralizes the tone of the more impersonal resume. The cover letter should be written as carefully as the resume as it may be used as a screening tool. It should be addressed to a specific person when possible.

As you explain what you can do for the prospective employer, emphasize what you can contribute to the organization. By using simple direct language and correct grammar, you can avoid being stiff and impersonal. The first sentence should catch the attention of the reader and the last sentence can suggest an interview.

The cover letter should include the reason for the contact. Are you responding to an advertisement? Are you writing at the suggestion of a mutual friend? If a specific skill was mentioned in the advertisement, refer the reader to the resume where your skill is described.

Lastly, review your resume and cover letter. They should project a positive, professional image that represents your unique personality. Resumes are a mainstay of modern business and are worth the effort spent in creating one that will advertise your skills.

PLANNING FOR A POSITION INTERVIEW

Within a university or college setting, there are many sources of information regarding possible positions following graduation. Once your resume is ready, begin exploring options and making appointments for interviews. Exposing yourself to several interviews gives you experience in the interview process and builds your confidence.

An excellent person with whom to begin your professional interview is the HIM manager at your affiliation or internship facility. Even though there may not be an opening at the facility, the manager may be willing to mentor you through this first interview. Also, asking a clinical supervisor or one of the instructors to critique your interview skills can create a great learning experience.

Guest lecturers in your courses also give good opportunities for interviews. A professional who gives time to students by lecturing is often willing to give you an interview and then critique your skills. Ideas for possible positions and future interviews may also come from guest lecturers.

Making the appointment for an interview should be at a time favorable for both of you. Choose a time when you can relax and not be rushed and certainly a time when the manager can give you his undivided intention. Set aside time to prepare for the interview. Learn details about the facility by reading reports, brochures, or newspaper articles. Become familiar with the vision of the facility, its success in maintaining that vision, and how the community needs are being met.

Preparing yourself to answer questions about technical details of the position for which you are applying is also crucial to success. This is enhanced by reviewing past experiences and using the 1-2-3 story technique to demonstrate your competence. This technique involves stating a problem that occurred, describing how you solved it, and then emphasizing the positive results of your action. You may even wish to write out some responses you would give to typical questions to reinforce your memory.

Planning your attire for the interview avoids last-minute problems. Professional conservative attire is a must but just as important is choosing well-fitting comfortable clothing that will allow you to focus on being yourself.

A winning resume, interesting cover letter, and professional attire will contribute to projecting the desired image employers are seeking. But it is the interview, where the chemistry between interviewee and the manager connects, that really counts. Expressions of confidence, interest, commitment, and competence will win the position.

PLANNING FOR POSITIVE PERFORMANCE EVALUATIONS

As new visions are anticipated, HIM professionals can prepare for making that growth step by maintaining a professional attitude, by wearing attire that projects a professional image, and by assuring that regular performance evaluations are a part of the personnel file. Busy managers and busy vice presidents to whom they report may not be documenting faithfully the spontaneous informal commendations that are verbalized or put in memos following rewarding efforts. Employees may maintain documentation and samples of positive performance to include in a professional portfolio or to serve as a reminder for the supervisor during performance evaluations.

PERSONAL TIME MANAGEMENT

This section brings into focus the importance of personal planning for effective time management. In Chapter 4 the more formal aspects of managing time are outlined. Additional informal aspects of time management are covered here.

Utilizing these aspects can lead HIM professionals to a better understanding of how they function at their best.

The technique of breaking down projects into several small or divided units will assist several of the organizational-type managers. Once the tasks are smaller, smaller blocks of time can be used effectively to complete the projects in manageable steps. Keeping these divided units together in a folder or tray until ready to put the project all together will keep time wasted to a minimum.

While most HIM managers will not fit neatly into just one of the personality organizational types depicted by Schlenger and Roesch, a personal appraisal of tendencies toward one or more of the types can lead to a conscious effort at reducing time wasters.

Professionalism Behaviors, appearances, attitudes, and actions in all aspects of the workplace.

Soft skills See professionalism.

PROFESSIONALISM

Professionalism is a concept that is important for all career fields, not just in health care. It includes the behaviors, appearances, attitudes, and actions in all aspects of the workplace. Another term used to describe professionalism as a skill set is **soft skills**. Table 21-1 provides some examples of the most commonly recognized aspects of professionalism.

TABLE 21-1	Professionalism in Action
Professionalism Aspects	**Examples**
Good hygiene	• No body odors • Teeth brushed • Facial hair neatly trimmed for men (some workplaces may prohibit facial hair) • Nails neatly trimmed (some workplaces may prohibit nail polish or acrylic nails)
Appearance	• No visible tattoos • No unconventional piercings showing (general rule of thumb is one ear piercing is acceptable)
Dress	• Appropriate uniform • Business or business casual, according to dress code • Shoulders covered • Skirts below mid-thigh • No open toe shoes • Socks or pantyhose may be required at some workplaces
Attitude	• Friendly • Positive • Loyal
Behaviors	• Offering help to others • Insightful to things that need to be done without having to be told • No gossiping
Work quality	• Neat • Complete • Compliant with regulations • Timely
Communication	• Respectful to others

Professionalism is noticed as a first impression when an applicant applies for a position with an organization. The quality and formatting of a resume can reflect a lot about attention to detail that an applicant may have in the workplace. When a workplace contacts an applicant for an interview, professionalism may be noted in the way the applicant answers the phone or even the type of message that the applicant has for voicemail. The interview is the next place where professionalism may be recognized in an applicant. This starts with physical appearance and the first personal impressions may include posture, handshake, eye contact, and voice control.

Outside of the Workplace

Professionalism does not stop when you leave the workplace. There are several things you need to keep in mind with your personal activities. Social media has made it possible for employers, or potential employers, to catch a glimpse into your personal life to see if you are the type of person they want to employ. Because of this, professionals should think twice before posting photos online (or allowing others to post pictures of them that may be tagged) of activities at parties involving drinking or other socially questionable actions.

Smoking

Smoking is generally not allowed on the property of health care providers. An increasing number of health care organizations now also have policies that prevent employees from smoking, even during their personal time. This is usually part of a wellness initiative. Employers may perform random testing for nicotine and other substances, and they may have policies regarding disciplinary action or dismissal if the test comes up positive.

Credit Checks

Another aspect of employees' personal lives that employers may be concerned with is credit history. There are some employers that require a credit check when they perform background checks prior to hiring.

The Remote Office

Technology has introduced the ability for employees to work from home. This is generally referred to as **remote work** since it is not performed on-site. There are several considerations for remote work related to human resources, technology requirements, and security that must be addressed when allowing an employee to work remote from the facility. Some of the major concerns, aside from the physical environment, which is addressed in Chapter 8 include working hours, productivity monitoring, childcare, and worker compensation.

Remote work
Work performed someplace other than at the facility.

Some organizations with remote employees require the employees to provide proof of childcare services in order to ensure the employee is not supervising their children while they should be working.

PROFESSIONAL GROWTH

HIM managers are constantly stressed by the need to monitor the latest computerized innovations or last week's technological systems change. This demand for ongoing new knowledge increases the need to review and glean information from health care and computer journals and magazines. They are valuable resources, and reading and scanning several at least monthly is a habit to begin now and to continue for the rest of your professional life. Becoming acquainted with successful HIM managers enhances the knowledge of new graduates; having them serve as mentors is a valuable growth experience. Seeing systems installed and functioning in facilities is another valuable resource. Visiting with vendors at professional meetings is an excellent avenue for obtaining current technological information.

Journals and newsletters from the American Health Information Management Association (AHIMA) and other associations are most beneficial. Examples of alliance associations are the Health Information Management Systems Society (HIMSS), the American Management Information Association (AMIA), the Healthcare Financial Management Association (HFMA), and the Healthcare Innovations in Technology Systems (HITS). Through networking experiences with other professionals, HIM managers can enhance their understanding of capabilities and trends in managing health care information into the future.

SUMMARY

Preparing well-written resumes using the 16 rules outlined in this chapter offers HIM professionals the opportunity to walk into a position interview with confidence. Other confidence-building items include a personalized cover letter and attire that creates the desired impression.

Resumes can be prepared using a chronological format where significant dates are included in reverse order. The functional format may prove advantageous when it is preferable to emphasize skills and abilities. A combination of the two formats may also be used where skills and abilities are emphasized selectively.

Major personality organizational types have been identified and play a role in how professionals organize work and utilize time. Understanding your organizational type can be helpful in using inherent strengths and downplaying weaknesses.

HIM professionals who make a personal effort to network with peers, read a broad range of literature, and attend professional meetings grow personally and professionally.

CRITICAL THINKING EXERCISES

1. Describe several tasks you will undertake in your personal planning for your first HIM position following graduation.

2. List the major features of a resume. Which format will be most appropriate for you?

APPLICATION OF THEORY EXERCISES

Create a resume that includes the elements discussed in this chapter.

INTERNET EXERCISE

Search for videos of mock job interviews online. Critique at least three videos, citing positive and negative aspects that you viewed.

CASE STUDY

You are getting ready to graduate with an associate degree in health information technology. You have never worked in the career field, but you have held previous positions at two different employers in food service. You were an excellent student in college, maintaining perfect attendance and frequently appearing on the dean's list. You just found out about an entry-level HIM position and plan to apply for it. Describe how you will organize your resume and list items you may wish to discuss in an interview to demonstrate why you would be a good candidate for the position, even though you do not have previous HIM experience.

GLOSSARY

A

accounting Collection, recording, and reporting of financial data.

accreditation Voluntary process that involves assessment of an organization's performance against established standards to evaluate the quality of operations and outcomes.

action plan The document that assists committee members with delegated responsibilities by reminding them of tasks and deadlines; prepared and distributed immediately following committee meetings.

ad hoc As needed.

adhocracy See organic design.

administrative data Coded information contained in secondary records, such as billing records, describing patient identification, diagnoses, procedures, and insurance.

aesthetics Aspects of the workplace that include color schemes, lighting, and other areas that impact the visual appeal of the environment.

agenda A document that provides the order of items to be covered in a meeting.

American Health Information Management Association (AHIMA) The professional organization for health information management professionals.

aggregate data Data extracted from individual health records and combined to form deidentified information about groups of patients that can be compared and analyzed.

attitudes Evaluative statements that reflect how an individual feels about objectives, events, or people.

authoritarian leadership The measure of a person's belief in status and power differences among people in organizations.

authority The rights inherent in a managerial position to give orders and expect them to be obeyed.

autocratic leader A leadership style that is stern, rigid, controlling, and does not welcome input from followers.

B

benchmarking The search for the best practices among like entities or past practices that lead to superior performance.

board of directors An elected or appointed group of officials who bear ultimate responsibility for the successful operation of a health care organization.

bottom-up budgeting process A philosophy that encourages participation of all employees in planning priorities and objectives for the budget year.

brainstorming Spontaneous generation of sometimes creative ideas.

broker A negotiator, an intermediary, or a person entrusted with the transmission of health care data.

business plan A plan that documents details of a proposed project or new business that includes a mission statement, a description, the proposed market, the budget, and a plan for evaluation.

bureaucratic leader A leadership style that is interested in the needs and concerns of followers, yet they maintain complete control in decision making.

bylaws Guidelines established by an organization for issues that may arise.

C

capital budget A budget developed for larger assets that are part of the strategic planning process.

cash budget The combined operating and capital budgets.

centralization of authority The concentration of decision-making authority that lies with upper-level management.

certainty A decision situation in which the manager can make a correct decision because the outcome of each alternative is known.

Certification Commission for Healthcare Information Technology (CCHIT) An independent, voluntary, private sector initiative organized as a limited liability corporation, which was awarded a contract by the United States Department of Health and Human Services (HHS) to develop, create prototypes for, and evaluate the certification criteria and inspection process for EHR products.

change management The formal process of introducing change, persuading others to adopt the change, and instill change organization-wide.

channel The medium by which a message travels from a sender to a receiver.

charge capture A process of collecting all procedures, supplies, and services provided during delivery of patient care.

charge description master (CDM) A comprehensive computerized list that contains information about several aspects of all items that the organization may charge for the health care services and procedures provided to patients.

charge reconciliation The act of reviewing all of the charges that have been entered for claims submission through charge entry.

chargemaster Charge description master.

chart tracking The process of signing out records and tracking them as they are transferred from one location to another.

chronological resume A summary of one's work and education experience in reverse date order.

closed systems Systems that are not influenced by their environment and do not interact with their environment.

cognitive dissonance An incompatibility between two or more attitudes or between behavior and attitudes.

committee structure A structure that brings together a range of individuals from across functional lines to solve problems or develop proactive alternatives before problems exist.

communication The transferring and understanding of meaning.

compensation All direct and indirect pay, including wages, mandatory benefits, and benefits such as medical insurance, life insurance, child care, elder care, retirement plans, and longevity pay

compressed work week A schedule where employees work four 10-hour days.

conceptual skills Skills that require higher-level intellect to be applied to planning, decision making, and problem solving.

concurrent review Review of records while the patient is still receiving services.

conflict The perceived incompatible differences that result in interference or opposition.

conflict resolution An action by managers to resolve conflicts through accommodation, force, compromise, or collaboration.

consistency perception The process of organizing and interpreting sensory impressions in order to give consistency and meaning to the environment.

consultant One who gives professional advice and services in the field of his or her specialty.

contingency approach An approach that recognizes and responds to situational variables as they arise.

continuous quality improvement A health care term that is patient or employee focused, used to describe a constant cycle of improvement.

controlling The management function that ensures activities are being accomplished as planned and corrects any significant deviations.

cover letter An introductory document that accompanies a resume sent to a prospective employer.

creativity A thinking process that combines ideas in a unique way to produce new and original concepts.

curriculum vitae A detailed history of work history, education, publications, presentations, awards, and other related activities.

cultural competence An awareness of cultural differences and practices specific to cultural groups.

customers Those persons who use the services provided or have a stake in the success of an organization.

D

decision-making process A series of steps that include identifying a problem, developing and analyzing possible alternatives, selecting the best alternative, and monitoring its effectiveness.

decoding The retranslating of a sender's message.

delegation Distribution of tasks and decision-making authority to others.

Delphi technique A group decision-making technique where members do not meet face to face.

democratic leadership A leadership style that maintains control of decision making but encourages followers to provide input and reflect that input plays a valuable role in decisions that are made.

demographic data Information used to identify an individual, such as name, address, gender, age, and other information linked to a specific person.

departmentalization The process of formalizing the structure by grouping employees together according to their specialized activities.

directing A component of the leading function of management that emphasizes giving assignments and instructions, guiding employees, and overseeing activities.

diversity Differences among people, such as age, race, nationality, gender, sexual orientation, or tenure with the organization or position.

diversity training Training that facilitates an environment that fosters tolerance and appreciation of individual differences within the organization's workforce and strives to create a more harmonious working environment.

division of labor See specialization of labor.

due diligence Process that involves taking the time in order to make a fully informed decision, including exploration of potential technical, financial, legal, and other consequences of doing business with a vendor.

E

effectiveness The degree to which stated outcomes are attained.

efficacy The degree to which a minimum of resources are used to obtain outcomes.

efficiency The degree to which a desired outcome is achieved within a minimal amount of time.

effort The mental and physical exertion required to perform job-related tasks.

e-HIM Management of health information through the use of electronic technology.

eighty-five/fifteen (85/15) rule Assumption that faults in the system are the cause of 85 percent of problems, and worker performance is only responsible for 15 percent.

electronic health record (EHR) A digital version of a patient record.

electronic meeting A committee or group meeting where decisions are made with linked computer technology.

employment at will A concept that employees can be fired at any time and for almost any reason based on the idea that employees can quit at any time and for any reason.

empowerment The process of increasing the decision-making discretion of employees.

encoding The converting of a message into symbols.

entrepreneur A person who conceives a product or service idea, pursues opportunities for innovation, and starts an organization.

ergonomics The design of products, processes, and systems to meet the requirements and capacities of those people who use them.

execution The phase of the project management life cycle that involves implantation of the plan.

expectancy theory of motivation A motivational theory based on the belief that an action will result in an outcome that is desired or expected.

external data Data coming from outside the facility that can be used to compare the facility with other similar facilities, such as quality of outcomes for various conditions being treated or surgical procedures.

external environment Outside forces that potentially affect a department or total organization's performance.

extrinsic motivation Performance of a task because of a potential reward or penalty.

F

facilitator A professional with expertise in leading group discussions, especially in quality improvement efforts.

facility access controls Policies and procedures that limit physical access to authorized staff to the work areas using computers for electronic information systems

feedback A process for determining whether the receiver of a message understood it.

fixed budget A budget that assumes a fixed level of services, sales, or productivity.

flex time Flexible work hours where employees work a specified number of hours per week, but are free, within limits, to schedule their own hours.

followership The theory that managers spend more time following leaders up the organization than in leading those down the organization.

formal leader The manager appointed to lead an entity and have responsibility for the activities within that entity.

formalization The degree to which an organization relies on rules and procedures to direct the actions of employees.

forming The team-building phase when team members first meet.

functional departmentalization The grouping of activities by functions performed.

functional resume A summary of a person's work and education experience that emphasizes skills and downplays dates.

G

Gantt chart A bar chart that graphically shows the work planned and completed on one axis and the time span on the other.

grapevine The informal communication network.

H

Hawthorne effect Workers are more productive when they know they are being observed and less productive when they are not observed.

health data Includes both clinical and administrative data (and perhaps other data associated with an individual's health care); also includes aggregate-level health data for secondary uses, such as quality and patient safety monitoring, population health monitoring, research, and reimbursement.

health information exchange (HIE) The electronic transmission or exchange of health information between health care providers, payers, and others, such as labs and pharmacies in order to facilitate coordination of care and provision of more efficient health care services.

Health Insurance Portability and Accountability Act of 1996 (HIPAA) The federal law that facilitates maintenance of insurance for health care consumers, protects privacy and security of health information, and controls administrative costs of health care delivery.

Health Level Seven International (HL7) An international standard development organization that provides standards that ensure the ability of EHR systems to be compatible for integration of components and exchange of information.

health literacy The ability to understand basic health information and make decisions related to personal health care management.

human relations approach An approach that emphasizes the important role humans play in the success of an organization and states that a satisfied employee will be a productive one.

human resources approach A managerial approach that focuses on human behavior.

hybrid health records Health records that consist of a combination of paper and electronic documentation.

I

incremental budget A budget that allocates funds to departments for the new budget period based on allocations of the previous budget period.

informal leader The leader chosen by members of the group to lead the group in certain attitudes and behaviors.

informal planning The planning done by managers that is not formally documented for present or future use.

initiation phase The beginning of the project management life cycle.

integrated model of management A model that uses the best features of information theories to develop a health care management model that integrates new technologies into the management model of the future.

integrated systems A system where data and information on separate automated applications are integrated to allow invisible transfer of information among them.

internal data Data from within the facility including administrative and clinical data.

internal environment Forces within the organization but outside the department that potentially affect the department's performance; factors within the department that affect its ability to perform effectively and efficiently.

interpersonal skills Skills used to communicate effectively with each other.

intrapreneur A person who creates an entrepreneurial spirit within an organization.

intrinsic motivation Performance of a task because it is personally enjoyable or personal value is seen in a certain behavior.

J

job characteristics model A framework for analyzing and designing jobs that identifies five primary job characteristics, their interrelationships, and impact on outcome variables.

job description The written statement summarizing what an employee does, how it is done, and why it is done.

job design The way in which tasks are combined to form a complete position.

job scope The variety of activities within a position description and the frequency with which each activity is repeated.

L

laissez-faire A management approach that has a low level of involvement by the leader, allowing followers to function on their own.

leadership The ability to inspire and influence attitudes and behaviors of group members in accomplishing objectives.

leading The management function involved in motivating employees, directing others, resolving conflicts, and selecting effective communication channels.

locus of control A personality trait with two components; internal, where people believe they control their own fate and external, where people believe they are pawns of fate.

longitudinal patient record The creation of a record that encompasses patient health care information from all sources, over time, for use and update by caregivers.

M

Machiavellianism A measure of the degree to which people are pragmatic, maintain emotional distance, and believe that ends justify means.

management A process of activities for creating objectives and for teaming with people to meet these objectives through efficient and effective use of resources.

management by objectives (MBO) A system where performance objectives are jointly planned by manager and employee with periodic review of progress and rewards based on this progress.

manual A book containing policies, rules, and procedures for a department, a section, a team, or an employee. Also called a handbook, guidebook, or data quality manual.

master patient index (MPI) A database of the name and unique identification number of every patient who has ever received services at the health care provider organization.

matrix organizational structure A design that assigns specialists from departments to work on one or more projects led by a project manager.

mechanistic design A structure that is high in complexity, formalization, and centralization.

Medicaid Assistance with medical coverage for low-income families and individuals, established by Title XIX of the Social Security Act.

medical necessity Documentation to justify that a medical procedure or service will benefit the patient's medical well-being or have a positive impact on the ability to diagnose and treat a medical condition and that the procedure or service is consistent with the medical community's accepted standard of care.

Medicare Federally funded program established to assist with health care costs for Americans 65 years of age and older and those with disabilities or end-stage renal disease, established by Title XVIII of the Social Security Act.

Medicare administrative contractor (MAC) Contracting entity that administers the Medicare program for designated regions.

mentoring Sharing knowledge, teaching skills, and encouraging others to promote professional growth.

merit raise A pay increase based on positive employee performance.

message A purpose to be conveyed.

minutes Documentation of key events in a meeting.

mission statement The documentation of the purpose of an organization.

moderator A person skilled in group techniques who leads a committee or group through a decision-making process.

monitoring A process of taking the action necessary to be aware of the quality and quantity of employee activities that may be performed by manual or electronic means.

motivation A willingness to exert high levels of effort to reach departmental goals, conditioned by the ability to satisfy some employee need.

multiskilled health professional A person cross-trained to provide more than one function, often in more than one discipline.

N

network structure An organization that chooses to rely on other organizations to perform some basic business functions on a contract basis.

new vision The creation of new professional career goals as the result of assessment and revitalization efforts.

noise Disturbances that interfere with the transmission of messages.

nominal group technique A method of generating ideas that involves anonymous submission of ideas followed by voting to rank the ideas.

noncompete clause A clause in an employment contract that may restrict the employee from seeking employment with a competitor, vendor, or client.

nonprogrammed decisions Decisions that are unique and thus require custom-made solutions.

norming The team-building step during which each team member comes to understand the roles of all members and how they will fit together to work for a common goal.

O

open-mode environment A specific work space that encourages creativity and original thinking.

open systems Dynamic systems that interact with and respond to forces in the environment.

operating budget A budget developed for the purpose of planning routine, and some nonroutine, expenses and revenue for the upcoming fiscal year.

operational approach to management A management approach that concentrates on improving efficiency of processes and elimination of waste.

operational plans Plans that detail the action of each department or team that will lead to achievement of the overall objectives.

organic design A structure that is low in complexity, formalization, and centralization.

organizational chart A graphic representation of an organization's formal reporting structure.

organizational development (OD) A system of techniques to motivate people and improve the quality of interpersonal work relationships.

organizing The management function that determines what tasks are to be done, who shall do them, the reporting structure, and at what level decisions will be made.

outsourcing Contracting with a company that enters into a contract with a health care organization to perform services.

P

paradigm shift The changes that take place as present models of activity no longer meet the needs, and pressure mounts for a shift to new models.

participative management A management style where managers consult with employees and use their suggestions in making decisions.

patient-focused centers Direct care units where multiskilled health professionals provide all of the patient activities and care, such as admitting the patient, performing diagnostic examinations, caring for the patient, and coding patient diagnoses.

patient portal A website that provides the ability for patients to access to information about test results and other personal health information without a health care professional needing to be available to answer questions or explain findings

perception The process of organizing and interpreting sensory impressions in order to give meaning to the environment.

performance evaluation Provision of feedback to an employee regarding quality of work.

performance evaluation and review technique (PERT network) A diagram that graphically shows the relationships among the various activities of a project and estimates the time needed for each activity.

performance standards Measurable criteria that is deemed acceptable regarding quality and productivity standards for each function performed in the position.

performing The phase in team building during which each team member is in a position to work toward achieving the team's stated goals.

Peter Principle Cynical belief that employees will advance to their highest level of competence and then be promoted to their level of incompetence, where they will remain.

planning The management function concerned with defining goals, establishing strategy, and creating plans to guide the coordinated effort of employees to meet the goals.

planning phase The second step in the project management life cycle.

point method A method of determining the amount or percentage of pay increase by the number of points in specified ranges on a performance evaluation

position depth A practice where employees are given an increased degree of control over their tasks.

position description See job description.

position design See job design.

position enlargement A practice that offers employees horizontal expansion of activities and an increase in scope.

position enrichment The practice of enriching positions by expanding the tasks vertically, usually with planning and evaluating responsibilities.

position rotation The practice of lateral transfers of employees among jobs involving different tasks.

power The capacity to influence the decision-making process.

probationary period A period of time during which the quality of work and competence are evaluated prior to assuming regular employment with the organization.

problem avoiders Managers who tend to ignore signs of problem eruption.

problem seekers Managers who actively look for opportunities to alleviate potential problems before they occur.

problem-solving process See decision-making process.

process approach to management A process where management performs the functions of planning, organizing, leading, and controlling in a circular and continuous manner.

productivity The overall output of products and services produced per employee hour that meet the established levels of quality.

professionalism Behaviors, appearances, attitudes, and actions in all aspects of the workplace.

programmed decisions A repetitive decision that is documented to handle routine problems.

project charter See statement of work.

project management Managing a significant project using a define set of procedures in order to plan and control all of the associated activities necessary to meet the project goals.

prospective review Review of records prior to delivery of services.

Q

quality The degree to which an activity produces a product or service that meets the standards set for that activity.

quality improvement The philosophy that processes, management, and employees all benefit from efforts to provide better service, products, and ideas focusing on the customer.

R

rational model in decision making A model where the manager behaves rationally in making decisions by following the steps and maximizing every alternative before the final decision is made.

recovery audit contractor (RAC) A governmental program whose goal is to identify inappropriate payments to providers for services delivered to Medicare beneficiaries.

recruitment The process of finding, soliciting, and attracting employees

reengineering The process of changing business practices to maintain quality, reduce costs, and improve performance that involves fundamental rethinking and redesigning processes.

remote work Work performed someplace other than at the facility.

request for information (RFI) A written document that is sent to a broad list of vendors.

request for proposal (RFP) A request for specific information about a vendor's product and proposed contract information.

resources An organization's resources are the skills and abilities of employees, the monies available for producing its products or services, and the physical plant and equipment.

results management See management by objectives (MBO).

resume A summary or brief account of one's background—work experience and education.

retrospective review Review of records following delivery of services.

revenue cycle A set of events that occur and repeat routinely as information and data about patient health and financial information moves through, into and out of a health care provider for the purpose of determining compensation, or reimbursement, for services.

revenue cycle management Management of all contributing functions, both administrative and clinical, in order to capture, manage, and collect revenue or payment from provision of services to patients.

revitalization A growth concept where professionals consciously stretch their horizons and gain new visions for the future.

risk The decision maker has some information but must calculate the likelihood of specific outcomes.

rule An explicit statement that requires definite action be taken or not taken in a given situation.

S

sampling The process of measuring productivity by making a series of observations at random.

scientific approach to management Scientific procedures for finding the best way to accomplish a task, introduced by Frederick W. Taylor.

scope All work processes and resources required to complete a project.

scope creep Phenomenon that occurs if the initially proposed scope of the project grows beyond previously defined limits.

section/team managers Managers whose span of control covers one section of a department or one team within a section or a department; also called team leader, team coordinator, section leader, or section coordinator.

self-esteem An individual's degree of like or dislike for him or herself.

self-evaluation An employee's critique of him- or herself against performance standards.

self-monitoring A personality trait that measures an individual's ability to adjust his or her behavior to external situational factors.

servant leadership model An approach taken by a leader who is in the position due to a desire to serve others by leading them.

service organizations Organizations that offer services to their customers in contrast with manufacturing organizations that offer products.

shift differential An increased wage paid to employees who work less desirable shifts.

sign-on bonus A monetary incentive used by a facility to encourage a candidate to accept employment.

single-use plan A plan that is created to cover a unique problem and is rarely used; also called a nonprogrammed plan or decision.

six Sigma A highly disciplined and data-driven methodology used for reducing or eliminating defects in any process.

soft skills See professionalism.

space modeling The layout model created to depict the plans and decisions made for a physical environment that includes ergonomic principles.

span of control The number of employees a manager can direct with efficiency and effectiveness.

span of management The number of employees a manager can direct efficiently and effectively. See also span of control.

specialization of labor An organizing concept where employees specialize in skilled tasks that may then be grouped for efficiency.

staff authority Authority that supports, assists, and advises managers of line authority.

stakeholder Any constituency in the environment that is affected by an organization's decisions and policies.

standing committee A committee established for the purpose of oversight of ongoing and sometimes cross-functional issues.

standing-use plan A plan that is created when repetitive or routine decisions are made; also called programmed plan or decision.

statement of work Definition of the broad scope and objectives of a project.

statistical modeling A model that uses information systems data as a base for quality improvement management.

storming The phase of team building when members examine their roles in the group.

strategic planning A planning process that documents long-range objectives, develops activities to achieve the objectives, and allocates resources to those activities.

stress A dynamic condition in which an individual is confronted with an opportunity, constraint, or demand related to what he or she desires for which the outcome is perceived to be both uncertain and important.

SWOT analysis An analysis involving an organization's strengths and weaknesses and the opportunities and threats in its environment.

systems approach to management A theory that views an organization as a set of interrelated and interdependent entities.

T

task force A temporary structure created to perform specific, well-defined, usually complex tasks using members from various organizational departments.

technical skills Skills focused on operational activities.

template A plastic pattern for drawing scaled layout furniture.

Theory X The assumption by managers that employees are not motivated by doing work but rather by monetary results of a paycheck to meet personal needs.

Theory Y The assumption by management that employees are intrinsically motivated by the work that they do and that the provision of optimal working conditions, including interpersonal relationships within the workplace, will enhance that motivation.

time management Skills of planning sufficient amounts of time for tasks according to appropriate priorities.

top-down budgeting process A philosophy where upper-level management plans the priorities and objectives for the budget year and disseminates these to others in the organization.

total quality management (TQM) A management philosophy that recognizes employee involvement in meeting customer needs and expectations.

train-the-trainer A commonly used method of training that involves training of certain individuals who, in turn, will be responsible for training others on a task or skill.

trainees New employees.

trait approach A leadership approach based on the premise that leaders possess a set of traits of qualities, setting them apart from nonleaders.

transitional planning A process that offers a new paradigm for planning that begins by designing a bridge to the future.

two-dimensional templates A set of scaled card stock cutouts, representing office furniture, for use in moving around layouts until desired configuration is taped in place.

U

uncertainty A situation where the decision maker has no certainty about the probabilities associated with the situation.

unity of command The principle that an employee should have one and only one manager to whom he or she is directly responsible.

universal process approach to management A management approach based on the assumption that all organizations, regardless of the size or type of ownership, are guided by the same general rational management processes.

V

values statement Communicate an organization's social and cultural belief system.

variable budget A budget that recognizes and gives consideration to adjusting costs as volume fluctuates.

vision An idealized goal that proposes a new future for an organization.

W

workflow The flow of several different processes, handled by more than one person, that are dependent upon each other.

work sharing A practice where work is shared across all shifts, or where one full-time position is shared by two part-time employees.

work transformation See reengineering.

Z

zero-based budgeting (ZBB) A budgeting system where each budget request requires justification in detail regardless of past allocation.

INDEX